$ 600

Twentieth Century America

FOURTH EDITION

VOLUME II
**THE TWENTIES
AND THIRTIES**

DAVID A. SHANNON
University of Virginia

Rand McNally College Publishing Company · Chicago

Current printing   (last digit)
10 9 8 7 6 5 4 3 2 1

Fourth Edition   1977

To Molly and Sarah

Preface

The writer of recent history, somehow always suspect in the eyes of peers who study more remote eras, is aware that the closer he comes to the present the greater the risk of error, superficiality, and unbalanced emphasis. He is likely to suffer from lack of sources; he has insufficient secondary material to learn from; perhaps worst of all, he cannot have sufficient time perspective. Will it really appear this way fifty or a hundred years from now? Should this, rather than that, receive special emphasis? Yet, someone must write recent history. Knowledge of recent history is imperative for the proper education of students, who need to put their own lives into context and thereby better understand themselves and their society.

At any time one should read skeptically and questioningly, but with an open mind; and a critical eye is especially necessary when reading recent history. Lest I seem to be advising readers not to believe anything in this book, I hasten to say that I have been especially careful and have tried to be as balanced in judgment as I can be in the preparation of this fourth edition. Writing the most recent history in these pages from abroad, I have perhaps in some measure compensated with geographical perspective what is unavailable in time perspective.

Some material from the third edition I have deleted and some I have expanded. I have also reorganized extensively. The material dealing with the period since late 1973 is entirely new.

This book is intended primarily for students in college courses in recent American history. I have taught such courses for many years, and this book grew from that experience. Explanations, examples, and methods I have found useful in the classroom are employed here. My thanks go to many who have helped me directly or indirectly, but it is to my students over the years I owe the greatest gratitude, for it is through their questions, responses, ideas, and implied criticism that I have sharpened and reshaped the way I look at the recent American past.

November, 1976   *D.A.S.*

Contents

CONTENTS

PART II

WAR AND BOOM
1917–1929

The War Comes—
and the
Yanks Who Went

. . . we are face to face with what appears to be a critical economic situation, which can only be relieved apparently by the investment of American capital in foreign loans to be used in liquidating the enormous balance of trade in favor of the United States. . . . My opinion is that we ought to allow the loans to be made for our own good. . . .

ROBERT LANSING, Secretary of State,
to Wilson, 1915

We are going into war upon the command of gold.

GEORGE NORRIS,
speech in the U.S. Senate, 1917

Chapter One

Americans have many legends about their past. One of them is that the United States was "isolated," at least from Europe's affairs, until it entered World War I. The previous chapter makes clear that America was not isolated from Latin American and Asian affairs, either diplomatically or economically, before World War I. Neither was it remote from, and disdainful of, strictly European matters, and it never had been. During the colonial period Americans had participated in three wars with the French and the Indians that were the American theater of "world wars." During the Napoleonic wars, the new republic fought on both sides, first against the French in an undeclared naval war in 1798 and then against the British in the War of 1812.

Although most Americans in the nineteenth and early twentieth centuries regarded the quarrels of the European powers as little more than exotic curiosities (unless they had to do with the western hemisphere), the United States had participated in European diplomatic conferences during this time. Roosevelt had played the peacemaker role between Japan and Russia in 1905. Almost simultaneously, Roosevelt was engaged in bringing about an international conference of the major European powers. Germany coveted the trade of North Africa, which the French were attempting to keep for themselves. In the spring of 1905 the Kaiser delivered a warlike speech at Tangier, Morocco, and European tension was such that war was entirely possible. The Kaiser requested that Roosevelt use his good offices and call a conference of the great powers, and in June, Roosevelt received the acceptances of France and England to meet with Germany at Algeciras in southern Spain. The United States had two official representatives at the conference which began in January, 1906. The Anglo-French alliance had the power to prevent Germany's demands at the Algeciras Conference, and Germany accepted the diplomatic results rather than go to war. The point is that the President of the United States had twice, once for the Russian-Japanese war and then for the Moroccan crisis, arranged an international conference to deal with matters in which the United States had little or no direct national security interest. Clearly, this was not "isolation."

3

The United States as a Neutral Power, 1914–1915

Americans were not excited when news came that a Serbian nationalist had assassinated the heir to the Austrian throne on June 28, 1914, at Sarajevo, in what today is Yugoslavia. It was too bad the man had been killed, but Americans thought that Balkan nationalists were crazy, and they had no love for the Hapsburg monarchy. But the nation was thoroughly shocked by the diplomatic chain reaction to the assassination. Austria declared war on Serbia on July 28. Russia mobilized, and Germany declared war on Russia on August 1. France was Russia's ally and itching to regain Alsace-Lorraine. When France replied unsatisfactorily to a German message, Germany declared war on France August 3. When the Belgians resisted the movement of the German armies on their way to France, Germany declared war on Belgium. Great Britain had an alliance with France dating from 1904, and Britain declared war on Germany August 5. The war was not only international madness, it was the bloodiest international war in the world's history. To say that Americans were shaken is an understatement. Europe, the seat of the world's richest culture, had gone berserk.

Neutrality and Divided Sympathies

On August 4 Wilson issued an official proclamation of neutrality and offered to mediate the conflicts but his suggestions were rejected. Fearful that the large number of foreign born would have unusual sympathies one way or the other, Wilson on August 19 made a personal appeal to the people to "act and speak in the true spirit of neutrality.... The United States must be neutral in fact as well as in name during these days that are to try men's souls. We must be neutral in thought as well as in act...." Practically everyone in the nation agreed that neutrality was the nation's only true course. Yet, thirty-two months later Wilson asked Congress for a declaration of war against Germany. What happened in the administration, in the changing international situation, and in American public opinion that led to the decision to abandon neutrality and become a full belligerent?

American sympathies for one side or the other existed despite Wilson's plea and were to become stronger as the war continued. Most Americans were more for the Allies—Britain, France, and Russia—than they were for the Central Powers—Germany and Austria. German-speaking Americans, particularly first-generation immigrants, hoped for a Central Power victory, but they were few in number compared to the general population which spoke the English language, had been brought up on English literature and history, and remembered with gratitude France's help to the colonies during the American Revolution. Russia was unpopular among Americans because of its autocratic Czar, its repression of internal dissent, and its anti-Semitism, but anti-Russian sentiment abated after the March, 1917, revolution. Britain was extremely unpopular among Irish-Americans, especially after its ruthless crushing of the Dublin uprising during Easter week of 1916.

Both the British and the Germans directed extensive propaganda campaigns in America, German propaganda was on the whole crude and ineffective. An official of the German embassy even left a briefcase of propaganda plans on a New York elevated train, and German efforts to foment strikes in munitions industries and a few efforts at sabotage caused more harm in public relations than they were worth to the German armies. Respected British scholars such as James Bryce wrote accounts of German atrocities to the Belgians, and the English supplied scores of competent speakers for American audiences and, to a considerable degree, controlled the journalistic reporting of the war after they cut the cable from Germany to the United States. Yet, all of the propaganda efforts probably did no more than intensify sympathies and hostilities that already existed. American public opinion was outraged by the German invasion of Belgium in defiance of a long-standing treaty which a high German official called "a scrap of paper." The Allies were on the defensive, the war was on French soil, and American sentiment usually goes to the underdog.

Economic Consequences of War in Europe

Economic considerations were more important to both sides than public opinion, and here the Allies because of Britain's naval power had the upper hand. Part of Britain's strategy was to strangle Germany with a naval blockade. The British navy effectively prevented American trade with the Central Powers. American industry was eager to sell abroad—there was a depression in this country when the war began in Europe—and the Allies were able to get practically all of the American war production. American trade with Britain, France, Italy, and Russia grew from $824.8 million in 1914 to $3 billion in 1916, an increase of roughly 390 per cent. During these same years, American trade with the Central Powers declined from $169.3 million to $1.2 million, a decline of over 99 per cent. The British navy also controlled the shipment of goods to neutrals such as Holland and the Scandinavian nations from which war material from America might have been transshipped to Germany and Austria.

Soon after the declaration of war, American exports to the Allies far exceeded its imports from them, thereby creating a need for the Allies to get loans or some kind of commercial credit in America. The month the war began, the Wilson administration imposed a ban on loans by American bankers to belligerent governments. In Wilson's mind the reason for the prohibition was concern for the domestic economy, which was momentarily disrupted with the outbreak of war; to Bryan the reason for the no-loan policy was to maintain absolute neutrality, although one might argue that the policy favored Germany, because only England had the physical means to transport American goods across the Atlantic. Wilson began to reverse the decision two months after it was made when he let it be known that he would not oppose extending short-term foreign credits. In March, 1915, the House of Morgan requested Washington's permission to grant a $50 million commercial credit loan to the French government. Wilson and Bryan approved. In September, 1915, after Bryan had resigned and Lansing had replaced him as Secretary of State, the administration approved a $500 million loan to an Anglo-French commission. Thereafter, private loans to the Allies became common. By the time the United States entered the conflict, American bankers had lent $2.3

billion to the Allies and only $27 million to Germany. These loans directly stimulated the American economy because the money was spent in the United States. The American economy thus became inextricably intertwined with the Allied war effort.

The British Blockade

In the first months of the European war practically all of the American diplomatic difficulties over the rights of neutrals in international waters were with Great Britain rather than Germany. Several issues divided the United States and the Allies, particularly Britain, about neutral rights: definition of contraband, rights of search and seizure, British freighters flying the American flag to avoid German attack (an old ruse that the United States had employed during the Civil War), and censorship of mail. Britain, though a legalistic nation, was struggling for her life and frequently went beyond the bounds of accepted international maritime law, saying that the new warfare rendered the old customs irrelevant. Britain refused to accept the Declaration of London, a code of maritime law adopted by an international conference at London in 1909, when Wilson suggested she accept it, because the code would have put greater limitations upon her than the older international law.

Britain gradually extended the contraband list to include commodities that had theretofore not been included: cotton, gasoline, and, most important, food. In April, 1916, Britain abandoned the distinction between absolute and conditional contraband, and for the next year practically all goods shipped from America were considered contraband. Britain also departed from custom with her blockade techniques. Instead of erecting a blockade near the German coast where her ships would have been vulnerable to coastal batteries, she took the more efficient alternative of blocking the entrances to the North Sea and then instead of searching American ships for contraband on the spot, taking them to English ports. British and French censorship of mail particularly irked American businessmen, who argued that censorship delayed the delivery of their letters, occasionally causing their bids on contracts to arrive too late and that the British used the trade information in their letters for their own advantage.

At the very outset of the conflict, Wilson was prone to take a stern position with Britain on American neutral rights, but Colonel House persuaded him to be moderate. Once Wilson accepted the general principle of the maritime system imposed by the British, saying that all differences could be arbitrated after the end of the war, the essentials were beyond further dispute. Wilson could only object to certain specific practices and incidents. Usually when Wilson objected he did so in a mild manner; even when he did send a strong note to London the American ambassador there, Walter Hines Page, a strongly pro-British literary man, often softened the blow by conciliatory statements to British officials. Page even told the British Foreign Office that he did not himself agree with the substance of some of Wilson's messages, that the messages were motivated by domestic politics, and that the British could find some way to circumvent Washington's objections without affecting the naval strangle on Germany.

On the whole, Americans, although annoyed with the British, did not feel nearly as strongly about British disregard for conventional neutral rights as they did about Germany's because of vital differences in British and German strategic positions and weapons. Britain's infringements of international law caused inconvenience, delay, and sometimes loss of profits to American shippers. Germany, which had to rely upon the submarine, cost American lives rather than business disadvantage when she tried to effect a stranglehold on the Allies.

German Submarines, American Lives, and American Ships

On February 4, 1915, the German Admiralty announced a submarine blockade of the British Isles. She said the use of submarines was necessary to counteract the recent British addition of food to the list of contraband and that if the British would revoke their food-as-contraband order she would call off the U-boats. The German announcement stated it would destroy all Allied ships within the blockade zone around Great Britain "although it may not always be possible to save crews and passengers." The statement also warned that neutral ships would be endangered because of the British practice of flying flags of neutrals on her merchantmen.

On February 10 Wilson sent a note to Berlin that was both strong and weak. It was strong in that he declared that if American ships were lost by submarine action, the United States would hold Germany to "strict accountability." This was a harder position than Wilson ever took with the British. But the note was weak in that it said nothing about the question of Americans who might be working as sailors or traveling as passengers on Allied ships, and it was here that most of the difficulty came. Wilson also tried to persuade the British to rescind their ruling on food as contraband. Ultimately, the British complied with important reservations, but by that time the activity of German submarines had created serious tensions between the United States and Germany.

Wilson's note was effective so far as submarine attacks on American ships were concerned. German forces attacked only two American vessels before February, 1917. Both attacks were in 1915. The *Cushing,* which was plainly marked as an American ship, was attacked by a German plane without loss of life. Soon thereafter, a German submarine torpedoed the *Gulflight,* a Gulf Oil Company tanker, which did not fly the American flag until just before the torpedo was fired and which was near a British ship. Two men on the *Gulflight* were killed and the captain died of shock. The ship reached port. Germany quickly apologized and offered compensation.

But loss of American lives on British ships was another matter. On March 28, 1915, a German submarine sank the British steamer *Falaba,* which was carrying passengers and munitions, killing one American passenger. The submarine commander had warned the *Falaba* to unload its passengers. Before the administration could settle differences within it about how to deal with the *Falaba* affair, the whole situation was changed. On May 7 a German submarine without warning sank the *Lusitania* off the south coast of Ireland just within the German submarine zone. The ship, the largest Atlantic liner then afloat and owned by the British Cunard Lines, sank in 18 minutes with a total loss of 1,198 lives, 128 of whom were American citizens. The *Lusitania* was carrying many cases of rifle cartridges, and the German embassy in Washington had advertised in New York newspapers that anyone sailing on British flag ships did so at his own risk.

There is no question but that the sinking of the *Lusitania* greatly turned American opinion against Germany, but there was considerable disagreement about what the United States should do about the sinking. On May 10 in a speech at Philadelphia, Wilson said, "There is such a thing as a man being too proud to fight." Being "too proud to fight" was a concept unfathomable to the furious Roosevelt, who declared Wilson was surrounded by "flubdubs," "mollycoddles," and "flapdoodle pacifists." Important Democrats in Congress, however, warned Wilson that the American people were not ready to go to war over the *Lusitania*. The first *Lusitania* note went out May 13 over Bryan's signature. The note virtually demanded that Germany refrain from submarine attack on unarmed merchant vessels. Bryan cautioned moderation and persuaded Wilson to issue a statement advocating arbitration of the *Lusitania* affair, but Wilson yielded under great pressure from less cautious advisers and recalled the statement which had already been cabled to Germany. The German Foreign Office replied to the first note evasively. Bryan resigned rather than sign the second note, which denied that Germany had a right to ignore "the rights of humanity, which every Government honors itself in respecting" because the British violated property rights on the high seas. A third note appealed to Germany to try to safeguard neutral lives and stated that a repetition of sinkings of unarmed vessels would be "deliberately unfriendly," a sharp diplomatic phrase that might lead to recalling of diplomats and possibly war. Finally, in February, 1916, the German government implicitly admitted liability and offered to indemnify the United States for the loss of American lives, but because Germany would not admit the sinking was illegal, Wilson refused to accept the German offer as adequate and the affair remained unsettled.

On August 19, 1915, the British *Arabic*, a ship that had been carrying contraband consistently, was sunk on a westbound crossing. Two American passengers were killed. Wilson resolved to settle the issue, and the tensions in German-American relations were extreme in both Berlin and Washington. Six days later, Germany announced that the submarine commander must have gone beyond his orders and that if investigation showed that it was a torpedo from a German submarine that sank the *Arabic*, Germany would immediately fully apologize and offer indemnity. It became known that more than two months before the *Arabic* sinking submarine commanders had been ordered not to sink large passenger liners. The Kaiser ordered the abandonment of unrestricted warfare against all passenger ships. On September 1 the German ambassador to the United States, Count Johann von Bernstorff, gave a written promise to Lansing that came to be known as the *Arabic* pledge: "Liners will not be sunk by our submarines without warning and without safety of the lives of noncombatants, provided that the liners do not try to escape or offer resistance."

The *Arabic* pledge was a major diplomatic victory for the United States, although it did not settle the question of American seamen aboard belligerent freighters. It apparently did not settle the question in Wilson's mind either. According to Colonel House, in September, 1915, the President told him "he had never been sure that we ought not to take part in the conflict and if it seemed evident that Germany and her militaristic ideas were to win, the obligation upon us was greater than ever." The best way to maintain American peace, Wilson apparently reasoned, was to try to end the war in Europe.

Attempts at Mediation, 1915–1916

Wilson made his first real attempt to end the war by mediation only a few months after the declaration of war. German Ambassador von Bernstorff hinted that the Kaiser might be receptive to mediation, might withdraw from Belgium, and give the Belgians an indemnity. After preparatory talks with Allied and Central Power diplomats in America, Wilson dispatched Colonel House to London, Paris, and Berlin in late January, 1915. House received the most encouragement from Berlin, but the terms the Germans wanted—parts of Belgium, a slice of the Belgian Congo, and an indemnity from France—were unacceptable to the French, and the British were in no mood for mediation after the sinking of the *Lusitania*.

House Peace Mission

In the fall of 1915 the Wilson administration embarked on another effort to bring a negotiated peace, but the effort was inept, less than candid with the American people and congressional leaders, not fully open and above board in its dealings with the belligerents, and finally, marked by contradictions and confusion with the administration. On October 8, 1915, Colonel House proposed to the President that the United States compel a settlement of the war or, should that fail, enter the war on the Allied side. Wilson did not veto the idea, and House took his silence as consent. Soon thereafter, House received letters from Sir Edward Grey, the British foreign minister, which implied that the Allies might consider a negotiated peace if America would join a League of Nations to prevent future wars. Wilson collaborated with House on a reply to Grey's letter. The reply asked Grey to inform House when he thought an American move for a negotiated peace would be propitious, and he promised that when so informed he would urge the President to begin action. House, upon getting Wilson's approval, would then confer with the British and go to Berlin to tell the German officials that Wilson wanted to stop the fighting but would not tell the Germans of the earlier understanding with the British. "If the Central Powers were still obdurate, it would probably be necessary for us to join the Allies and force the issue." Wilson inserted the "probably." Grey replied, seeking some clarification and asking for a pledge to a League of Nations. Wilson approved the League idea.

In December, 1915, without any word from Grey that the time was ripe, Wilson decided to send House on a peace mission. At that time relations between Washington and Berlin were sorely strained—Germany was requested to recall Franz Von Papen and Karl Boy-Ed, its military and naval attachés in Washington, for plotting against American neutrality, and a complete break in relations seemed possible. House arrived in London on January 6, 1916. He received no commitments from the English but was encouraged nevertheless and went on to Berlin. The German leaders said they would participate in no peace negotiations that did not include assurances of French and British indemnities and German control of Belgium and Poland, harder terms than they had laid down a year before.

9

Actually, both sides expected major victories in the summer campaigns and neither was eager to bring peace. House went on to Paris and back to London where he and Grey in February prepared a memorandum of the Anglo-American understanding. The House-Grey memorandum stated that when France and England declared the time opportune, Wilson would propose a peace conference. Should the Allies accept and Germany refuse, "the United States would probably enter the war against Germany." If both sides accepted a conference, the peace meeting would secure "terms not unfavorable to the Allies; and, if it failed to secure peace, the United States would leave the Conference as a belligerent on the side of the Allies, if Germany were unreasonable." Again, Wilson had the "probably" inserted. Within a few months after this memorandum, Britain became quite optimistic about its chances of success on the battlefields of France and in August flatly rejected House's suggestion of a conference. House's negotiations were not known outside the Wilson administration, not even by the Democratic leadership in Congress.

While House was in Europe seeking a kind of pro-Allied peace, Lansing and Wilson were taking actions in Washington that, at first, brought Germany and the United States more closely together. Consistency was not among Wilson's virtues in early 1916. The White House also precipitated a major explosion on foreign policy in Congress.

Armed Merchant Ships and the Submarine

The main issue was over the arming of merchant ships. Early in the war, before the beginning of the German submarine campaigns, the State Department had classified armed merchant ships as peaceful and therefore free to enter neutral America's ports. In the summer of 1915 the British began to arm her freighters and even her liners and ordered them to attack submarines. For America to insist that German submarines observe the same rules toward these armed merchantmen that naval surface craft observed—warning and search for contraband—was to expose the relatively defenseless surfaced submarine to great danger. On January 18, 1916, therefore, soon after House arrived in London, Lansing proposed in notes to the Allies a new *modus vivendi*, or implicit working arrangement for maritime warfare: the Allies would remove arms from their non-naval vessels and the German submarines would observe the rules of surface craft. The British could not understand the House negotiations and the new Lansing proposal coming at the same time, for they considered that to disarm the merchant ships would serve Germany's advantage.

Soon Lansing and Wilson would back off from their new proposal but only in such a way as to heighten German-American tensions and bring about a congressional crisis. On January 26 Lansing told an Austrian diplomat in Washington about his proposal to the Allies. The Austrian replied that the Central Powers were contemplating a declaration of unrestricted submarine warfare against armed merchantmen and asked Lansing if he thought such a declaration advisable in view of his proposal to the Allies. Lansing answered that he thought such a German and Austrian declaration should be issued soon. On February 10 the Germans made the following announcement: beginning on February 29 their submarines would attack armed Allied freighters without warning. Having led the Central

Powers to issue the declaration, Lansing now reversed himself and on February 15 told the press that although he still thought it best for the Allies to disarm their merchantmen, if they did not do so the United States would not press the issue and would not warn its citizens against traveling on armed Allied ships. Two days later Lansing and Wilson rejected the German proposal for indemnity for the American lives lost on the *Lusitania*.

Now Democratic leaders in the Senate and House concerned with foreign affairs became alarmed and had an interview with the President. They wanted to know what Wilson would do if a submarine without warning sank an armed Allied ship on which American citizens were traveling. Wilson replied he would hold Germany to strict accountability but would not press the Allies to disarm their merchant ships. This was too warlike for Congress. The House Foreign Affairs Committee unanimously agreed to bring to the floor a resolution already offered by Representative Jeff McLemore of Texas which warned Americans against traveling on armed ships of countries at war. Senator Thomas P. Gore introduced a similar resolution in his chamber. The resolutions were strongly supported. House Speaker Clark said the McLemore resolution would carry by two to one if it came to a vote. But Wilson pressured Congress not to pass the resolutions by using his patronage powers extensively and succeeded in having both of them tabled.

The German government refused to revoke its declaration of unrestricted submarine warfare, even though Lansing was by this time unsuccessfully urging Wilson to break off diplomatic relations. On March 24 a German submarine torpedoed the *Sussex*, an unarmed French passenger ship, in the English channel. The boat made port, but there was a heavy loss of life. None of the American passengers was killed, but several were injured. At first the German diplomats, misinformed by their naval people, evaded responsibility for the attack. Lansing and House urged severe measures upon Wilson. On April 16, 1916, a note to Berlin declared that unless Germany "should now immediately declare and effect an abandonment of its present methods of submarine warfare against passenger and freight-carrying vessels," the United States "can have no choice but to sever diplomatic relations." Wilson went before Congress and repeated the ultimatum. This was a long way from Lansing's proposal about disarming merchantmen three months earlier.

The Germans were then eager to avoid war with the United States and backed down part way. On May 4 the German government replied to the note of April 16 saying that it would thereafter observe the rules of visit and search before sinking merchant vessels, but that if the United States did not make the British cease violations of prewar international law "the German government would then be facing a new situation in which it must reserve itself complete liberty of decision." Wilson replied to this so-called *Sussex* pledge on May 8 by saying that friendly relations between the two powers depended upon German observance of its statement and the United States did not recognize the conditional provision that it should hold the British to compliance with international law. There the matter stood. The tension abated. But Wilson had placed himself in a position that required a diplomatic break if the Germans resumed unrestricted warfare.

For the balance of 1916 German-American relations were relatively peaceful.

But Anglo-American relations deteriorated badly. The suppression of the Irish rebellion in April heightened American popular disapproval of the English, and Wilson was distressed by the final British refusal to accept a peace conference at that time. Furthermore, in July, 1916, the British published a list of eighty-seven American companies with whom British subjects were forbidden to deal because they had done business with the Central Powers. In retaliation against this blacklist, Wilson secured legislation that empowered him to refuse American port facilities to ships that discriminated against the forbidden American companies. These difficulties with the English, however, were not so emotional as had been the situation with Germany in the spring, and the elections of 1916 were held without a threat of imminent war.

Preparedness

Almost from the beginning of the European conflict there had been demands for strengthening the American military and naval establishment from both economic conservatives such as Henry Cabot Lodge and from followers of the chip-on-shoulder Roosevelt. In the fall of 1914 the Army League, the Navy League (both old militaristic organizations), and the new National Security League urged Congress to increase American armed strength. Most people were apathetic or opposed, and the White House was then opposed to an increase in armaments. The advocates of preparedness argued that America could best preserve her neutrality by building strong defenses.

But the thousands of people in peace organizations believed that the argument of neutrality through strong defenses was specious because its proponents frequently urged intervention when there was a crisis in relations with Germany or Mexico. Furthermore, with the exception of the Roosevelt group, the advocates of preparedness were conservatives in domestic affairs, and most of the peace organizations were dominated by Democratic progressives or Republican agrarian progressives. They feared that preparedness would mean militarism and an end of progressivism at home.

As the German submarine disputes became serious in 1915, Wilson began to shift ground toward preparedness. He also was surely not unmindful that he and the Democrats would be in an advantageous position for the 1916 elections if he yielded some to the preparedness advocates and yet preserved the peace. In July, 1915, he asked the Secretaries of War and of the Navy to prepare recommendations for strengthening national defense. Their reports recommended building a navy to be the equal of Britain's by 1925, increasing the size of the regular army, scrapping the state-controlled National Guard, and erecting in its place a national reserve force, the Continental Army, of four hundred thousand men. The President made the program public in November, and when Congress met the next month Wilson made patriotism and preparedness the main topics of his annual message. The Democratic leader of the House, Claude Kitchin, and a considerable group of Democratic congressmen from the South and West sharply opposed Wilson on preparedness and controlled the House military affairs committee. Wilson went on a speaking tour of major cities of the Midwest to whip up enthusiasm for preparedness but he failed to excite much support.

12

In March the House passed a bill to increase the regular army from 100,000 to 140,000 men but killed the Continental Army idea, which had aroused widespread opposition as a militaristic notion, in favor of granting War Department control of the state National Guard units. The next month, however, the Senate added to the limited House increases against the background of the *Sussex* crisis, and the final law passed in May raised the regular army to 11,327 officers and 208,338 enlisted men. The law also integrated the National Guard into the War Department and authorized total National Guard strength of 17,000 officers and 440,000 enlisted men. On the whole, the Army Reorganization Act was a substantial step toward preparedness, although Kitchin regarded the bill as a personal victory and extreme preparedness advocates such as Roosevelt denounced it. The National Security League even urged Wilson to veto the bill and demand stronger legislation.

The congressional naval affairs committee postponed action until the army bill went through. Then the House ignored the executive request for a five-year building program but authorized more tonnage the next year than the White House had requested. The Senate put the five-year program back in and stepped up the schedule to three years. Wilson pressured the House into concurring in the $500 million plus measure. The act provided for the construction the first year of four battleships, four battle cruisers, four cruisers, twenty destroyers, and thirty submarines. The White House also obtained passage of the Merchant Marine Act of 1916 which created a United States Shipping Board empowered to spend as much as $50 million on building or purchasing merchant ships suitable as naval auxiliaries, to operate shipping lines, and to charter its ships to private companies. Shipping companies objected to the bill, calling it "socialism," never dreaming that the Shipping Board in time would be a tremendous subsidy to them.

The opponents of preparedness had lost almost everything on the defense program except for omitting the proposed Continental Army. At the same time, however, Wilson urged a series of domestic reform measures and acquiesced in the progressive demand that the cost of the armament program be paid for by higher taxes on big incomes of individuals and corporations, as described in chapter three (volume I). It is difficult to say with any certainty if a majority of the people supported the preparedness program or not. Washington sponsored several "preparedness parades" and other patriotic demonstrations in 1916, but much of the enthusiasm for these spectacles seemed synthetic. Wilson's efforts to turn the Democratic national convention into a patriotic preparedness rally backfired completely, and it actually became more of a peace demonstration. Undoubtedly, the fact that the nation was still at peace on election day had more to do with Wilson's re-election than the fact that he had led the struggle for greater armament.

The War Comes

When Wilson could again turn his full attention to foreign affairs after the election, the situation in Europe had changed. The German offensive at Verdun in the spring of 1916 had failed, as had the Allied Somme counteroffensive, but in the late fall of 1916 the Germans gained on the eastern front and occupied Romania. The Germans, of course, did not know that the first Russian revolution would come the following March and that Russian resistance would collapse soon thereafter. In the immediate situation it seemed to both sides that they must intensify the use of their best weapons: for Germany, the submarine campaign to disrupt the economic base of British strength; for Britain, the stranglehold of economic blockade.

The British tightened their hold through bunker agreements; neutral shippers agreed to adhere to the regulations of the British Admiralty in exchange for the privilege of buying British coal at ports of the world. From November, 1916, until the end of January, 1917, Anglo-American relations were their most strained.

At a high-level conference of German leaders in late August, 1916, the naval officials had urged an all-out submarine campaign, arguing that they could knock out about 40 per cent of the British sea freight capacity within five months and that the campaign would meanwhile keep many neutral vessels at home. Civilian and army leaders, however, argued that a submarine campaign probably would bring the United States into the war and vetoed the German Admiralty's suggestion for the moment. Germany first would try direct negotiations for peace.

The Second Peace Proposal

Wilson also decided that another effort to bring peace was in order. He realized that the House-Grey memorandum was dead, and to Colonel House's question as to what he would do if the Germans accepted peace overtures and the Allies did not—House even suggested the Allies might declare war on America —he replied that he did not think the Allies would declare war but that if they did he would not back away. The Germans had already urged Wilson to take the initiative for peace, and in late November, 1916, Wilson began to draft a note to urge a peace conference.

Wilson's first draft of the note is interesting in view of later developments. He wrote that the reasons for the war were obscure, that neutrals still did not know what the war was all about, and that the belligerents ought to state their war aims. Lansing and House persuaded Wilson to redraft and tone down the note which went out on December 18. It asked only that the belligerents state their objectives.

Both the Allies and Germany were evasive, dilatory, and less than candid in stating their war objectives. The day after Wilson sent his note, the British prime minister, David Lloyd George, told the House of Commons that the Allied peace terms were "complete restitution, full reparation, and effectual guarantee" of peace in the future. The British foreign secrtary, Arthur Balfour, in a confidential memorandum whose contents did not become known until years later, was more specific. The objectives were to weaken the Central Powers by breaking up large parts of Central Europe into several nations on the basis of nationality—Alsace-Lorraine back to France, Constantinople for Russia, a semiautonomous Poland with close Russian connections and to include parts of Germany and the Austrian provinces—and to secure reparations for the submarine sinkings and war damages in Belgium, France, and Serbia. The Germans were reluctant to reveal their aims until after they had already made the decision for an all-out submarine campaign, and further made clear they did not want Wilson at any peace conference that might develop. To the Germans, his function was merely to force the Allies to a peace conference. The German war objectives Wilson received on January 31, 1917, were territorial changes in East Europe to protect Germany from Russia, additional colonies, indemnity from the Allies for war damages, and German withdrawal from France and Belgium but with financial compensation and re-drawing the boundaries to Germany's advantage. Clearly, neither side in the winter of 1916–17 was willing to settle for a draw, a "peace without victory" such as Wilson urged in a speech to the Senate on January 22 while delicate negotiations were still in progress.

Resumption of All-Out Submarine Warfare

When Wilson gave his "peace without victory" address Germany had already decided, on January 9, 1917, that a negotiated peace on the terms she wanted was out of the question and that she would begin her attempt at a knock-out blow by submarine on February 1. The German government informed its ambassador in Washington, Bernstorff, on January 16, of its decision and instructed him not to notify the Wilson administration until January 31. Bernstorff presented both the notice of the submarine campaign and the final statement of German war objectives at the same time. The submarine note declared that effective February 1 German submarines would attack all ships, Allied or neutral, in a war zone around Great Britain, France, Italy, and the eastern Mediterranean. The United States would be permitted to send one passenger ship a week to Falmouth, England, if it bore certain designated markings. In other words, Germany had revoked not only the *Sussex* pledge of May, 1916, but the practice observed since the spring of 1915 of avoiding attacks on American ships. The German government took this decision with recognition that it would probably mean American military intervention on the side of the Allies. Germany's hope was that the submarine campaign and an offensive on the western front would end the war before American military power could tip the balance for the Allies.

Wilson had committed himself to breaking diplomatic relations with the resumption of intense submarine warfare at the time of the *Sussex* crisis. On February 3 Wilson announced in a speech to Congress that he had taken steps to end all diplomatic relations with Germany. The immediate economic effects of his action are worth noting. The stock market, which had been depressed during the peace efforts, immediately started up, and Wilson received messages of congratulations from the House of Morgan, United States Steel, Bethlehem Steel, and the Remington Arms Company. But Wilson's support was far wider than just among the interests that stood to profit from a war. On the whole, he had the support of the Midwest and the West, which theretofore had been primary centers of neutralist sentiment. Only very few people, however, called for a declaration of war.

Wilson was by no means ready for war. In fact, he made an unsuccessful and desperate attempt to divide Austria-Hungary from Germany and to bring peace by a promise it could retain its prewar empire, an attempt which was interesting in view of Wilson's ultimate peace conference position. He also made it clear to the British that the United States was still neutral when, on February 17, he notified them that international maritime law was still unsettled and that America reserved the right to enter claims for damages to American citizens incurred

15

by British action. Wilson was waiting for an overt act by German submarines. The first attacks on American ships did not come until March 12.

Arming American Ships

On February 7 Wilson refused to use the navy to convoy ships through the war zone. Shipping companies began to cancel sailings, and, as material began to pile up in Atlantic ports, there was considerable pressure on the administration to arm merchant ships. In cabinet meetings Wilson resisted a decision to ask Congress for authority to arm them until February 25. He then changed his mind upon learning from Ambassador Page in London the contents of a note from the German foreign minister, Alfred Zimmermann, to the German minister in Mexico City which the British had intercepted and decoded.

On January 17 Zimmermann had sent to his minister in Mexico via Ambassador Bernstorff in Washington instructions to be followed in the event of war between the United States and Germany. Upon a declaration of war the minister should propose to the Mexican government an alliance in which Mexico would declare war upon the United States and recover Texas, New Mexico, and Arizona. Mexico was also to ask the Japanese to join the new alliance. Ironically, the German foreign office had asked for and received permission to send the message over the wire connecting the American embassy in Berlin with the State Department. After the British had intercepted and decoded the note, it delayed informing the United States of its contents until an advantageous moment. The day after learning of the proposed German-Mexican alliance, Wilson went to Congress and asked for authority to arm American merchant ships.

Wilson's speech was not warlike. He did not mention the Zimmermann note, pointed out that there had not yet been a submarine attack on an American ship, and expressed a hope for peace. Yet he asked for authority to arm the merchant ships and for broad authority to use "any other instrumentalities or methods" to safeguard lives and commerce. There was little sentiment in either house of Congress for arming the merchant vessels, but the extreme neutralists in the Senate, led by LaFollette and Norris, threatened to filibuster the whole armed ship bill if it granted the President broad powers. Congress was then in a "lame duck" session which had to disband by March 4, and a filibuster could be successful. Indeed, a group of Republican senators had already decided to filibuster an appropriations bill so that the "lame duck" session would be ended and Wilson would call the new Congress, elected in November, 1916, into a special session. The Republicans called off their filibuster plans and let the LaFollette-Norris group bear the odium of the delay. The House foreign affairs committee would grant the power to arm merchantmen but not the broad powers, despite great White House pressure.

When it appeared that neither house would give him the powers he asked, Wilson released the Zimmermann note to the Associated Press, which published it on March 1. A great wave of hostility to Germany swept the country, and immediately the House passed the armed ship bill by an overwhelming margin but without a broad powers provision. Senate majority leaders urged the passage of a grant of broad authority, but the neutralists talked the bill and the session of Congress to death. On March 9 Wilson announced he would arm the merchant ships upon the authority of an antipiracy law of 1819. The gun crews on the ships were ordered to fire upon any submarine that came within range. He also called the new Congress to meet on April 16. On March 12 a German submarine sank the *Algonquin*, an unarmed American merchantman, without warning. The same day there came the first revolution in Russia. American public reaction was quite favorable, partly because it gave a greater aspect of democracy to the Allied cause, and the United States officially recognized the new government on March 22. On March 18 German submarines sank three more American merchant vessels.

Wilson's War Message

At a cabinet meeting on March 19 Wilson did not announce a decision for war despite the cabinet's urging of a war message. When Lansing argued at the meeting for a war declaration upon ideological grounds, to save democracy from German militarism, Wilson replied that he did not see how he could invoke democracy in a war message to Congress. The next day, however, Wilson moved up the opening date of the new Congress to April 2, "to receive a communication concerning grave matters of national policy." His decision to deliver a war message became clear when he called the National Guard of the eastern, midwestern, and Pacific Coast states into federal service and authorized the Secretary of the Navy to begin working out plans for coordinating American and British naval operations. He went to work on his war message, but only with a heavy heart and well aware of what war would mean for the country. As he had told his friend Frank Cobb, editor of the New York *World*, "Once lead this people into war and they'll forget there ever was such a thing as tolerance. To fight you must be brutal and ruthless, and the spirit of ruthless brutality will enter into the very fibre of our national life, infecting Congress, the courts, the policeman on the beat, the man in the street."

Wilson delivered his war message to a joint session of Congress the evening of April 2. He asked Congress to recognize that a state of war already existed between the United States and Germany. He had changed his mind since the cabinet meeting of March 19 about putting the message on ideological grounds and declared, "The world must be made safe for democracy. Its peace must be planted upon the tested foundations of political liberty." The Senate adopted a war resolution on April 4 by an 82 to 6 vote; the House passed the resolution on April 6 at 3:12 in the morning by a 373 to 50 vote. Wilson signed the resolution the afternoon of April 6, and the United States was officially at war. America did not declare war on Austria-Hungary until December 7, 1917, hoping meanwhile it might divide the Central Powers. The United States never declared war on Germany's other two partners, Turkey and Bulgaria, although it broke diplomatic relations with Turkey. An era of American history had ended.

Why did the United States go to war with Germany? Few people would assert that there can be a simple or definitive answer to the question. The submarine campaign of early 1917 triggered American intervention, but the gun was already cocked. What cocked the gun? Many things. One was majority sentiment for the Allied cause, a belief that German victory was inimicable to democracy and that an Allied victory, while not necessarily cause for democratic jubilation, was at least more desirable. Akin to this underlying cause of the war was American belief in a right, even a duty, to set the world aright—a missionary impulse which for many meant molding the rest of the world in the American image. Economic factors were certainly another basic cause. Loans and sales to the Allies, long before the war declaration, had been the basis of American prosperity, and the United States had a considerable economic stake in an Allied victory. This does not imply a banker-munitions manufacturer plot to trick the nation into war; it merely means that societies are basically conditioned by their economic foundations. American national security in the sense of protection of its shores from foreign attack was not truly a major consideration, although many people regarded the Zimmermann note, which was to be executed only in the event of a declaration of war, as a threat to national security.

Could American entrance into the war have been avoided? In other words, what would have happened if different decisions had been taken from the time of the outbreak of war in Europe? No one can ever know for sure, and the conditional tense is not the one for historians. One can only speculate. Some have speculated that if the Russian revolution had come earlier, thereby encouraging German victory, Germany would not have resorted to all-out submarine attacks and the United States would not have become involved. One can speculate that if the United States had placed its very highest priority on remaining neutral and submerging other considerations, it could have avoided war. The grounds for this speculation lie in the relatively small amount of damage incurred by the United States as a result of German naval attack, which was the factor that precipitated the final declaration. Between the outbreak of war in 1914 and April, 1917, 209 American citizens died as a result of German attack, more than half of them on the *Lusitania*. Only 28 Americans lost their lives on American ships. The contrast with the Scandinavian nations, which remained neutral, is striking. Norway lost over 3,000 sailors and about half of its merchant marine, and foreign commerce was more important to that small nation than it was to the United States. Yet to expect the complicated and vast nation that was the United States to have unitedly submerged all else for neutrality would be unrealistic.

The Yanks Who Went to War

The first United States contribution to the ultimate Allied victory was on the seas. (America, incidentally, was careful not to make any permanent alliances and always referred to herself during the war as an "Associated Power" rather than one of the Allies.) Admiral William S. Sims conferred with British naval officers in London even before the declaration of war, and thereafter the United States navy worked as an integral part of British operations rather than independently.

The primary naval tasks were to protect the sea lanes and transport troops, which meant that the main enemy was always the submarine. There were no major naval battles such as the British had fought with the Germans at Jutland in the spring of 1916. In May, 1917, therefore, the United States abandoned its general shipbuilding program and concentrated on destroyers and other anti-submarine craft. It was important that the American navy get into the war against the submarine quickly. In April, 1917, alone, German submarines sank over 880,000 tons of shipping. In May the first American destroyers began operating with the British, and by the end of the year losses to submarines had been cut in half. After the first year of American naval operations, shipping losses never amounted to more than two hundred thousand tons a month.

The Contribution of the U.S. Navy

The United States navy made two main contributions to Allied naval strategy: the convoy technique for trans-Atlantic merchant and troop shipping and a partial blockade of the entrance to the North Sea by a mine field. The British had not had enough destroyers to protect convoys and had thought it impossible to keep merchant vessels in formation in the foggy North Atlantic, but American officers insisted that the trick could be done and ran the first convoy to Britain in May, 1917. From the summer of 1917 until the end of the war, Allied shipping went by convoy. The British navy at first rejected the American suggestion of a mine field between the Orkney Islands and Norway, but cooperated in the venture in early 1918 after the development of an improved mine. The two navies had not completed laying the field by the end of the war, but the mines nevertheless destroyed about 10 per cent of the German submarines that tried to go through the huge sea gate, and many others suffered damage.

Conscription

When the United States first declared war, few citizens thought that American participation would go beyond naval support, shipping, and material. French and British army missions, however, explained that the Allies were getting low on manpower and had to have American troops. Wilson and his Secretary of War, Newton D. Baker, were determined that the raising of the army would be somewhat more efficient than had been earlier American efforts, when individuals were allowed to raise volunteer units such as the Rough Riders and conscription had been only a last resort. The administration asked for a conscription law soon after the war declaration, but the bill ran into considerable opposition in Congress. Speaker of the House Champ Clark vigorously opposed the draft, remarking that where he came from conscripts and convicts were regarded as remarkably similar. Congress opposed the War Department demand for conscription of men aged nineteen to twenty-five and set the registration for all men between twenty-one and thirty. Congress also authorized volunteer units, although it did not force the administration to take them. The prohibitionists showed that they were going to use the war to their advantage by banning the sale of liquor at or near army camps, but, as French bistro keepers soon learned, the dry camps did not diminish the American doughboy's taste for alcohol. Roosevelt wanted desperately to raise his own division and take it to France although he was fifty-eight years old and blind in one eye. When Wilson and Baker refused him and all other volunteer units, the ex-President was convinced that Wilson acted only from personal malice.

The draft bill became law on May 18, 1917; the first registration under it was on June 5. The administration remembered the opposition to the draft during the Civil War, anticipated violence on registration day, and obtained the cooperation of local sheriffs and police, but 9,500,000 men registered that day without major incident. On August 31, 1918, conscription was extended to all men between eighteen and forty-five. No enlistments were permitted after August 9, 1918. By the end of the war, 24,234,021 men had been registered and 2,810,296 drafted. On April 2, 1917, there were 378,619 men in all the armed forces; on Armistice Day the figure had increased to 4,791,172.

To get men in the armed forces was easier than training and equipping them. In June, 1917, construction began on 16 new army camps, each one to be a complete unit for the training of 48,000 new soldiers. They went up remarkably quickly but were far from ready when the first draftees arrived in September. Training officers was more difficult than training enlisted men, and the system used at Plattsburgh, New York, and other such centers where college students and a few others became "ninety-day wonders" was never fully satisfactory. Although American industry performed miracles during the war, it was never able fully to meet the demands of the services. Most of the artillery used by the American Expeditionary Force in France was of French manufacture, and only a small proportion of the aircraft used was produced in the United States.

The AEF

Wilson bypassed General Leonard Wood to make General Pershing commander of the American Expeditionary Force (AEF). Pershing arrived in Paris in mid-June, 1917, to announce, "Lafayette, we are here," but "we" consisted of only about 14,500 troops, whose chief immediate value was for Allied morale. Pershing insisted to the British and French commands that the AEF be an independent unit, working with the Allies in general strategy of course, but a unit unto itself with its own independent function at the front. There was little the Allies could do under the circumstances but submit to Pershing's demand, and they grudgingly granted the AEF a quiet sector to defend near Verdun in the fall of 1917. Some battalions had already had some battle experience serving with the French.

In the fall of 1917 the German armies began a series of attacks which became increasingly serious as the Germans shifted divisions from the eastern front. The second, or Bolshevik, Russian revolution came in November, 1917, and the Russians were soon out of the war altogether. Not until the Germans concentrated on the western front did the Allies create the Supreme War Council to direct all western military operations. During the winter of 1917–18, Pershing and Wilson were under considerable pressure from the Allies to allow elements of the AEF to be used as replacements in defense against the German attacks, but they successfully held to their demand for an independent American command.

On March 21, 1918, the Germans launched a series of attacks which they hoped would end the war. The first attack, against the British on the Somme sector, rolled thirty miles the first week, a greater gain than either side had made in such a short period since 1914. The Allies and Wilson then named Marshal Ferdinand Foch as supreme commander of the western forces, and Pershing offered him all of his resources. At the time Pershing had four divisions plus necessary supporting units. By the Armistice on November 11 he had forty-two divisions and slightly over two million men.

The AEF First Division went into the Somme sector in late May with orders to take the village of Cantigny. This was the first rough action American troops had been in, and the Allies were eager to see how the doughboys acquitted themselves. They did well. They captured Cantigny on May 28 and successfully defended the strategically important village at the tip of the German offensive against seven counterattacks in three days.

On April 9 the Germans unleashed a major attack on the British toward the northern end of the front, and although they made advances and captured many prisoners the British held their lines. Then on May 27 the Kaiser's army unleashed a dangerous campaign against the French between Soissons and Rheims. In three days, the Germans were at Chateau Thierry on the Marne River, only fifty miles from Paris. Foch threw in the AEF Second Division and American marines. They pushed the Germans back across the Marne and in June cleared them out of Belleau Wood.

A word needs to be said about the nature of the fighting on the western front, which was different from most subsequent American military action. Each side in times of relative quiet settled down to trench warfare, a dirty, cold, and thoroughly unpleasant life for the soldier, which only got worse when either side made an attack. Preceding an attack the artillery would lay down a terrific barrage, and then the infantry would go "over the top" in an effort to dislodge the enemy from its stronghold. Casualties were concentrated and very heavy.

In mid-July, 1918, the Germans made a desperate attack on the sector between Soissons and Rheims, the Marne offensive. About 85,000 American troops were in the Marne pocket, and in three days the Germans had been stopped. The Germans had spent their last offensive strength in one final effort. Pershing and the Allied commanders realized the German position and soon began a series of offensives that finally ended the war.

The offensives extended the length of the front; American troops were engaged in two drives near the southern end, the St. Mihiel salient southeast of Verdun and the Meuse-Argonne sector west of Verdun. The Germans had been dug in at the St. Mihiel salient since 1914 and were well fortified. The AEF attacked it on September 12 and within four days had control of the area. Pershing wanted to push on to Metz, but Foch moved the AEF's main strength to the Meuse-Argonne sector, where the objective was to capture the railroad behind the German lines upon which the Kaiser's armies depended.

The battle for the Argonne was one of the bloodiest of the whole war. The AEF had twenty-four miles of the two-hundred-mile front when the counteroffensive opened on September 26. It sputtered at first and had to be reorganized eight days later. Then one sustained and hard push for the rest of the month pushed the quickly weakening Germans back to the Meuse River and beyond at some points. Allied arms had similar success in other sectors, and the Germans were on the run.

Armistice, At Last

The Central Powers began to fall apart. Bulgaria agreed to an armistice on September 29 and Turkey on October 30. On November 3 Austria gave up, and the end was in sight for Germany. On November 7 a German detail of officers passed through the lines to discuss armistice terms, and on November 11 at 11:00 a.m. the long and horrible war ended at last.

For years after 1918 Americans fruitlessly argued with British and French citizens over who won the war. It was easy for Americans to say they had won because victory came after they had thrown their full force into the battle. Indeed, American power was decisive although it was only the straw that broke the German camel's back. When the Germans began their last offensives in the spring of 1918, they had a numerical superiority. By the fall, the heroic measures taken to get American soldiers across the Atlantic and to the front had given the Allies superiority in numbers and firepower.

The statistics were appalling. Slightly more than 50,000 American soldiers lost their lives in battle. Another 75,000 died from other causes, largely the influenza epidemic that swept the world and killed about 10,000,000 people. Over 200,000 American troops were wounded; about 85 per cent of the wounded, thanks to efficient medical services, returned to active duty. Yet the American losses were minor compared to those of the other belligerents. Germany lost 1,600,000 men and Austria 800,000. On the other side, the Russians suffered the worst losses, 1,700,000 killed, a fact that was no small factor in bringing about the Bolshevik revolution. The French lost 1,385,000 and the British, with her empire troops, 900,000. It was no gross exaggeration to say that the flower of the western world's young generation lost its life blood on the soil of European nationalism. And, as everyone soon would see, the war had not made the world safe for democracy.

The Home Front
and the Peace

*The President . . . did not permit himself ever to refer to
the nations by whose side we fought as "allies," but
always as "nations associated with us in the war." . . .
Now, in the twinkling of an eye, while passion and
emotion reign, the Washington policy is to be entirely laid
aside and we are to enter upon a permanent
and indissoluble alliance.*

HENRY CABOT LODGE,
speech in the U.S. Senate, 1919

Chapter Two

The history of a war is not completed when the military and naval action has been described. Success or failure in battle underlies all a nation's decisions and policies during wartime, of course, and to the men engaged in battle nothing else in the world is as important. Yet, apart from the basic condition of victory or defeat, what happens to a nation economically, politically, socially, and diplomatically during a war has a more lasting impact than the events of conflict. What happens at home has even a more permanent effect upon the soldier himself, provided he survives in reasonably good condition.

The United States that returning servicemen found in 1919 was not the United States they had left in 1917. Nor would it ever be again. Progressivism was all but dead. Intolerance had replaced freewheeling dissent and rebellion. The economy had changed significantly and was to change still more. And the peace that was made held little promise of preventing another war.

The Economic Impact of War

The stimulus of war contracts, both for American use and for the Allies, brought a high level of prosperity. Unemployment, which had not been any serious problem since mid-1915 when sales to the Allies ended the 1914 recession, practically disappeared, and women and young people who had theretofore not been on the labor market took jobs in industry. Work was regular, and the take-home pay of industrial workers rose considerably. High prices wiped out a large part of the gain in money income, but not all of it; real wages—wages in relation to cost of living—improved. With a better market in the cities and a huge market for their products abroad, farmers' real income increased by about one-fourth. Furthermore, a speculative boom in farm property made it possible for those who sold their farms to make huge returns on their investment. On the other hand, those who bought farm acreage at inflated prices incurred large debts that would later bring agricultural disaster.

Financing the War

Before the war the federal government's annual budget had never exceeded $750 million, but the average for fiscal 1918 to 1920 (July 1, 1917 through June 30, 1920) was $12.5 billion. Increased taxes and borrowing—at a ratio of about twice as much in bond sales as in taxes—paid for the war. Left progressives wanted the war to be paid entirely from increased taxes, and business wanted at least four-fifths of the cost to be financed by bonds. Congress passed the first War Loan Act two weeks after the war declaration. It authorized government borrowing of $2 billion in short-term notes and $5 billion in Liberty Loan bonds. Later in the war there were three other Liberty Loan drives, and a Victory Loan came after the armistice. Altogether these bond sales brought the Treasury about $21 billion.

The Treasury was eager for the Liberty bonds to have a wide general sale, both to prevent banks and other financial institutions from holding all the debt and for propaganda purposes. The Department organized huge bond-selling drives and publicized them extensively. Local Liberty Loan committees organized brigades of "four-minute men" to give speeches at public gatherings to boost bond sales, and frequently the committees resorted to high pressure tactics and intimidation to reach their quota. People who did not purchase as many bonds as the community thought they should were likely to be labelled "slackers," the great smear word of the era, and, especially, if they had a German name, might find their home smeared with yellow paint during the night. School boards cooperated by selling students thrift stamps in small denominations.

The revenue measure adopted soon before the war declaration had to be buttressed with a new tax law in October, 1917. The new law levied excise taxes on tobacco, liquor, insurance, transportation, automobiles, and other less revenue-producing items. The act lowered income tax exemptions to $1,000 for single people and $2,000 for married couples, raised the normal tax to 4 per cent, and increased the maximum surtax (on incomes of over $2 million) to 63 per cent. It also increased the inheritance tax to a maximum of 25 per cent and levied an excess profits tax on corporations that ranged from 20 to 60 per cent. Late in the war, the administration asked for an increase in taxes, but the next revenue act did not become law until soon after the armistice. It raised the normal income tax to 6 per cent (on incomes up to $4,000), hit receivers of huge incomes a little harder by lowering the highest income bracket level to $1 million and increasing the maximum surtax to 65 per cent, and increased the excess profits tax slightly. Although families with unusually large incomes paid far greater taxes under the war tax laws than they had ever before, families with low and moderate incomes provided the bulk of revenues for the war.

Directing the Economy

Before the war it was apparent that an unusual amount of federal direction of the economy would be necessary even to meet the demands of the preparedness program. When the war came, the government realized that the nation's economic system was far from adequate to produce and transport what was necessary. The administration only gradually and piecemeal took over direction of the economy and never fully controlled it, but by the end of the war the federal government had become the nation's economic coordinator and regulator. World War I was the United States' first experiment with a planned economy.

Congress created the Council of National Defense in 1916 as part of the preparedness program. The Council, composed of six cabinet members and its Advisory Commission, which did most of the actual work and which consisted of transportation, engineering, mercantile, financial, and labor specialists, made an inventory of the nation's productive capacity. In late March, 1917, it created the Munitions Standards Board to standardize munitions production, which after the war declaration was renamed the General Munitions Board and empowered to supervise the purchase of all munitions for the services.

It became obvious, however, that government control would have to go farther than munitions, and on July 28, 1917, the Council of National Defense abolished the General Munitions Board and created the War Industries Board (WIB) to coordinate all relevant production, allocate materials and power, and supervise labor-management relations. The new system did not work at first because the WIB had insufficient power. The first WIB director, Frank A. Scott, broke down and resigned in October, and his successor, Daniel Willard of the Baltimore and Ohio Railroad, left the position in January, 1918, just as a Senate committee revealed chaotic inefficiency in the industrial war effort. Instead of resorting to laissez-faire as the Senate committee suggested, Wilson drafted a bill that granted him very extensive powers to reorganize the war agencies and to direct the nation's industrial effort. The bill became the Overman Act in April, 1918. In March Wilson named Bernard M. Baruch, a highly successful Wall Street speculator who was a member of the Council of National Defense, to be director of WIB and granted him emergency powers.

Baruch used his great powers to rationalize American industry, something that had to be done to get material produced and transported. Some individual firms, most of them large ones, had already rationalized their production, but Baruch found it necessary to rationalize whole industries and coordinate the various industries into an efficient national production system. The WIB accomplished a great deal of efficiency merely by standardizing sizes and reducing them to a minimum. For example, it reduced the number of sizes and types of automobile tires from 277 to 9, steel plows from 312 to 76, and buggy wheels from 232 to 4. It also experimented successfully with regulating the size of packages so that box car space would be most fully put to use. Businessmen frequently grumbled at taking orders from Washington bureaucrats, but they made good profits. "Dollar-a-year men," businessmen who gave their services to the government for a nominal salary while they remained on the payroll of their corporation, frequently were not above the temptations of their conflict of interest. "Cost plus" government contracts, which allowed a fixed percentage of profit on the gross costs of production, encouraged reckless spending and, sometimes, dubious accounting methods.

Dealing with Shortages

Wilson and the Council of National Defense in April, 1917, brought Herbert Hoover, who had been director of the Belgian Relief Commission during the neutrality period, into the administration to serve as chairman of the committee on food production and distribution. His function was at first only advisory, but in May he became Food Commissioner and was granted slightly more power. The Lever Act of August, 1917, created the office of Food Administrator with broad powers over the production and distribution of food, feed, fertilizer, farm implements, and fuel. The law also forbade the manufacture from foodstuffs of all alcoholic beverages.

Hoover's main food problems were with wheat, sugar, and pork. The wheat crops of both 1916 and 1917 were poor. The Lever Act set a minimum price of $2.00 a bushel for wheat, but Hoover offered to buy the 1917 crop, through the new United States Grain Corporation, at $2.20 a bushel. This price encouraged greater wheat production in 1918, but it was short throughout 1917, and families were urged to observe "wheatless Mondays and Wednesdays," as well as "meatless Tuesdays" and "porkless Thursdays and Saturdays." Practically every day was "sugarless," as the price of sugar soared beyond reason and grocers were ordered not to sell more than two pounds per person per month. Hoover urged families to grow "war gardens" even in their front yards. Hoover did as good a job of efficient food distribution as could be done under the law. But the distribution of food would have been more equitable had the federal government been empowered to control prices and ration critical items.

Coal became seriously short in the winter of 1917–18. In August, 1917, Wilson established the Fuel Administration and named his friend Harry A. Garfield, president of Williams College, to head it. Garfield was able to bring about an increase in coal production by raising its price, which made it profitable for operators to work mines that had become marginal. But coal soon ran into a major transportation problem during the unusually cold winter. Some steel plants ran short of fuel and had to cut back production, and, in January, thirty-seven freighters laden with munitions were stranded in New York harbor by lack of coal. Garfield ordered all manufacturing plants except those engaged in vital war production to close down for five days in mid-January and to observe nine subsequent "heatless Mondays." Businessmen roared but the drastic action, plus a far-reaching railroad reorganization, got the economy past the crisis.

Railroads and Shipping

Wilson put all rail transportation under the control of the United States Railroad Administration in the closing days of 1917. William McAdoo resigned as Secretary of the Treasury to become its head. The railroads were in a terrible mess at the time. Eastern freight yards were jammed to capacity and manufacturers elsewhere needed empty cars. Heavy snows and frozen switches created chaos throughout the transportation system. To meet the crisis, McAdoo operated all the nation's railroads as if they were one integrated system and cut back passenger schedules to a minimum. When it became evident that the railroads' equipment and facilities were inadequate—sometimes actually dangerous—the federal government spent over $500 million on improvements.

The production of ships was not satisfactorily solved before the armistice. The Emergency Fleet Corporation was created as a subsidiary of the United States Shipping Board in April, 1917, but the chairmen of the two bodies argued with one another over wooden ships versus steel ships and accomplished little. Wilson fired them and appointed Edward N. Hurley of the Federal Trade Commission to head both agencies. Hurley pressed ahead on the construction of both wooden and steel ships and even some concrete vessels. Despite great efforts, however, ship production did not become adequate until the end of the war. The shipping agencies accomplished more in the prosecution of the war by rationalizing schedules and putting into service the German ships that had been caught in American ports by the declaration of war. The administration also took command of ships under construction in private shipyards.

Labor Relations

Efficient war production was dependent upon peaceful labor relations. Wilson recognized the importance of labor when he appointed Samuel Gompers to the Council of National Defense in 1916. Gompers and other AFL leaders were so impressed by being treated as respectable members of the nation that they perhaps overdid their cooperation with the President. For example, the lengths the AFL leadership went to in order to minimize the influence of Socialists in the labor movement were sometimes absurd. AFL leaders even rented all of the meeting halls in some cities so that Socialist trade unionists would have no place to meet.

Throughout 1917 the federal agencies to deal with labor relations were scattered and uncoordinated. Perhaps the most effective was the President's Mediation Commission, led by Felix Frankfurter. In April, 1918, Wilson created the National War Labor Board under the joint chairmanship of ex-President Taft and Frank P. Walsh, a prominent labor attorney. The Board served mostly as a labor disputes court, although it lacked real authority to do so. It averted many strikes by informing both management and labor, after a hearing, what it thought the terms of agreement should be. If the executives and labor leaders involved did not heed the Board's recommendations, Wilson could resort to his emergency powers. When the management of Smith and Wesson Arms Company refused a Board recommendation, the War Department simply took over the Smith and Wesson Springfield, Massachusetts, plant. When a local of the International Association of Machinists at Bridgeport, Connecticut, threatened a strike against a Board decision, Wilson announced that he would revoke the draft deferments of the war production workers and put them into the army.

The National War Labor Board's tasks were too great for it to accomplish alone, and in May, 1918, Wilson established the War Labor Policies Board with Frankfurter as head. Its function was to determine general war labor policy, standardize wages and hours, and, insofar as it could, allocate manpower. Its most effective allocation of manpower was through the newly established United States Employment Service in the Department of Labor, which placed 3,700,000 workers in war industries.

America's World War I experience indicated that an essentially laissez faire economy was inadequate in a national emergency. It indicated, furthermore, that planning and central direction, while difficult, nevertheless could produce and distribute the necessary goods and services, but that half-way measures could not do the job. In order to meet the demands, the Wilson administration increasingly had to resort to greater federal action. Where it fell short it was because it never took the next obvious step, such as rationing and price control, or took it too late to avert an industrial bottleneck, as in the transportation crisis of the winter of 1917–18. The experience also indicated that the economy could be directed without gravely injuring individual freedom. Liberty and freedom received body blows during the war and immediately thereafter, but the centralized economy was not the reason for them.

Public Opinion and Civil Liberty

No one has ever known what percentage of the American people supported the war and what proportion thought the decision to intervene was a serious mistake, and no one has ever known how many of those opposed to the war were prepared to do anything against the war effort. Probably a majority of the people favored the war declaration, although many of them reluctantly, and it is clear that support for the war increased as the conflict progressed, particularly after Wilson stated the nation's war aims in January, 1918. But there is considerable evidence that a sizable minority was lukewarm or even opposed.

A total of fifty-six Representatives and Senators voted against the war resolution, and, although some of them probably voted their convictions against the wishes of a majority of their constituents, surely some of their districts supported their vote. Some citizens of recent German and Austrian background undoubtedly opposed the war, although their opposition was never as open as that of the Socialists and other radicals, few of whom were of German background. The Socialist party, in a convention that met as Congress declared war, stated its opposition but did not state what the party would do about it. A referendum of the membership overwhelmingly supported the convention. Some members quit the party over its antiwar position, but they were relatively few. In the municipal elections of 1917, the Socialists in several midwestern and eastern cities polled the best votes in the party's history. The fact of considerable opposition to the war led to an unusually shrill prowar propaganda campaign and a widespread disregard of constitutional rights.

A week after the war declaration, Wilson created the Committee on Public Information with George Creel, a Denver journalist, as its chairman. Creel conceived his task to be "to sell the war to America" and to publicize the American cause abroad. The extent of the CPI's activities was tremendous: more than 7,500,000 speeches, and thousands of pamphlets and magazine articles in several languages. The Creel committee endeavored on the one hand to picture the American war effort as eminently Christian, decent, and democratic and to picture "the Hun" as depraved, bloody, and cruel. The CPI whipped the war spirit to a fever. Many schools abolished the teaching of the German language, and a few colleges allowed students to acquire credits in German by cultivating war gardens. There was an unsuccessful effort to rename sauerkraut "liberty cabbage." A popular song of the day was entitled "I'd Like To See the Kaiser with a Lily in His Hand." The regents of the University of Wisconsin rescinded an honorary degree they had once awarded the German ambassador, Johann von Bernstorff, and many Wisconsin faculty members signed a public letter condemning Senator LaFollette for his vote against the war declaration. Even before the war declaration, Professor Charles A. Beard resigned at Columbia University over a matter pressed by the "patriotic" university administration.

In this atmosphere, words such as "traitor" and "disloyal" were thrown about recklessly, and vigilante organizations came into being in every state. The National Security League and the American Protective League sent voluntary agents to meetings of radicals and German-American organizations and received the cooperation of the Department of Justice. Wilson's administration proved the validity of his prediction to Frank Cobb that war would bring intolerance. Three wartime laws were the authority for most of the prosecutions of war objectors. The Espionage Act of June, 1917, provided penalties of up to twenty years' imprisonment and fines of up to $10,000 for convictions of inciting rebellion in the armed forces, obstructing recruitment of servicemen or operation of the draft, or making false reports to aid the enemy. The law also authorized the Postmaster General, Albert S. Burleson of Texas, to deny the use of the mails to materials which in his opinion advocated treason, insurrection, or resistance to law. The Trading-with-the-Enemy Act of October, 1917, was primarily to control foreign trade, but it gave the Postmaster General wide powers to censor the domestic foreign-language press. An amendment to the Espionage Act in May, 1918, often called the Sedition Act, extended the ban to the spoken word and provided that a conviction under the Espionage Act would be legitimate if words or actions "tended" to bring violations of law, whatever their actual consequences.

Famous Sedition Cases

The most famous cases under these laws were the conviction of the Socialist leader Eugene V. Debs in 1918 and the conviction in a mass trial of one hundred leaders of the IWW. The speech for which Debs was convicted, before the Ohio state convention of the Socialist party at Canton, was actually rather mild. Debs's appeal to the Supreme Court was futile, and he went to prison in early 1919. Wilson refused to commute his sentence and release him despite considerable support in the cabinet for such action, and Debs remained in an Atlanta penitentiary—even ran for president from there in 1920—until Wilson's successor commuted his sentence on Christmas, 1921. In the IWW trial the jury took only four hours to find all guilty as charged, and the judge, Kenesaw Mountain Landis, sentenced fifteen of the leaders to twenty-year terms, thirty-five others to ten years, and imposed fines totalling $2.3 million. Judge Landis also presided at the trial of the Socialist leader Victor Berger; a higher court found his conduct of the trial prejudiced and set Berger free. Higher courts, however, upheld nearly all the convictions under these laws, and the Supreme Court after the end of the war found the laws constitutional. The opinion of Justice Oliver Wendell Holmes in the Schenck case in 1919 deserves special consideration because he introduced a judicial concept in free speech cases that later was to have wide application. Schenck admitted advising resistance to the draft. Speaking for a unanimous Court, Holmes was faced with the problem of squaring the Espionage Act with the First Amendment which states, "Congress shall make no law . . . abridging the freedom of speech, or of the press. . . ." Holmes ruled that Congress had the constitutional power to prevent speech and publication that constituted a "clear and present danger." Schenck's activities, he ruled, did in fact constitute such a danger. Holmes apparently intended the "clear and present danger" doctrine to hamper the prosecution of persons whose violations of the laws were minor. Critics of the doctrine have pointed out that it, in effect, said that a person could say whatever he pleased only so long as he was ineffective.

Suppressing Dissent

Postmaster General Burleson greatly hampered radical organizations by denying their publications the use of the mails, even sometimes of first-class mail. He banned the IWW weekly newspaper as well as several publications with Socialist connections. He also suppressed anti-British Irish nationalist publications and even forbade the circulation of one issue of a Henry George single tax journal.

Surely no administration in American history ever went farther in suppressing dissent and prosecuting critics. Wilson himself was as unrestrained as his less constitutionally minded subordinates. In 1918 he suggested to Attorney General Thomas W. Gregory that something be done to "bring to book" the editor of the Kansas City *Star* for publishing a letter from Mrs. Rose Pastor Stokes, wife of a prowar millionaire Socialist, that said "the government is for the capitalists." Gregory assured the President that the editor had violated no law. Mrs. Stokes was later imprisoned for the Kansas City speech her letter to the newspaper was intended to clarify.

War passions did not cool with the end of hostilities. If anything, the public and the federal administration became even more intolerant in 1919 and early 1920 than it had been during the war. Wartime hostility to "the Huns" was now directed exclusively against "the reds"; and the wave of hysterical fear and intolerance is usually called the Red Scare.

The Red Scare Period

The Bolshevik revolution of November, 1917, divided the American Socialist movement. The extreme left wing of the party wanted to redesign the Socialist party along Bolshevik lines; a majority and practically all the leaders, while not opposing Bolshevism for Russia, wanted to keep the organization oriented toward democratic socialism to be achieved by parliamentary means. At a convention of the Socialists in the summer of 1919 the party split forever, the minority bolting and constituting themselves as the Communist Labor party. Another group called itself merely the Communist party. Several months later they merged, under Moscow direction, as the Workers' party, later renamed the Communist party. Even in 1919, before the Communists of various kinds suffered serious reverses, total membership of all the left parties was less than .2 per cent of the population. But the Communists, seeing the success of their idols in Russia and their idea spreading in eastern Europe, were convinced that revolution was just around the corner, and many conservatives hysterically agreed with them on this point. Both far left and far right interpreted the 1919 steel strike in terms of revolution.

A general strike in Seattle, Washington, in February, 1919, and a series of bombs in April set the country aflame. The black maid of a Georgia senator had her hands blown off when she opened a package addressed to her employer. A search of the mails uncovered thirty-six bomb packages addressed to prominent political and business leaders. The guilty person or persons were never caught, but everyone assumed it was "the reds," and the public rarely made any distinctions among the many kinds, who fought one another usually more vigorously than they did those contented with capitalism. Antiradical mobs became common. Sometimes the mobs rounded up local radicals, roughed them up, and forced them to kiss the flag. Others were somewhat more serious. On May Day, 1919, a mob of servicemen invaded the offices of the Socialist daily newspaper in New York City, *The Call,* and destroyed the equipment. On Armistice Day, 1919, gunfire from an IWW hall in Centralia, Washington, killed three paraders in an American Legion demonstration. The Legionnaires said the attack was unprovoked; the IWW members said they were defending their hall from attack and destruction as it had previously been attacked. Twelve IWW members were arrested. A mob lynched one of them, and the others received sentences of from twenty-five to forty years. Other mobs elsewhere in the Pacific Northwest destroyed IWW halls and local police arrested over one thousand members. Mobs, federal prosecution during the war, and so-called criminal syndicalism laws adopted by thirty-two states outlawing membership in revolutionary organizations practically killed the IWW. Twenty-eight states also forbade the display of red flags.

As it had during the war, the Wilson administration led in the postwar drive against radicals. A law passed in the last month of the war authorized the Secretary of Labor to arrest and deport any alien who advocated revolution or belonged to a revolutionary organization. During 1919 Secretary William B. Wilson rounded up a considerable number of such alien radicals, and the *Buford,* popularly called "the Soviet ark," left the United States with 249 radicals bound for Finland, there being no regular relations with Russia. Attorney General A. Mitchell Palmer, who succeeded Gregory in 1919 and had his eyes on the White House, soon made Secretary Wilson seem a model of restraint by comparison. Palmer had turned the Federal Bureau of Investigation into a red-chasing organization, but despite horrifying reports he sent to Congress he had been unable to get Congress to enact a bill that would have made it illegal to say or write anything that tended to incite sedition. Without the knowledge of Secretary Wilson or the Assistant Secretary, Palmer obtained from an agent in the Department of Labor warrants for the arrest of three thousand alien radicals. On the night of January 2, 1920, the "Palmer raids" rounded up thousands of radicals in thirty-three cities from coast to coast. (The Republican District Attorney of Chicago, hoping to steal some limelight from the Democratic Attorney General, jumped the gun by twenty-four hours.) A second series of raids came on January 5. Everyone found in the offices of revolutionary organizations, whether citizen or alien, warrant or not, was put under arrest. In some cities even those who visited the arrested persons in jail were locked into cells. Altogether more than 5,000 people were arrested. Secretary Wilson took over the deportation proceedings, weeded out thousands of innocent victims of Palmer's ambition, and deported 556. The states prosecuted about one-third of the others. Both Communist parties went underground.

In this hysterical mood the Vice-President of the United States saw evidence of subversion when the Radcliffe College debating team took the affirmative in an intercollegiate debate on the subject, "Resolved, that the recognition of labor unions by employers is essential to successful collective bargaining." It was inevitable that legislative branches of government would reflect the popular intolerant mood. A special joint committee of the New York legislature headed by Clayton R. Lusk investigated radicalism, and its four-volume report, *Revolutionary Radicalism*, amply revealed how broadly it defined its terms. The legislature passed several sweeping laws against radicalism, but Democratic Governor Alfred E. Smith vetoed them. The New York legislature also refused to seat five assemblymen from New York City solely because they had been elected on the Socialist ticket. Congress refused to seat Victor Berger after his election to the House in November, 1918, actually because he was a Socialist, ostensibly because he was then under indictment under the Espionage Act. When the House declared the seat from Berger's Milwaukee district vacant and ordered another election, Berger entered the second election and defeated a candidate who had combined Democratic and Republican support. Still the House refused Berger. After Berger won again in 1922, the House seated him without incident.

In early 1920 it seemed that the Red Scare might go on forever, but it faded quickly during the year, especially after lawyers of unimpeachable respectability, many of them conservative in economic matters, denounced intolerant excess. Charles Evans Hughes in a New York Bar Association report denounced the refusal of the legislature to seat the five Socialists as a denial of representative government. A committee of twelve distinguished lawyers and law professors in May issued a severe denunciation of Palmer's administration of the Department of Justice, charging that "the office of the Attorney General . . . has committed continual illegal acts" and regularly denied due process of law. So quickly did the immediate manifestations of intolerance fade that when by far the most outrageous bombing of the era occurred in September (the detonation of a wagonload of explosives outside the offices of the House of Morgan on Wall Street, killing thirty-eight, injuring two hundred, and destroying $2 million in property) the reaction was surprisingly slight. But intolerance itself did not disappear by any means, and the war and demobilization period left a legacy of distrust, reaction, and violence that was to plague American society for years. One famous case begun during the Red Scare involving two Massachusetts anarchists, Nicola Sacco and Bartolomeo Vanzetti, was to divide the nation and arouse hostility to the United States abroad for several years.

The Peace: Diplomacy During the War

Long before the United States entered the war, Wilson made public statements about the kind of peace he hoped would be created. In a speech to a meeting of the League to Enforce Peace in May, 1916 (the League was an American organization founded by ex-President Taft and A. Lawrence Lowell, president of Harvard, in 1915 to work for a postwar international organization), Wilson committed himself to American participation in a postwar organization of nations. In his "peace without victory" speech to the Senate in January, 1917, Wilson reiterated his belief in an international organization and further made clear he was opposed to indemnities.

Wilson's failure to get all he wanted from the Allies at the peace conference began when he blundered in bargaining, or failing to bargain, with the Allies immediately after the American declaration of war. The decision to become a belligerent did not commit the United States to military participation in France. It would have been quite possible for the United States to have restricted her operations to the seas. This the Allies realized when they came to Washington in April, 1917, to seek American military intervention. Arthur Balfour, the British foreign minister, headed his Washington delegation. Balfour apparently expected to have to make concessions to Wilson on the peace conditions to get military help, and he informed Wilson and Colonel House about the secret treaties and agreements the Allies had made since the outbreak of fighting in 1914. Summarized, these agreements were as follows: (1) Russia was to get Constantinople and the Asian shore of the Bosporus and the Dardanelles, reserving the right of transit of the straits for all nations; (2) Italy was to get control of the Adriatic, the Alpine passes to Austria, parts of Albania, and parts of the Turkish empire; (3) Romania was to get some Serbian-populated areas in the Austrian-Hungarian empire, but these were abrogated by her defeat and separate peace with Germany in 1918; (4) Great Britain was to get the conquered German islands in the Pacific south of the equator, Japan was to get those north of the equator plus the German rights in the Chinese province of Shantung; and (5) Russia and France were to have a free hand in drawing their boundaries with Germany, which meant that France would get Alsace-Lorraine at least and Russia at least a slice of German Polish provinces. But Wilson did not press Balfour for a postwar agreement, apparently on Colonel House's advice, and committed the United States to military action without guarantees. Wilson rationalized that by the end of the war the Allies would be so much in debt to the United States that he could force them to accept his peace terms.

The Bolshevik revolution in November, 1917, not only created a new situation so far as the conduct of the war was concerned but for the peace as well—and, when the Bolsheviks in time showed they were going to survive and retain control of Russia, for the whole shape of the postwar world. Hoping that the people of the world would overthrow their governments, stop the war, and form communist governments when they became aware of the hypocritical secret treaties, the Bolsheviks published the treaties in December, 1917. The publication did not bring the expected reaction, and the Bolsheviks began peace negotiations with Germany.

Wilson's Fourteen Points

Wilson's reply to the publication of the secret agreements was his Fourteen Points address, a statement of war aims intended not only for shaping the peace but as a propaganda weapon, delivered before Congress January 8, 1918. To the Germans, Wilson held out the hope of a just peace. Summarized, the Fourteen Points were as follows:

1) No secret diplomacy—"Open covenants of peace, openly arrived at."
2) Freedom of the seas during both peace and war.
3) "The removal, so far as possible, of all economic barriers and the estab-

lishment of an equality of trade conditions among all the nations consenting to the peace and associating themselves for its maintenance." (The Open Door, in other words, for nations adhering to point 14.)

4) Reduction of armaments.

5) Impartial adjustment of all colonial claims, "the interests of the populations concerned" to have "equal weight with the equitable claims of the government whose title is to be determined."

6) Evacuation of Russian territory and opportunity for Russia to develop herself however she sees fit without foreign interference. "The treatment accorded Russia by her sister nations in the months to come will be the acid test of their good will, of their comprehension of her needs as distinguished from their own interests, and of their intelligent and unselfish sympathy." (This point would be ironic before the end of 1918.)

7) Evacuation of Belgium and full Belgian sovereignty.

8) Evacuation of French territory and "the wrong done to France by Prussia in 1871 in the matter of Alsace-Lorraine . . . should be righted."

9) Redrawing of the Italian boundaries "along clearly recognizable lines of nationality."

10) Free opportunity of autonomous development of the nationalities within Austria-Hungary.

11) Evacuation and restoration of the Balkan nations and access to the sea for Serbia.

12) Sovereignty for the Turkish parts of the Ottoman empire, but opportunity for the autonomous development of other nationalities within the empire and the Dardanelles to be open to the commerce of all nations.

13) An independent Poland with access to the sea.

14) A League of Nations. "A general association of nations must be formed under specific covenants for the purpose of affording mutual guaranties of political independence and territorial integrity to great and small states alike."

Liberals everywhere regarded the Fourteen Points as a great manifesto. Creel had thousands of leaflets containing these war aims dropped by airplane behind the lines in Germany and Austria. They undoubtedly were a factor behind the Central Powers' decision to seek an armistice.

In early October, 1918, Germany and Austria-Hungary approached Wilson, not the Allies, to propose an armistice based upon the Fourteen Points. The German generals hoped to trick Wilson into a cessation of hostilities during which they could regain their strength and attack again. Wilson headed off this possibility by dilatory tactics and insistence upon a German civilian administration. The Central Powers' position was deteriorating badly, both on the western front and at home, where communism was growing rapidly, especially in Berlin and Hungary. On October 20 Prince Max of Baden, the new German chancellor, informed Wilson that Germany accepted all of Wilson's conditions. Wilson replied three days later that he would transmit the appeal for an armistice to the Allied governments and implied that Germany would be well advised to abandon its monarchy and establish a republic. The Kaiser abdicated on November 9 and fled to Holland.

Colonel House dealt with the Allies on the armistice terms in Paris. They at first professed not to know what the Fourteen Points were, and House informed them. The British prime minister, David Lloyd George, flatly rejected Point 2 on freedom of the seas. The French insisted upon the right to impose reparations for German-inflicted damages to civilian property. House headed off further Allied objections by raising the threat of a separate peace between the United States and the Central Powers. Germany agreed. Thus on November 11, 1918, each side laid down its arms and agreed to a peace to be negotiated between the Allies and Associated Powers on the one side and Germany on the other on the basis of Wilson's peace pronouncements, with the two exceptions of the abolition of Point 2 and German reparations to France.

Point 6 of the Fourteen Points, pertaining to Russia, had already disappeared. After the Treaty of Brest-Litovsk in the spring of 1918, chaos enveloped Russia. Civil war broke out at many points between the supporters of the old Czarist government—the Cossacks or Whites—and the Bolsheviks' Red armies. A band of fifty thousand Czechs, formerly Russian prisoners of war, formed themselves into a military unit and began to beat their way to Vladivostok, Russia's port on the Pacific, hoping ultimately to get to the western front. Neither the Reds nor the Whites effectively controlled Siberia, and Japan was preparing to take the territory for herself. The Allies were eager for the overthrow of the Bolsheviks. After weeks of hesitation, Wilson consented in the summer of 1918 to participate in Allied expeditions in Russia, one in Siberia and one in northern European Russia around Murmansk and Archangel. Wilson's concern for Siberia had as much to do with heading off the Japanese as protecting the Czech force, the ostensible reason for the Siberian intervention. The ostensible reason for the northern intervention was to prevent the Germans from getting the military supplies in the port cities. The United States had 9,000 troops under the command of General W. S. Graves in Siberia before they began to leave in January, 1920. There were 4,500 American troops in the northern expedition, which had no justifiable strategic reason for being there after the armistice but which remained until May, 1919. The United States did not participate in an Allied intervention into Russian territory near the Black Sea made after the armistice. Actually, the Allied armies aided the efforts of the Russian Whites. The Allied policy of helping the anti-Bolsheviks, which was not vigorous enough to defeat the Bolsheviks, only left an understandable Soviet legacy of hostility toward the West.

The Peace Conference

Wilson, who had on the whole displayed political finesse in his first five years in office, yielding when he had to, pushing and demanding when he had to, committed a series of political blunders beginning in the late fall of 1918 that were to make most of his second term a personal nightmare and insure the doom of his peace program. In politics, at least, nothing succeeds like success and failures snowball; Wilson's failures came all at once.

First, Wilson injected partisan politics into the peace issues. If, eventually, it was partisan politics that defeated his program, it was Wilson who first tried to make political capital from international policy. During the campaign for the congressional elections in 1918, Democratic hopefuls asked him to lend their candidacies a helping hand with public endorsements. Wilson was busy with the war and early armistice negotiations, and he decided to make a blanket appeal for his party's candidates. This decision was probably mistaken, but he made it worse the way he did it. On October 25, 1918, the newspapers carried this statement from the White House:

> If you have approved of my leadership and wish me to continue to be your unembarrassed spokesman in affairs at home and abroad, I earnestly beg that you will express yourselves unmistakably to that effect by returning a Democratic majority to both the Senate and the House of Representatives. ... The return of a Republican majority to either house of the Congress would ... be interpreted on the other side of the water as a repudiation of my leadership.

If Wilson's primary purpose was to have a cooperative Congress, he would have been wiser to have asked the voters to elect men who supported his position, irrespective of party; if his main concern was to have a Democratic Congress, he would have been politically more astute if he had not spelled out so clearly what a Republican victory would mean. Why the voters cast their ballots the way they did was of course a multiple mystery. Local issues, vague dissatisfaction with the war, and discontent about wartime restrictions played a part in causing citizens to vote Republican. It also should be remembered that the GOP was then the majority party and Democratic victories depended upon Republican division and the cross-over vote. At any rate, the new Congress was Republican, 49 to 47 in the Senate and 237 to 191 in the House. By Wilson's own terms, the citizenry repudiated his leadership.

A week after the armistice, Wilson announced that he would head the American peace conference delegation and go to Paris. Republicans raised an outcry against his decision (no president had ever before gone to Europe during his term of office nor had personally conducted peace treaty negotiations), but, if his decision to participate personally was a blunder at all, it was not so serious as his failure to include a prominent Republican in the peace commission. The other commissioners were Secretary of State Lansing, Colonel House, General Tasker H. Bliss, and Henry White. White was an experienced diplomat and a Republican voter but not an influential Republican politician. If he had wanted to avoid Senator Henry Cabot Lodge of Massachusetts, which was understandable, he still could have named Taft, Elihu Root, or Hughes. Besides not naming a Senator to the commission, Wilson did not even confer with Senators about the appointments. And, as Senator Lodge pointed out, the Senate would have to ratify the treaty.

The Conference at Paris and Versailles

On arriving in Europe, Wilson made a tour of Paris, London, and Rome which demonstrated he had considerable popularity among the European masses, but it is doubtful that his popularity made much difference to his skilled and cynical adversaries at the conference—Lloyd George, French Premier Georges

Clemenceau, and Italian Prime Minister Vittorio Orlando. These three and Wilson constituted the Big Four, who made most of the important decisions at the conference. The peace conference cannot be fully understood without seeing its background. There were the Allied representatives, in varying degrees old-fashioned nationalists and colonial imperialists, trying to establish a postwar world as much as possible like the prewar world minus German power. There was Wilson, a middle-class, liberal idealist with something of a Messiah complex, who wanted to amend the old order considerably and reform it along the lines of Open Door empire. Not represented at the conference, but very much in the minds of the peace negotiators, was a new force, symbolized by the new Soviet government, which wanted to create a communist world. Marx had exaggerated a bit when he wrote in the Communist Manifesto in 1848, "The specter of Communism is haunting Europe" but the specter very much haunted the conference at Paris and Versailles. It haunted Wilson as much as it did the Allies. The Allies and Wilson had their differences, important differences, but they were united in their opposition and fear of the new force and endeavored to create a fresh era which would minimize it. The peace conference did not come to terms with Bolshevism or with the conditions which created it. The conference only shut it out and tried to isolate it. For decades to come, communism and various reactions to it were to be the main issues of world politics.

The first plenary meeting of the conference was on January 18, 1919. Twenty-seven nations, all enemies of the Central Powers during the war, had representatives. Such a large group was unwieldy, and a Council of Ten, representing the United States, Britain, France, Italy, and Japan, met separately and made the important decisions. Sixty commissions, in which small nations were represented, attended to details of special questions. Wilson returned to the United States early in the conference and was not at the conference from February 15 to March 14. Lloyd George was gone part of this time, and Clemenceau was incapacitated by an anarchist's attack. Orlando went home in a huff in late April. The Council of Ten was abandoned on March 24, and the Big Four decided important questions until it became the Big Three with Orlando's departure. The Treaty of Versailles was completed by the end of April and presented to Germany in early May. Germany made some written objections and counterproposals, and the conference made some minor changes in the document. In June the German cabinet resigned rather than approve the treaty. General Foch was ordered to march on Germany, which had continued to suffer under the blockade over the winter, unless she accepted within three days. On June 23 the Germans capitulated and signed the treaty in the famous Hall of Mirrors at Versailles.

The Treaty and the Fourteen Points

These are the bare bones of the conference. What did the treaty provide? How did Wilson and his Fourteen Points fare at the peace table? In summary, he won his objectives or partially won them on several points and lost badly on others. The treaty was a Wilson-Allies compromise.

Wilson partially lost Point 1, "open covenants openly arrived at," on the first day of the conference when the press was shut out from the meetings. At the end of each day the press received a bare, very brief summary of the day's activities. ~~His main victories were the redrawing of the map of Europe along general lines of "self-determination of peoples" and the League of Nations.~~ Ethnic boundaries and political boundaries were by no means identical after the treaty, but the lines were more nearly congruent than they had ever been before. At least some of the new national states were created to serve as buffers between Central Europe and the Soviet Union.

~~The League was Wilson's primary desire.~~ He won assent to the League in principle and presented a draft of the League constitution or covenant to the conference before his brief return to America. He later had the League thoroughly tied into other treaty provisions so that to accept the treaty meant necessarily to accept the League. The League covenant called for an Assembly in which each member nation, no matter what its size, would have one vote and a Council consisting of four small nations on a rotating basis and five permanent seats for the United States, Great Britain, France, Italy, and Japan. The League was empowered to create a Permanent Court of International Justice and deal with several matters such as disarmament, world health, and labor conditions, but its main function was to preserve peace. The covenant provided that members of the League would submit any controversy between them (not with non-League members) likely to lead to war to arbitration or investigation by the Council and not resort to war until at least three months after a report or award had been made. If all League members other than the interested parties agreed to certain recommendations, no League member would go to war with a nation that complied with the recommendations. A League nation that went to war in defiance of the covenant would be liable to economic sanctions, and the Council could recommend joint military action against the offender. Wilson regarded Article 10 as "the heart of the Covenant": ~~"The Members of the League undertake to respect and preserve as against external aggression the territorial integrity and existing political independence of all Members of the League.~~ In case of any threat of danger of such aggression the Council shall advise upon the means by which this obligation shall be fulfilled." This provision was to be central in the battle over Senate ratification.

Now for the other main provisions of the treaty. ~~Great Britain and the dominions of the empire wanted to keep the German colonies they had won in Africa and the Pacific. This involved Point 5 of the Fourteen Points.~~ The upshot was that the former German colonies would be governed by League of Nations mandates, the nation to hold the mandate to be named by the League. In every case, the League awarded the mandate to the nation that had conquered the colony or had been promised it by a secret treaty. ~~At best, Wilson won only a paper, legalistic victory on the issue; at worst, there was little difference between governing a colony under mandate and ruling it by outright possession.~~ The decision was not between colonialism and anticolonialism but who should have colonies and how. ~~The colonial people were not granted the right of self-determination.~~

The mandate scheme was used to settle the question of Japan and Shantung. Japan wanted two things: an explicit statement of racial equality in the League covenant, which she did not get, and Shantung, promised her by a secret treaty, which she got by mandate. Wilson did not like the Shantung settlement but agreed to it, which, as one of the historical specialists on the conference, Professor

Thomas Bailey, has written, "lent point to Clemenceau's alleged remark that Wilson 'talked like Jesus Christ but acted like Lloyd George.'" At another point in the conference the cynical Clemenceau was supposed to have remarked, in reference to Wilson's Fourteen Points, that even *le bon dieu* had but ten.

Wilson grossly violated his "self-determination" principle in assenting to a secret treaty that awarded Italy the Alpine passes to Austria, areas populated by Austrians. Wilson resisted Italian demands for the port city of Fiume, necessary for the new state of Yugoslavia. The conference ended with the Fiume question unsettled. A 1920 treaty between Italy and Yugoslavia made a compromise, and four years later, after Benito Mussolini became Italy's Fascist dictator, Italy took Fiume by force.

Reparations

The toughest opposition Wilson faced was Clemenceau's insistence upon French security against Germany in the Rhineland and huge German reparations. Wilson, with Lloyd George's help, gained a compromise with Clemenceau on the boundary question but lost nearly everything on reparations with hardly a fight. France demanded removing Germany from the west side of the Rhine and creating French-controlled buffer states there. In the end France had to be satisfied with the return of Alsace-Lorraine, demilitarization of a zone of Germany extending thirty miles east of the Rhine, and a fifteen-year joint Allied occupation of the west bank of the Rhine. Clemenceau agreed to this arrangement only if the United States and Great Britain would sign a treaty with France pledging them to come to her aid if Germany attacked. Wilson and Lloyd George agreed and signed such a treaty which provided that the alliance would not become effective unless ratified by all three parties. Britain and France ratified. The United States Senate never put the treaty to a vote, and Wilson did not push the issue.

The reparations matter was to be an international issue for years. The Allies would have liked to have made Germany pay the whole cost of the war. The final provisions were not so harsh as that, but they were severe. The armistice understanding had left open the possibility, which under the circumstances meant the probability, of German reparations for civilian damages to the Allies. Now Wilson further agreed that Germany should pay the Allies a sum sufficient to pay their servicemen's separation payments and pensions and to extend the responsibility on damages to include damage to Allied government property as well as civilian property. France also got ownership of the coal mines in the Saar province of Germany, the Saar to be governed by a League commission for fifteen years. At the end of that time there would be a Saar plebiscite to determine whether the area would be German or French. Finally, the treaty itself did not determine the size of the reparations or set a maximum amount. The reparations bill would be drawn up by a special commission instructed to make a report no later than May, 1921. When Germany signed the Treaty of Versailles, she in effect signed a note of unknown size. The reparations commission in 1921 set the bill at $33 billion.

Was the Treaty of Versailles consistent with the Fourteen Points? Clearly, it violated them in several respects but did not wipe them out completely. Was it the best that Wilson could have achieved? The question has been debated at length but remains unanswered, as it must, because one can only speculate. Was it a more equitable treaty because of Wilson's role in its writing? Probably France would have imposed a more Carthaginian peace without Wilson's restraint, but, again, one cannot say what might have happened. It has been argued that the treaty was neither harsh enough to prevent a German resurgence of strength nor fair enough to prevent German demagogues from exploiting popular dissatisfaction with it. Certainly, the treaty did not bring stability and peace, but one cannot lay the blame for the growth of Hitlerism and extreme German nationalism entirely upon the Treaty of Versailles. The most valid criticism to be made of the treaty was that it was based upon a conception of the world that was no longer relevant, if indeed it had ever been. It failed to treat constructively the questions of communism and nationalist revolt of colonial peoples. If the Treaty of Versailles and the thinking behind it were ever suitable to the facts of the world, it was the world sometime between 1815 and the 1890's.

The United States Rejects the Treaty

The most common interpretation of the Senate's rejection of the Versailles Treaty and the League of Nations is that the defeat of the treaty instituted an era of "isolationism" that lasted for about twenty years. The term "isolationism," however, is too broad and vague to be useful as a tool of communication. It is far more accurate to say that the treaty's defeat was a victory for the opponents of collective security. Certainly, the United States was not "isolated" economically between the two World Wars. For that matter, despite America's refusal to enter the League of Nations, the nation was not entirely aloof even from the idea of collective security during the two inter-war decades.

The Opponents' Reasons

The reasons why opponents of the treaty and the League took the position they did were many. Most were alarmed by the degree of collective security implicit in the League and feared that membership entailed a limitation on the power of the United States to make its own decisions. A few were true "isolationists," who believed America should concentrate on its own problems, ignore the rest of the world, and withdraw from it. A few were critics of Open Door empire and thought that the wave of communist revolution and nationalist revolts of colonial peoples required a fundamental revision of American policies and that the treaty only solidified the old policies. Some represented special interests which were slighted by the treaty. Here, for example, were many Irish-Americans, who were aroused by the treaty's failure to provide Irish independence, as well as Zionists disappointed by the absence of provisions for a Jewish national state in Palestine. Still others were motivated by Republican partisanship and hatred of Wilson as a Democratic leader. But the sharpness of the conflict over the League—and it was bitter—should not obscure the fact that Wilson and most of his opponents were in fundamental agreement about the basic shape of American foreign policy. They nearly all agreed implicitly in Open Door empire or informal imperialism. Wilson and his enemies differed more over means than ends, the opponents of the treaty holding that the League jeopardized American economic opportunity abroad.

The President's Difficulties with the Senate

Wilson's difficulties with the Senate over the League began well before the treaty had been entirely drafted. Wilson, rather belatedly, conferred with the Senate and House foreign relations committees during his brief return to Washington in late February, 1919. He did not satisfy the objections of some Republican Senators to his League proposals. The Democratic "lame duck" Congress was then in session, and Republicans in the Senate filibustered an important appropriations bill to force Wilson to call a special session of the Republican-dominated Congress that had been elected in November. On the last day of the old Congress Senator Lodge released a round robin signed by thirty-nine Senators or Senators-elect, well over the one-third plus one needed to reject a treaty, that declared "it is the sense of the Senate that . . . the constitution of the league of nations in the form now proposed to the peace conference should not be accepted by the United States. . . ." The letter also stated that the United States should first conclude a peace with Germany and then consider a league. The main stated objections to the League at that time were that the League covenant contained no procedures for a nation to withdraw, made no explicit recognition of the Monroe Doctrine, and provided no specific guarantees that the League would not consider member nations' internal affairs. Wilson revealed how uncompromising he would be on the League issue on the night the round robin was released by telling a Madison Square Garden audience, "When that treaty comes back, gentlemen on this side will find the covenant not only in it, but so many threads of the treaty tied to the covenant that you cannot dissect the covenant from the treaty without destroying the whole vital structure." And upon his return to Paris Wilson did inextricably tie the League into the rest of the treaty, although he arranged for some modifications in the covenant to meet a few of the objections. The final covenant expressly stated that nothing in the League affected the validity of "regional understandings like the Monroe Doctrine" and provided a method for a nation to withdraw from the League with two years' notice.

The revised League covenant, however, did not satisfy Senator Lodge, and he was chairman of the Senate Foreign Relations Committee in the new Congress. Furthermore, nine of the ten Republican members of the committee supported Lodge's position, as did one of the seven Democratic members. When the Senate began to consider the treaty in July, 1919, public opinion seemed to be for the League. Two-thirds of the state legislatures and governors had gone on record supporting it. A *Literary Digest* poll of newspaper editors in April had shown overwhelming League support. The odds against Lodge in the Senate were long, for more than two-thirds of the members of the upper chamber were for membership in some kind of a league. Only seven of the forty-seven Senate Democrats were unwilling to support Wilson on the League issue to the hilt. A group of twelve to fifteen so-called irreconcilables, led by Senators Hiram Johnson, William E. Borah of Idaho, and Robert LaFollette were opposed to the League altogether. Another group of Republicans, led by Senator Lodge, were for strong reservations to the League covenant, some of which, in the eyes of Wilson's supporters, emasculated the document. Most Republican Senators favored ratification with only mild reservations.

This being the situation, Lodge saw that his best strategy was to stall for time until League opponents could muster greater support. He even consumed two weeks by reading aloud the 246 large pages of the treaty at committee meetings. Extensive hearings took another six weeks. Meanwhile, anti-League propaganda, financed by Henry Clay Frick and the Pittsburgh banker and majority stockholder in the monopolistic Aluminum Corporation of America, Andrew Mellon, began to make inroads in public opinion.

Wilson Takes to the Stump

After Wilson conferred with several Republican Senators on August 19 he realized that Lodge was gaining. Most of the Republicans who conferred with the President were mild reservationists concerned about Article 10 of the covenant. Wilson pointed out that Article 10 provided only that the League could "advise upon" means to be taken against an offending power and that, unless the United States were a party to a controversy, the permanent American seat on the League Council provided a veto. And although Wilson had said in the past that Article 10 was the "heart" of the covenant—he sometimes changed his anatomic figure of speech and called it the "backbone"—he told the Republican leaders that Article 10 provided only "a moral, not a legal obligation." He also told the conference that he would not object to resolutions that stated the Senate's interpretation of the treaty, but that he did not approve of amendments to the treaty itself because they involved acceptance by the other signatory nations. When Lodge continued to oppose, Wilson decided that an appeal to the people was necessary to carry the day.

On September 3 he began a speaking tour of the Midwest and Far West that in twenty-two days took him eight thousand miles. He delivered thirty-seven major addresses. His health had not been good when he started the tour, and he left Washington against his physician's advice. He had been very sick while in Paris and had suffered from headaches during the summer. At Denver, on September 25, he was so near collapse that his physician ordered his immediate return to Washington. One week later he suffered a stroke that paralyzed his left side and nearly killed him. For weeks he was unable to perform the responsibilities of the presidency. Besides raising the serious constitutional problem of how to proceed when the president was incapacitated, a problem not yet solved, Wilson's stroke and slow recovery was a serious handicap to the treaty's chances in the Senate.

The Vote on the Treaty

The Senate Foreign Relations Committee reported the treaty on September 10. Ten of the seventeen members of the committee signed the majority report, which called for forty-five amendments to the treaty; the minority report recommended ratification without change. A coalition of Democrats and mild reservationist Republicans voted down the forty-five amendments, the main argument against acceptance of the amendments being that they were so sweeping that the peace conference would have to reconvene and begin over again if they were adopted. On November 6 Lodge, acting as committee chairman, presented fourteen reservations. Most of them were unimportant, but one declared that the United States would assume no obligations under Article 10 of the covenant or use its armed forces under any article of the treaty unless Congress authorized such action by joint resolution. Another withheld approval of the treaty provisions for Shantung. The Senate approved the Lodge reservations by an almost solid party division. There was not yet a vote on the treaty itself. Thus the ball was tossed to Wilson and the Democratic Senators.

Democratic friends of the League urged Wilson to accept at least some of the Lodge reservations in order to get ratification. Colonel House urged Wilson to compromise but with no effect. The Democratic leader in the Senate, Gilbert M. Hitchcock of Nebraska, twice visited Wilson in his sickroom and twice found him unwilling to yield. Illness seemed only to strengthen Wilson's Calvinist will. On November 18 Wilson released a public letter to Hitchcock that declared the Lodge reservations do "not provide for ratification, but, rather for the nullification of the treaty. I sincerely hope that the friends and supporters of the treaty will vote against the Lodge resolution of ratification."

The following day the Senate voted for the first time on the treaty itself with the Lodge reservations. The Democrats were almost solid against Lodge's ratification resolution and were joined by the "irreconcilables." The Senate defeated ratification, fifty-five to thirty-nine. Hitchcock then offered a resolution of ratification with five reservations which embodied the critical Lodge objections, but this too went down, fifty-one to forty-one. Then the Senate voted on the treaty without reservations at all, and the vote was fifty-three to thirty-eight.

There the matter stood at the end of 1919, but no one yet considered the treaty and League issue dead. After all, almost four-fifths of the senators were for the League either with or without reservations. How many of the strong reservationists really hoped to defeat the treaty is impossible to say. One cannot even be certain what Lodge's objective was. But, in any case, it was apparent that to get ratification, Lodge's reservations, or most of them, would have to be accepted. Wilson was under considerable pressure from his party to bend and accept the inevitable, but Wilson was not a man to bend when he thought the right was entirely on his side. The British sent former foreign secretary Sir Edward Grey to Washington as a special ambassador to urge Wilson to compromise, and Wilson refused to see him. When Grey wrote a letter to the London *Times* saying that failure of the United States to join the League would mean the wrecking of the international body and that the Allies would accept the Lodge reservations without new negotiations, Wilson only became angry. Public opinion demanded that the Senate reconsider the treaty and that ratification in some form or another be made.

The Senate began debate on the treaty again in mid-February, 1920. By this time Wilson had recovered his health sufficiently to lead a more active life, and he used much of his regained vigor to hold out against compromise. On March 19 ratification came to a vote again. This time there were fifteen reservations, one having been added that advocated Irish independence. Twenty pro-League Democrats who figured that ratification would either be with the Lodge reservations or not at all braved White House wrath and voted for the resolution. Most Senate Democrats remained in line. Ratification failed, forty-nine voting for the resolution and thirty-five against it. If seven more Democrats had joined the twenty who deserted Wilson on the vote, the treaty would have been ratified and the United States would have been a member of the League of Nations.

Technically, the United States still was at war. To remedy this situation and to curb Wilson's wartime powers, Congress, on May 15, passed a joint resolution, the so-called Knox resolution, that merely rescinded the declarations of war. Wilson vetoed it. Treaty ratification was thereafter practically dead. Wilson had in effect demanded total victory or total defeat. He received total defeat.

There remained one anticlimactic chapter to the treaty fight. In January Wilson had sent a message to a Jackson Day dinner in Washington in which he said that if the Senate refused to ratify the treaty without reservations the election of 1920 would be a "great and solemn referendum" on the issue. This was a serious lapse on the part of the former professor of political science, for American presidential elections are not referendums on a single isolated issue and certainly they are not "great and solemn." The issues of 1920 were many. The Democratic candidate endorsed the League. The Republican platform was deliberately vague, and the Republican candidate was evasive. Republican friends and opponents of the League both thought that he agreed with them, and the Republicans won a landslide victory. The Senate did not consider the treaty again. On July 21, 1921, Congress passed a joint resolution declaring the war was over.

The Politics
of Business,
1919–1929

*The successful business man among us . . . enjoys the
public respect and adulation that elsewhere bathe only
bishops and generals of artillery. . . . He enjoys an
aristocratic immunity to most forms of judicial process. He
wears the legion d'honneur, is an LL.D. at Yale, and is
received cordially at the White House.*

H. L MENCKEN, 1927

Chapter Three

America in the 1920's belonged to the businessman. It was a business civilization. The business community had always been extremely influential, and it had at times so thoroughly controlled national politics that it regarded Washington as a branch office. But never before in American history had business influence been so unhampered and so pervasive. Politics, economic affairs, foreign policy, social relationships, and popular thought all reflected the triumph of the businessman. Two Republican slogans, each of which was taken as a profound statement of social philosophy, indicated the pedestal of prestige that business basked upon: Harding's slogan, "Less government in business, more business in government" and Coolidge's statement, "The business of America is business."

The Republican party installed three of its figures in the White House during the decade, Warren Gamaliel Harding, Calvin Coolidge, and Herbert Clark Hoover. Coolidge was Vice-President under Harding, and Hoover was Secretary of Commerce and one of the most important cabinet advisers under both Harding and Coolidge. The differences among the three men reflected three evolutionary stages in the relationship of government to business. Harding was first and foremost a politician, not a businessman. He had no serious disagreements with the business community, and he accepted business as an ally, but he owed his career to his political activities. In many ways, Harding was the last of the nineteenth-century presidents—a political figure who usually did what business expected of him but was actually more interested in the political spoils of office. Harding let business down because he was too much of a political wardheeler; the scandals of his administration, revealed after his death in office, jeopardized the stability of business control of government. Coolidge, too, was from a political background and a friend of business, but he had even less personal force than Harding. He surrounded himself in Washington with business rather than political figures, and he smacked less than Harding of the political clubroom. Hoover was the ultimate in business and government. Rather than an agent of business, he was business. Himself an experienced engineer and a highly successful mining investor, Hoover as Secretary of Commerce and as President used his positions to further the business community's interests in a more positive way than had his predecessors. Hoover brought the economic traditions of Alexander Hamilton to twentieth-century fruition. As cabinet member and chief executive, he instituted a new order. And when the crisis of 1929 came it was the new order's responsibility. Rather than the old order of politics and business represented by U. S. Grant and Daniel Drew, or William McKinley and Mark Hanna, or Warren Harding and Harry Sinclair, it was a new order symbolized by Herbert Hoover and anonymous corporation executives.

Demobilizing the Economy

Conservative reaction to the Progressive Era, both in economic matters and civil liberties, began long before the election of a Republican president in 1920. The last two years of Wilson's second term, when there was a Democratic executive and a Republican Congress, was a period of bipartisan conservatism.

During the war left progressives had regarded the federal government's transportation and communications role with approval and hoped that with the coming of peace the government would stay in these businesses, as was the general practice in Europe. Businessmen, however, decried government operation of the railroads and the communications industry as socialism and demanded the return of their properties. In communications, railroads, and shipping, the federal government got out of business on terms quite favorable to the property owners. Telegraph and telephones were simply returned to private operation on August 1, 1919, with only the condition that rates should not be raised for four months.

The Railroads

The return of the railroads could not be accomplished so simply. Never before had the nation's railroads operated as efficiently as they had under government operation, and many people demanded that the government stay in the railroad business. McAdoo, Railroad Administrator until January, 1919, and his successor, Walker D. Hines, recommended that Washington continue to operate the railways for another five years and that meanwhile an investigation be made of the whole transportation problem. The railroad brotherhoods threw their weight behind the Plumb Plan, a scheme for the socialization of the railroads worked out by the brotherhoods' legal counsel, Glenn Plumb. Plumb suggested that the government buy the railroads with funds to be raised through bond sales and operate them through a board representing the public, labor, and management. Half of the earnings of the roads would be used to pay off the bonds, the other half would be divided among all employees, labor and executive alike, as a bonus to wages and salaries.

While the public debated the question, Wilson announced on Christmas Eve, 1919, that he would return the railroads to private management on March 1, 1920, no matter what action or lack of it there was in Congress. Congress passed the Esch-Cummins Act at the last minute. The law and its operation were complex, but in general it returned the roads to private operation on terms favorable to management. For six months the government guaranteed the railroads a profit equal to the rent they had received from the Railroad Administration, and during this period all rates and wages were to remain as they were. The government financed improvements were to be paid for by the railroads over several years, and the law established a fund of $300 million to be lent to the railroads on liberal terms. The Interstate Commerce Commission, enlarged from nine to eleven members under the Act, received greater powers to regulate railroads, but railroad law was changed in such a way that the ICC's new power did not necessarily cause opposition from railroad managers.

Although the ICC now had power to ban the issue of new securities and the construction of new facilities, it also could set aside the rates fixed by state regulatory commissions, which in many cases in the past had been tougher on the railroads than the ICC. The law also empowered the ICC, in an effort to build consolidated railroad systems, to lift the ban on long haul-short haul price discrimination and permit pooling. Indeed, the feature of the act that aroused the most controversy, the "recapture clause," involved a kind of pooling. The commision divided the nation into districts and fixed rates at such a level as to bring railroads within the district a fair return on their investment, in practice 6 per cent. An efficient railroad would make a higher return at a given district rate than an inefficient one. The "recapture clause" met the situation by providing that half of the profits in excess of 6 per cent should be set aside for the road's reserve fund and the other half turned over to a general contingent fund, supervised by the ICC, from which loans to inefficient railroads could be made or from which the ICC could purchase new equipment to be leased. The stronger railroads objected to the plan, and eventually the "recapture clause" was repealed and the contingent fund returned to its contributors.

The Esch-Cummins Act provided that the ICC should evaluate railroad properties and use that figure as a basis for calculating a fair return on investment. Agrarians had long demanded that the worth of railroad property should be determined by its original cost, and railroads had pleaded that the evaluation should be in terms of contemporary replacement cost. Because of generally rising costs, the later the base year for figuring replacement costs the higher the total and, therefore, the higher the rates allowed to meet a fixed percentage of profit. The ICC set 1914 as the base year for calculating replacement costs; the railroads argued for current replacement costs. In 1929 the Supreme Court, in a case involving the St. Louis and O'Fallon Railroad, accepted the railroad's contention. One final provision of the Esch-Cummins Act: it created a Railroad Labor Board representing labor, management, and the public to settle labor disputes. The board failed to prevent a shopmen's strike in 1922, and in 1926 Congress abolished the board and established a Federal Board of Mediation with less power.

Shipping

The problem of what to do with merchant ships was somewhat different because some two thousand ships totaling fifteen million tons had been built and operated by the federal government rather than rented from private companies as in railroading. The experience of the war had shown that an efficient merchant marine was vital to national defense. The crux of the issue was: should a merchant marine be maintained, as it had been built, through government enterprise, or should it be turned over to private hands and subsidized? Subsidies seemed necessary if shipping was to be private; unsubsidized shipping before the war had resulted in only a feeble merchant fleet.

Congress and the President chose to turn the fleet over to private business and to subsidize it. The Jones Merchant Marine Act of June, 1920, directed the Shipping Board to sell its ships quickly and on easy terms to American-owned corporations and ordered the Emergency Fleet Corporation to operate the ships until they could be sold. The law also stimulated private shipping by setting up a $25 million loan fund to be lent to American shipping companies, providing extremely liberal mail contracts, exempting marine insurance companies from the operation of the antitrust laws, excusing shipping companies from excess profits and corporation income taxes if the money thus saved were used for the construction of new ships in American shipyards, and, reminiscent of English mercantilism during the colonial period, granting American ships a monopoly on shipping between colonial territories and the mainland. Under the act, shipping companies purchased wartime built ships at ridiculously low prices. A fleet of two hundred wooden ships brought what it had cost to build one. Henry Ford bought 199 ships and used them for steel scrap. But even with these generous government subsidies, American shipping was unable to compete with the merchant marines of other nations, and in 1928 Congress passed the Jones-White Act. This law restricted the bargain-basement sales of government ships but provided government loans of up to 75 per cent of the construction costs of new ships and increased subsidies for mail carrying. Under this law the American merchant marine flourished briefly, but it was hard hit by the depression of the 1930's and was in poor condition at the outbreak of World War II.

Labor

Government was generous to business in its economic demobilization, but labor organizations found both government and the public cold to their demands. With the end of the war most working men had less regular work and therefore less income, but prices continued to rise until the fall of 1920. In 1919 the cost of living was 77 per cent higher than it had been in 1913, the last full prewar year; in 1920 the figure rose to 105 per cent. Labor in many industries sought higher wages, and when it found almost universal resistance among employers resorted to strikes. Over four million workers were on strike sometime or other during 1919, but labor won no important victories and suffered some major defeats. The public confused labor unionism with Bolshevism, and employers took advantage of the Red Scare to advance their own interests.

In the fall of 1919 three strikes held the nation's front pages: the strike of the Boston police, not very important economically but psychologically and politically significant, and strikes in the basic steel and coal industries. In the summer of 1919 the Boston police, disturbed by their low pay, asked the AFL to grant a charter to their Boston Social Club. Police Commissioner Edwin U. Curtis had previously warned the police against any union affiliation and now threatened to suspend nineteen officers of the policemen's organization. Democratic Mayor Andrew A. Peters offered a compromise, but Curtis refused to yield and proceeded to suspend the police leaders. After a vote in which only two policemen dissented, the police went on strike. That evening gangs of youthful vandals disrupted Boston's peace and there was some looting, but losses amounted to only an estimated $34,000 for the entire strike. On the second day of the strike, Mayor Peters called out Boston residents of the state guard for street patrol, and Harvard students put on arm bands and served as auxiliary policemen. Order returned to Boston with this action, but Mayor Peters publicly criticized Governor Calvin Coolidge, a candidate for re-election, for inactivity. Coolidge then called out the rest of the state guard and asked Washington for federal troops if the strike should spread. On the fourth day, the striking policemen saw they were defeated and prepared to return to duty, but Commissioner Curtis refused to reinstate any of the strikers and prepared to recruit practically an entire new force. Samuel Gompers tried to intercede against the lockout, but Governor Coolidge supported Curtis and sent a public telegram to Gompers in which he said, "There is no right to strike against the public safety by anybody, anywhere, any time." Public opinion in 1919 was such that this statement not only helped Coolidge's re-election, for which he received congratulations from the Democratic President, but lifted him into contention for the 1920 Republican presidential nomination.

Hours, wages, and working conditions in the steel industry were more than usually bad. Roughly one-half the nation's steel workers received wages below those considered by the federal government to be the minimum necessary to maintain a family with a minimum decent living standard. Average hours of work in the entire industry were 68.7. The industry operated on a two-shift basis, and many steel workers worked a twenty-four-hour shift every other Sunday when they changed from the day to the night shift. In the summer of 1918 Gompers created a National Committee for the Organizing of the Iron and Steel Industry and named William Z. Foster, a former Socialist and syndicalist who supported the war and was then a Chicago AFL official, as its chairman. In 1921 Foster joined the Communist party and later became its national leader. By the summer of 1919 the steel workers' committee claimed one hundred thousand members and demanded an end of the twenty-four-hour shift, an eight-hour day, and a six-day week. Judge Elbert H. Gary, chairman of the board of United States Steel and leader of the whole industry, refused to negotiate with Foster or Gompers or any other union official and dismissed known union members. The union voted to strike on September 22. Wilson urged the AFL to postpone the strike. Gompers was willing to do so, but Foster and the steel workers were not. On the appointed date, 343,000 steel workers walked off the job, most of them in the Chicago-Gary steel district, but some in the Ohio, Pennsylvania, and New York steel centers.

The strike was never fully effective, and steel management found that crying communism and exploiting nationalistic rivalries among the predominantly immigrant steel workers both brought public opinion to its side and created dissension among the strikers. Violence broke out at Gary in November when United States Steel imported thousands of southern Negroes to break the strike. The governor of Indiana sent the state guard to Gary to protect the entrance of the strikebreakers into the plant, and when violence persisted he appealed to Washington for federal troops. General Leonard Wood arrived in Gary with an army contingent and declared martial law. The strike in Gary was defeated. The steel workers' committee gave up entirely in January, 1920, and the steel industry was not to become organized until 1937.

During the strike the Industrial Relations Department of the Interchurch World Movement made an extensive investigation of the strike and working conditions in the industry and issued a report that supported labor's contentions. The report was not issued in time to influence public opinion during the course of the strike, but in subsequent months public opinion turned against steel management. The steel companies denied the accuracy of the churchmen's conclusions, but in 1923 they partially surrendered to public opinion and, upon President Harding's urging, abolished the twelve-hour day.

The coal strike of 1919 was interesting because of the attitude of the Wilson administration and the emergence of a new personality in the labor movement, John L. Lewis, who had just become president of the United Mine Workers. Bituminous coal miners had not had a wage increase since 1917 despite the soaring cost of living. A convention of the UMW in September, 1919, called for the termination of the 1917 wage agreement and negotiation for a thirty-hour week and a 60 per cent wage increase. Coal mine operators refused these terms, and despite Wilson's assertion that a strike would be "morally and legally wrong," the miners left the pits on November 1.

Attorney General Palmer, acting upon Wilson's recommendation, secured a sweeping labor injunction. Lewis called off the strike, saying, "We cannot fight the government." But most of the miners refused to return to work. In December Palmer conferred with UMW leaders and achieved agreement with a compromise solution of an immediate small wage increase and arbitration of other issues. Ultimately, the miners received a 27 per cent pay increase but no change in the hours of work.

Harding and the Election of 1920

Republican victory in the congressional elections of 1918 and Wilson's unpopularity heartened the GOP and heightened the struggle for the 1920 Republican nomination. The front runner for the nomination was General Leonard Wood, who wore the mantle of the deceased Roosevelt as much as anyone and was a militaristic nationalist, independent of the bosses of the party. Just behind him was Governor Frank Lowden of Illinois, a former Congressman whose main support was in the Midwest. There was a host of other hopefuls: Hiram Johnson, Senator LaFollette, Governor Coolidge, Hoover, Nicholas Murray Butler, and Senator Warren G. Harding of Ohio. A Senate investigation, prompted by Senator Borah, revealed just before the convention that Wood had spent $1.8 million in working for the nomination, much of it raised by the soap manufacturer William C. Procter, and Lowden had spent $414,000.

In the first balloting at the Chicago convention the Wood and Lowden forces battled to no conclusion, and the convention seemed likely to deadlock. Senator Lodge, the convention chairman, successfully maneuvered an adjournment early in the evening of Friday, June 11, and a group of Republican bosses met in George Harvey's suite at the Blackstone Hotel to pick a dark horse. Harvey was the publisher who had first sponsored Wilson for the presidency and then turned strongly against him. Others in the famous "smoke-filled room" were Lodge,

Senator Boies Penrose of Pennsylvania, and Republican National Chairman Will Hays of Indiana. Late that night the group decided upon Harding because he had always been a party regular, made a good personal appearance, was extremely pliable, and had been so inconspicuous in the Senate as to make no strong enemies. The bosses summoned Harding and asked if there were any reason the GOP should not nominate him. Harding adjourned to an adjoining bedroom, thought for ten minutes, and emerged to say that his record was clean. Later it would be charged that he was only recently the father of an illegitimate child. The next day the powers of the GOP easily put across Harding's nomination. The convention balked at the inner-group's attempt to force the nomination of Senator Irvine Lenroot of Wisconsin as vice-president, but the measure of its rebellion was indicated by its choice of Governor Coolidge as Harding's running mate. The platform was evasive on the League but promised support of the World Court. It endorsed the recent railroad and merchant marine laws and promised aid to the farmers, lower taxes, higher tariffs, and reduced government expenditures.

The Democrats met at San Francisco later in June. The race for the Democratic nomination had been confused. Wilson had acted as if he were a contender for a third nomination without ever saying so, which put the front runner, his son-in-law McAdoo, at a disadvantage. Attorney General Palmer and the three-term governor of Ohio, James M. Cox, had considerable preconvention strength. McAdoo led for the first thirty-seven ballots, but Palmer was not far behind. On the next ballot Palmer withdrew and most of his delegates went to Cox, who was the favorite of the city bosses because he opposed prohibition. The nomination went to Cox on the forty-fourth ballot. Cox chose the Assistant Secretary of the Navy, Franklin D. Roosevelt, for the vice-presidential place on the ticket.

Cox and Roosevelt campaigned hard and supported the League, but the Republicans were ahead throughout the campaign. Harding had made a statement before the convention that proved popular and indicated the way the Republican nominee saw the presidency. What the country needed, said Harding, was "not heroism but healing, not nostrums but normalcy [Harding always suffered from acute suffix trouble], not revolution but restoration, not agitation but adjustment, not surgery but serenity, not the dramatic but the dispassionate, not experiment but equipoise, not submergence in internationality but sustainment in triumphant nationality." Precisely what that meant was anyone's guess, but obviously Harding did not want much action—and neither did the electorate. Harding conducted a front-porch campaign reminiscent of McKinley's in 1896 and won in a landslide. He received 16,152,200 votes for 404 electoral votes to 9,147,353 popular and 127 electoral votes for Cox. Cox carried no state outside of the former Confederate states except Kentucky and lost even Tennessee. In twenty states, among them Massachusetts, New York, Michigan, and California, Cox failed to carry a single county. The GOP also won overwhelmingly in the congressional elections. It had a majority of 22 seats in the Senate and 167 in the House.

Harding as President

Harding's tragedy—and the country's—was that he had risen in politics far above the level his abilities warranted, and he knew it. Raised on an Ohio farm, he had married a widow of moderate wealth and strong will and become owner and publisher of the Marion, Ohio, *Star*. A hearty extrovert, Harding had gone into local politics, then served in the state legislature and as lieutenant-governor. He was defeated for the governorship in 1910. He went to the Senate in 1914. His chief political manager and supporter was Harry M. Daugherty, leader of the "Ohio gang" who aspired to play the role of president-maker. Harding was not an evil man; he was only a weak one.

Harding's cabinet revealed the blend of political mediocrity and big business conservatism that characterized his administration. Harry Daugherty became Attorney General and Senator Albert B. Fall of New Mexico, around whose person there had long been the political odor of oil, became Secretary of the Interior. The most distinguished member of the Harding cabinet was Charles Evans Hughes, who became Secretary of State only after the outcry against Harding's suggestion of Fall for that post proved overpowering. Two able businessmen-politicians, Hoover and Andrew Mellon, became Secretaries of Commerce and the Treasury, respectively. The appointment of political hacks was to ruin Harding and make his administration second only to Grant's for political scandal and corruption.

Democratic and insurgent Republican gains in the 1922 elections, primarily the result of a short but sharp depression, reduced GOP majorities to eight in the Senate and eighteen in the House. But it was Harding's friends rather than his enemies who caused most of his problems. In June, 1923, Harding left Washington for a speaking trip through the West and a vacation in Alaska. He was worried and exhausted, and he could not get his mind off his treacherous friends in Washington. Upon returning to Seattle in late July, he nearly collapsed on the platform while making a public address. His physician reported that he was suffering from ptomaine poisoning from eating spoiled crabs. The ship on which he traveled from Alaska did not report any crabs on its manifest. The presidential party went on to San Francisco, where Harding got pneumonia. When the pneumonia crisis seemed over, he had a stroke and died on August 2. The close-mouthed rural Yankee, Coolidge, then on a vacation at his father's Vermont farm, took the presidential oath of office. His father, a rural justice of the peace, administered it.

Soon the causes of Harding's worries would become public knowledge. A woman named Nan Britton wrote a book entitled *The President's Daughter* in which she alleged that Harding was the father of her illegitimate child. Senate investigators revealed graft and corruption in the Harding administration so startling that it was years before Harding's hometown could persuade a prominent Republican to dedicate its Harding Memorial. There were unsubstantiated charges that Mrs. Harding had poisoned the President; there was better evidence that Harding's health broke from worry caused by his cronies in office. He told the Kansas publisher William Allen White before he left on his last trip that he had no trouble from his opponents, "But my damned friends, my God-damn friends, White, they're the ones that keep me walking the floor nights!"

The Harding Scandals

Although Harding's friends in the "Ohio gang" were involved in a wide variety of corrupt practices, some of them as petty as bootlegging liquor from government warehouses, the main cases brought to light were in the Veterans Bureau, the Department of the Interior, the Department of Justice, and the office of the Alien Property Custodian. Harding knew at least part of the Veterans Bureau scandal before he died. The head of the Bureau, Charles R. Forbes, a Harding appointee, had enriched himself and some close friends by about $250 million of Bureau funds. One of his practices was to label certain veterans hospital goods as worthless, sell them to friends at a low price, and have the Bureau buy them back later at a high price. Another was to accept bribes and grant special favors to contractors engaged in building veterans hospitals. Honest contractors who were discriminated against began to talk of Forbes's corruption and rumors reached Harding. Harding called in Forbes, got some of the story from him, and allowed him to go abroad and resign in February, 1923. The following month the Senate heard the rumors about the Veterans Bureau and began an investigation, whereupon the Bureau counsel, Charles F. Cramer, committed suicide. After Harding's death, the Senate revealed much more of Forbes's corruption. Forbes was convicted of fraud and was sentenced to two years in the penitentiary.

The most famous of the Harding scandals involved the naval oil reserves at Elk Hills, California, and Teapot Dome, Wyoming. Presidents Taft and Wilson had set aside these oil lands for the navy's future use. Soon after Harding's inauguration, Secretary of the Interior Fall, upon a pretext, got Harding secretly to transfer administration of the two reserves from the Navy Department to his jurisdiction. The Secretary of the Navy, a nonentity from Michigan named Edwin Denby, did not protest. He apparently did not know of Fall's plans. In 1922 Fall leased, again secretly, the Elk Hills reserve to the Pan-American Petroleum Company, owned by Edward L. Doheny, and the Teapot Dome reserve to the Mammoth Oil Company, owned by Harry Sinclair. News of the leases leaked out, Senator LaFollette demanded a Senate investigation, and the Senate named Thomas J. Walsh, Democrat from Montana, to head the inquiry.

Walsh investigated the existing situation thoroughly before he began open hearings in October, 1923, two months after Harding's death. Witnesses conveniently suffered attacks of bad memory and resorted to unusually evasive replies, but Walsh slowly and painfully dug out the story. Doheny's son had given Fall a "little black bag" containing $100,000 in currency as an unsecured "loan." Sinclair had given Fall $223,000 in Liberty bonds, $85,000 in cash, and some prize cattle for Fall's New Mexico ranch. Fall resigned, and the government began prosecution, circumventing the Department of Justice because Attorney General Daugherty was already in trouble in another scandal. Conspiracy and bribery indictments were charged against Fall, Sinclair, and Doheny in June, 1924. Delays and appeals of various kinds postponed final action for years, but Fall was finally convicted of accepting a bribe and sentenced to a year in prison and a fine of $100,000. Doheny and Sinclair, the bribers, managed to get acquitted, but Sinclair got three months for contempt of the Senate and six months more for contempt of court when he hired detectives to shadow the jurors. The government, after carrying the case to the Supreme Court, got the Doheny and Sinclair leases invalidated.

Fall and Denby resigned from the cabinet; Daugherty not only refused to resign but set the FBI to investigating Senators who were investigating executive corruption. Daugherty's downfall came in 1924 in a case involving the American

Metal Company, a $6.5 billion German corporation the government had seized during the war. Early in the Harding administration, a German representative paid John T. King, a prominent New York Republican, $441,000 in the hope that the company would be returned. King turned over $50,000 to the Alien Property Custodian, Thomas W. Miller, an "Ohio gang" member who had been prominent in the American Legion. Another $50,000 in Liberty bonds was deposited to a joint account held by Daugherty and his close Ohio friend, the "unofficial attorney general" Jesse Smith. When the case broke in March, 1924, King had already died and Smith had committed suicide in Daugherty's Washington apartment, thinking he was about to be discovered in another fraud. Daugherty refused to testify before a Senate investigating committee, citing the Fifth Amendment right to withhold testimony that might be self-incriminating. Coolidge then demanded and received Daugherty's resignation. In 1926 Daugherty refused to testify at his trial, saying that his silence was to protect the confidence of the late President. He was acquitted. The next year Miller was convicted.

Coolidge as the New President

The surprising thing about the Harding scandals was that they did not significantly harm the Republican party. The public, in general, took the attitude that only the individuals involved were responsible. Harding's death and the succession of the puritanical, tight-fisted, taciturn Coolidge had a great deal to do with the public's reaction. Harding's views of government and business had been consistent with the majority public mood. His only trouble, thought most people, was that he surrounded himself with crooks, and they regarded Coolidge as a kind of honest Harding, New England division. Indeed, there were similarities between Harding's and Coolidge's careers. Both were country boys who had moved to small towns, pursued professional careers, and slowly worked their way up through local and state politics more because of their party regularity than their ability. Coolidge had been born in rural Vermont in 1872, had gone to Amherst College, and had settled down to practice law in Northampton, Massachusetts. He had gone to the state legislature where in the course of time he became speaker and then governor. There was nothing distinguished nor colorful about him. A sour man who said little, probably because he had little to say, Coolidge was always essentially a narrow, inhibited, conservative, rural Vermonter, almost the stereotyped Yankee of jokes. The title of William Allen White's biography of Coolidge well summarized the man: *A Puritan in Babylon*.

The Election of 1924

Coolidge's nomination by the 1924 Republican convention was entirely predictable. He received the nomination at the Cleveland convention on the first ballot, and all that prevented his nomination by acclamation was the opposition of the Wisconsin and North Dakota delegations. The Coolidge demonstrations lacked fire and conviction because it was difficult to get excited about the man. Charles G. Dawes, a Chicago banker and former Director of the Budget who swore masterfully and smoked a peculiar underslung pipe, received the vice-presidential nomination and lent color to the ticket. The platform was a safe, conservative document, adopted when the convention defeated a more progressive platform submitted by the Wisconsin delegation.

The Other Two Nominees

The badly divided Democratic convention at New York's Madison Square Garden offered far more fireworks. Prohibition and the anti-Catholic Ku Klux Klan widened already existing Democratic cleavages. The eastern urban wing of the party supported Governor Alfred E. Smith of New York, a son of Irish immigrant parents, a Roman Catholic, and, in the language of the day, a "wringing wet" on the prohibition question. He was anathema to the southern and western wings of the party, which supported McAdoo. McAdoo might have received the nomination had he not lost the support of progressives in the party who disapproved of his serving as Doheny's lawyer in the oil scandals. The balloting went on for days while the noisy Tammany galleries thoroughly alienated the rural delegates. Smith and McAdoo withdrew after the ninety-fifth inconclusive ballot. On the one hundred and third ballot the nomination went to John W. Davis, an able and prominent Wall Street lawyer originally from West Virginia. To placate the agrarian wing of the party, the convention nominated Governor Charles W. Bryan of Nebraska, brother of the Great Commoner, for the vice-presidency. The platform, except for criticism of the last Republican tariff and a promise of Philippine independence, which the Democrats had failed to enact in 1916, was as conservative and conventional as the Republican platform. The biggest fight within the platform was over a resolution sponsored by Smith's followers which called the Klan an un-American organization. The convention defeated the resolution by one vote.

The only real excitement in the 1924 campaign came from the independent candidacy of Senator LaFollette. Progressivism had by no means died out completely among the agrarians of the upper Mississippi Valley. The National Non-Partisan League had spread from North Dakota into neighboring states. Founded in 1915 by an ex-Socialist named Arthur C. Townley, the League had won the governorship of North Dakota in 1916 and the legislature as well in 1918. It partially enacted its semisocialistic program, creating a state-owned flour mill and grain elevator. In 1920 the League had made common cause with agrarians in Minnesota and North Dakota and nominated a Farmer-Labor party ticket. Most farmers gave up an old-fashioned agrarianism in the postwar depression and supported the American Farm Bureau's farm bloc tactics, but in early 1922 a group of agrarians, railroad brotherhood officials, Socialists, and a few urban reformers met in Chicago and formed the Conference for Progressive Political Action. The CPPA considered launching a third party, but abandoned the idea in favor of working for selected candidates in the major parties in the 1922 congressional elections. CPPA-endorsed candidates did very well.

Had the Democrats not been so badly divided and had they not neglected economic issues for prohibition and the Klan, they might have been able to capitalize on the agrarian movement of the upper Midwest. They did not, however, and after the agrarians were thoroughly repudiated at the 1924 Republican convention, there was nowhere for them to turn. The CPPA met in convention at Cleveland on July 4. It decided to defer the question of the formation of a permanent third party until after the election, but it nominated LaFollette for the presidency and later named Senator Burton K. Wheeler, Democrat of Montana who had been prominent in investigating Harding scandals, as its vice-presidential candidate. LaFollette dictated the platform. It was for elimination of monopolies, federally owned water power, direct election of federal judges, the child labor amendment, and a prohibition of the labor injunction. The Socialist party, the Farmer-Labor party, and the AFL endorsed the LaFollette-Wheeler ticket, although the AFL did practically nothing to help LaFollette and Gompers all but withdrew the endorsement just before the election. The Communists, who had been denied seats at the CPPA convention, offered their support, but LaFollette vigorously repudiated them.

The Campaign and After

Most of the electorate was disinterested in the campaign. The Republican slogan, "Keep Cool with Coolidge," was well adapted to the majority mood. Coolidge campaigned little, and Davis' speeches were dull. LaFollette worked hard in the Midwest and the Far West, but much of his potential vote was scared away by the Republican argument that a strong LaFollette vote would produce no electoral majority and throw the election into the House of Representatives, as had happened in 1824. Only half of the qualified voters bothered to go to the polls on election day. Coolidge received 382 electoral votes and 15,725,003 popular votes, Davis 136 and 8,385,586, and LaFollette 13 and 4,826,471. The new Senate was composed of 50 Republicans, 40 Democrats, and 6 LaFollette Progressives; the House of 232 Republicans, 183 Democrats, and 20 Progressives. Davis carried only the eleven former Confederate states and Oklahoma. LaFollette carried his home state of Wisconsin and ran ahead of Davis in eleven other states, all of them in the West. Davis faded to political obscurity. In 1954 he was the attorney for the segregationists in the school integration cases before the Supreme Court.

Although the LaFollette Progressives did very well for an independent candidacy, a meeting of the CPPA early in 1925 decided not to attempt to form a permanent third party. LaFollette died a few months later, to be succeeded in the Senate by his elder son, Robert M. LaFollette, Jr. With the collapse of the LaFollette movement, independent political Progressivism receded to its lowest ebb since the Civil War. Both parties were under the control of standpatters, and most of the public did not seem to care. Yet it is easy to exaggerate the strength of political conservatives in the 1920's. A handful of progressives from each party remained in Congress, especially in the Senate, and in combination with farm bloc congressmen who frequently stood pat on nonfarm issues, these progressives were able to block or modify part of the conservatives' legislative program. Their position was strengthened after the 1926 elections, when the GOP majority was cut to forty in the House and the new Senate contained forty-eight Republicans of various hues, forty-seven Democrats of similar variegation, and one Farmer-Laborite.

The progressives were able to give Coolidge and the regular Republicans a great many headaches. For example, early in 1925 the Senate twice rejected

Coolidge's appointment of Charles B. Warren to the Attorney Generalship. In 1927 led by Senator Norris, the Senate progressives blocked the seating of two conservative Republicans, William S. Vare of Pennsylvania and Frank L. Smith of Illinois, who had been elected with huge campaign funds. They also were able to defeat the Coolidge administration's plan to sell the power site at Muscle Shoals on the Tennessee River and thereby save the area for development by the Tennessee Valley Authority in the 1930's. But the most the progressives could do in the Coolidge administration was to throw an occasional monkey wrench into the conservative gears, and business had good reason to be happy with Coolidge and his cabinet.

The Republican Administrations and Business

It frequently is said that the Republican administrations of the 1920's favored laissez-faire. This is true only if one defines "laissez-faire" as the absence of government restraint on business. In many areas, these administrations used the power of the federal government to aid business enterprise. Some of the aid was by the executive branch of government alone; some was through legislation.

The Federal Trade Commission

Needless to say, the Department of Justice in the 1920's did not embark upon any trust-busting campaigns, but in this respect it did not differ from the Wilson administration. In fact, the government instituted more antitrust actions during the eight years of the Harding and Coolidge administrations than it did during Wilson's eight years. Indeed, in many ways the attitude of the executive branch toward business in the 1920's was the logical extension of Wilson's policies. For example, Wilson never intended the Federal Trade Commission to be a militant regulator of business, and his appointees to the FTC were safe conservatives. Under Harding and Coolidge the FTC became only more active in its probusiness activities. From 1921 until 1925, however, the FTC was more restrained in its aid to business than was the Department of Commerce under Secretary Hoover. Then in 1925 Coolidge appointed William E. Humphrey of Washington to the FTC, and he was able to convert it to an all-out aid for business agency. As late as 1924 the FTC could issue a report critical of Mellon's Aluminum Corporation of America, but after 1925 its regulation consisted of no more than clamping down on the most flagrantly fraudulent of advertisers.

The FTC after 1925 worked closely with Secretary Hoover in helping business to minimize competition through trade associations, so much so that Senate progressives like Norris demanded that the FTC be abolished. Hoover had accepted the Commerce post from Harding only on condition that he be given a free hand on all matters pertaining to business and that he have an unofficial veto in foreign policy. Both under Harding and Coolidge he operated without White House restraint, a kind of subpresident for business affairs. The trade association, of which there were already about two thousand in existence in 1921, was Hoover's favorite device for achieving business stability and minimizing competition. Hoover called many industrial conferences and explained to them the advantages of the device for businessmen, published a handbook that explained how to organize a trade association, and helped the associations gather statistics and other information (which was published at government expense) that was necessary for businessmen efficiently to restrict production, maintain prices, and divide markets, as well as to rationalize production and distribution. The FTC worked closely with the trade associations to advise them what was and what was not contrary to the antitrust laws. In other words, the FTC conceived its function, after Humphrey joined it, as showing business how legally to minimize competition. When the courts changed interpretations of antitrust law, the FTC and the Department of Justice advised business of the effects of the new judicial interpretations on their operations. Operating from shared information supplied by Washington and the trade associations, business in the 1920's, as we shall see in greater detail in chapter four, was enabled to become practically self-governing and to establish an oligopolistic structure in the important industries.

The Tariff

The main legislative aids to business in the 1920's were the traditional ones of tariff protection and a tax structure favorable to wealthy individuals and corporations. Wilson and his three Republican successors did not see eye-to-eye on the tariff, although they substantially agreed that the purpose of tariff revision was to benefit American business; they disagreed on the tariff as a means, not as an end.

With the advent of the postwar depression, the Wilson administration was under considerable pressure to increase tariff duties, especially on agricultural products. Farmers, subjected to generations of high-tariff propaganda, were blind to the fact that with few exceptions foreign farm commodities could not compete with their products in the domestic market even if there were no duties whatsoever. Wilson resisted the pressure for raising the tariff, saying, "If we want to sell, we must be prepared to buy." That was indeed the situation unless another way could be devised to get purchasing power in foreign hands. But it should be noted that Wilson's objection to increased tariffs was that higher duties would hurt American markets abroad. In the last days of the Wilson administration, Congress rushed through a new tariff bill that raised duties on several agricultural commodities. Wilson vetoed it on March 3, 1921, his last full day in office. The new Congress, after receiving a special message from Harding in favor of tariff protection, dug out the rejected bill, revised it slightly, and submitted it to Harding, who promptly signed it. This measure, the Emergency Tariff of 1921, raised duties on meat, wool, sugar, corn, and wheat to about the levels of the Payne-Aldrich Tariff of 1909.

But the Emergency Tariff was only a temporary measure until a more comprehensive tariff bill could be prepared. Steered through the House by Joseph W. Fordney of Michigan and the Senate by Porter J. McCumber of North Dakota, the new tariff bill was the highest yet in America's history. In exchange for almost meaningless increases in duties on farm products, Congressmen from rural districts supported increases in duties on manufactured goods. A number of raw materials on the free list of the Underwood Tariff, hides, leather, coal, iron ore, and cotton, were kept without duty since manufacturers did not want to pay a premium on their own imports. The biggest increases in the duties on manufactured goods were for chemicals, textiles, chinaware, toys, and jewelry. Even books printed in the English language were taxed almost 25 per cent; and scientific laboratory equipment had a duty of 40 per cent. The bill enjoined the tariff commission to keep an eye on the relative costs of production of domestic and foreign manufacturing and to advise the president, who under the bill could raise or lower duties by as much as 50 per cent. Coolidge accepted the tariff commission's suggestions only when it recommended an increase in duties. Harding signed the Fordney-McCumber Tariff in September, 1922.

Despite the Democrats' condemnation of the 1922 tariff in their 1924 platform as the "most unjust, unscientific, and dishonest tariff tax measure ever enacted in our history," the act actually removed the tariff from serious political differences during the 1920's. Battles over domestic taxation were much hotter. Many businessmen were beginning to see that, with American industry becoming increasingly dependent upon foreign trade, raising the tariff amounted to cutting one's own throat. They clamored instead for a reduction of taxes, and in Secretary of the Treasury Mellon they found a kindred spirit.

Tax Reductions

In order to cut taxes there had to be a reduction in government spending. Through ruthless trimming and refusal to undertake new expensive programs, the federal government was able in the 1920's to cut its expenditures to about $3.6 billion each year from 1922 until the depression. This figure was well above the spending of the prewar years—higher prices and a greater population made return to the old budgets impossible—but it was less than one-third of the budgets of the war years. Despite tax cuts, the government still spent less than it received and reduced the war debt by about one-third, from about $24 billion to about $16 billion. This record earned Mellon the popular title of "the greatest Secretary of the Treasury since Alexander Hamilton." Certainly his view of who should pay taxes was reminiscent of Hamilton and the whiskey tax.

Almost all political groups urged tax cuts. The question that divided them was who should receive the lion's share of the cuts. Mellon, soon after he came to office, sent Congress a series of messages in which he urged abolition of the excess profits tax, a slight compensatory increase in the regular corporate tax, gradual reduction of individual income taxes until the maximum was 33 per cent, repeal of the wartime excise taxes, and a new tax on automobiles. The House and the Senate finance committee went along with Mellon's recommendation, but a group of agrarian Republicans combined with the Democrats to write their own tax bill and informed Mellon and the White House that they must accept their bill or get none at all. The final law eliminated some of the excise taxes, left the individual income rates where they were, and raised the personal exemption for married couples from $2,000 to $2,500. Some Congressmen asked Mellon why personal exemptions should not be raised to excuse the taxation of incomes less than $5,000. Mellon's Hamiltonian reply was, ". . . nothing so brings home to a man the feeling that he personally has an interest in seeing that Government revenues are not squandered, but intelligently expended, as the fact that he contributes individually a direct tax, no matter how small, to his Government."

In 1923 Mellon urged a reduction of the surtax on large individual incomes and a drastic cut in the inheritance tax. He argued that wealthy people would not invest in industry if income taxes took a large share of their return. He declared that tax-exempt bonds of municipalities took such a share of total investment that industry suffered, an assertion hardly borne out by corporate balance sheets. Coolidge urged Congress to amend the Constitution to abolish tax-exempt securities. But again a combination of farm Republicans and Democrats made their point of view prevail. The tax law of June, 1924, cut the maximum surtax on individual incomes from 50 to 40 per cent, but it also cut the normal tax of low and middle incomes by half, left corporation taxes where they were, and raised the maximum inheritance tax from 25 to 40 per cent. In addition, it imposed a new gift tax, a device to prevent the circumvention of inheritance taxes by giving fortunes to heirs before death.

The general prosperity of 1925 to 1929 brought increased tax revenues and surpluses to the federal government and helped Mellon in his program to reduce taxes on large incomes. The Revenue Act of 1926 lowered the normal tax on incomes, reduced the maximum surtax to 20 per cent, reduced corporation taxes, cut the inheritance tax by half, and eliminated the gift tax altogether. The act of 1928 left personal income taxes at the 1926 rates but reduced corporation taxes further. Neither measure raised personal exemptions, consistent with Mellon's theory that the more people who paid taxes the better. But Mellon's tax program reduced taxes on large incomes so much that a million-dollar income after 1926 would pay less than one-third as much in taxes as in 1921.

Conservatives of today's heavily taxed generation look back wistfully to the taxes of Mellon's days and maintain that Mellon was a paragon of fiscal wisdom. Some even favor abolition of the income tax altogether. However, one can make a strong argument that it was economically unwise to reduce taxes on high incomes at all. Much of the income thus saved from the tax collector went into land and stock speculation and contributed to the crash of 1929. If wealth had been taxed at the rate it was during or soon after the war, more of the national debt could have been retired or, possibly, the higher revenues could have been used for a vigorous government farm program and an economically healthier distribution of income. Prosperity might have lasted longer. Part of the responsibility must fall on the progressives, who never seriously put forward better proposals for dealing with the annual government surplus.

The Farm Problem and Politics in the 1920's

Agriculture, in general, did not share in the prosperity of the 1920's. As already described, farmers overextended their investments during the war. When the government withdrew wartime price supports from wheat in May, 1920, agriculture's wartime prosperity came to a sudden end. By the end of 1920 wheat prices had fallen to $1.44 a bushel as compared to $2.15 at the end of 1919, corn from $1.25 to 68 cents a bushel, and cotton from 36 cents a pound to 14 cents. Farming never truly recovered until World War II. Although farm prices subsequently rose, they did not go up as much as the prices farmers had to pay for manufactured goods nor as much as local taxes on their land. Total farm income amounted to a smaller percentage of the national income, falling from 16 per cent in 1919 to 9 per cent in 1929. Farm tenancy and mortgage indebtedness became increasingly serious.

The decline of farm prices and income was attributable to several factors. An important one was that increased mechanization and use of better seed, fertilizer, and breeding stock greatly increased farm yields. At the same time, there was no compensating increase in farm markets. Indeed, demand for many farm commodities declined during the 1920's. For example, the widespread use of rayon and the fashionable abandonment of numerous petticoats and long, fully cut dresses seriously reduced demand for cotton. Even diet changed. Americans in the 1920's ate less bread and fat than they had before the war. Further, population increase slowed down and less land was needed to produce feed for draft animals.

Thus far we have been considering the total farm picture. The situation of the small farmer was worse than the national average. The small farmer in the 1920's was a victim of the new technology. He could not produce as efficiently or compete with the bigger farmer whose mechanized efficiency reduced his costs per unit of production. As the optimum farm size and the optimum investment increased, the smallest and least efficient farmers experienced great difficulty. Many left farming altogether; the total farm population decreased by over 3 million in the 1920's. Farmers tried to meet their new situation through two means: cooperative marketing and politics.

Cooperative Marketing

Aaron Sapiro, who became general counsel of the American Farm Bureau Federation in 1923, was a strong advocate of cooperative marketing. He had already helped dairy and tobacco farmers to organize cooperatives. To be successful, a marketing cooperative had to be able to force nearly all producers of a commodity for a particular market to agree to work within the organization and not sell privately, and that required law behind the cooperative. Kentucky passed the first Cooperative Marketing Act in 1922, and most other agricultural states soon followed suit. Cooperative marketing worked well—sometimes too well for the public's economic welfare—when the production of a commodity was fairly well concentrated. For example, the California Fruit Growers' Association was able to dictate prices about as it chose. But the scheme did not work for commodities that were produced in large areas of the nation, and the majority of farmers raised such widely produced commodities as wheat, corn, hogs, beef, and cotton. These farmers had to resort to politics.

The Farm Bloc

In May, 1921, at the suggestion of the head of the Farm Bureau, Grey Silver, a group of Congressmen from agricultural states met in the Bureau's Washington office and organized the farm bloc. Senator William S. Kenyon of Iowa was its first leader; he was succeeded by Senator Arthur Capper of Kansas. In the Senate the bloc consisted of fourteen Republicans and twelve Democrats, all from the West and the South. For the next few years the bloc stuck together and was able to pass a series of laws designed to aid the farmer.

The farm bloc got through Congress some beneficial measures that protected farmers' interests in stockyards and grain exchanges and that extended more government-backed credit to farmers. But these laws failed to get at the basic problem: low farm prices. Farm economists reasoned that the root of the farmer's problem was the low world price of farm commodities and that the answer was to provide the farmer the kind of protection from world prices that the government had already granted manufacturers with the protective tariff. An ordinary tariff on agricultural imports would not work because the goods imported were only rarely in competition with American farm products. Tariff protection for corn was mythical if no one imported corn, and no one did. The four McNary-Haugen bills of 1924 to 1928 were efforts to build an effective tariff for farm products—to institute a two-price system, one price for the United States and another for the rest of the world.

The McNary-Haugen Bills

The McNary-Haugen bills, named for their sponsors Senator Charles McNary of Oregon and Representative Gilbert Haugen of Iowa, can be traced to the ideas of George N. Peek and Hugh S. Johnson, president and general counsel, respectively, of the Moline Plow Company. Each of these men was to become prominent in the early New Deal. They realized that to sell agricultural implements to farmers, the farmer had to have more income. The McNary-Haugen bills differed in detail, but they all had this rather complicated basic feature: a federal farm board would be established which would buy up the surplus of designated farm commodities at a price based upon prewar averages, when prices farmers received were in better relation to prices farmers paid. This price would be about equal to the world price of the commodity plus the existing tariff. The government-owned surplus could then be stored for a lean year or sold abroad at the world price. Thus the domestic price would be higher than the world price by the amount of the tariff. The loss to the government incurred by selling at a lower price than it had bought would be met by an equalization fee to be paid by producers of the commodity. The net return to the farmers, the plan's proponents argued, would be higher than under the existing practice of selling all the crop at world prices whether at home or abroad. The total equalization fees would not equal the increase of the domestic price unless exports equaled domestic consumption.

McNary and Haugen introduced their first bill in January, 1924. It had the support of nearly all of the farm organizations and of Secretary of Agriculture Henry C. Wallace. When Wallace died later in the year, Coolidge replaced him with a man whose views on farm economics were more nearly like his own. But Congress defeated the first bill, as well as the second one in 1926, largely because the bills covered only commodities produced in the Midwest and West and omitted southern cotton and tobacco. A third bill, which satisfied southern Congressmen, passed in February, 1927, only to run into a veto from Coolidge. In May, 1928, Congress passed a McNary-Haugen bill again and drew a second veto. Advocates of the plan were insufficient to override either veto. Coolidge's second veto, coming in an election year, made farm relief one of the issues of the campaign, but other factors in the election so clouded the picture that the Republican party's continued opposition to McNary-Haugenism did not constitute a real referendum.

The National Grange suggested still another scheme, the "export debenture" plan, to give effective tariff protection to farm commodities. It never was able to get its plan through Congress. The idea was for the federal government to pay an export subsidy on designated commodities equal to one-half of the tariff duty on the commodity in the form of "debentures" which would be accepted by customs collectors for any import. After receiving their "debentures," according to the plan, farm associations would sell them at a discount to importers and thereby receive benefit from duties on manufactured goods.

Whether the McNary-Haugen bills or the export debenture scheme would have effected a lasting solution to the farm price problem is dubious. Neither plan provided for an effective means of limiting agricultural production, of eliminating the surplus by growing less. Not even the production controls of the farm laws adopted in the 1930's and later successfully met the problem of the surplus, and it is safe to assume that the plans of the 1920's would not have either. Nor did the farm plans of the 1920's promise much for the small farmer confronted with the superior resources and efficiency of the big-scale farmer. For that matter, no subsequent legislation met that problem either. In the 1920's "factories in the fields" were beginning to become important economically. The Campbell Farming Corporation of Montana operated over one hundred thousand acres and could plow one thousand acres and seed or harvest two thousand acres in a single day. The farm relief plans of the 1920's and the opposition to them from the eastern wing of the Republican party did, however, have a political impact: they demonstrated conclusively to western farmers that eastern Republicans had a double standard for government aid to business. Eastern Republicans would help commerce and manufacturing but deny real aid to agriculture as a violation of laissez-faire. When a general downswing in the business cycle after 1929 made farm conditions much more desperate, the political chickens hatched by the McNary-Haugen vetoes came home to roost.

The Economics
of Business,
1917–1929

One of the oldest and perhaps the noblest of human
aspirations has been the abolition of poverty. By poverty I
mean the grinding by undernourishment, cold, and
ignorance, and fear of old age of those who have the will
to work. We in America today are nearer to the final
triumph over poverty than ever before in the history of
any land. The poorhouse is vanishing from among us. We
have not reached the goal, but, given a chance to go
forward with the policies of the last eight years, we shall
soon with the help of God be in sight of the day when
poverty will be banished from this nation.

HERBERT HOOVER, acceptance speech,
Republican National Convention,
August 11, 1928

Chapter Four

The era from the beginning of World War I until the Great Depression was more prosperous than any the American people had previously known. They had more money and more of the things that money could buy than ever before. There were blemishes on prosperity's beaming face, but the period was nevertheless one of unprecedented comfort.

Merely to describe prosperity, however, is to miss some highly important developments in American history, to ignore some facts from the past which helped mold the way Americans live today and the material basis of American society. Put most generally, business in the 1920's brought the big corporation to a new state of development and in so doing modified the whole nature of the economic system. This basic economic change did not develop overnight. It had developed slowly. The large business corporation might be dated from the establishment of United States Steel in 1901. But in the period from 1917 to 1929, big businesses came into their own. When Herbert Hoover and others referred to the economy of the 1920's as the New Economic Order or the New Era, they did not exaggerate. It was new, and it was of overriding importance. One of the most perceptive of scholars, Professor Thomas C. Cochran, writing on the history of American business, has justifiably described the rise of the large business corporation as "one of the major changes in history, comparable to the rise of medieval feudalism or of commercial institutions at the close of the middle ages. . . . Corporate enterprise gradually altered the meaning of property, the circumstances and motivations of economic activity, and the careers and expectations of most citizens."[1]

Prosperity and Wealth

Real per capita income (the dollar value of total national income divided by population and adjusted for price changes) increased from $517 for the period

---

[1] Thomas C. Cochran, *The American Business System* (Cambridge, Mass.: Harvard Univ. Press, 1957), p. 51.

1909–18 to $612 for the years from 1919–28. Real per capita income in 1921 was $522; it grew to $716 in 1929. This was a notable gain, but the increase was not steady. One major and two lesser dips in the business cycle during the 1920's interrupted economic growth. The boom created by war orders sustained itself on reconstruction loans and pent up consumer demand until mid-1920. Then the economy went into a sudden decline that was as sharp a drop as any America had ever before experienced. The postwar depression was at its worst in 1921, when unemployment reached 4,750,000 and national income was off roughly 28 per cent from the previous year. But the economy righted itself rather quickly and by late 1922 the depression was over. Since agriculture did not regain its normal level, the growth of national income by 1923 to the 1919 level indicates how strong the recovery was in industry. Slight dips in industrial production in 1924 and 1927 were no more than the usual fluctuations of the business cycle, which does not climb steadily in the best of times.

ECONOMIC GROWTH, 1919–1929

	Industrial Production	Cost-of-Living Index 1929 = 100	National Income Billions of Dollars	Real Income per Capita, 1929 Prices
1919		101.6	64.2	543
1920		116.9	74.2	548
1921	58	104.2	59.4	522
1922	73	97.7	60.7	553
1923	88	99.5	71.6	634
1924	82	99.8	72.1	633
1925	90	102.4	76.0	644
1926	96	103.2	81.6	678
1927	95	101.2	80.1	674
1928	99	100.1	81.7	676
1929	110	100.0	87.2	716

Construction and Manufacturing

Construction and manufacturing boomed more than other parts of the economy. The amount of new building was tremendous after 1922. In that year more than $12 billion worth of building materials were used by the industry. In 1928 the figure stood at $17.4 billion, but it dropped over a billion dollars in 1929 to a level below that of 1926. Construction used more new capital than any other industry, employed between 5 and 6 per cent of the labor force, and accounted for 7.5 per cent of total payrolls. A large part of the construction boom was the result of road and bridge building made necessary by the greater number of automobiles. By the end of the 1920's, about one-fifth of America's three million miles of roads were hard-surfaced one way or another. More than eighty thousand miles were paved with concrete. The Portland Cement Association used high-pressure sales tactics on many municipal and township governments, and some of the new roads were unwarranted. Others were poorly constructed—too narrow, improperly drained and banked, and insufficiently reinforced at the edges—and had to be rebuilt in another age. Yet most of the roads were a vital necessity to the new automobile age. The states' share of the costs of new road construction came mostly from registration taxes on cars and on gasoline taxes, which ranged from two to six cents a gallon. In 1930 gasoline taxes totaled nearly $500 million. But residential, hotel, and office building construction also boomed during the decade. Real estate men opened thousands of new suburban developments, usually called something innocuous and homey like Elm Grove or Green Highlands, and Sinclair Lewis was wise to make Babbitt a "realtor." Much of the hotel, some of the office, and a bit of the housing construction was more the result of rosily optimistic speculation than the fulfillment of real need.

Manufacturing increased its output during the decade by 64 per cent. Because of an improvement in labor productivity of 40 per cent, this increased production was the work of fewer workers. There was a small absolute decline in the number of people engaged in manufacturing between 1919 and 1929. It has been estimated that between 1920 and 1929 manufacturing dispensed with the labor of thirty-two men out of every one hundred employed per unit of production, but that twenty-seven of them were absorbed in increased total production. Most, but not all, of the workers displaced from industry found jobs in service or trade, which accounted for a larger percentage of the labor force.

Two trends in manufacturing during the 1920's stimulated speculation, and speculation had doleful implications for the future. Manufacturing corporations, particularly big ones, were able to finance a larger part of their expansion from their own reserves and thus were less dependent upon bankers than they had been before the war. "Finance capitalism" was being undermined in the decade of its greatest success. Corporations kept their reserves in bank time deposits, rather than demand deposits, which enabled banks to lend a greater amount of money for essentially speculative purposes. Brokers' loans, to be considered in greater detail in the discussion of the stock market boom in chapter 8, constituted a considerable part of the capital for speculation on Wall Street. The other trend was that industry in general invested relatively less money in new physical equipment; there was a decline in the percentage of the national income going into capital formation. This decline in the last five years of the boom was particularly marked, so much so that there was an absolute decline in new investment. In 1924 financing for new physical equipment was 76 per cent of all new financing; in 1929 it was only 35 per cent. The dollar total declined from $3.5 billion in 1924 to $3.2 billion in 1929. This decline occurred despite the great growth of a few industries, such as automobiles, chemicals, electric power, and electric appliances. At the same time total savings increased. The lag in capital investment, therefore, stimulated speculation of all kinds, primarily in stocks and bonds and in real estate.

Savings and Speculation

The pattern of income distribution had much to do with savings and speculation. The share of income received by the richest 10 per cent of the population had been increasing ever since about 1910. Between 1919 and 1929 the share received by the wealthiest 1 per cent of income receivers increased by 13 per cent. People with low and middle incomes necessarily spent whatever additional income they received for consumer goods, but people with large incomes did not add appreciably to consumption when they received more income. In the 1920's what happened to the increased share of total income that accrued to the wealthiest families of America was almost the sole decision of the business community. Government played only a small role in investment; its expenditures were low and federal taxes on wealth declined during the period. Business leaders decided not to invest in new capital equipment at the rate they had earlier. They had many reasons for their decisions, but the fundamental one was that the market did not, in their opinion, warrant expansion at the old level; and a basic reason why the market did not warrant expansion was the incomes of the great majority of consumers were not sufficient to absorb the production that would result from a greater rate of investment in capital plant. Thus the pattern of income distribution tended to increase the volume of speculation, both by creating larger discretionary sums and by influencing investment decisions. The resulting speculation was spectacular.

Speculation in securities became major after mid-1924. The stock market climbed rather steadily until 1926, declined slightly, and then from 1927 to 1929 zoomed to unprecedented heights. Salesmen for stocks and bonds scoured even small towns for people with savings and encouraged them to get into the market and get rich fast. John J. Raskob, a member of the Democratic national committee and chairman of the board of General Motors, wrote in *The Ladies' Home Journal*,

> If a man saves $15 a week, and invests in good common stocks and allows the dividends and rights to accumulate, at the end of twenty years he will have at least $80,000 and an income from investments of $400 a month. He will be rich. . . . I am firm in my belief that anyone not only can be rich, but ought to be rich.[2]

If Raskob were right, and a great many people thought he was, this was a return on investment of over 400 per cent. A big electric sign above New York's Columbus Circle declared that every man fifty years old should have $50,000.

Land speculation probably involved more people than stock speculation. Small town promoters appealed both to desire for financial gain and local pride when they organized hotel-building ventures. These economic white elephants, many of them financed with contributions as low as $500 to $1,000, still ornament hundreds of court house squares. Florida had the most spectacular land boom of the decade. If everyone who had a normal amount of sense was going to be rich, thought many speculators, then they would want to vacation in Florida. Promoters put up palatial resort hotels of pseudo-Spanish design, drained swamps and called the drainage ditches lagoons, and fleeced the unwary. One promoter in Coral Gables paid William Jennings Bryan to sit on a raft under a beach umbrella and lecture on the glories of Florida's climate. He attracted a crowd for

---

[2] Samuel Crowther, "Everybody Ought To Be Rich" (An Interview with John J. Raskob), *Ladies' Home Journal* (August, 1929), 9.

Bryan with the popular dancer Gilda Gray. Speculators bought and sold titles and options for unseen lots and acres, some of which, it later developed, were under a few feet of swampy water. Bubbles like the Florida land boom have their foundation in mass delusion and greed and are easily broken. A disastrous hurricane in 1926 broke the Florida mania. By the early 1930's, when few people could afford Florida vacations, some communities of the state were ghost towns with abandoned hotels and grass in the streets.

Prosperity's record in the 1920's was extremely spotty. On the one hand, total compensation to employees increased from 1922 to 1929 by about 40 per cent while the cost-of-living index rose only from 97.7 to 100. This was probably the best record in improved living standards of any previous eight-year period. But on the other hand, some economic areas were depressed throughout the decade. The trials of the farmer have already been discussed. Coal mining was a sick industry, as was the New England textile industry. Unemployment in 1928, the last full boom year before the crash, was 1,900,000 out of a labor force of 47,900,000, roughly 4 per cent unemployment. A brief description of income distribution in 1929 indicates how fair prosperity was from being universal and illustrates how the boom was based upon a narrow foundation. Of the approximately 27,500,000 American families of 1929, 16,350,000 received less than $2,000 income; 11,653,000 families received less than $1,500; 5,775,000 families received less than $1,000. At the other end of the scale, the most fortunate 1 per cent of income recipients received 14.5 per cent of the total and the top 5 per cent received 26.1 per cent.

New and Expanded Industries

In the 1920's the automobile industry grew more and had more far-reaching effects on the economy and the way people lived than any other industry. The industry introduced no startling new inventions during this period, but it enormously improved its product through better machining and engineering. At the end of the war, machine tools in the auto industry were still so crude and allowed such tolerances that a hand-finished auto engine could develop as much as twice the horsepower as a standard, machine-made one. By the end of the 1920's, due to better cutting tools and the use of the Swedish Johansson measuring blocks, hand finishing offered little mechanical advantage.

The following table indicates the expansion of the industry during the postwar decade. Imports of foreign cars amounted to practically nothing; in 1926, the year of largest auto imports after 1920, only 813 entered the United States. There is no better way to indicate the central position the auto industry began to take in the economy than to cite some statistics. In 1929 the industry accounted for 12.7 per cent of all manufactures, employed 7.1 per cent of all manufacturing wage earners, paid 8.7 per cent of manufacturing payrolls, and used 15 per cent of total steel production. These figures do not include the expansion that autos brought in oil, rubber, glass, textiles, and nickel. According to one estimate, the industry directly or indirectly was responsible for the employment of 3,700,000 workers in 1929. After 1923, when Detroit for the first time produced more closed

EXPANSION OF AUTOMOBILE INDUSTRY, 1915–1930

Year	Total Automobiles Manufactured	Number Registered
1915	970,000	2,446,000
1920	2,227,000	9,232,000
1925	4,428,000	19,937,000
1929	5,622,000	26,501,000
1930	3,510,000	26,524,000

cars than open models and sales began to boom, financing car purchases became a significant part of the national credit structure. In 1925, 68.2 per cent of all new cars were bought on time.

At about the same time the sale of used cars began to be economically important. The used car market doomed Ford's Model T, for prospective car buyers could buy a larger and more comfortable used car for the price of a new Model T. Ford's dealers pleaded with him to manufacture a fancier model, but he refused to change until his competitors began to eat seriously into the Ford market and Model T sales fell. Ford ended production of the Model T in 1927 and was out of production for a year before he put the Model A on the market. The industry concentrated on ever bigger and more powerful cars and shunned smaller, less expensive models. Rather than use the savings brought by more efficient production to lower prices, lower costs were absorbed by more complicated and elaborate models. This pattern became the usual one for American production of complicated and durable consumer goods.

The auto industry was a prime example of developing oligopoly. An oligopolistic industry is one dominated by a few large firms and characterized by a lack of price competition although competition for sales may be intense. In the industry's early days there had been numerous small companies, none of them with a major share of the market. Then Ford concentrated on a mass-produced inexpensive car and became the industry's giant. In 1908 William C. Durant of the Buick Company, a former wagon company executive, organized General Motors with a minimum of Wall Street financing by combining seventeen independent firms. General Motors at first concentrated on medium-priced to expensive cars, the Buick, Oakland, Oldsmobile, and Cadillac. Continental Motors, a mass-production parts maker, provided parts at wholesale prices to small firms, which merely assembled them and sold them under their own brand names. One of these small firms was run by Louis Chevrolet. Small firms could sell a medium-priced car in competition with larger companies but were at a disadvantage nevertheless because they could not afford large-scale advertising campaigns or attract sufficient dealers to provide a network of convenient service garages.

The DuPont interests, in chemicals and explosives, came into General Motors in 1917 and acquired control of it in 1921. General Motors acquired Chevrolet and made it a competitor to Ford's Model T. Selling for a little more in the early 1920's, it offered much the Model T could not meet, such as four-wheel brakes and a standard gear shift. The growth of Chevrolet sales more than anything else forced Ford to abandon the Model T, but his Model A never caught up with its GM competitor. GM operated as a huge industrial empire governed by a federal system. Executives of its component divisions had considerable autonomy and competed with one another, but a committee of the central organization determined general policy. Despite GM's ties to DuPont, it provided much of its own financing for expansion by plowing back its profits. It reinvested about 47 per cent of its profits between 1909 and 1926. Profits in the industry were high. The profits of the thirty-two auto companies that operated throughout the period 1919 to 1928 ranged from a high of 25.3 per cent in 1922 to lows of 16.1 in 1927 and 1928.

Walter P. Chrysler, a former GM executive, formed the Chrysler Corporation in 1923 when he acquired control of the failing Maxwell Company. He manufactured a line of cars under his own name and acquired Dodge Brothers in 1928. In 1929 Chrysler got control of Plymouth and made it a competitor to Ford and Chevrolet.

By 1923 the ten largest auto manufacturers produced 90 per cent of all cars and trucks. By 1930 Ford, GM, and Chrysler produced 83 per cent of the output. Of the 181 auto manufacturing companies of 1903, only 11 survived in 1930. Studebaker, Nash, Packard, and Hudson were secure small manufacturers, but dozens of others slowly died out. Some disappeared altogether, such as the Moon and the Dort. Others were absorbed or turned to specialized production. Reo converted to truck manufacture entirely, but big over-the-road trucking did not begin to become economically important until the late 1920's and early 1930's.

The Big Three and the independents competed vigorously but not in the traditional ways. Because the intricacies of production required planning for changed models far in advance of actual production, each firm knew well what its competitors were planning. Secrets were difficult to keep when thousands of employees were involved. All companies except Ford belonged to the National Automobile Chamber of Commerce and provided the Chamber with monthly reports of sales. Until 1925 the auto companies maintained a patent pool, and any firm could use any patent without royalty. Success in the business depended more upon salesmanship than upon engineering.

The Chemical Industry

The chemical industry received a great stimulus from the war. Military orders for explosives provided good profits, and companies like DuPont invested its increased revenues in new endeavors, frequently using research to develop entirely new products and markets. The war also provided an opportunity to overtake the German chemical industry, the most important in the world before 1914. During the war, the federal government confiscated German chemical patents and sold them to American firms. Formulas for dyes were the first German patents exploited, but so far behind Germany was American chemical engineering that it was years before American firms could produce dyes comparable to those of German manufacture at reasonable cost. The Fordney-McCumber Tariff put a high duty on dyes, and ever since, the chemical industry has advocated a high tariff, although, since World War II, at least, it has been in a strong competitive position with foreign producers even on a free trade basis.

The most dramatic development in the chemical industry after the war was the proliferation of synthetics. Synthetics were nothing new. Celluloid had been developed in 1869 and was used widely early in the twentieth century for combs, novelties, and even men's collars. Bakelite, also developed before the war, became increasingly important in the 1920's as an insulator in radios and electric appliances. Rayon, another prewar product, was not commercially used to a significant extent until the early 1920's when it was produced cheaply enough almost to replace silk in women's clothing. Celanese, another artificial silk synthetic, went on the market in the mid-1920's, as did cellophane, first produced commercially by DuPont in 1924. George Washington Carver, the best known Negro scientist of the day, concentrated on finding uses for materials found in surplus farm commodities. From peanuts and sweet potatoes he synthesized a wide range of products from paste to shaving lotion.

Measuring the growth of the chemical industry during the 1920's is impossible because the definitions of the census of manufactures were arbitrary and meaningless. The chemical industry, in a sense, knows no boundaries. Chemistry is universal, like mathematics. One specialist, however, for what his figures are worth, estimated the industry's production in 1929 as worth $3.8 billion, a growth of over 50 per cent since 1914.

The Electric Industry

The electric industry, both the generation and transmission of power and the manufacture of electrically powered machinery and appliances, was one of the big growth industries in the 1920's. Electric power generated more than doubled between 1920 and 1929.

As more households gained access to electricity—from 16 per cent of the population in 1912 to 63 per cent in 1927—there developed a vast market for home electrical appliances. Two giants dominated the industry. In 1897 General Electric, itself a consolidation of several smaller companies, and Westinghouse Electric signed an agreement to share one another's patents. They were thus enabled to gain practical control over the heavy equipment field, but in the 1920's the market for home appliances became too large for them to keep out competition, although they continued to dominate the appliance industry. In 1926 an estimated four-fifths of homes with electricity had an electric iron, three-eighths had a vacuum cleaner, and one-fourth had a washing machine. Electric refrigerators were uncommon until late in the 1920's. The working-class housewife's work was cut down considerably by some of these appliances. Certainly electric ironing was more efficient and easier than lifting the old heavy irons back and forth from the stove, and piloting a vacuum cleaner did a better job more easily than a hand broom or a carpet beater. For middle-class housewives, however, it is dubious that these work-saving appliances actually simplified her life. They may have made it harder. One could send out the laundry and ironing for quite a long time for the price of an electric washer, and hiring someone to do the cleaning was easier than doing it oneself even with an electric sweeper. Rising labor costs for domestic services more than convenience made purchase of electric appliances economical for middle-class families.

The Radio Industry

Home radio was a completely new postwar industry. Many cities claim to have been the first to have had a radio station. The Wisconsin state station on the University campus broadcast experimentally in 1919, and in the summer of 1920 *The Detroit News* started broadcasting news bulletins for the benefit of local radio "hams." The first commercial station was KDKA operated by Westinghouse Electric from East Pittsburgh. It began broadcasting on November 2, 1920, just in time to give the first election returns by radio. By 1922 three million homes had a radio, usually a heavy, bulky battery set. Sales of radios that year amounted to $60 million. By 1929 about 40 per cent of America's families owned a radio and sales amounted to over $400 million.

General Electric and Westinghouse, through their creation and control of the Radio Corporation of America (1919), held the basic patents and controlled both radio manufacture and one of the national radio networks. In the mid-1920's RCA created the National Broadcasting Company and arranged with the American Telephone and Telegraph Company to use its long-distance telephone lines to transmit broadcasts to stations in the network. When the number of broadcasting stations multiplied—there were over five hundred by 1924—something obviously had to be done by the federal government to prevent broadcasters from using the same wave lengths. The Department of Commerce began to assign wave lengths in 1924, but it ran into an adverse court decision in 1926 and stopped the practice. In 1927 Congress created the Federal Radio Commission to license broadcasters and bring order into the chaos. The new commission soon ran into difficulty when the Los Angeles evangelist Aimee Semple McPherson (a cultural phenomenon who combined sex appeal and religion and called herself "the world's most pulchritudinous evangelist") declared that her radio wave length came from Divine authority, the government of the United States to the contrary.

Broadcasting was a profitable business after station WEAF in New York City began to sell time to advertisers in 1922. A New York real estate company had the dubious distinction of sponsoring the first radio commercial. Most of the other nations of the western world forbade radio advertising and subsidized broadcasting from revenues gained by a tax on radio receivers. If commercial radio had begun a decade earlier or later perhaps American radio programing would have developed along similar lines.

Supercorporations and the "New Competition"

By the end of the 1920's the supercorporation was the norm in the critical areas of the American economy: manufacturing, railroad transportation, communications and other public utilities, and finance. The large corporation also was becoming increasingly important even in retail trade. Small and medium-sized businesses were far more numerous than their big brothers, and they remain so today. Big businesses did not even employ a majority of the wage-earners. Only about one-sixth of them, in fact, were on big business payrolls. But large corporations had a grip on the most important parts of the economy. To use military terms, they were the main sources of supply, except for food products (and big corporations were growing quickly there), and they controlled the "narrows" of the economy, the economic bridges, passes, and straits.

In the 1880's an ordinary citizen might come into contact with a supercorporation only when he purchased Standard Oil kerosene for his lamps. By 1929 he might awaken in a house built of lumber supplied by the Weyerhaeuser Timber Company and financed by a mortgage from the Bank of America, glance over his newspaper published by a unit of the Hearst chain while he ate a breakfast bought at the A&P and prepared on a General Electric or Westinghouse stove which used electric power generated by a link in the Insull empire, and drive to work in a Big Three car burning Standard Oil gasoline. In the evening he and his family might have an Armour ham for dinner and listen to a radio program sponsored by United States Steel and carried to his city over American Telephone and Telegraph Company lines. Like as not, he would then go to bed, priding himself on his "rugged individualism" and thankful that he did not live in a centralized society.

The Two Hundred Largest Corporations

Statistics are necessary. In 1929 the two hundred largest business corporation possessed almost half of the total wealth of corporations, just under two-fifths of the total business wealth, and one-fifth of the total national wealth. These two hundred companies grew three times as fast in assets and income as small corporations. A major study of the corporation made by Adolph Berle and Gardiner C. Means published in 1932 estimated that if the two hundred largest corporations continued their rate of growth they would own half of the national wealth and four-fifths of the corporate wealth by midcentury. Thousands of small corporations disappeared as separate entities by merging with others or by selling out to larger corporations, usually for stock in the purchasing company. Between 1919 and 1930 over eight thousand businesses in manufacturing and mining disappeared. In 1926 and 1927 alone 1,940 public utility firms disappeared as separate businesses. Retail outlets did not disappear, but chain stores steadily accounted for an increasing share of total sales. Chain-store units increased from 29,000 in 1918 to 160,000 in 1929. In 1929 they sold 27 per cent of the country's food, 19 per cent of its drugs, 27 per cent of its clothes, 30 per cent of its tobacco, and 26 per cent of its general merchandise. A&P had about 15,000 retail stores. Drug, Inc. had 10,000 Rexall stores and 706 Liggett stores, as well as control of Bayer Aspirin, Bristol-Myers, and Vick Chemical. Chain stores were to grow even more in the 1930's.

Banking

Banking experienced a concentration in the 1920's that made the old "money trust" seem juvenile. In 1921 there were 30,812 banks; in 1929 there were only 25,330. Failures accounted for much of the shrinkage. Bank failures never fell below 367 a year in the 1920's, and 976 banks failed in 1926. Almost all these closed banks were fairly small and in depressed agricultural areas. Branch banking became important in states that permitted it. Branch banks approximately tripled in number during the decade. Far and away the biggest bank chain was the Bank of America, centered in San Francisco and founded by A. P. Giannini. New York banks, many of which merged during the 1920's, remained the most powerful of the country. In 1929 the biggest 1 per cent of the banks controlled 46 per cent of the nation's bank resources.

Holding Companies

The holding company was the most common device of concentrating economic control. Of the ninety-seven biggest industrial corporations in 1929, ninety-four were holding companies. Twenty-one were purely holding companies that did not themselves produce anything. Among the prominent companies of this sort were United States Steel, Eastman Kodak, and Allied Chemical & Dye. Most of them were operating companies themselves but owned controlling stock of other corporations in their industries. In manufacturing, the holding company seldom extended above one level. But in public utilities—and to a lesser extent in railroading—pyramid holding companies were the rule. In 1930 ten holding-company structures dominated 72 per cent of the nation's electric power.

The huge and enormously complicated holding-company pyramid of Samuel Insull, an immigrant from London who settled in Chicago, was the nation's biggest. Insull was chairman of the board of 65 corporations, and there were 111 separate corporate entities within his pyramid. The structure was so complicated with its 24 levels of holding companies between the top and the firms that actually generated electric power that it is doubtful if anyone, including Insull, fully understood the giant's anatomy. Owen D. Young, chairman of the board of General Electric from whom Insull sought advice, said of the Insull empire, "It is impossible for any man to grasp the situation of that vast structure . . . it was so set up that you could not possibly get an accounting system that would not mislead even the officers themselves." If Young could not understand the system, certainly the thousands of investors did not. But investors were eager to buy stock in Insull companies because they thought the stock would appreciate quickly—and it did until late 1929. By having controlling interest of the first-level holding company, whose stock was owned by another Insull-controlled company, and so on up for 24 layers, Insull achieved powerful leverage all the way down through the pyramid. With each dollar he invested in the top company, Corporation Securities Corporation, Insull controlled over $2,000 in assets of a generating company at the bottom.

The Van Sweringen railroad empire was not as big or complicated as Insull's, but it was built with less cold cash. O. P. and M. J. Van Sweringen, Cleveland brothers who had made a fortune in real estate, parlayed $500,000 of their own money and a like sum from a group of associates into control of several railroads with over twenty-nine thousand miles of track. They bought control of the Nickel Plate Railroad from the New York Central for $8 billion, one-fourth in cash which they borrowed through the House of Morgan, the rest payable in ten years. Collateral for the loan was the Nickel Plate stock acquired with the loan. They organized a holding company and sold stock in it to raise the funds for the balance of the Nickel Plate price. Then they branched out. In 1930, just before their whole structure collapsed, the Van Sweringens controlled the following railroads through minority stock holdings: the Nickel Plate, the Chicago and Eastern Illinois, the Erie, the Wheeling and Lake Erie, the Chesapeake & Ohio, the Hocking Valley, the Kansas City Southern, and the Pere Marquette. They also had majority control of the Missouri Pacific, which in turn owned half the stock of the Denver & Rio Grande. Here is an example of Van Sweringen leverage: the brothers owned 80 per cent of the stock of the Vaness Company, which owned 50 per cent of the stock of the General Securities Corporation. The Van Sweringens owned another 40 per cent of General Securities in their own name. General Securities controlled the Allegheny Corporation by owning 8.61 per cent of its stock. Allegheny controlled the Chesapeake Corporation in which the Van Sweringen equity was only 4.1 per cent. The Chesapeake Corporation controlled the Chesapeake & Ohio Railroad, of which the Van Sweringen equity was .98 per cent of the stock. The C&O controlled the Hocking Valley. Van Sweringen equity in the Hocking Valley amounted to only .04 per cent of its ownership. Like Insull, the Van Sweringens were dependent upon large numbers of small stockholders to retain their control of the whole structure.

Trade Associations

So far in this section we have considered the diminution of full competition only by the acquisition of at least some of the stock of a potential competitor. Competition was also reduced by cooperation of firms completely independent of one another so far as ownership was concerned, and the usual instrument of such cooperation was the trade association. Trade association members competed with one another for markets, but through advertising rather than underselling each other. They sometimes referred to this kind of cooperation as "the new competition," taking the term from a 1912 book by that name by Arthur Jerome Eddy, the same Chicago lawyer who purchased the "Nude Descending a Staircase" at the Armory Art Show. Eddy's book, which went through five editions in three years and favored trade associations, asserted that the main difference between old-fashioned competition and "new competition" was that the old employed secrecy and conspiracy and that the new was open. The new was also usually more efficient because it generally embraced all the economically important firms in a market. The contrast between the methods of a trade association and the older means of price setting may be illustrated by describing the steel industry's Gary dinners and the association "open price" system. Early in the twentieth century, steel executives met irregularly and informally for dinner at the home of United States Steel chief Judge Elbert H. Gary and set prices for their products. Once when a small firm began to cut prices against the Gary dinner set it was warned that if it continued its "unreasonable and destructive competition" the industry would have to resort to the law of the jungle in which only the fittest would survive. The threat was sufficient. The Gary dinner system could not work in an industry with a greater number of smaller firms with less punitive power.

Trade association members furnished the association with their price information, and the association made it available to all either through publication or letters. Associations also persuaded members to use standard cost-accounting methods and instructed members in the use of uniform formulas to calculate costs for contract bidding. Under the guidance of Hoover's Department of Commerce, associations urged standardization of product sizes and shapes, for such standardization was necessary to achieve price uniformity. Over two hundred sizes and shapes of bottles were cut to ten, varieties of brick shapes declined from sixty-six to seven, and numerous other commodities were similarly standardized. This standardization was only a continuation of War Production Board policies, the benefits of the efficiency now to accrue to manufacturers in the interest of profits rather than in the interest of better prosecution of the war. The Supreme Court in a series of cases in the early 1920's ruled, in effect, that exchanging price information and other knowledge among "competitors" was within the law unless the purpose was explicitly to raise prices.

The "Managerial Revolution"

As corporations grew larger and their stock ownership became more diverse and as trade associations increasingly assumed corporate functions of determining price and nature of production, the ownership of a firm became separated from actual control. Let us take an extreme example for illustration. General Motors was a huge corporation with hundreds of thousands of stockholders, most of whom owned only a tiny proportion of the outstanding stock. Each share had one vote in elections to GM's board of directors, and each stockholder was legally entitled to attend the annual stockholders meeting and speak his mind. But in actual fact most stockholders did not care one way or another about the thousands of decisions, big and small, that the corporation had to make each week. Most stockholders were interested only in dividends and appreciation of their shares on the stock market. Most GM owners who did care about the corporation's decisions were ill prepared to make a decision, for example, on whether the 1928 Chevrolet should have wire-spoke or disc wheels, what advertising agency should handle its account, what the FOB Detroit price should be, or what the wage rate should be for tool and die makers. Decisions, major and minor, in all large corporations came increasingly to be made by salaried corporation officials who did not necessarily own any stock at all. Several corporations in the 1920's sold stock which had no voting rights; owners of nonvoting stock did not have even a legal or theoretical right to participate in making decisions. Owners of voting stock in a company such as the Hocking Valley Railroad were likewise powerless to defy the Van Sweringen interests in the company although the brothers personally had only a very small equity in the firm. Thus the traditional concept of private property, in which the owner was inhibited in his decisions about how to use his property only by law—he could not legally use his gun to shoot his neighbor, for example, nor use his ships in smuggling—became considerably modified. Paradoxically, the development of American capitalism, based upon private ownership, was to change the nature of property ownership.

The shift of substantial control from owners to corporation executives has been called a "managerial revolution." Business administrators—"corporation bureaucrats"—were a new breed of businessmen. They endeavored to make administration a precise and specialized science and resorted to a complicated division of labor and specialization. At the same time as the blue-collar worker "on the line" in an automobile plant became a human cog, something similar happened to his white-collar colleague in the plant's offices. Some administrators became specialists in personnel work and applied psychological principles to put square pegs in square holes for the benefit of the corporation's efficiency. Others became specialists in some small part of production, or advertising, or cost accounting, or sales, or purchasing of supplies. Top managerial positions tended to go to men who had specialized in some aspect of sales because the decline of price competition heightened the importance of persuading the public to buy the corporation's products by some other means.

One kind of corporation administrator with special implications for society was the public relations specialist. His function was to get the public's good will for the corporation, to mold public opinion so as best to promote his corporation's interest. The best of them, who usually founded independent firms and contracted with corporations much the same way as advertising agencies, were surprisingly successful in forming what they in time came to call a favorable "public image." The wartime Creel committee was a training school for several of the public relations specialists of the 1920's, who now sold a corporation rather than the war. Edward Bernays, one of the cleverest of the image-molders, was a graduate of the Creel committee and a nephew of Sigmund Freud, whose psychological theories sometimes were applied to advance corporate interests.

Improved Efficiency and Its Beneficiaries

The question of efficiency of production and distribution is a central one in forming a judgment about corporatism. There is little question that most large corporations produced and distributed more efficiently than most small ones. Because they could achieve greater production with mass methods, they could decrease costs of production. Many of them had research departments that developed new products and more efficient methods of producing old ones, and the fruits of some of this research improved the population's material standard of living. Management specialization resulted in miracles of production. Bigness, it was apparent, had its limits. A factory could become too large and complicated to operate at maximum efficiency. Optimum size depended upon markets and the state of technology, both of which changed constantly. But a single corporation could efficiently operate a number of optimum-sized production units. There were dangers of bureaucracy, however, even in a huge corporation that divided its production into efficient separate units. Some became inflexible and unwieldy. In industries with high overhead costs, such as steel, corporations sometimes had to retain production methods that management knew were not as efficient as a new process because too much was invested in the old to make changing to the new profitable.

Sometimes concentration of control had no effect whatsoever on the efficiency of the industrial process. Samuel Insull did not erect his crazy-quilt power empire to improve the generation and transmission of electricity, nor did the

Van Sweringens integrate operations of their many railroad lines. The purpose of these businessmen was to profit by shuffling around paper evidences of property ownership. Only the disadvantages of concentration operated in cases such as these.

It should be noted that the growth of supercorporations by no means meant the extension of absolute or total monopoly of a market. Sometimes it did, but on the whole there was less absolute monopoly in the 1920's than there had been early in the century when Standard Oil stood virtually alone in the oil business and United States Steel controlled a larger proportion of the nation's steel capacity. Indeed, chain stores often broke local monopolies of small merchants, and consumers' burdens had not been lighter merely because they had been exploited by a small monopolist.

But after assuming that large corporations and other forms of economic concentration did increase efficiency with certain exceptions noted, one is confronted with the question of who was the beneficiary of the improved efficiency. The facts indicate that corporation officials and stockholders received the lion's share of efficiency's benefits during the 1920's. Workers' incomes increased 11 per cent from 1923 to 1929 while corporate profits rose 62 per cent and dividends 65 per cent. Prices were fairly stable, but the consumer usually got a better product. A 1929 car was a better machine than a 1923 flivver, and the price was about the same.

The administered prices that came with the "new competition" were to have great implications for the next decade of depression. In classical economic theory, depressed economies right themselves automatically because prices drop, thereby increasing demand and bringing it again into balance with supply. Whether this classical theory ever actually and perfectly described the actual situation is dubious, but it certainly did not conform to the facts of the Great Depression. In industries where the "new competition" obtained, corporations tended to keep prices stable and to restrict production. Restricting production meant unemployment, and unemployed workers had only a minimum of purchasing power.

There were also political issues in the New Economic Order. Was it right, asked some critics, for a relatively small group of corporation directors and salaried officials, who wielded great power without any mandate from the population, to make economic decisions which affected almost everyone? The sum of decisions made by businessmen—whether or not to cut prices, cut production, expand research, move a factory to another part of the country, or expand foreign investments—probably had more to do with the way citizens lived than the decisions of the politicians for whom they could vote. Others replied that the consumer voted every time he made a purchase. To a limited degree this was true. He could vote against Henry Ford by buying a Chevrolet if he did not like black cars. (Ford had once said that a Model T buyer "can have a Ford any color he wants—so long as it's black.") But the consumer's veto power had tight boundaries. If he disliked a firm's labor policies and organized a boycott, he ran afoul the law. Protective tariffs limited his freedom to buy foreign products. An industry that administered its prices left him only the choice of not buying at all. The consumer's veto was at best an imprecise one.

But in the palmy days of the late 1920's few questioned corporate policies or expressed concern about corporate power. Public opinion put top corporation officials upon a prestige pedestal, and neither government nor labor organizations made serious inroads upon their prerogatives.

Labor in the Business Decade

Although workingmen did not receive as great a share of the economic expansion of the postwar decade as their employers, they made a substantial gain in their living standards. Average real wages in 1919 were 105 on an index in which 1914 was 100; in 1928 real wages had risen to 132. This method of measuring living standards disregards unemployment. Prosperous eras usually stimulate the effectiveness of labor organizations because employers, eager for uninterrupted production when sales prospects are bright, are more likely to make labor concessions than they are when they are pessimistic about business. But organized labor suffered severe defeats in the depression of 1920–21 and failed to recover thereafter.

The Open Shop and Welfare Capitalism

Employer associations opened a vigorous "open shop" campaign during the postwar depression in an effort to drive labor unions out of their cities and industries. Employers actually wanted more than the open shop; they wanted elimination of unions altogether. And they had considerable success. Unions in industries only recently organized were the most vulnerable, but well-established unions in the printing and building trades also retreated. Bethlehem Steel Company President Eugene G. Grace announced in late 1920 that his firm would refuse to sell fabricated steel to building contractors in New York and Philadelphia who did not have an open shop and that he would not recognize a union and bargain with it even if 95 per cent of his employees belonged. Businessmen were seldom so extreme in their public statements, but many were equally opposed to unionism.

Employers also dampened enthusiasm for unionism through what was commonly called *welfare capitalism*. Welfare capitalism included everything from sports programs, soap in the toilets, and water coolers to good company housing and group insurance. Several companies introduced employee stock-purchase plans in which employees bought the corporation's nonvoting stock on the installment plan. Employers hoped the scheme would lead employees to adopt stockholders' viewpoints rather than those of labor organizations but the idea backfired after 1929 when employees lost not only their jobs but their savings.

The AFL in the Twenties

By such devices total union membership, both within and outside the AFL, fell from about 5,100,000 in 1920 to about 3,600,000 in 1923. Organized labor had not received such a blow in the twentieth century. From 1923 until the depression, union membership was fairly stable, neither growing nor shrinking significantly. Employers' counterattacks and prosperous complacency had much to do with labor's failure to grow during the boom, but labor's leadership must also share some of the responsibility. Samuel Gompers died in 1924, and William Green, of the United Mine Workers and Chillicothe, Ohio, succeeded to the AFL presidency. Green was not the man Gompers had been. Surely UMW president John L. Lewis exaggerated when he said of Green in the late 1930's, "I have done a lot of exploring of Bill Green's mind, and I give you my word there is nothing there." There was something there, but not much originality nor imagination. He and such colleagues as Matthew Woll, AFL vice-president, and John P. Frey, head of the Metal Trades Department, were far more interested in appearing respectable to the public and in maintaining the economic status of the craft unions' skilled members—"labor's aristocracy"—than in extending unionism to the 90 per cent of the working force that had no organization.

Union-sponsored banks, one of organized labor's few experiments during the 1920's, reflected labor's business outlook. At the height of the labor bank movement in 1926 thirty-five labor banks had combined resources of over $126 million. The bank established by the Brotherhood of Locomotive Engineers, perhaps the most "aristocratic" of all unions, got into the Florida land bubble. It invested heavily in what was to be a model project at Venice, Florida. When Venice land values fell disastrously in the general Florida collapse, the engineers' bank went on the rocks. Most of the labor banks were poorly managed, and only a few of them survived the bank crisis of the early depression. Those that did stand the shocks of the Great Depression did so because they operated much as conventional banking institutions. Labor banks made one contribution both to people of little income and to general banking practice. They pioneered in making small loans at reasonable interest rates, thereby saving their borrowers from the much higher rates of finance companies and the usury of illegal "loan sharks." When commercial bankers saw labor banks enjoying a high rate of repayment from small loans, increasing numbers of them followed the labor banks' example. Labor banks also stimulated the growth of credit unions, special associations of employees to receive members' deposits and make small loans.

The Clothing Industry Unions

The most notable exceptions to general timidity and lack of imagination in the labor movement were the activities of the needle trade unions, particularly the two biggest such unions, the Amalgamated Clothing Workers in the men's clothing industry, of which Sidney Hillman was president, and the International Ladies Garment Workers Union, of which David Dubinsky was president. The clothing industry was characterized by sharp competition and a myriad of small entrepreneurs who could start a business on a contracting or subcontracting basis with a minimum investment. Labor usually finds it difficult to organize such an industry because failure to capture the whole industry usually puts the employer who pays union-scale wages at a competitive disadvantage. The needle trade unions largely solved this problem by pioneering in introducing Taylorism in the industry, sometimes even lending employers the funds necessary to introduce new and more efficient methods, and vigorously organizing all firms in the industry. Having much of the brains of the industry as well as its labor and being almost the only industry-wide association in the fragmented field, the Amalgamated and the ILGWU came to provide what stability and leadership the industry had.

The needle trade unions were among the first to win the forty-hour week, to build cooperative housing projects, and to gain unemployment compensation. It was largely these unions, composed mostly of Jewish and Italian immigrants, that kept alive the tradition of labor militancy between the setbacks of 1920–22 and labor's revival in the Great Depression.

Coal Strikes

Labor conducted relatively few strikes after the immediate postwar strike wave. The most important ones during the 1920's were in coal and textiles. Most coal mining was done in isolated, small communities marked by constant friction between miners and owners. Competition in the industry was sharp, and during the 1920's the whole industry became sick as coal lost ground to natural gas and oil as fuel. Mine operators were in no position to be generous, and miners, the world over a tough breed hardened by backbreaking work and constant danger, were in no mood to compromise. Isolated from the enlightened and pacifying influences of urban civilization, both operators and miners frequently used violence to try to achieve their ends. Violence was particularly sharp in the coal field of West Virginia and eastern Kentucky from 1919 to 1921. When armed battles between striking miners and company guards broke out, the governor of West Virginia declared martial law and called out the state guard. In 1921 battles between guards and miners became serious, and Harding sent the army into the troubled area.

Both anthracite and bituminous miners went out on strike when old contracts expired in April, 1922. Operators had tried to reduce wages during negotiations for a new contract. The strike was peaceful until June, when a large coal company in "Bloody Williamson" County, Illinois, imported strikebreakers and mine guards killed two strikers attempting to keep strikebreakers out of the pits. The strikers retaliated by killing nineteen strikebreakers in a company stockade. In mid-August, about one-fifth of the soft coal operators gave in and most of the other operators soon followed suit, but the United Mine Workers had been unable to make much headway in organizing the West Virginia and Kentucky field.

The 1922 contracts were due to expire in April, 1924. Before the contract expired, the operators of the central competitive field, Illinois, Indiana, Ohio, and western Pennsylvania, signed the Jacksonville agreement with the UMW. The agreement maintained wages, but the understanding was that the operators of the region would not extend the wage agreement when it expired in 1927 if the UMW had not meanwhile organized the southern or West Virginia-Kentucky field whose coal competed with that from UMW areas. The miners were not only unsuccessful in organizing the southern field, due largely to wholesale injunctions and yellow-dog contracts, but the southern field expanded its production. In 1924 three-fifths of the nation's soft coal came from the central district's union mines; a year later the non-union southern field produced three-fifths of the total. At the same time, Lewis faced a revolt within the UMW in Illinois, and when the 1927 negotiations came up, the UMW, after an unsuccessful strike, had to accept a wage cut. The UMW remained weak until new federal legislation in the 1930's enabled it to organize better the southern field.

86

Textile Strikes

Textiles were as sick or sicker than coal. Faced with a shrinking market, textile firms in the North shifted their operations to the cheap-labor southern Appalachian region. Despite appeals from southern AFL organizations, the national AFL and its United Textile Workers made little more than half-hearted efforts to organize the South until 1928. By that time the Communists' National Textile Workers' Union had already made progress. The next year violent and unsuccessful strikes occurred in Elizabethton, Tennessee, and Marion and Gastonia, North Carolina.

Girls in the Elizabethton rayon mill worked a fifty-six-hour week for from sixteen to eighteen cents an hour. They walked out and obtained a verbal agreement for a slight wage increase, but they did not get union recognition. The employer soon violated the verbal agreement. Two AFL representatives who went to Elizabethton were beaten by a mob of businessmen and local civil officers, taken to the state line, and warned not to return. Workers in the Marion mill went out on a United Textile Workers strike against low wages and the "stretch-out" which required employees to tend more machines. Feelings ran high when the company evicted the strikers from their company-owned homes, and the governor sent in the national guard to supplement a large force of deputy sheriffs. In a brawl between unarmed pickets and the national guard deputy force, five unarmed pickets were killed and nineteen wounded. Strike leaders and the responsible law officers were arrested, but the accused killers were acquitted and the most prominent local labor leader sent to prison. The Communist-run strike at Gastonia was the best publicized. The strike, which began in April, collapsed in October when seven Communist strike leaders were convicted of the second-degree murder of the Gastonia police chief. One of the convicted Communists, Fred Beal, jumped bail and went to Russia, but became disillusioned with Communism while there and returned to serve his sentence.

The Foreign Policy of
a Business Government

*America seeks no earthly empire built on blood or force.
No ambition, no temptation, lures her to thought of
foreign dominion. The legions which she sends forth are
armed, not with the sword, but with the cross.*

CALVIN COOLIDGE, Inaugural Address, 1925

*There is no question that if the revolution continues
American investments and business interests in Nicaragua
will be very seriously affected, if not destroyed. . . . I have
deemed it my duty to use the powers committed to me to
insure the adequate protection of all American interests in
Nicaragua, whether they be endangered by internal
strife or by outside interference. . . .*

CALVIN COOLIDGE, message to Congress, 1927

Chapter Five

Foreign policy is the extension of a nation's domestic problems and policies. We do ourselves a disservice and make understanding impossible if we conceive of foreign policy as the pursuit of abstract principles separate from other considerations, decided upon by a small group of rarified experts studying and discussing calmly in the foreign offices of the world's capitals, and put into action by suave, striped-trousered, formal diplomats over teacups or cocktail glasses. True, the Department of State and foreign offices of other major powers maintain staffs of experts on various subjects, and, true, diplomatic tradition is more encrusted with protocol established in another century than most other governmental functions. But foreign relations are real, diplomacy is earnest, and the form is not the goal. A nation's policies with other nations are subject to all kinds of domestic pressures, and the overwhelming bulk of foreign policy activities has to do with mundane dollars-and-cents matters.

With corporation businessmen controlling the federal government during the 1920's and less strength in agriculture, labor, and reform than there had been since the 1890's or earlier, American foreign policy was the policy of American business. The primary molders of the nation's foreign policy, Secretary of State Hughes and Secretary of Commerce Hoover, were confronted, first and foremost, with problems of economic expansion and then war debts, reparations, and maintenance of peace.

Business and Foreign Policy, 1919–1929

The outstanding difference between the postwar and the prewar international balance of power was the tremendous growth, both absolutely and relatively, of American strength. In 1929 United States national income was greater than the combined national incomes of France, Great Britain, Germany, Japan, Canada, and seventeen smaller nations. Before the outbreak of war in 1914 the United States had been, on balance, a debtor nation despite huge investments abroad. On July 1, 1914, nationals of foreign countries had $3.68 billion more invested within the United States, either directly or in loans, than Americans had invested abroad. By December 31, 1919, private investment had shifted until the American advantage amounted to $2.97 billion, and there was a further net foreign debt due the United States government of $9.59 billion. The accompanying table gives more detail. Washington's international power, in other words, had become remarkably stronger as a result of the war. New York and Washington had become the world's economic centers of gravity, taking the position that London had enjoyed from 1815 to 1914.

AMERICA'S INTERNATIONAL CREDITS AND DEBTS
(in millions of dollars)

	July 1, 1914	December 31, 1919	July 1, 1929
Private credits:			
Securities	862	2,576	7,839
Direct investments	2,652	3,880	7,553
Short-term credits	. . .	500	1,617
Private debits:			
Securities	5,440	1,623	4,304
Direct investments	1,310	900	1,400
Seized enemy property	. . .	662	150
Short-term credits	450	800	3,077
Net private debit or credit	—3,686	2,971	8,078
Intergovernmental debt:			
Owed to United States	. . .	9,982	11,685
Owed by United States	. . .	391	. . .
Total net debit or credit	—3,686	12,562	19,763

Economic Expansion Abroad

How did the Republican administrations of the 1920's desire to use this new power? What were the objectives of their foreign policy? Actually, they did not differ substantially from the objectives of Democratic administrations either before or after them, although they sometimes differed from the Democratic administrations in methods. Most important during the 1920's was extension of the Open Door empire, informal imperialism, economic expansion abroad, or whatever one chooses to call it. This expansion was necessary to make the domestic economy function smoothly. As Hoover put it, "We must find a profitable market for our surpluses." As Harding put it, American businessmen must "go on to the peaceful commercial conquest of the world." But such expansion was not only an objective; it was partly a means to other ends. As Hoover, Hughes, and their presidents saw it, expansion, peace, and the prevention of revolution were irrevocably dependent upon one another. One of the results of war was revolution, and revolutions could result in war. Peace and stability were necessary for economic expansion. But economic expansion and the use of American strength also could be used to effect a *Pax Americana*. Peace, order, national stability, and expansion of American business opportunity abroad—these were the main objectives of American foreign policy.

Operating on the theory that revolution was an export commodity, American foreign policy makers in the 1920's sought to prevent such disruptive upheavals partly by isolating the Soviet Union. (Communists too thought revolution emanated only from Moscow and imitated the Bolsheviks' methods. One effect of this conservative-Communist area of agreement was to make every successful revolution in the world enhance the influence of the Soviet Union.) Throughout the 1920's the belief persisted in America that the Soviet regime would not last. The conclusion of many people in the western world was that the Soviet regime was such a negation of the values of western liberal society that it could not in the nature of things long endure. Disapproval and the assumption of impermanence were behind the American policy of refusal to recognize the Soviet state. The immediate and ostensible reason for nonrecognition was Soviet repudiation of the pre-revolutionary Russian debt and confiscation of about $443 million in American-owned property. The czarist government had sold about $75 million worth of bonds in America, and the United States had lent the Kerensky regime $178 million in 1917. Nonrecognition was bipartisan; Wilson had begun the policy, and his Republican successors continued it. Wilson and his successors were under some domestic pressure to recognize the Russian regime, although the pressure did not become strong until after the crash of 1929. Some of the pressure was ideological; some of it was from businessmen who wanted to trade with Russia and thought trade could best be done under normal diplomatic arrangements. During the 1920's Hughes and Hoover, without publicity, permitted some economic relations between American businessmen and the Soviet Union in the belief that these activities would both undermine the Bolsheviks and increase American influence in the new government to be established after their collapse. Ironically, these economic relations actually helped Russian economic recovery and thereby bolstered the Communists.

American Exports and Imports

Before the war, when the United States had been, on balance, a debtor nation, its exports had exceeded its imports. This was normal for a debtor nation, the only way under ordinary circumstances that, over a period of years, interest and dividends could be paid to foreign investors. During the war and immediate postwar reconstruction years, while European investors were liquidating many of their American investments and the federal government was lending billions to European governments, United States exports continued to exceed imports. This was a normal war condition. But even after the war and reconstruction, when the United States was the greatest creditor nation of the world,

American exports still exceeded imports, and this was *not* a normal condition. The tariff acts of 1921 and 1922, plus the efficiency of American production and the distance of the American market from Europe, prevented the United States from assuming the normal position of a creditor nation, an excess of imports over exports.

This being the situation, how could nations in debt to the American government and American private investors pay for their imports from the United States and pay their American debts? The answer was that, ultimately, the debtor nations could not pay their debts, even after the United States scaled down the war and reconstruction debts. But meanwhile, such "invisible" American payments as shipping fees to European freighters, American tourist spending abroad (which amounted to a surprising amount in the late 1920's), and remittances from American immigrants to their families in the Old Country helped to lessen the dollar gap but fell far short of closing it. The greater part of the annual European dollar deficit from 1919 to 1929 was covered by further American investments, either direct investments or loans. Thus American capital subsidized American exports. A large amount of world trade was dependent upon the outward flow of American capital. So long as American capital continued to flow, trade went well enough. But with the depression the flow of capital largely dried up and world trade collapsed. The whole western world had become extremely sensitive to fluctuations in the American business cycle. This was the over-all structure of America's world economic role. Let us now consider various aspects of the scheme, imports and exports, loans abroad, and direct foreign investments.

Imports into the United States increased during the 1920's, although not so much as did American exports. In 1914 imports amounted to $1.9 billion. By 1923 when the abnormal conditions of war, reconstruction, and postwar depression were over, imports totaled $3.8 billion. By 1929 they had grown 16 per cent to $4.4 billion, considerably more than double the 1914 figure. Most imports were raw materials for manufacturing, finished manufactures for American manufacturing use (newsprint, for example), and food. Of consumer goods imported in 1929, less than 6 per cent were finished manufactures for direct consumption. These finished consumer imports were mostly luxury items. The main raw material imports were silk, crude rubber, tin, copper, tobacco (for blending with domestic tobacco), and hides and skins. The quantity of imports followed almost exactly the curve of American manufacturing. This fact not only shows American manufacturing's dependence upon foreign sources for many items, but it indicates how dependent were the economies of other nations upon the health of American manufacturing. In 1929 the United States received about one-eighth of the world's total imports. Only Great Britain, a nation lacking many important raw materials, accounted for a larger proportion of total imports.

The pattern of American exports since the Civil War had been characterized by a steady growth in the proportion of manufactured goods to the total. This trend accelerated in the 1920's. From 1911 to 1915 manufactures each year had averaged 30 per cent of American exports; the proportion increased to 36 per cent for the period from 1921 to 1925 and to 45 per cent from 1926 to 1930. When one compares average export figures for the first half of the 1920's with the second half of the decade, one sees that every farm product dropped in dollar volume and that practically every industrial product increased.

Foreign Loans and Investments

More than half of the dollar gap was covered by loans and much of the balance by direct foreign investments. From 1925 through 1929 American investors bought foreign bonds totaling about $5.1 billion. The war had accustomed Americans of moderate income to buying bonds, and an estimated one-eighth of the population had an interest in foreign securities of some kind. Banks scoured the world searching for likely borrowers, sometimes resorted to questionable methods to persuade foreigners to take a loan, and then dispatched thousands of bond salesmen to beat the American bushes for bond buyers. One village in southern Germany, bankers discovered, needed to borrow about $125,000; the village burghers were persuaded to borrow $3 million through bonds sold in America. Competition among banks for the privilege of handling bond issues was intense. When Budapest decided to borrow, thirty-six banks, most of them American, competed for the commission; fourteen banks competed for the flotation of a Belgrade bond issue. All too often investment houses floating the bonds were more interested in their underwriting profits than in the wisdom of the loan, either from the point of view of the borrower or the lender. Since many of the loans were risky, interest rates were frequently high, and foolish American investors, attracted by the interest rate, bought bonds unlikely ever to be paid in full. When the whole flimsy international trade structure collapsed in 1929, millions of dollars worth of bonds were defaulted, and broke but wiser American investors muttered about their valueless "Brazilian 6½'s" or the "Peruvian 7's."

The biggest borrowers, in descending order of the total of their loans, were Germany, Canada, Italy, Australia, Chile, Argentina, Brazil, Colombia, Japan, and Poland. Some of these loans, especially those in Canada, went for projects that increased productive capacity; others went for monumental public works that had the effect of bolstering the political regime. Frequently, the regime aided by the loan was utterly undemocratic, such being the case in Mussolini's Italy and several of the Latin American nations. That democratic forces in these countries were disillusioned with America as a democratic force was not surprising.

Direct foreign investments in the 1920's were not as great as loans, but they were more lasting and had greater permanent influence on foreign nations and on United States foreign policy. In 1919 new foreign direct investments amounted to $94 million. Big profits and undistributed corporate earnings during the 1920's —the latter averaged about $2.5 billion a year—enabled industrial corporations to increase their investments abroad independent of bankers. Their investments increased, particularly in the latter part of the decade, until in 1929 new foreign direct investments amounted to $602 million. During the decade American corporations invested about $3 billion abroad. In general, it was the big corporations that made most of the foreign investments.

Canada took much of the American corporate expansion in the 1920's. The corporations' motive here was largely to get inside the British imperial preference system. By building factories across the river from Detroit, Ford and General Motors were far better able to compete with British products in Great Britain and throughout the empire. Each company also began production on the European continent itself and vastly increased its sales and service organization there. Separating their domestic production from their foreign market, besides reducing costs by moving nearer to the market and taking advantage of generally lower wage scales, enabled Ford and GM to tailor their product to the desires of the foreign market.

Oil companies, particularly Standard Oil of New Jersey, made the most dramatic foreign expansions of the decade. Oil companies in the 1920's usually bought into already existing foreign corporations. Thus during the Wilson and Harding administrations American oil corporations got into the Turkish oil field by buying stock in the Turkish Petroleum Company. An Anglo-Dutch petroleum corporation, Royal Dutch Shell, began operations in the United States just before the war. In the late 1920's this firm and Standard of New Jersey together with another British oil company, formed a cartel that carved out world markets and quotas.

Indeed, cartel arrangements with European companies became common and enabled large corporations to extend their "new competition" to the world scene. Two sulphur companies, Texas Gulf Sulphur Company and Freeport Sulphur Company, between them controlled practically all American production and sulphur deposits. In 1922 they formed together the Sulphur Export Corporation (not a violation of the antitrust laws after the passage of the Webb-Pomerene Act of 1918) and made a cartel agreement with an Italian firm that controlled most of the supply of the rest of the world. DuPont, through complicated arrangements on patents and sales agencies, had a link with the huge German chemical cartel I. G. Farben.

In nations where American corporate investments were large, it was natural for people to form their idea of what the United States was and what it stood for by observation of the corporations near them. Venezuelans and Mexicans who worked for American oil companies in their countries easily transferred their antagonism for the boss to the United States generally and learned to hate "Yanqui imperialism." Liberians who sweated on the Firestone Tire and Rubber plantations were not blind to the profits that went to Americans rather than Liberians. In general, it is accurate to say that the United States set the main outlines of its economic policy toward underdeveloped nations in the 1920's, and the policies were such that would naturally make popular political movements in these countries suspicious of America.

War Debts and Reparations

During the war the United States government lent the Allies a total of about $7.08 billion. Soon after the war the government lent another $2.53 billion for reconstruction. A considerable part of the postwar loans went to new countries created after the war. Most of the money had come originally from purchases of government bonds by Americans, and the debtor European governments had spent about 90 per cent of the money for food and war supplies in the United States. Total governmental indebtedness to the United States amounted to $10,350,-479,074. Most of the loans had been at 5 per cent interest, the terms of repayment to be worked out after the war with interest to be paid meanwhile. Great Britain ($4.3 billion), France ($3,404,818,945), and Italy ($1,648,034,050) were the biggest borrowers. In addition to these loans from the United States, the Allies had lent one another considerable sums. The whole picture of intergovernmental debt was enormously complicated and further confused by the Soviet Union's repudiation of the debts incurred by previous Russian governments. The United States government had incurred no debts to another power during the war and reconstruction years.

The War Debts Problem

Soon after the war, the debtor nations started a campaign to have the war debt cancelled or at least scaled down. They argued that for America to cancel the loans would only make her war contribution more nearly equal to their own, for they had fought longer and lost far more men and property. They also pointed out that most of the money borrowed had been spent in the United States. Further, the Europeans reasoned, how could the debts be paid even if they agreed they should be paid? Payments in gold were impossible for most of the powers. The United States owned much of the world's gold already, and what Europe had was necessary to stabilize its currencies. To pay in goods was difficult because of American protective tariffs. For that matter, American industrialists did not want payment in goods they themselves produced. At the peace conference the British suggested unofficially that all war intergovernmental debts be cancelled or, if that idea were not acceptable, that payment of the Allied debts be tied to collection of reparations from Germany. Wilson refused to consider either idea. His successors down until World War II followed Wilson's policy in the matter. Coolidge summed up the United States view with his typical Vermont spare language: "They hired the money, didn't they?" More articulate Americans pointed out that the Allies had received territory either directly or in mandates from the peace treaty as well as German reparations and that the United States received neither.

Late in 1921 Harding asked Congress for authority to make a settlement of the principal and interest not yet paid, and in February, 1922, Congress created the World War Foreign Debt Commission, authorized to fund the debt and extend the time of payment. Soon the Debt Commission, of which the Secretary of the Treasury was chairman, received delegations from debtor powers and began negotiations. In every debt settlement, the Debt Commission agreed to terms more liberal than those provided by the enabling act, but in each case Congress ratified the settlement. The settlements consisted of extending the time period and reducing the interest rate. At 5 per cent, interest payment of the debts was manifestly impossible; capital at 5 per cent interest compounded annually doubles itself in fifteen years.

Great Britain in June, 1923, was the first to arrange a debt settlement. The old arrangement had been 5 per cent payable over twenty-five years. The new settlement extended the period to semiannual payments over sixty-two years and reduced the interest to 3 per cent for the first ten years and 3.5 per cent for the last fifty-two years. This amounted to about a 30 per cent cancellation of the debt as it stood before funding. The French, who remembered that the United States had never completely paid off the French debt incurred during the American Revolution, were tougher in negotiations. In a 1926 funding settlement, which the Chamber of Deputies did not ratify until 1929, the French interest rate was cut to 1.6 per cent. "Ability to pay" was the principle followed in reducing the interest, and under this principle Mussolini's Italy got the best bargain. Italy's interest was reduced to 0.4 per cent, which meant a reduction of 80.2 per cent of the entire debt. The various funding agreements cut the aggregate debt due the United States slightly more than 50 per cent. At the same time the Debt Commission was funding the debt to America, the European powers made funding settlements with one another for the inter-Allied indebtedness.

German Reparations

At no time did the United States agree that the war debt question was in any way connected with German reparations, although as a matter of practical fact rather than legal theory the two matters were thoroughly related. It will be recalled from chapter two that the Reparations Commission set up by the Allies at the peace conference presented Germany on May 1, 1921, with a reparation bill of $33 billion. The payment scheme called for Germany to pay the Allies at the rate of $375 million each year from 1921 to 1925 and at least $900 million a year thereafter. Any interest charge not paid on the bonds Germany had to give the Allies would be added proportionately to the capital indebtedness. The Reparations Commision was to collect by supervision of Germany's foreign trade and controls over her internal economy. Any willful default of reparations was to be punished by military occupation of German territory, a provision of the peace treaty.

In 1922 Germany was unable to pay the next reparations payment and French troops, over the objections of the British, occupied the Ruhr—Germany's coal, steel, and general heavy industry region. Germany's economic condition was desperate. Her currency became wildly inflationary, so much so that German workers demanded they be paid at the end of each hour so that they could pass their wages out the window to their wives who rushed to stores before prices went up again. Nor did France profit from the occupation. The German workers offered passive resistance and production fell sharply. The State Department was alarmed at the situation, which promised only to get worse. Hughes persuaded the French to agree to work out a new reparations system more nearly consistent with Germany's ability to pay.

The United States officially had nothing to do with the Reparations Commission, but three American citizens, Charles G. Dawes and Henry M. Robinson, both bankers, and Owen D. Young, joined a Commission committee. In April, 1924, the committee presented the Dawes Plan, which was ratified in August. Under this scheme Germany was to pay reparations the following year of $250 million and in increasing amounts thereafter as the German economy was able to stand it. American and Allied bankers were to lend Germany $200 million in gold to be used to hasten industrial recovery and to back a new currency issue. As Germany's payments became larger and she saw no visible end of reparations, she asked for a further reduction in reparations. Again American citizens, officially without government connection, worked out a plan. The Young Plan, adopted December 22, 1928, reduced the German obligation to $153 million a year until 1988, there also to be additional "conditional payments" depending upon the strength of the German economy. The Allies agreed to leave all German territory and to relinquish controls over the German economy.

The Dawes and Young plans worked well enough in one sense; Germany paid reparations to the Allies. But, on the other hand, the plans started a crazy circular financial motion. The Dawes Plan, by stabilizing German currency, made German bonds attractive to American investors. Between 1924 and 1930 American private investors bought German bonds of the German central government, municipalities, and corporations totaling about $2.5 billion. With these outside loans Germany was able to pay approximately $2 billion in reparations to the Allies. With help from reparations, the Allies were able to pay approximately $2.6 billion on their war debts to America. Thus the money, after unknown numbers of exchanges, interest payments, broker's commissions, and underwriting fees, went from America to Germany to France, Britain, or Italy and then back to America again. European need for American money kept the circle going. The State Department frowned upon private investments to nations in default on their war debts, thereby levering them into keeping up their payments. Europeans began to refer to Uncle Sam at Uncle Shylock.

Based ultimately upon American private investment, the whole reparations and war debt system was dependent upon the continuation of American prosperity. When American prosperity came to an abrupt end, the whole structure collapsed.

Japan and the Open Door in Northeast Asia

Japan's desire to control Asia, at least northeastern Asia, ran head on against the American Open Door policy, and the United States was by no means willing to abandon the Open Door, the basis of her foreign policy everywhere. Japan had strengthened her position and expanded her influence and control considerably between the outbreak of war in Europe and the early 1920's, but she had continually run into an American stumbling block. Situations which would lead to war between Japan and the United States two decades later were already beginning to take shape; on both sides as early as 1920 there was talk that war might come to pass.

Japanese-American Relations

Japan had become angry with Wilson at the peace conference when he opposed inclusion in the League convenant of an explicit statement of racial equality. Wilson had compromised his stated principles and yielded on the question of a Japanese mandate of Shantung, but the Japanese, in view of their secret treaty on Shantung, did not regard the mandate solution as a total victory. In 1917 Wilson had revived the idea of an international bankers' consortium to keep an eye on the Japanese in China and to keep America's foot in the open door. The Japanese agreed to the consortium only after reserving for themselves special commercial privileges in Mongolia and Manchuria, and the final signing of the consortium agreement came in October, 1920.

A large part of the reason for America's participation in the armed intervention into Soviet Siberia in 1918 had been to block the possibility of Japan's taking complete advantage of the power vacuum created in northeastern Asia by the Russian Revolution. A point of conflict in that part of the world was control of the Chinese Eastern Railway which ran across Manchuria toward Vladivostok and had been controlled by Russia until the revolution. Japan coveted the railroad for herself, but the Allied command of the Siberian expedition successfully put it under the control of an Inter-Allied Railway Commission. When the United States and the other western powers evacuated Siberia in the spring of 1920, the Japanese occupation force remained. The Railway Commission continued to control the Chinese Eastern, but the Japanese had the only foreign troops in the vicinity.

In March, 1920, the Japanese also extended their occupation to the rest of Sakhalin, the northernmost island in the Japanese chain just off the Siberian coast. Japan had received the southern half of Sakhalin at the end of the Russo-Japanese war in 1905; Russia retained the northern half. When Bolshevik troops massacred a Japanese garrison in Siberia, the Japanese retaliated by rushing north across the Russian-Japanese border on Sakhalin to hold it, they said, as security until the Russians agreed to a satisfactory restitution for the massacre. They did not leave until 1925, and then only after wresting concessions from Russia for coal and oil rights in northern Sakhalin as well as fishing rights in Siberia.

One other territorial matter disturbed Japanese-American relations: control of a tiny island in the western Pacific with the unlikely name of Yap. This little dot on the map was of potential use as a cable station. Wilson had argued unsuccessfully at Paris that Yap be made international territory. Instead it had become one of the Japanese mandates. Through late 1919 and 1920, the United States had pressed Japan for rights to establish cable operations there, but the Japanese were adamant.

Naval Armament

Perhaps the most potentially explosive matter between Japan and America was naval armament, a question made more complicated by the existence of the Anglo-Japanese Alliance of 1902. In 1916 the American government had made plans for building a huge navy as part of the preparedness program. During the war, paradoxically, the plan had been laid aside. The 1916 idea had been to construct a huge, balanced fleet with battleships and other capital ships as the central core. The war had forced the navy to concentrate upon immediately needed destroyers and other smaller craft. With the end of the war, the navy wanted to resume its earlier program and even expand it. The British were not likely to sit back and let the United States build a navy superior to hers, and the Japanese expanded their naval construction. Admirals and other big-navy advocates, however, faced strong political opposition to a great naval expansion. Congress in 1919 and 1920 had cut back the navy's plans considerably. In May, 1921, the Senate overwhelmingly passed a Borah resolution that requested the administration to negotiate with Japan and Great Britain on naval disarmament, and the House concurred the following month. If a full-scale naval armament race actually got under way, reasoned the State Department, the United States might well lose the race because of domestic opposition.

Even if no naval race developed, there was the possibility that two of the three naval powers in the Pacific—Japan, Britain, and the United States—might combine to harm the third. The alliance between Japan and Britain provided that if either power became involved in a war brought on by "an unprovoked or aggressive act" anywhere the other should help its partner. When the alliance was renewed in 1911, the British insisted upon including a clause that exempted operation of the alliance in the case of a war with a nation with which either Japan or Britain had a general arbitration treaty. This was the cue for the United States to remove herself from the possibility of war against combined British and Japanese power. President Taft negotiated an arbitration treaty with Great Britain, but the Senate involved the treaty with other matters and did not ratify it. When Japanese-American relations deteriorated, Canada became excited over the possibility that her imperial connection with Britain and the Anglo-Japanese alliance might involve her in a war with her southern neighbor. Britain did not want to be forced into a war with the United States because of her alliance with Japan any more than did Canada. It was high time, thought the British, for clearing the air on the whole matter of naval armament and Pacific questions. It seemed the same to Secretary of State Hughes.

A New Complex of Treaty Arrangements

On July 5, 1921, the British Foreign Office suggested to the American ambassador, George Harvey of "smoke-filled room" fame, that Harding invite the major powers to a disarmament conference. Harvey cabled the suggestion to Washington on July 8. Earlier that same day, Hughes had cabled Harvey with instructions to ascertain if the British would agree to meet at a disarmament conference. Upon receipt of Harvey's cable, Hughes released a statement to the press and issued informal invitations to the other major powers to meet in Washington to discuss not only naval disarmament but general problems of the Far East and the Pacific. Japan qualified and delayed her reply, but Hughes announced that all invited powers had accepted. From the Washington Conference were to come three major treaties—the Five Power Naval Treaty, the Four Power Treaty, and the Nine Power Treaty—as well as a series of small agreements.

The Five Power Naval Treaty

The Conference met for its first plenary session on November 12, 1921, in Washington's large Memorial Continental Hall. Quite in contrast to the secrecy and formality of the Paris Conference, the press and hundreds of others who were not delegates, including many Congressmen, were invited to the Washington meeting. The American delegates, led by Hughes, were Senator Lodge, Democratic Senate minority leader Oscar Underwood, and Elihu Root. Harding opened the meeting with the kind of inane welcoming address of which he was a master and yielded the floor to Hughes. The audience prepared for the usual ceremonial opening speech of felicitously phrased banalities.

But Hughes flouted diplomatic convention and came straight to the point. He proposed a ten-year holiday on the construction of new capital ships and the scrapping of some already built or under construction so that the number of capital ships of the three largest naval powers, Britain, the United States, and Japan, would be maintained at the existing ratio of 5–5–3, respectively. Then he declared the United States was prepared to scrap thirty capital ships with a total tonnage of over 800,000. He went on to describe just what Japan and Britain should turn to scrap. As an English newspaperman put it, Hughes destroyed more of the British fleet in a few minutes than the armadas of the world had been able to in centuries. Under the plan Britain would discard capital ships totaling about 583,000 tons and Japan about 449,000 tons. The delegates were thunderstruck.

In mid-December, the British, American, and Japanese delegates announced essential agreement. But then the French became difficult when Hughes tried to get them and the Italians to agree to accept their existing 175,000 tons apiece as their maximum. The French, under the illusion they were still a national power of the first magnitude, had already shown they were touchy when they objected to where their delegates were seated at the conference table, and Hughes had not improved matters when he made an aside about France's ability to pay her debts. The French delegates insisted upon a maximum capital ship tonnage of 300,000. The British leaked this demand to the press, and the reaction of the world was strongly against the French. Hughes then appealed over the heads of the French delegates directly to Premier Aristide Briand, who had gone back to Paris after the conference opening, and was able to persuade him to accept the 175,000 ton maximum.

The Five Power Naval Treaty, signed in February, 1922, provided for a roughly 5–5–3–1.7–1.7 ratio of capital ships: for Britain and the United States, a maximum of 525,000 tons; for Japan, a maximum of 315,000; for France and Italy, a maximum of 175,000. In addition, Britain and America could have up to 135,000 tons of aircraft carrier, Japan 81,000 tons, and France and Italy 60,000 tons each. The signatory nations agreed to stop capital ship construction for ten years and, importantly, to maintain the *status quo* on naval bases and fortifications of Pacific islands except for Hawaii and those immediately off the powers' coasts. The treaty limited the size of smaller naval vessels but imposed no restrictions about their number.

The Four Power Treaty

Senator Lodge proposed at a plenary session in December, 1921, that Japan, Great Britain, France, and the United States agree to a treaty under which the signatory nations would respect one another's possessions in the Pacific and confer if any disputes among them or with an outside power threatened to break the peace. Lodge, who just two years before had led the fight against the League as an "entangling alliance," surprised the public with his proposal. The resulting Four Power Treaty, signed in February, 1922, also abrogated the Anglo-Japanese alliance effective upon ratification by all powers. The Senate ratified the treaty the following month after making the reservation that the treaty imposed no American obligation to commit armed forces.

The Nine Power Treaty

The Washington Conference's Nine Power Treaty, also signed in February, 1922, was an international recognition of the Open Door in China. The United States, Britain, Japan, France, Italy, China, Belgium, Holland, and Portugal pledged themselves to respect the "sovereignty, the independence, and the territorial and administrative integrity of China" and to "refrain from taking advantage of conditions in China in order to seek special rights or privileges which would abridge the rights of subjects or citizens of friendly states, and from countenancing action inimical to the security of those states." The Nine Power Treaty did not commit its signatories to action in case of violations.

Two days before the nine powers signed their treaty, China and Japan signed a treaty that Hughes had been strongly urging upon them. Japan agreed to return the Shantung peninsula to China, but China agreed to honor the many private contracts that Japanese businessmen had already made in Shantung and to buy from Japan the railroad the Germans originally had built. Japan also announced she would withdraw her troops from Siberia. Finally, the Japanese allowed the United States to build a cable station on Yap and agreed to abrogate the Lansing-Ishii agreement of 1917, supplanted by the new Nine Power Treaty.

What can one say of the Washington Conference treaties? During World War II many considered the naval limitation idea a mistake, but this judgment was a reflection of war passion. True, the United States sacrificed potential naval supremacy in the Pacific waters. If Japan and the United States had engaged in a naval armaments race, surely America could have built the more powerful navy because her wallet was thicker. But it is dubious that the United States actually would have built a superior fleet. She did not in fact even keep her fleet up to the limits imposed at the Washington Conference. If Japan gained a little in actual naval strength under the agreement as it was observed, she backed at least part of the way out of Shantung and recognized the Open Door principle more strongly. Of course, the Washington treaties did not get at the root of the difficulty in the Far East: commercial rivalries and the conflict of the American Open Door empire and the British formal and informal empire on the one hand, with Japanese colonial empire ambitions on the other. And they did not prevent war in the long run. But, given the basic policies of the Pacific powers concerned, they clarified the situation, saved a great deal of money by limiting naval armament, and preserved peace for a decade.

Later Naval Conferences

In 1927 President Coolidge rather hastily decided to call another international conference to limit naval armament. The Five Power Naval Treaty had not prevented unlimited building of cruisers and other ships smaller than battleships and aircraft carriers, and the three greatest naval powers had begun to build heavy cruisers. The French replied that they preferred to work for naval disarmament within the League of Nations and declined to attend the conference which began at Geneva in June. Italy also declined to participate. Planning for the conference had been inadequate, and Britain, America, and Japan could not agree. The conference broke up with no accomplishments. Two years later it was revealed that armament and steel manufacturers had retained a lobbyist named William B. Shearer to try to sabotage the conference. The sensational revelation prompted a congressional investigation, but it was not at all clear that Shearer's activities were what had caused the conference to fail.

In 1929 the new prime minister of Great Britain, Ramsay MacDonald, visited

Hoover, and the two agreed to call another naval conference to meet in London. The London Conference of 1930 extended the ban on capital ship construction for another five years (to the end of 1936) and continued limitations to smaller vessels. Japan objected to the old 5–5–3 ratio for smaller ships but agreed to a compromise that kept the old ratio for heavy cruisers, increased the ratio for light cruisers and destroyers to 5–5–3.5, and granted Japan equality on submarines. France and Italy would not ratify the London Treaty.

Such negotiations and agreements as the naval disarmament treaties suggest that even in international political affairs, the United States did not pursue an isolationist foreign policy during the 1920's. America only drew back from entering any international agreement or organization that might in any way obligate her to use her armed power in a dispute in which she had no immediate interest. The decision of 1919 not to join the League of Nations was never rescinded; the United States never officially joined the organization. Yet America had a great deal to do with the League. In 1922 Hughes sent "unofficial observers" to meetings of special League commissions and agencies, and at these meetings the American participants spoke and argued but could not vote. Two years later the administration named official delegates to the League's Second Opium Conference. By 1931 the United States had five permanent delegates to League agencies at Geneva and had participated officially in more than forty conferences. American opponents of the League had some justification for their charge that the United States had taken the back door to Geneva; certainly, American policy was not isolationist by any reasonable definition of the term.

Kellogg-Briand Pact

In 1927 the State Department led in an international effort—pathetically futile as it turned out a few years later—to "outlaw" international war. Aristide Briand, after earlier conversations with Professor James T. Shotwell of Columbia University and the Carnegie Endowment for International Peace, announced that his nation was prepared to agree with America never to war with the other. Secretary of State Frank B. Kellogg, who succeeded Hughes in March, 1925, was at first cool to the idea but yielded to popular pressure. Kellogg extended the idea to include other nations. Subsequently, France and the United States drew up a document which declared that "they condemn recourse to war for the solution of international controversies, and renounce it as an instrument of national policy in their relations with one another" and invited fourteen other nations to sign the document with them jointly. The other nations were Belgium, Czechoslovakia, Germany, Italy, Japan, Poland, and Great Britain and her self-governing dominions. These nations signed the Pact of Paris (or Kellogg-Briand Pact) on August 27, 1928. Later the Soviet Union and several other nations signed. The public record of the negotiations made clear that the pact imposed no ban upon a war of self-defense, although since almost every nation in the world ultimately signed, self-defense would in theory be unnecessary.

International Courts

Kellogg went on to make bilateral arbitration treaties with eighteen nations which provided that certain kinds of disagreements between the signatory powers would be submitted to the Permanent Court of Arbitration at The Hague, usually called The Hague Court. The treaties provided that arbitration might be undertaken by any other "competent tribunal." This phrase was a reference to the Permanent Court of International Justice, usually called the World Court and with no connection to The Hague Court. The World Court had been established as a fully independent agency of the League of Nations.

In 1924 public opinion for American participation in the World Court was strong enough that both major parties supported the Court in their platforms. Early in 1925 the House by an overwhelming vote passed a resolution favoring United States adherence to the World Court. Debate in the Senate was extensive, and the upper chamber modified the resolution to include five reservations. The modified resolution passed the Senate in early 1926. At the time the Kellogg arbitration treaties were drawn, it was assumed that the United States would soon be a participating member of the World Court. A committee of the League appointed an international committee of jurists, of whom one was Elihu Root, to revise the World Court protocol so as to meet the American reservations. In 1930 and again in 1935 the revised protocol, already agreed upon by the President and the Department of State, failed to get the necessary two-thirds vote of ratification in the Senate. Thus, the United States never joined the World Court.

Slowly Learning to Behave in Latin America

During the 1920's the United States improved her relations with Latin American nations. When Hoover left office early in 1933, the situation was considerably better than it had been when Wilson left the White House in early 1921. Two factors seem to have operated in the gradual growth of better United States manners in Latin America. Public opinion at home turned increasingly against armed intervention south of the border, which by the time the United States entered the war had become a matter of ordinary routine. The newspaper sentence, "The marines have landed and the situation is well in hand," had become a cliché. Part of the reason for the gradual shift in public opinion was that only by the wildest flight of imagination could anyone see a threat to the nation's security in events to the south. The other factor was that businessmen, who greatly increased their investments in Latin America during the prosperity decade, began to learn that over the long run a policy of cordiality with firmness on economic matters was financially wiser than bulling one's way through with reliance upon armed force. One might gain in the short run by resort to force, but the reservoir of ill will that resulted, businessmen learned, would in the long run harm their economic influence. Armed intervention came to be a last resort. However, relations with Mexico and Nicaragua did prove to be trying problems in the postwar decade.

Mexico and Oil Lands

Petroleum's odor permeated United States diplomacy in Mexico. During the 1920's, before the Venezuelan and Middle Eastern oil fields were in full production, Mexico was second only to the United States in world oil production, and American and British corporations accounted for roughly two-fifths of Mexican oil output. To protect United States oil investments was the primary objective of the State Department's Mexican policy. As Hughes said in a 1924 public statement, the "fundamental question" was "the safeguarding of American property rights . . . against confiscation."

During the war President Carranza decreed that Article 27 of the Mexican constitution of 1917 would be put into effect. This article provided that all subsoil rights to land owned or leased by foreigners belonged to the Mexican nation, even holdings acquired before promulgation of the new constitution. Article 27 actually was a return to historic Mexican practice. In Spanish nations it was the common rule that subsoil resources were the property of the nation rather than of the owner of the lands, and Mexico had followed this general rule until the late nineteenth century. Foreign oil corporations would have to seek new concessions from the government, which was likely to be tougher in dealing with foreign interests than had been the prerevolutionary Diaz regime. The State Department and the British Foreign Office protested strongly enough to get Carranza to postpone enactment of the retroactive feature of the article.

In the spring of 1920 a revolutionary movement headed by General Alvaro Obregón overthrew Carranza. Obregón was actually more friendly to foreign oil interests than Carranza, but when he did not immediately agree to keep the status quo on foreign oil investments the Wilson administration refused to recognize his regime. This was the situation Hughes inherited in 1921. Two years later Hughes began negotiations with the Obregón government which ended with the signing in September, 1923, of two claims conventions. In these agreements Obregón conceded that subsoil rights to property held by American firms before 1917 would remain in American control and that American owners of land expropriated under another provision of the 1917 constitution should be granted fair compensation. The numerous monetary claims of American citizens against the Mexican government and vice versa would be settled by special claims commissions. In return the United States diplomatically recognized Mexico again and thereby facilitated private American loans. Soon thereafter, when the Obregón regime was threatened by a revolt led by General Adolfo de la Huerta (not to be confused with Victoriano Huerta with whom Wilson had had difficulty early in his first term), Hughes consented to sell a limited amount of arms to Obregón and deny them to de la Huerta. The Mexican government put down the revolt, and when the new Mexican president-elect, Plutarco Calles, visited Washington in October, 1924, all seemed rosily optimistic for Mexican-American relations and the interests of United States oil companies.

Secretary of State Kellogg and James Sheffield, the new ambassador to Mexico, quickly created trouble again. Sheffield, who was close to the biggest American oil interests in Mexico, reported that the Calles government was not respecting American property rights. Kellogg issued an incredible public statement that implied that if the Calles government did not do the State Department's bidding on oil matters the United States would support any revolution against the Mexican government that might develop. Calles, perhaps figuring that working with Washington was impossible, yielded to Mexican popular opinion in December, 1925, and got laws through the legislature that for all practical purposes rescinded subsoil rights to land held before 1917. The laws were to go into effect January 1, 1927. Throughout 1926 the Mexican government negotiated with

American oil companies, regaining oil and mineral rights for the Mexican nation and granting fifty-year leases. Nearly all the American companies but the Mellon-Sinclair-Doheny group complied, but this group remonstrated strongly with the State Department. Kellogg asserted that Mexico was supporting rebels in Nicaragua, where the United States was simultaneously embroiled, and in January, 1927, he charged that the Calles government was Bolshevik-controlled and working with Russian agents to endanger the Panama Canal. The situation was further irritated by the heated opposition of American Roman Catholics to the anti-clericalism of the Calles government. Some people even expected war. But in late January the Senate indicated what it thought of Kellogg's charges when it, without a dissent, passed a resolution calling for arbitration of the whole Mexican oil problem.

Sheffield resigned in June, and Coolidge replaced him with Dwight Morrow, a House of Morgan partner who had unusual skills of persuasion and diplomacy. Within a few months Morrow was able to arrange a way in which subsoil rights on pre-1917 holdings would stay in private foreign hands and Calles could appear not to reverse himself. Morrow also brought about a truce in the battle between church and state and thereby quieted anti-Mexican feelings in the American Catholic community. Apparently no small part of Morrow's success was due to his arranging for Charles Lindbergh to make a goodwill flight to Mexico City in December, 1927. The young flier, soon to become Morrow's son-in-law, had become a world hero the previous May when he became the first man to fly solo and nonstop across the Atlantic.

Nicaraguan Problems

Resolution of the difficulties in Nicaragua was somewhat cruder. Both concern for the Nicaraguan canal possibilities and American investments were behind United States interests in that Central American hotbed of palace revolutions. Marines had been stationed there since the Taft administration. An American collector of customs had stabilized Nicaraguan finances, and in 1923 Hughes promised that if the Nicaraguans conducted an honest election the next year, the marines would be withdrawn. The election was held under a law written by a United States citizen, the Liberal party under Carlos Solórzano was formed, and the marines departed in August, 1925. Soon after their departure, another palace revolution forced Solórzano to resign and Vice-President Juan Sacasa to leave the country. But the State Department refused to recognize the new government led by a Conservative party leader, Emiliano Chamorro. Such was the state of Nicaraguan politics that the Nicaraguan Congress deposed Chamorro and elected another Conservative, Adolfo Díaz, an old friend of American interests, and the State Department promptly recognized the Díaz government.

At this stage of the matter, former Vice-President Sacasa returned, claimed to be president, set up his own government, and began warfare with the Díaz regime. The United States responded by sending in five thousand marines, more than had been there before they left the previous year. Sending the marines back was highly unpopular with most of the American population. In the spring of 1927 Coolidge sent Henry L. Stimson, who had been Secretary of War under Taft, to Nicaragua in an effort to resolve the conflict between the Conservatives and the Liberals, who did not capitulate when the marines arrived. Stimson brought an end to most of the fighting when he persuaded Díaz to accept Liberals in his cabinet and guaranteed fair elections in 1928. The American military forces supervised the election and prevented "repeaters" by requiring every voter to dip his fingers in a red dye upon leaving the polls. The Liberal candidate won. The marines were employed for several months trying to capture a Liberal rebel group led by Augusto Sandino who refused Stimson's terms, but they were gradually withdrawn after 1931.

New Interpretation of the Monroe Doctrine

Elsewhere in Latin America the United States behaved not quite so imperiously, and late in the decade it even repudiated the Roosevelt corollary to the Monroe Doctrine. The last American marines withdrew from the Dominican Republic in 1924, although American control of Dominican finances continued until 1940 and marines remained in Haiti on the other half of Santo Domingo. At a Pan-American Conference in 1923 Hughes supported a proposal for peaceful settlement of disputes among American republics but refused to budge from the traditional United States position that only it could invoke the Monroe Doctrine. But he also said in a speech before the American Bar Association in 1923 that the Monroe Doctrine as he understood it "does not infringe upon the independence and sovereignty of other American states." "Misconception upon this point is the only disturbing factor in our relations with Latin American States." However exaggerated this second statement was, the speech was nevertheless at least a step backward from the Monroe Doctrine as interpreted by Theodore Roosevelt.

At the next Pan-American Conference at Havana in 1928, Hughes again led the United States delegation although he had left the cabinet three years earlier. Representatives of Caribbean and Central American republics pressed strongly for a commitment from the United States that it would not intervene in the affairs of other American nations. Hughes refused even to allow the topic to come into official conference discussions, and with the help of South American nations below the equator smothered discussion. At the same time, Coolidge requested J. Reuben Clark of the State Department to define precisely what the Monroe Doctrine was. Clark's memorandum, not published until 1930, clearly repudiated the Roosevelt corollary.

Just how much difference Hughes's and Clark's interpretations of the Monroe Doctrine actually made would have to be determined by later administrations. It was now official State Department policy that the Monroe Doctrine could not be used to justify intervention into Latin American affairs, but at the same time both Hughes and Clark made clear that intervention could be justified on other grounds, notably self-preservation and defense of the Panama Canal. However, as shallow a concession as this was, it made easier the adoption in the 1930's of what another Roosevelt called the "Good Neighbor policy."

The Business Civilization and Its Critics

It would give me great pleasure to vote for a Tory candidate for the Presidency . . . one voicing the sincere views of the more civilized section of the propertied class, not a mere puppet for usurers. Unfortunately, no such candidate ever offers himself.

H. L. MENCKEN, 1920

Chapter Six

Between World War I and the depression, a wide gulf separated the values of the nation's intellectuals and artists from the rest of the population. Before the war, novelists, for example, had written on political and social themes that both reflected and stimulated a general concern for such matters among less articulate people. Painters, like social workers and progressive politicians, discovered poverty and made it central to their work. But after the war popular tastes and values went one direction while most intellectuals went another. People of an artistic or literary bent frequently referred to more conventional people as "philistines." H. L. Mencken, a Baltimore newspaperman and magazine editor who was extremely popular in the 1920's among young people with intellectual aspirations, called the ordinary, unintellectual, popular mass the "booboisie." The philistines and the booboisie retaliated with condemnations of "long-haired men and short-haired women."

Practically everyone on both sides of the cultural fence agreed that those with conventional values, ideals, and ideas—the philistines—both reflected the dominance of businessmen in American society and set the nation's cultural tone. So, too, did foreign observers, many of whom were fascinated but repelled by American society and wrote books about the country. André Siegfried, a French author (*America Comes of Age*, 1927), Arthur Feiler (*America Seen Through German Eyes*, 1928), and an iconoclastic London philosopher, C. E. M. Joad (*The Babbitt Warren*, 1927), were probably the three best-known foreign authors who wrote about the United States in the 1920's. These men differed on many particulars but were unanimous in commenting that culturally conventional, intellectually shallow, artistically ignorant, and socially primitive businessmen dominated America and set the framework for its formal culture. (Joad, incidentally, the most vivacious but irresponsible of the three, did not think it necessary to visit the United States before writing his book.)

Yet, looking back at the period from a greater time perspective, one notices that the creators of enduring works, those who have become accepted as major intellectual or artistic figures, were not in the dominant cultural stream. The major figures divided into two camps, each of them scornful of popularly accepted values. One intellectual camp attacked convention by explicitly criticizing the direction of American life. Sinclair Lewis, for example, brought a new word into the vocabulary with his book about *Babbitt*, a well-meaning but bigoted and culturally hopeless businessman. The other camp revealed its disgust by retreating from American society in one way or another. Many of them actually lived abroad; others of them turned inward into their chosen field, working out their artistic or intellectual problems, ignoring society as much as possible; still others concentrated upon form more than upon content. A popular slogan of this last group, whether they were artists or not, was "Art for Art's sake."

But for all the social critics and *avant garde* bohemians or mandarins, respected by a relative few in their own day but honored by many in a later generation, the 1920's popular honors went to defenders of the cultural *status quo*, particularly to those who glorified the man of business. To be a "go-getter," a "success," a "live wire" was the generally accepted ideal. Writers who enthusiastically supported these ideals reaped large rewards. A book by Bruce Barton, partner in the advertising firm of Batton, Barton, Durstine, and Osborn, entitled *The Man Nobody Knows: A Biography of Jesus*, was a best seller in 1925 and 1926. The dust jacket reprinted enthusiastic endorsements from many of the country's outstanding clergymen. Jesus, according to Barton, was "the founder of modern business." He was the greatest salesman of His age, the "most forceful executive" of His world. He demonstrated His genius for personnel work in the manner in which He chose His disciples. Although Barton's readers in a later day waver from incredulity to dismay to hilarity, he was taken seriously and at face value in the 1920's. Most of his readers were not sure whether Barton's primary purpose was to sanctify the businessmen or to pay Jesus his ultimate compliment, but they disagreed with neither intention.

Most of this chapter will be concerned with those who dissented from the dominant values and thought of the 1920's since these dissenters were the ones who carried formal American culture along through the decade. The next chapter on various aspects of the era's social history will concentrate to a greater extent upon dominant, popular currents. The reader should remember, however, that for every person to whom a Sinclair Lewis or T. S. Eliot was a hero there were a dozen who honored a Barton.

Education

The outstanding development in public education during the 1920's was a tremendous increase in the number of years young people went to school. Increases in enrollments of primary grades were more the result of a larger population than an increased percentage of school attendance. Increases at the junior and senior high school level were due mostly to an increased proportion of that age level continuing formal education. High-school enrollments approximately doubled during the decade. By the late 1920's, about half the population of high-school age was in school, a proportion unsurpassed elsewhere in the world.

Teacher salaries had lagged far behind the sharp increase in the cost of living from 1917–20, but after the postwar depression salaries improved. By the end of the decade teachers' average real income was better than before the war. Yet teacher incomes did not improve as much as incomes in other fields requiring a similar amount of training. One result of this situation was that men teachers became fewer. Those who had families felt obligated to go into fields where they could better support them. While certainly a teacher's sex makes no difference in ability, the predominance of women in teaching did make it more difficult for the field to acquire the characteristics of other professions. Women frequently taught for a few years and then quit to marry. Many school boards refused to appoint married women and dismissed single women who did marry. But teaching increasingly acquired one of the aspects of a profession—special graduate education. Most of the schools of education in the state universities offered graduate work in the 1920's. Thousands of teachers attended graduate school each summer, and, particularly in the high schools of the cities and larger towns, master's degrees became commonplace.

Better automobiles and roads made it possible for the first time to abandon the rural one-room elementary school and to bring secondary education to country youth. The nation's school transportation bill each year amounted to more than $20 million. "Busing," to use a term that became popular in the 1970's, originally had wide support because it bettered the education of rural youth.

With thousands in high schools who in an earlier day would have quit school at the elementary level, the high schools were forced to modify their standards and curriculum. More modification came in the next decade as high school enrollments continued to rise, but by the late 1920's many schools had introduced ambitious vocational training programs for the students who were poorly equipped for or uninterested in the usual academic program. The best of these vocational programs turned out young people prepared to take jobs in commercial offices, the building trades, print shops, and automobile garages; others merely taught the use of hand carpentry tools and the rudiments of mechanical drawing. The equipment required for vocational education made its costs greater than those of academic courses, and most school systems were unable or unwilling to make a sufficient investment.

The Broadened Role of the School

Preparation for an occupation was only one of several aspects of the broadening function of the public schools. The school had originally served for intellectual or academic training altogether; no other social institution—the family, the church, the trade union, the social club—was able to fulfill the intellectual training function. But by the end of the 1920's the school had taken on a number of other social functions. In an agricultural society the family had provided vocational education and a measure of social preparation, the family and the church had at least endeavored to provide moral training, and the family and the doctor had taught the rudiments of health and hygiene. But in urban and industrial society the family had tended to become less powerful as a social organization at the same time that life became infinitely more complex and education for that life therefore more difficult. The school, as a result, came to assume functions in the education of the young theretofore alien to it. Pressures for modification of school programs came from many directions. Educators themselves brought some of the changes. Patriotic organizations insisted upon nationalistic citizenship training. Society in general demanded that the school become the main agency for Americanization of immigrants. Insurance companies pressured school administrators to set aside student time for instruction in safety. Prohibitionists enlisted teachers in the campaign against alcohol. In the assumption of these many tasks the school often neglected its original academic function.

Many people became alarmed by the changes in the school, saw the changes as all for the worse, and, confusing all change with John Dewey's ideas, lashed out against "progressive education." According to the more old-fashioned intellectuals, the school produced a more inferior intellectual product each year, a deterioration that dated from the educational golden age when the critics themselves had sat at student desks. Actually, most objective comparisons of the academic knowledge of children in the 1920's with that of school children a generation earlier showed no deterioration and sometimes an improvement. But this was because teachers had become more effective rather than because they put an equal emphasis upon academic subject matter. With the better methods, textbooks, and libraries there is reason to believe that a much higher level of achievement could have been reached if the school had retained its academic function exclusively.

Despite all the talk of Dewey and "progressive education," there was relatively little of Dewey's theory put into practice in most school systems. For the most part, one had to go to experimental schools operated by universities or teachers colleges to find Deweyism. Yet there were many innovations, particularly in private schools in the large cities, that went under the name of "progressive education," innovations so wildly different from convention that their label of "progressive" damaged Dewey's popular reputation. Most of these wilder innovations derived more from a revolt against Victorian mores and misunderstanding of Sigmund Freud than from pragmatism.

The Scopes Trial

It was the anti-evolution crusade of religious fundamentalists rather than progressive education that caused the big headlines about schools in the postwar decade. The post-Civil War generation had engaged in an enormous controversy over Charles Darwin's theory of evolution that most people in the cities by 1920 had assumed to be a dead issue. Biological evolution was generally accepted, and the urban churches had accommodated their doctrine to the scientific view of man's origin. But rural America, particularly in the South, revived the controversy in a startling way in the early 1920's. William Jennings Bryan became the popular leader of the fundamentalist crusade against evolution. He engaged in an extended public controversy with E. A. Birge, a biologist and the acting president of the University of Wisconsin, that rallied him strength in the country but only disdainful amusement from the cities. In 1922 the Kentucky legislature came within one vote of passing a bill to outlaw teaching evolution in the schools. Antievolutionists won minor successes in North Carolina, Florida, and Oklahoma, and Governor "Ma" Ferguson of Texas herself blacklisted biology textbooks when the legislature refused to do so. Then in 1925 Tennessee's legislature made it illegal for a teacher in the public schools "to teach any theory that denies the story of the divine creation of man as taught in the Bible." Mississippi and Arkansas soon enacted similar statutes. The American Civil Liberties Union offered free counsel to any Tennessee teacher who violated the act, and a young high-school biology teacher of Dayton, Tennessee, accepted the ACLU offer. The teacher, John Scopes, became the least important figure in the trial as the ACLU provided him the services of Clarence Darrow, the most famous criminal defense lawyer of the day, Dudley Field Malone, and Arthur Garfield Hays as counsel and Bryan acted as a special assistant for the prosecution. The "monkey trial" attracted national headlines, and H. L. Mencken wrote brutal attacks upon Bryan, referring to him, among other things, as a "sweating anthropoid." Darrow made Bryan look like a fool, getting him to contradict himself in his defense of his proposition that the Bible was in every respect literally true. The jury found Scopes guilty of violating the law, which clearly he had, but the state supreme court threw out the case on a technicality and thereby dodged a decision on the constitutionality of the law. The heat at the trial, held in July, was oppressive, and Bryan so exhausted himself that he died a few days later. It was tragic that the Great Commoner died when his reputation was at its lowest point, when he appeared to be an ignorant, anachronistic, rural clown rather than the leader of one of the nation's major political parties and a Secretary of State.

The College Attendance Boom

The biggest problems confronting the colleges and universities arose from rising costs and a huge expansion of enrollments. In 1920 the campuses were jammed with about six hundred thousand students, many of them war veterans whose education had been interrupted or delayed. But the increased enrollments were not temporary, as they were expected to be. By 1930, there were roughly twice as many students in college. Although some employers still fumed that college was a waste of time, specialization in engineering and other professions made college attendance a practical necessity. In some lines of business the social polish and associations that one could acquire at certain campuses were more important vocationally than whatever knowledge and intellectual discipline might have been developed within the walls of ivy. Young women and their mothers realized that one's chances of attracting a desirable bachelor improved by pursuing a bachelor's degree. But for whatever reasons, intellectual or otherwise, hundreds of thousands of new students arrived on the campuses each fall, and higher education in the United States became mass education. And as faculties increasingly expected the Ph.D. degree as a condition of appointment and industry began major research laboratories, expensive graduate education became ever more common. In 1920 American universities awarded slightly over five hundred Ph.D. degrees; by 1930 the figure had quadrupled.

So much has been written and put onto film about campus life in the 1920's, the Charleston, raccoon coats, hip flasks, and Stutz Bearcats, that little need be said. The popular accounts were grossly exaggerated. Men and manners, maidens and morality, differed enormously from campus to campus and from group to group upon a single campus. Some professors thought that there was less drunkenness in the 1920's than there had been before the war, but surely professors were not in the best position to know all that went on in either period. One thing is indisputable about campus life during the boom: never before had football loomed so large as a university activity. Men like Harold

"Red" Grange of Illinois, Albie Booth of Yale, Ernie Nevers of Stanford, and Coach Knute Rockne of Notre Dame came to be known to far more people than the professors or presidents of their institutions.

Literature and Prosperity

If there was anything that most major literary figures of the 1920's could agree upon—and there was not much—it was that America was a mess. Harold Stearns, a disgruntled literary critic, edited a volume in 1922 entitled *Civilization in the United States* in which thirty American writers in various fields looked about them and unanimously concluded that American life was esthetically barren, intellectually superficial, and stiflingly oppressive. Middle-class values, worship of technology and material wealth, Victorian morality, and glorification of outmoded ideals had, they said, made it impossible for art and intellect to flourish. That they had a point any objective observer would agree. Yet by the decade's end any accountant of culture would have to agree that the years had brought forth an unusual burst of creative energy, a frenzy of intellectual and artistic excitement, and a few masterpieces.

The Major Writers of the Prosperity Decade

A few writers dedicated the decade to documenting the conclusions of the Stearns volume. The most famous and widely read of these were Sinclair Lewis, Sherwood Anderson, and H. L. Mencken. Lewis skyrocketed to national attention in 1920 when he painted a grim picture of a small midwestern town in *Main Street*. Two years later he did a similar job on a larger city in *Babbitt*. In *Arrowsmith* (1925) he was critical of the medical profession, in *Elmer Gantry* (1927) he ripped the clergy to shreds, making them all either fools or knaves, and in *Dodsworth* (1929) he featured the soul sickness of a businessman who had wrecked his life pursuing the dollar and neglecting his own development. In 1930, Lewis became the first American novelist to receive a Nobel prize.

Sherwood Anderson, who had more impact upon intellectuals but less of a popular following than Lewis, was best known for his *Winesburg, Ohio* (1919). A legend about Anderson which he himself encouraged was illustrative of one intellectual fad of the 1920's. Anderson had, it was said, walked out of his paint factory in Elyria, Ohio, one afternoon in 1912, thoroughly sick of his middle-class way of life, set his face toward the sun of culture and art, and never turned back. The fact was that Anderson had a nervous breakdown. But hundreds of young writers treasured the legend and romantically honored him for breaking with convention, and, probably, hundreds of frustrated young businessmen envied him for the courage they thought he had.

Henry Louis Mencken, "the bad boy of Baltimore," was the rage among young would-be sophisticates of the 1920's. Mencken became an editor of *The American Mercury* in 1924 and soon every sophomore who yearned for Montmartre and despised his hometown carried the green-covered magazine. If anything was sacred to Mencken besides beer and Johann Sebastian Bach, he concealed the reverence. Voting was ridiculous, wrote Mencken, and politicians were only "beaters of breasts." He defended prostitution, declared that boot-leggers were nature's noblemen, and proposed to sink the Statue of Liberty. The more he shocked dominant middle-class America, the more subscriptions he received. Quite apart from his social and literary commentaries, Mencken was a respectable philologist, and his studies on the American language received critical acclaim.

But most of the major writers of the prosperity decade did not regard America's cultural shoddiness as even worthy of serious direct attack. Henry Adams, a descendant of a great family, in his 1918 autobiography included a perceptive criticism of American culture from the Civil War to the World War and then retreated to the Middle Ages, attracted by that period's spiritual unity and repelled by modern materialism. T. S. Eliot was thinking of more than business when he wrote The Waste Land (1922) and The Hollow Men (1925), but his despair certainly included the United States. This expatriate, whose poetry forms had a great impact on young people, also retreated to medievalism. Scott Fitzgerald, whose novels became the symbol of "flaming youth" and the "lost generation," occasionally made explicit criticisms of American life but was for the most part concerned with individual and personal matters.

Concern for the Individual and Self

Indeed, emphasis upon the individual in one way or another to the almost complete exclusion of concern for society, was an outstanding characteristic of letters during the decade. It was quite a reversal from the dominant pattern before the war and in contrast to what was to come in the 1930's. Even the writers who were expressly critical of America saw the problems of the nation in individual rather than social terms. The same was true of their solutions, to the degree they offered solutions. Most saw no hope whatsoever and, therefore, no possible solution. When Stearns turned in the manuscript for his Civilization in the United States, he issued no manifesto, called no writers' congress, organized no intellectual school or community. He embarked for France. The drama critic George Jean Nathan, a friend and associate of Mencken, stated the view of most major writers well if in exaggerated form:

> The great problems of the world—social, political, economic and theological —do not concern me in the slightest. If all the Armenians were to be killed tomorrow and if half of Russia were to starve to death the day after, it would not matter to me in the least. What concerns me alone is myself, and the interests of a few close friends. For all I care the rest of the world may go to hell at today's sunset.[1]

Such views, if sincerely held, automatically threw reform out the window. Before the war the arty set, the bohemians, had mingled happily with the reformers and the social radicals. The left-wing Masses had combined social radicalism with literary and artistic innovation. Greenwich Village had been a neighborhood for both kinds, and the distinction between artist and radical had been

---

[1]William E. Leuchtenburg, The Perils of Prosperity, 1914–1932 (Chicago: Univ. of Chicago Press, 1958), p. 150.

difficult to make. Again in the 1930's radicals and artists were to move back together for a while. But in the 1920's they had little in common. They fused around the Sacco-Vanzetti case but little else. To the artistic temperament, reform was old hat and radicalism was an irrelevant museum piece. John Chamberlain, a newspaper book reviewer, wrote a survey of American social protest movements in 1929 which was vaguely sympathetic but condescending. He buried social protest, he thought, with his title: *Farewell to Reform*. For Chamberlain personally reform was buried indeed; he later moved farther to the right. Max Eastman, a Greenwich Village young genius who before the war was both literary and radical as a *Masses* editor, became exclusively literary for a while in the 1920's. He later became an editor of *The Reader's Digest* and a warrior against the left. Lincoln Steffens, the muckraker who had moved steadily leftward and had hailed the Bolshevik revolution, announced that the Hoover administration would bring all the material goals for the poor that the Socialists had agitated for.

The main tendencies of literature and intellectual life in the 1920's—remembering always that we are here considering relatively few people, not the mass popular Bruce Barton school of thought—flowed naturally from rejection of reform and social problems for concern with the individual and particularly for one's self. The main tendencies, but one can discern others, were hedonistic pursuit of pleasure, Freudianism or distorted forms of it, primitivism, and anti-democracy.

Hedonism

Edna St. Vincent Millay wrote a short poem, "Figs from Thistles," which became one of the most widely quoted verses of the decade. It well expressed the hedonistic mood that extended far beyond the intellectual, would-be intellectual and artistic community.

> My candle burns at both ends;
> It will not last the night;
> But, ah, my foes, and oh, my friends—
> It gives a lovely light.

Scott Fitzgerald's novels, *This Side of Paradise* (1920), *The Beautiful and the Damned* (1922), and *The Great Gatsby* (1925), and the facts and legend of his career were perhaps the best example of postwar hedonism. Fitzgerald's characters found life meaningless, they had been tragically disillusioned by the war, they conceived of themselves as "the lost generation" and they abandoned themselves to pleasures of the moment. To be "free" and "gay" were their goals. Until the crash, Fitzgerald and his wife even lived the life of their determined-to-be-carefree characters. They were in France much of the time with hordes of other American expatriates. Their money went farther there, and France had no prohibition or puritan tradition. Ernest Hemingway, the best stylist of the "lost generation," also lived in France and developed fictional characters who found their world without meaning and therefore gave up and pursued pleasure for pleasure's sake. His *The Sun Also Rises* (1926) and *A Farewell to Arms* (1929) had a huge impact on young intellectuals of his day and upon successive generations of them, both in America and throughout the western world. Most people, however, were only shocked by his use of four-letter words and his explicitness about sex.

Freudianism

A few American intellectuals had discovered Freud before the war, but only a few. After the war Freudianism became widespread, although far less so than it would become after World War II. One of its greatest influences upon literature was through the stream of consciousness technique. The dramatist Eugene O'Neill even used this technique on the stage. His *Desire under the Elms* (1924), *The Emperor Jones* (1920), *The Great God Brown* (1926), and *Strange Interlude* (1928), while they puzzled their audiences, disseminated Freudian ideas to a wide circle. Easily the outstanding American playwright of the decade (perhaps of all time), O'Neill's stature at home and abroad has grown with the years.

Primitivism

Primitivism received a stimulus from the notion that civilization was thoroughly sick and rotten. If man had any dignity at all, primitivists held, it would be found among people whose contact with civilization had been small, for to civilize was to spoil. A strong primitive streak ran through Hemingway's novels. The characters he most admired were men of muscle and violence and unfettered sex urges, people who operated by their emotions rather than by their reason. When they had intelligence, it was the cunning of a jungle animal rather than cultivated insight. Thus boxers, hunters, soldiers, rum runners, and bull fighters peopled his pages. One aspect of primitivism of the 1920's was a cult of the Negro. During the decade there was a considerable black literary renaissance. Some white intellectuals sponsored and praised black artists, novelists, poets, and musicians mainly because they were black. Carl Van Vechten was the leading white sponsor of black literature, and Countee Cullen was the best known black poet. In some white circles in New York City people prattled of atavism and "earth rhythms" and spent their evenings in the night clubs of Harlem. The Cotton Club soon became too well known for the true connoisseur of black life who sought out his jazz and gin in smaller and more esoteric Harlem speakeasies. It is interesting to note that these primitivists did not oppose segregation in one sense; they thought it would be tragic if the Negro became so much a part of American life that he would lose what they considered unique and inherent Negro qualities. France, perhaps through the influence of the expatriates, also had a wave of black primitivism. French intellectuals raved about *le jazz hot* until the French masses and American whites also discovered jazz.

Antidemocracy

Antidemocratic attitudes revealed themselves in a great deal of the decade's literature. In Fitzgerald there was an element of elitist thinking. When one reads today the detective novels of S. S. Van Dine one is astonished by their snobbery and racism. The poet Ezra Pound ultimately became a Mussolini fascist, and some who retreated into medieval culture did so largely because they found the democracy of later eras distasteful. Mencken included democracy among the favorite targets of his literary meat axe. The clearest and best reasoned attack upon democracy in literary circles, however, came from a group of critics called the "new humanists." Led by Paul Elmer More of Princeton and Irving Babbitt of Harvard, the "new humanists" rejected the naturalism and sensuality of the literary innovators of the decade as well as old-fashioned progressivism and defenders of the business civilization. They deplored the direction of the modern world since the late eighteenth century. The best of all possible worlds, they at least implied, was one such as prerevolutionary France, where a cultured elite with wealth and leisure patronized unadulterated art and literature.

The Exceptions

In a culture as dynamic and diverse as American culture was, however, there were many exceptions to the literary trends noted here. Magazines like *The Nation* and *The New Republic* more than held their own. Reform was not altogether dead even among writers of fiction in the Coolidge era. Upton Sinclair, for example, wrote steadily throughout the decade and had a wide audience, although he was regarded as old hat by many. Theodore Dreiser never lost hope for social regeneration despite his gloominess, and his *An American Tragedy* (1925) was one of the greatest novels of the era. Carl Sandburg's and Edgar Lee Masters' sense of identification with ordinary people never left them, and the same might be said for the more conservative Robert Frost. There even was a considerable amount of good literature in the older genteel tradition. Willa Cather's *Death Comes to the Archbishop*, her best and most famous novel, was published in 1927. Her *The Professor's House* (1923) remains one of the best novels about academic life, although dozens of them were written later. Perhaps the most striking exception to the dominant literary trends of the period by a young man was Stephen Vincent Benét's *John Brown's Body*, a masterful epic poem of the Civil War which won a Pulitzer prize in 1928. Benét, like so many others of his generation, had fled to France. But instead of cursing and despairing of America he wrote a beautiful reaffirmation of old American values without in any sense being old-fashioned.

The Twenties and Music

The history of music in the United States in the twentieth century is largely the story of the development of its own musicians of all kinds, including composers. Then, when the basis of an American music had been laid, much of the story had to do with efforts to produce a distinctively American music, to evolve musical expression less dependent upon European traditions. America's musical history has been roughly analagous to the industrial strivings of economically underdeveloped nations of South America, Africa, and Asia. During the 1920's, however, there were several important developments in the effort both to develop American musical personnel and to create a unique musical tradition.

American musical development was tied in with the growth of an American musical audience. To use an economic analogy again, there had to be a market before there could be production. Further, American musicians could not come into being from a musically arid society. In the 1920's prosperity and technology stimulated the domestic market for music. Phonographs became more widely owned than they had been before the war, and the introduction of electrically transcribed recordings in 1925 considerably improved their fidelity to the sound as it had come from the musicians' instruments or voices. Radio made it possible for millions to hear music who had never heard it extensively before, and the variety of music that one could hear from the radio was much wider than anyone could have from recordings. Prosperity made possible live music in towns that had previously had a minimum of professionally produced music. In 1920 Henry P. Harrison of the Redpath Chautauqua and Lyceum Bureau of Chicago began to organize groups in several towns and cities that he called Civic Music Associations. The Associations sold subscriptions for a season's concerts, and Harrison supplied the artists. He soon had several imitators. The performers, it is true, had to cater to rather unsophisticated popular tastes and had to feature dramatic selections that involved as much showmanship as music—one will never know how many times Fritz Kreisler and Albert Spaulding, the nation's favorite violinists, had to play Saint-Saëns's "Ghost Dance"—but their programs and musicianship were clearly superior to the old traveling troupes of Swiss bell ringers.

Schools of Music

Three major schools of music opened their doors during the decade. The Eastman School of Music at Rochester, New York, began in 1921, founded by an endowment from the photographic equipment manufacturer George Eastman. After Howard Hanson became director of the Eastman School in 1924, it quickly became noted for its vigorous composition department. New York's Julliard School of Music opened in 1923. Philadelphia's Curtis Institute accepted its first students in 1924. Graduates of these schools, both performers and composers, were to become the equal of their counterparts from Europe.

The Performers

By the end of the 1920's American symphony orchestras contained many American born and educated instrumentalists. The Metropolitan Opera Company still found it necessary to contract with European singers for most of the stars of the company, but during the decade John Charles Thomas, Lawrence Tibbett, and Rosa Ponselle sang important roles on the Metropolitan's stage and were well received. Marion Talley, originally from Missouri, captured the public imagination when she sang her first major role at the Metropolitan in 1926. In 1927 The King's Henchman, one of the first American operas to make an impact, was a New York hit. Deems Taylor was its composer, and Edna St. Vincent Millay wrote the book.

The Composers

Three young American composers in the 1920's became the first to achieve national and world esteem, Aaron Copland (born 1900), Howard Hanson (born

1896), and George Gershwin (born 1898). Both Copland and Gershwin tried to adapt jazz or elements of jazz to symphonic forms. Gershwin was easily the more widely heralded of the two, largely because he was already known as a composer of popular music and songs for musical comedies, but also because he had the backing of Paul Whiteman, a popular orchestra conductor who stood between the jazz and "serious music" worlds. Whiteman, a symphony violinist, endeavored to tame jazz and play it as concert music. At a 1924 New York concert the Whiteman orchestra first played Gershwin's "Rhapsody in Blue." Ferde Grofé, later to gain a name for himself for his symphonic suites on American themes, orchestrated Gershwin's composition. The same concert introduced a sticky suite entitled "Serenades" which Victor Herbert had especially written for the occasion. The comparative lasting qualities of the two compositions well reveal which kind of music better reflected American interests and characteristics. The New York Symphony, an organization that later merged with the New York Philharmonic, first played Gershwin's "An American in Paris" in 1928.

Hanson soared across the musical sky like a rocket and became a dean of American composers while still a young man. A son of Swedish immigrant parents, reared in Wahoo, Nebraska, Hanson won an American Prix de Rome and studied abroad for three years. He then returned to the United States to direct the Eastman School. He composed his "Nordic Symphony" in the 1920's as well as his symphonic poems "North and West" and "Pan and the Priest."

Jazz

Jazz, or more precisely jazz-influenced popular music, swept the country after the first years of the decade. Real jazz, unadulterated by Tin Pan Alley, also gained in the decade after the war, but it was little heard on the radio, and the record companies separated it from popular music by creating "pop" divisions in their firms and relegating jazz to what they called "race records" sold mostly in black neighborhoods. Neither was respectable, and jazz devotees were not fully successful in their efforts to make it respectable with concert performances and learned articles in highbrow and middlebrow magazines. But the vitality of jazz and its reflection of the dynamic and disturbing new machine America, a hustling, break-neck urban civilization, made it attractive to young people whose tastes had not been formed by the Victor Herbert version of Viennese music. Sweet string music simply did not fit the America of the second quarter of the century. The brassy, blaring, wailing, and nervous rhythms of jazz did fit modern America, and jazz needed only time to live down older prejudices and become widely accepted.

Prosperity and Art

The business cycle and art are intimately related, although many artists might deny any connection. Prosperity and local civic pride in the 1920's led almost every fair-sized city in the country without an art museum to establish one. Between 1921 and 1930 sixty new art museums were formed in the United States. At the same time there was an expansion of the private art market. Once only a relatively few families of enormous wealth had bought paintings. The greater number of rich families during the boom decade considerably widened the market, and art-buying extended downward a little into less wealthy income groups.

Most of the money, however, went for purchases of old and traditional European painters. Portraits by eighteenth-century English painters became a vogue in the bigger "English manor" style houses that went up in the new suburbs. Probably the most famous painting in the United States was Gainsborough's "Blue Boy" at the Huntington Library at Pasadena. Winslow Homer's "Eight Bells" brought $50,000 at a New York sale, and an Inness brought $60,000 soon thereafter, both new highs for American paintings. Significantly, however, no contemporary American painter ever received more than a small fraction of such prices. French modernism caught on with a relatively small public, and the collector John Quinn, who had a tremendous modern collection by French and American artists, sold it in 1927 for $700,000. Still we must remember that the market for contemporary art in America never approached what it would become in a few decades. The French in 1925 asked President Coolidge to send an American exhibit to the Exposition des Arts Décoratifs. Coolidge replied that the United States had no contemporary art to send. He clearly was badly misinformed, but few people knew that he was.

Modernists and experimentalists dominated American art in the 1920's. The trend was consistent with the main directions of literature and music during the period. Modernism meant a great many things. There were several modernist schools, but they had certain similarities. They did not attempt lifelike representations, but their subject matter was usually recognizable. Only a few were completely abstract. The modernists emphasized formal harmonies, and they expressed subjective emotions. It was a new way of looking at things, a new vision, greatly influenced by new schools of painting abroad, especially in France, and to some extent by new perspectives offered by the camera and the microscope. In New York, where most of the modern painting was done, modernism created a spirit of excitement.

The Individualists

Three major painters with highly individualistic styles who were outstanding in the 1920's were John Marin, Georgia O'Keeffe, and Max Weber. Marin, who was to live until 1953 and become the dean of American artists, specialized in modernist water colors. During the twenties, his style reached its most abstract point, but generally the form was recognizable—usually scenes of New York City or the Maine coast. But the form was not the most striking aspect of his work. It was rather his sweeps of bright color which gave his paintings a dynamic quality.

Miss O'Keeffe painted with a clean, austere line that heightened reality. Even when she did completely abstract things she kept her edges sharp and clean, almost camera-like. She has been criticized for too often becoming merely decorative, but her best canvases, such as her "The American Radiator Building" done in 1929, have been of lasting importance.

Weber is considered here because he first came to attention in the 1920's.

He continued to be one of America's foremost painters for many years, especially after World War II. Weber painted in a variety of styles. He was influenced by Oriental art as a student, and when he studied in Paris he became interested in primitive and Middle Eastern art. Matisse was his teacher in Paris, but Cézanne became his idol. Cézanne, incidentally, was the most important single influence on American painters in the 1920's. Back in America, Weber painted in many of the styles of modernism and was criticized for not being himself. He was eclectic, but in all his styles his own distinctiveness was apparent.

Cubism

Three painters of the 1920's who had a marked similarity in subject matter and in general approach were Charles Demuth, Charles Sheeler, and Joseph Stella. Sometimes called the cubists-realists, they emphasized geometric forms to be found in architecture and machinery. Cubism was a school of painting, originally French, in which emotion was subdued and, in its simplest interpretations, broke down all physical reality into its basic structural elements: cubes, cones, and cylinders. Demuth, who painted in a flat style with little perspective, distorted reality by stripping his vision down to the essentials. The result was a very stylized rendition of a perfectly recognizable building or machine, made more elegant by the distortion. Sheeler's work emphasized depth or perspective. One gets the feeling in looking at them that one is looking through a strong lens. Sheeler first made his living as a photographer, and his emphasis on perspective, light, and shadow learned with his camera carried over to his canvases. In 1922 he made a film entitled "Manahatta" with the photographer Paul Strand who, along with Edward Steichen, was at the forefront of art photography during the decade. One of his most famous paintings, "Church Street El," done in 1920, emphasizes light and shadow under an elevated railway to such an extent that at first glance the composition seems abstract. Later in the decade, Sheeler became increasingly realistic. He did a series of photographs of Ford's River Rouge plant and then painted many of the scenes with the photographs as notes. His work did much to popularize industry as subject matter for painting, and *Fortune* magazine later did many covers in this stylized fashion. Stella's pictures gave more feeling of movement than Demuth's and Sheeler's. He particularly liked to do suspension bridges and port scenes, and the big cables swooping down and across the canvases gave them a dynamic quality.

Several other American painters prominent in the 1920's went through cubist phases. Alfred H. Maurer, who did cubist still lifes, is attributed by some to have done the most interesting and advanced cubist work of any American painter, but he is also known for his sad stylized portraits in the manner of Matisse. Maurer never received the recognition during his lifetime that he deserved, and he committed suicide in 1932. Andrew Dasburg did cubist interpretations of the desert landscapes of the American Southwest which must have amazed the New Mexicans who might have looked over his shoulder. Stuart Davis, who was in Paris for most of the decade, was the most radical of the American cubists. Some of his paintings, for example "Egg Beater No. 1," were such departures from surface reality in their attempt to portray reality in the cubist sense that viewers felt grateful, if puzzled, by their titles.

Arthur Dove had been influenced by cubism, but he did not fit into that school precisely. He was a daring innovator. His colors were on the drab side, but his forms were frequently completely abstract. He also experimented with collage in a manner that was almost surrealist. Dove was so dedicated to the avant-garde that seeing his collages a generation later, with their use of pieces of steel spring, pages torn from old Bibles, fragments of needlepoint, and bits of weathered wood, one is struck by the degree later offbeat artists only repeated ideas he worked out in the 1920's. His collages have rotted and rusted to such an extent that their main interest today is historical.

Marsden Hartley, although he painted a great many mediocre pictures, did some of the most emotionally intense canvases of the decade. Hartley had studied in Germany, unlike most American artists, and his painting showed the influence of German expressionism. He did some powerful pictures of the southwestern desert, featuring twisted trees and barren landscape. Another artist influenced by German expressionism, strangely enough, was a Japanese-American, Yasuo Kuniyoshi. He came to America from Japan when a boy and had all of his training in the United States. Because of his background, many have proclaimed that he combined western and Oriental art, but it is doubtful that a Japanese artist would see anything familiar in his paintings.

Popular Modernists and Realists

Modernist, but far more in keeping with popular tastes, were a group of painters who continued to take the human face and form for subject matter. Walt Kuhn had been a realist associate of George Bellows. He was greatly affected by the Armory Show, which he helped to organize, and for a while experimented with radical modernism. Then in the 1920's he returned to representational portrayal of people only slightly distorted or stylized. His favorite subjects were stage and circus people, but his portraits were of types rather than of actual people. Bernard Karfiol specialized in nudes that were much like Renoir in their style.

Realists worked throughout the decade, but they were fewer in number than they had been before the Armory Show or would be in the 1930's, and they did not attract as much public attention. John Sloan and George Luks were active as realists, but had given up their Ash Can tradition. In the late 1920's, a considerable group of realists, including Reginald Marsh, Morris Kantor, and the Soyer brothers, who were to come to national prominence in the depression, had shows in New York. Social protest art during the decade was restricted almost entirely to illustrators for left-wing magazines, and they, too, would attract greater attention with a reversal of the business cycle.

On the whole, American painting during the 1920's was in the art-for-art's-sake tradition, and it was much influenced by Europe, especially Paris. Cubism, fauvism, and other French styles seldom were taken wholly by American painters, but they had a strong impact.

Sculpture and Architecture

In both sculpture and architecture, especially for public buildings, there was relatively little experiment or departure from tradition. Perhaps the economics of these fields made them differ from painting. Paintings usually were purchased by one person to be hung in the home or perhaps given to a museum, frequently for speculation. But it was government commissions, corporations, or civic clubs that instigated public buildings and statues. Committees were involved; purchasing or commissioning a design was an organization enterprise. In such circumstances, daring was the last thing to be expected. So sculptors maintained a safe and diplomatic conformity to precedent—designs which the public would approve. The sculpture in the many World War I memorials of the 1920's differed from the memorials to the Civil War mainly in that they indicated more action than the old general-on-a-horse pose and they were more nationalistic in feeling.

One of the best-loved sculptures of the decade was Daniel Chester French's enormous and romantic statue of Lincoln in the Lincoln Memorial at Washington. The public clearly liked representations of Lincoln consistent with the Lincoln legend. A 1917 magazine poll to determine the public's favorite Lincoln statue rated a realistic work by George Gray Barnard that emphasized the Emancipator's ungainliness at the bottom of the list; Augustus Saint-Gaudens' romantic likeness in Lincoln Park, Chicago, was the easy winner. Gutzon Borglum was the best-publicized sculptor of the 1920's. Borglum agreed to do a monumental chiseling of the side of Stone Mountain, Georgia, and transform its stone front into likenesses of Confederate heroes. After a disagreement with some of the project's sponsors, Borglum temperamentally left the job to be completed by others. He later did an even bigger work of mountain sculpture on Mount Rushmore in the Black Hills of South Dakota. More of a geological and sculptural stunt than a work of art, the Mount Rushmore monument has representations of Washington, Jefferson, Lincoln, and Theodore Roosevelt.

In 1924 Louis Sullivan died broke and broken in a run-down Chicago hotel. Not far away was rising Colonel Robert R. McCormick's *Tribune* Tower, about as complete a negation of Sullivan's skyscraper idea as possible that could still be called a skyscraper. It was capped with pseudo-Gothic decoration. To combine skyscraper and Gothic architecture was about as sensible, critics said, as an airplane pilot's wearing a monk's robe, but there were other examples of this combination before the decade ended. The University of Pittsburgh erected in the steel city's Civic Center what came to be known as the "Cathedral of Learning," a hybrid between a Gothic cathedral and an office skyscraper. Other universities, too, taught twentieth-century knowledge and ideas in Gothic surroundings. Yale built its medieval Harkness Quadrangle deliberately dilapidated. The cigarette king James B. Duke endowed Trinity College of Durham, North Carolina; it became Duke University, abandoned its old campus, and built a new Gothic one.

In university schools of architecture, however, students and faculty showed an interest in architectural functionalism and modernism that in a generation's time would make it almost impossible to study traditional architecture in the United States. The commission for *Tribune* Tower had been awarded after a competition that attracted 260 proposed designs from 23 countries. Second prize went to a Finnish architect, Eliel Saarinen. Saarinen's design was far more exciting to architectural educators than the winning entry and thereafter the University of Michigan invited Saarinen to join its faculty.

The People
and
Their Tensions

The issue in Kansas this year is the Ku Klux Klan. . . .
It represents a small minority . . . and it is organized for
purposes of terror . . . directed at honest, law-abiding
citizens, Negroes, Jews, and Catholics. . . . They are good
citizens, law-abiding, God-fearing, prosperous, patriotic.
Yet, because of their skin, their race, or their creed,
the Ku Klux Klan in Kansas is subjecting them
to economic boycott, to social ostracism, to every form of
harassment, annoyance and every terror that
a bigoted minority can use. . . .
WILLIAM ALLEN WHITE, announcing his
independent gubernatorial candidacy, 1924

Chapter Seven

The social history of the 1920's offers so much that is colorful that it has become a favorite subject of popular writers. Babe Ruth, the Hall-Mills murder case, "Lucky Lindy," flappers, speakeasies, Rudolph Valentino, and Floyd Gibbons receive a full measure of treatment in these accounts, some of which are accurate, well written, and entertaining. It is interesting that the emphasis of popular and nostalgic social history of the 1920's is on aspects of urban life, almost to the exclusion of the country and the small town. Yet a large part of the population lived in rural communities and was not much involved in jazz age life. In many ways the countryside in the 1920's made its last losing battle to preserve its values and traditions as the national standard. Many of the social conflicts of the decade—struggles over immigration, over prohibition, over religion, and over individual morality—were related to urban-rural division.

The decade's prosperity brought little social harmony and stability. Changes in the way people lived, especially in the cities, were greater from 1919 to 1929 than during any decade between the Civil War and World War I. Rapid social change invariably brings anxiety and conflict between those who approve of the new ways and those who resist them. The postwar decade was marked especially by conflict between immigrants and old-stock Americans, Protestants and Catholics, and those who wanted a homogeneous, stable society and those who saw America's greatness in its heterogeneity and dynamism.

Immigration Restriction

For years a combination of forces as diverse as Boston blue bloods and organized labor had converged in an effort to restrict immigration. Gradually they had been able to get legislation through Congress that excluded certain persons deemed undesirable, the most important law being the illiteracy test act that Congress had passed over Wilson's veto in 1917. Immigration had declined to unimportant proportions during the war, and its opponents were determined that the stream should not flow again when the war ended. Soon after the armistice, however, thousands of Europeans departed for the New World. Immigration figures for 1920 were almost as high as they had been for the peak years from 1905 to 1914. Renewed immigration stirred restrictionists to legislative action, and they received additional public support because of widespread fear of communism. Most people associated radicalism with immigrants.

The Quota System

Restrictionists pushed a bill through Congress in the last days of the Wilson administration. The House passed a bill late in 1920 introduced by Representative Albert Johnson of Washington to suspend immigration for a year while new restrictive legislation was prepared. The Senate amended the bill to provide a quota system. Wilson refused to sign the bill, however. Harding favored restriction, and Congress passed a slightly revised Johnson bill in May, 1921. The new law was a radical departure from previous immigration legislation. It provided that the number of immigrants from any nation who might be admitted each year should be no more than 3 per cent of the number of foreign-born of that nationality living in the United States in 1910. The law further provided that no more than one-fifth of the quota could be admitted in any single month. This led to a ridiculous situation when steamers loaded with immigrants waited outside New York harbor and raced for Ellis Island as the old month expired.

The Johnson Act, sometimes called the Emergency Quota Act, rigorously reduced immigration. In its first year of operation, immigration declined roughly 62 per cent to about 300,000 persons. This was still too many for extreme restrictionists, and it did not discriminate sufficiently against southern and eastern Europeans to meet their demands. By the base year of 1910 millions of immigrants from Italy, the Balkans, and the Russian empire had migrated to America. Under the law the maximum quota for eastern and southern Europe was about 160,000 and the maximum for northern and western Europe about 200,000. In the first year of its operation, more than half of the quotas for northern and western Europe had gone unused, but 95 per cent of the other quotas had been filled. Restrictionists demanded a more severe law, as did Coolidge in his State of the Union message in December, 1923. "America," said Coolidge, "must be kept American," by which he meant white, Anglo-Saxon, and Protestant.

National Origins Act

The National Origins Act of May 26, 1924, also introduced by Representative Johnson, had two major parts, the first to apply until 1927 (later delayed until 1929), and the second to operate thereafter. For the first years, immigration quotas were figured at a maximum of 2 per cent of the foreign-born population for each nationality as revealed by the 1890 census. This new quota system reduced the total legal European immigration to about 164,000, and it further discriminated against the "new immigration." Putting the base year at 1890 cut back quotas for southern and eastern Europe from the 1921 level because most immigration from there had been after 1890.

The system to go into effect July 1, 1927, was even more restrictive. It put maximum immigration each year at 150,000. The quotas within this maximum were arrived at by figuring the ratio of "the number of inhabitants in the continental United States having that national origin" to the total population in 1920. Note that instead of figuring quota on the basis of foreign-born, as in earlier workings of the quota system, it now was to be on the basis of "national origin." Calculating these quotas, a task of the executive branch, involved genealogical chaos. Who could say what a family's "national origin" was when it had been in America for several generations and had intermarried? This scheme even further reduced quotas for eastern and southern Europe because the new basis included those whose forefathers had come to America as long ago as 1607 and immigration from other than the British Isles had been small until the 1840's. The executive branch of the government wrestled with the genealogical problem unwillingly and tried to get Congress to amend the law to make it administratively more convenient. Congress refused to budge, but it consented to extend the deadline until July 1, 1929. When the new quotas finally were announced, there was considerable consternation in some quarters. Great Britain's quota almost doubled, but Germany's and Ireland's declined by half and Sweden's, Norway's, and Denmark's fell by two-thirds. There had been many people of German, Irish, and Scandinavian background who were perfectly willing to exclude Italians, Slavs, and Jews to "keep America American," but they had not foreseen how the new formula would discriminate against their own kind. Their protests availed them nothing. Congress was not particularly happy to see Great Britain get the lion's share of the 150,000 maximum, but it feared that to reopen the whole matter might allow substantial numbers of "new immigrants" to reach American shores.

One provision of the National Origins Act simplified the tasks of officials and removed one source of immigrant hardship. When immigrant ships had raced one another to docking space at Ellis Island, immigrants over the quota had been turned back and families had become separated. Under the new law, United States consuls at European port cities had responsibility for the acceptance of immigrants.

The law provided for no quota whatsoever for Asian countries, not even the token quota of one hundred granted countries such as Luxemburg. The law forbade the entry of any person not eligible for citizenship, and the Supreme Court had only recently reaffirmed that Japanese, for example, were not eligible. The Court had ruled that Japanese, being neither "free white persons" nor persons of African birth or origin, could not be naturalized under existing law. While Congress debated the National Origins bill, Japan sent the State Department a note which reminded the United States of the Gentlemen's Agreement of the Roosevelt administration and stated that absolute exclusion would have "grave consequences." In the conventions of diplomatic note writing "grave consequences" is a strong phrase. Secretary of State Hughes sent the note on to Congress. He had calculated that the Japanese quota would be about 250 a year if she were allowed one at all, constituting something surely less than a "yellow peril" to California. But West Coast newspapers demanded Japanese exclusion, and Congress by an overwhelming vote kept the exclusion clause in the bill. Passage of the law set off anti-American demonstrations in Japan, and when the new law went into effect, Japan observed the day as one of national humiliation.

The End of Immigration and Its Effects

The law's purpose was to freeze permanently the national composition of the American people. The great tide of humanity that had flowed from Europe to America for a century was now completed. It may have been almost finished anyway. Several European nations restricted emigration in the 1920's and 1930's, and some of those that did not never filled their quotas. The law did not apply to immigration from other American nations. During the 1920's, about nine hundred thousand Canadians moved to the United States, many of them French-speaking Roman Catholics and precisely the kind of immigrants the laws were designed to exclude. Almost a half million immigrants from Mexico went through the formality of being counted. How many others moved across the border without the Immigration Service's knowledge was not known, nor was there an accurate estimate of the number of Mexican laborers who entered the United States on temporary work permits to take stoop-labor agricultural jobs but escaped federal supervision and did not return. In 1930 the Mexican-American population was about two million.

With the practical end of immigration came inevitable changes in established immigrant institutions. The many fraternal organizations of immigrant groups waned in vigor as their source of new members declined to a trickle and children of immigrants felt less identification with the parent nationality. Foreign language newspapers continued to be published by the score in the major cities, but these also changed. First the comics and the school news appeared in English, then the sports page, and eventually much of the general news. Immigrant churches began to conduct two services, one in the European tongue and one in English. One aspect of America's diversity began slowly but steadily to disappear.

Black Americans, South and North

The most important development among American Negroes during the war and the 1920's was a huge migration out of the South. In the long run, this migration had tremendous implications. First, it enabled blacks to receive a better formal education than they would have had in the South, and educated blacks could give their race better leadership. Second, by moving where they could vote, blacks in time gained political leverage in national politics.

Migration to the North first became significant in 1915. It grew during the war and increased still more in the 1920's. In 1910 only about 850,000 blacks lived outside the South; in 1920 the figure was about 1,400,000; in 1930, it was about 2,300,000. The percentage of nonsouthern blacks to the total increased from slightly less than 10 per cent in 1910 to 20 per cent in 1930. Various pulls from the North and pushes from the South got the migration under way and kept it going. Prosperity created jobs in the North, although for the most part blacks got the worst jobs available. Fewer European immigrants provided them the chance to get employment that had once gone to "greenhorns." In the South a combination of circumstances made blacks want to leave more than before and made it possible to do so. The boll weevil made cotton farming more precarious than usual, and white men increasingly moved into occupations that had traditionally been reserved for blacks. More widespread elementary black education in the South sharpened aspirations and provided the literacy necessary for most urban employment. Prosperity created jobs in southern cities as well as northern ones, and thousands of blacks moved from their rural homes to the nearest city where they got the cash necessary to go north. Most of the northward migration was from city to city, and most of it was to the nearest northern city. Thus blacks in the southeastern states tended to go to Washington, Baltimore, Philadelphia, and New York, and those in the central South tended to move to cities of the Midwest. Black migration to the West Coast had not yet become significant.

The war itself wrenched thousands of blacks from their homes and their old ways of living. Roughly 400,000 black men served in the armed forces during World War I, and about half of them served overseas. Once moved from behind a plow and shown something of the outside world (including the racial equality of France) the young black was not likely to return to his old life. In fact, many stayed in France. Far more moved to northern cities.

Outbreaks of Violence

The disruption of traditional patterns in the South during the war and the appearance of large numbers of blacks in the North brought an appalling outbreak of violence. In the South most interracial violence was lynching; in the North most of it was rioting. Lynching was usually rural and small-town; rioting was usually urban. Lynchings increased from 34 in 1917 to 60 in 1918 and to 70 in 1919. Several of the victims were soldiers or veterans, some of them in uniform. Simultaneously in the South, the Ku Klux Klan revived and terrorized blacks, sometimes only frightening them but often beating them.

So many riots occurred in the North in the summer of 1919—more than a score—that black publications referred to it as the Red Summer. The worst of the riots began in Chicago in late July when a fight began between some young blacks and whites at a Lake Michigan beach. The violence went on for almost two weeks before the National Guard and the police restored order. White gangs invaded black neighborhoods to beat victims, loot stores, and burn buildings and black gangs ranged out of their ghettos into neighboring slums to do the same. When it was at last over, 15 whites had been killed and 178 injured and 23 blacks had been killed and 342 injured. In the nation's capital a mob of white soldiers, having saved the world for democracy, roamed black neighborhoods to destroy property and beat up those who resisted.

Lynching and rioting were almost altogether a lower-class phenomenon. Both white and black leaders deplored violence, and following the 1919 violence, they formed interracial commissions in both the North and the South in an effort to prevent further outbreaks. The National Association for the Advancement of Colored People undertook a campaign for the enactment of a federal law against lynching, violators of the law to be tried in federal courts. When lynchers were arrested at all, their trials in state and local courts were farces.

In 1921, in the face of strong public opinion, the House passed an antilynching law, but southern Senators filibustered it to death. Their stated reason for opposition was that a federal law on the subject would be an invasion of state rights.

Marcus Garvey

It was against this background of strife and bloodshed that millions enlisted in the first black nationalist movement to amount to anything in the United States. The leader was Marcus Garvey, a remarkable man from Jamaica who saw himself as the Moses of his people. In 1914 Garvey founded the Universal Negro Improvement Association, but when he moved to Harlem two years later his idea struck little response. He went to Europe until 1918, and when he returned his organization caught on and spread quickly. It was at its height in 1920 and 1921, although it did not die out until the mid-1920's. He claimed to have six million followers; four million was a better estimate.

Garvey was a thorough nationalist who exalted all things black and had contempt for all things white. God and Jesus Christ were black, said Garvey, and it was humiliating for blacks to worship a white God. He vigorously opposed integration, declaring that it was a scheme of the whites and that black leaders who worked for assimilation were accommodationist Uncle Toms. He proposed a kind of black Zionism. American blacks should flee to Africa and establish a black empire. To do so meant that the white rulers of Africa would have to be driven out, and he organized the Universal African Legion, the Black Eagle Flying Corps, and the Universal Black Cross Nurses complete with uniforms and officers. Transportation would be needed, and he organized the Black Star Line and purchased ships. In 1921 he proclaimed the Empire of Africa and was inaugurated as its provisional president. He tried to get the "nation's" acceptance into the League of Nations and negotiated with Liberia as a fellow-state. If these plans seemed ridiculous it was only because Garvey ultimately failed. Had he been as successful as the Zionists, his grandiose plans would have indicated great foresight.

Garvey as a political leader was an interesting phenomenon, but his tremendous reception by American blacks was even more interesting. And this was despite almost unanimous opposition from the black press, the churches, and the leaders of the racial organizations. Black intellectuals, both educators and others, were particularly outraged. But when he counterattacked, asserting that these leaders were traitors to their race and worse, hundreds of thousands of his followers believed him. Part of the explanation of the response to Garveyism lay in the techniques of the movement. The uniforms and ritual had appeal for people who led drab lives. But apparently it was an illusion of probable success that was Garvey's greatest attraction. The established black organizations had not yet achieved success with their programs. Nine years after the NAACP's foundation had come the worst wave of lynchings since the 1890's. The achievements of the black labor movement were still pathetic. Most black ministers still emphasized only salvation after death. Black educators had done a great deal to help the race to lift itself by its bootstraps, but as late as 1929 there were only about 15,000 black college graduates and only forty who held a Ph.D. The momentum of the Garvey movement made quick success seem possible.

The movement died out rather quickly, probably because it became apparent that the difficulties facing the Empire of Africa were insurmountable. Garvey's several business ventures either failed or involved him in legal tangles. The Department of Justice prosecuted him for using the mails to defraud in selling stock in the Black Star Line. Garvey foolishly conducted his own case at the trial. After a long series of legalistic holding actions, he went to prison in 1925 for a two-year term. Upon his release he was deported back to Jamaica. The Universal Negro Improvement Association collapsed. Garvey himself faded into obscurity and died in London in 1940, forgotten and broke.

The Communists Court the Blacks

Black history for the rest of the war-to-depression period offered nothing as spectacular as the immediate postwar violence and the Garvey movement. A few leaders moved into left-wing politics during the decade. A. Philip Randolph, who was later to become an outstanding and effective leader of his people, published a left-wing magazine and joined the Socialist party which was extremely weak in the 1920's.

The Communists began to make a determined effort for black support in the late 1920's, but they met with little success. Perhaps the strongest reason for Communist failure among them was suspicion that they were being used. Nor did the Communist program of "self-determination for the Negro people in the Black Belt" make much sense to American blacks. An attempt to transplant Josef Stalin's theory on the various nationalities in the Soviet Union, "self-determination" meant to establish an autonomous black republic in the most densely black area of the South. This involved a kind of supersegregation, and blacks came to call the plan "Red Crow."

Prohibition: Wets, Drys, Crime, and Politics

We have already seen in chapter five how the prohibition movement gained strength and how, by 1917, it had succeeded in banning the sale of liquor in a large part of the United States. In 1917 the Lever Act prohibited the manufacture of alcoholic beverages in order to conserve grain for food. The prohibition movement had strength and momentum, and the wartime mood with its special kind of idealism further strengthened the prohibitionist principle.

It should be noted that prohibition movements were not unique to the United States. Most of the nations of the western world in the first third of the twentieth century had at least a temperance movement, and several of them legislated prohibition. Great Britain's dry movement was strong, and it succeeded in decreasing the hours that pubs could remain open and creating a chaotic schedule of opening and closing hours that defied reason. Sweden, Norway, and Iceland imposed absolute prohibition. The Soviet Union, under quite a different rationale, outlawed liquor. Even the French, for all their professed amazement and amusement by American prohibition—"But, yes, next *les américains* will regulate the marriage bed"—had a modest temperance movement and outlawed the manufacture of absinthe.

The Eighteenth Amendment, Its Violations and Violators

On December 17, 1917, Congress passed the Eighteenth Amendment to the Constitution and submitted it to the states. "After one year from the ratification of this article, the manufacture, sale, or transportation of intoxicating liquors within, the importation thereof into, or the exportation thereof from the United States and all territory subject to the jurisdiction thereof for beverage purposes is hereby prohibited." (Congressmen in 1917 did not write as clearly as the founding fathers of 1787.) The amendment further provided that it should become inoperative if three-fourths of the state legislatures did not ratify it within seven years. Given the pitch of prohibitionist sentiment, the seven-year provision did not give wets even a sporting chance. The thirty-sixth state ratified the amendment in January, 1919. In October, 1919, Congress passed the Volstead Act over Wilson's veto. The law extended wartime prohibition until the Eighteenth Amendment went into effect the following January and defined "intoxicating liquors" as any beverage that contained as much as 0.5 per cent of alcohol by volume.

Prohibitionists were ecstatic in their victory over what they called John Barleycorn or The Demon Rum. The new Prohibition Commissioner promised that his administration would be so strict that no liquor would be manufactured "nor sold, nor given away, nor hauled in anything on the surface of the earth or under the earth or in the air." He was wrong on almost all counts, although not much was given away. Actually, it is impossible to say precisely how well—or how badly—the law was observed and enforced. It was observed best in rural areas and small towns that were overwhelmingly Protestant. But it was possible in even the driest of regions to buy a bottle if one used some ingenuity. In the rural upper South and the southern Midwest, both predominantly Protestant, it was possible in several places to leave some money on a special stump in the woods and return after a respectable interval to get the moonshine that an obliging "alky cooker" had provided. Doctors reported fewer deaths from alcoholism and police blotters recorded fewer arrests for drunkenness than before prohibition. But, obviously, the Eighteenth Amendment was the most widely disobeyed part of the Constitution—except perhaps the Fifteenth Amendment, which forbade racial discrimination in the right to vote. Paradoxically, on another level, Constitution worship was a major fetish of the decade.

Particularly in the late prohibition period, one could buy liquor and beer without difficulty. Patrolling the whole Mexican and Canadian border was impossible. Whole fleets of boats imported Canadian whiskey across the Great Lakes. Running rum from Cuba was more difficult but was commonly done. Bootleggers in many cities offered delivery service, and the saloon merely became more or less secretive and known as a speakeasy. In cities with a large foreign-born population speakeasies operated fairly openly. Strangers sometimes asked policemen for the address of the nearest one. Much of the stuff that was sold had only an alcoholic similarity to what it was labelled. Burnt sugar and iodine added to watered pure grain spirits looked similar to bourbon. Some of the concoctions were dangerous, and blindness, paralysis, and internal bleeding were their consequences. Making one's own beverages was common. Copper stills were for sale in many hardware stores, and one could buy drops or powders at drug stores which flavored the distillation however one wished—gin, rum, bourbon, or scotch. Making beer in the basement became a great indoor sport. Crocks, bottles, and bottle cappers were easily purchasable; malt companies took full-page advertisements in national magazines and sold their product through groceries. Families sometimes bought equipment cooperatively, and children hauled it about from family to family in their toy wagons.

The Bootlegger Gangsters

In the nation's big cities gangsters consolidated the bootlegging business upon the same economic principles as general business. But since they operated altogether outside the law and had no resort to conventional legal procedures for enforcing contracts, they used their own private force as a business auxiliary. In 1920 Al Capone, a New York hoodlum, moved to Chicago and began a bootlegging business. He became the most important of the Chicago beer barons who divided the market amongst themselves. By 1927 Capone had a $60 million business with a private army of nearly one thousand gangster troops to protect the market and raid other territories. Bootlegger gangsters thoroughly corrupted the administration of Republican Mayor William H. Thompson. In 1926 and 1927 there were 130 gang killings in Chicago; not a single one of the murderers was caught and brought to trial. A group of Sicilian brothers, the six Terrible Gennas, sought to underprice their competitors and engaged the services of five police captains and four hundred policemen. Their corruption of the police, however, was not enough to save three of the brothers from being killed in typical gang fashion. Dutch Schultz's organization in New York collected protection money from speakeasy operators and had an alliance with Tammany Hall and the Democratic Jimmie Walker administration. Bootleggers of Philadelphia, long a center of commercial propriety, organized their own court system with a "judge" who held bootlegger court, complete with attorneys and precedent, and whose decisions were enforced by thugs. Prohibition has sometimes been blamed for indirectly creating this kind of organized crime, but the allegation is unfair. Organized crime existed before prohibition and after repeal; it only moved into the liquor business during prohibition because of the fat profits to be made. And if organized crime flouted the law more openly and successfully during prohibition than at other times it was because of the venality of public officials and lack of moral indignation in the public at large.

Waning Support of Prohibition

Popular support for prohibition was at its greatest in 1918 and early 1919 when the amendment was before the states and when wartime faith in the millennium was high. Its popularity waned steadily thereafter. A poll of almost two million people in 1926 indicated that less than one-fifth supported the Volstead Act completely, almost one-third were for outright repeal ("wringing wets" in the parlance of the day), and half wanted the law modified to permit light wines and beer. Yet prohibition of all liquor remained for another seven years. Why? Basically, because the prohibition question had become involved in partisan politics and a number of other social conflicts, between city and country, Catholic and Protestant, black and white. Thousands of people who regularly used bootleggers' services and grumbled about the poor quality and high price of their purchases voted for candidates who were politically dry—and sometimes also personally wet. The most outspoken opponents of prohibition, both before its adoption and after, were immigrants and those of recent immigrant background. Among Germans, beer at meals was as routine as salt; among Italians, wine was the table beverage. These immigrants, for the most part, lived in industrial cities of the North and West.

Many middle-class persons privately violated prohibition but approved of it as a means to keep liquor away from the working class, either out of compassion for working-class wives and children whose breadwinner might drink away his wages or from vague fear that liquor might unleash class violence. Again, the industrial working class lived mostly in the northern cities. Because the Republican party's main strength was rural or small town and urban middle-class, that organization remained steadfastly for prohibition until the bitter end. The Democratic party divided badly over prohibition. The urban parts of the party were wet, from slightly damp to wringing wet. The western rural Democrats usually agreed with their Republican neighbors on the issue. The South remained firmly dry, not because the term "bourbon" for a southern Democrat did not have a logical linguistic basis, but because white supremacists wanted to keep liquor from blacks. A drunken black was less likely to be docile than a sober one. As the comedian Will Rogers, a man who made many shrewd political observations, said, "Mississippi will vote dry and drink wet as long as it can stagger to the polls." The Democratic party compromised in 1924 and did not put repeal into its platform, but in both 1928 and 1932 its platform advocated the end of prohibition. In both 1928 and 1932 differences between wets and drys played such an important part in the campaigns that more important issues were obscured and submerged, although prohibition was by no means the only issue in the campaign. John Dewey exaggerated only a little when he wrote after the national conventions of 1932, "Here we are in the greatest crisis since the Civil War, and the only thing the two national parties seem to want to debate is booze."

Ironically, prohibition faded quickly while Hoover, who called it a "noble experiment," was in the White House. Soon after he took office, he appointed a commission headed by former Attorney General George W. Wickersham to investigate prohibition's enforcement and to make recommendations. Testimony given to the commission indicated that enforcing a widely unpopular law was next to impossible short of police-state measures. The Commission, however, refused in its 1931 report to recommend repeal. It instead offered several suggestions to make federal enforcement more efficient. But enforcement was already deteriorating quickly. Three states, New York, Maryland, and Wisconsin, had already repealed their "baby Volsted Acts" and ceased state enforcement. Other states practically abandoned enforcement as the depression cut into state government revenues seriously. After the electorate overwhelmingly elected a Democrat on a repeal platform in 1932, the end was in sight. On February 20, 1933, a lame-duck Congress passed the Twenty-first Amendment, which repealed the Eighteenth. A new Congress made the manufacture and sale of weak beer legal the next month, and the thirty-sixth state ratified the repealing amendment on December 5, 1933. Prohibition on a national scale was finished.

Manners and Morals

Many writers have concluded that standards of behavior changed so radically during the 1920's that the change amounted to a "revolution in morals." They point out that older people whose standards had been formed in a more sedate society expressed considerable dismay about "flaming youth" and "flappers." The automobile, they suggest, offered young people greater freedom from social supervision than they were once allowed. Rudolph Valentino, a rather oily film star who played great-lover roles in desert "sand and sex" pictures, was the most popular male Hollywood figure of his day, and thousands of women rioted at his funeral in 1926. These writers often assert that popular songs of the day indicated drunkenness and passion—"Show Me the Way To Go Home," "Makin' Whoopee," "Hot Lips," and "Hot Mama."

That there were significant changes in manners is clear, but it is not at all clear that society in the 1920's underwent a "revolution" in sexual morality. Each generation from time immemorial has regarded the next one as more degenerate than itself. Statistics on sexual matters are elusive at best. The questionnaire studies of Dr. Alfred Kinsey of Indiana University done a generation later indicated, for what they were worth, that women who matured in the 1920's had only a slightly higher incidence of premarital and extramarital sexual relations than those who matured in an earlier day. In general, it seems that the "revolution in morals" has been grossly overstated and overemphasized, but the whole truth is impossible to discover.

Obviously, there was less prudery in the most commonly accepted code of manners and dress after the war than there had been previously. Where mother would never have said the word sex, at least in mixed company, and might even have referred to the legs of a table as its limbs, daughter tossed around Freudian terms as if she understood them. Women's figures were far less concealed. Dresses at the end of the war were fully cut tentlike garments that extended to the ankles. Stockings were dark, petticoats numerous, and corsets forbiddingly hard. By the late 1920's skirts came to slightly above the knees, stockings were flesh colored, and corsets were reserved for dowagers. Certainly there was less prudery in the subject matter and language of fiction, although it was fairly tame in comparison with what was to come after World War II. But what, if anything, the new code signified about personal morals is moot.

When one makes class and urban-rural distinctions and considers feminism as a relevant factor, the thesis of a "revolution in morals" seems even less justifiable. The main changes in behavior were most pronounced in the urban middle class. Except for women's fashions, rural and small-town life had little of the jazzy flapper age. The ways of working-class youth, male and female, changed less than their wealthier neighbors. Prudery had never been as strong among immigrant working people as it was in more comfortable circles with rural and Protestant backgrounds. The way older critics referred to the behavior of "flaming youth" as "common" suggested an impression of blurred class mores. Much of the change in manners can be explained in terms of feminism, the gradual adoption of a single standard of conduct by middle-class urban girls. If society was not shocked by the young men's drinking, smoking cigarettes, and general lack of parental control, feminist young women figured they too should have a similar freedom.

Indeed, the fashions and ideal feminine types of the 1920's suggest that feminine equality rather than sex was the main factor in changing manners. The flapper costume was anything but sexy, with its sackish lack of waistline, a roll of stocking just below the knees, and hat that looked like a too large Viking helmet. Women looked like dressed-up little girls, or even little boys, especially when they wore their hair bobbed. Florenz Ziegfeld chose flat-chested girls for the nudes in his famous Follies, a fact the Freudians of the age could have speculated upon gaily. Nor were the famous dances of the period erotic in any sense. The Charleston and the Black Bottom were boisterous but hardly bawdy. Only one thing is certain: sex was more freely discussed in the 1920's than it had been before the war.

Rural and small-town people resisted the new folkways more than their more hedonistic city cousins. Rural people did not enjoy as much prosperity or as much leisure. When rural youths revolted, they were likely to move to the city and thus be less subversive of traditions in their home communities than city young people were to theirs. The automobile and better roads, to be sure, changed rural life, but lack of money, the necessity of hard work and long hours, the family, and the church braked the speed of rural social change. The city changed rapidly, the country changed slowly, and the differences in their ways of life broadened.

"One Hundred Percentism"

Rural America and urban America had one important social-political trait in common during the 1920's: extreme nationalism, "one hundred per cent Americanism." Twenty years of Theodore Roosevelt on the national scene and the forced-draft patriotism of the war had had their effects. Nationalism has two aspects: externally, a strident chip-on-the-shoulder attitude toward other nations and other peoples of the world; internally, a glorification of national institutions, superpatriotism, lack of tolerance, and efforts to bring about conformist unanimity. During the 1920's the government itself pursued economically nationalist policies, and the electorate displayed a generally hostile attitude toward the rest of the world. But "internal nationalism" was even stronger.

Nationalism in the cities differed in its emphases from that of the country, but each was nationalistic. Perhaps William Hale Thompson, mayor of Chicago in the 1920's, got more political mileage from a nationalistic stance than any other urban figure. By any standard Thompson's administration was disgraceful. The Chicago schools suffered badly from lack of funds and political interference. Its officials' alliances with bootlegger gangsters made it the most lawless large city in the United States. Chicago acquired a deserved reputation abroad for corruption and violence which has not entirely dissipated yet. But despite the gross inadequacies of his administration, Thompson's political opponents were ineffective because the mayor's political organization was good and his flamboyant nationalism was popular. He led a campaign to remove "pro-English" history textbooks from the schools.

He gained international notice when he offered to "punch King George on the snoot." Such statements, designed especially for the Irish vote, had a much wider appeal. Patriot organizations such as the Daughters of the American Revolution and the American Legion were as popular and as powerful in all but the biggest cities as they were in small towns. City dwellers, perhaps more than people in the country, had great praise for the Italian dictator Benito Mussolini, primarily because of his extreme nationalism, his anticommunist policies, and the supposed efficiency of his government. Not until the 1930's was Mussolini's fascism regarded as a menace by most American publications. The historical novelist Kenneth Roberts wrote a highly laudatory series on Italian fascism for the *Saturday Evening Post,* and the American Legion invited Mussolini to address its 1923 convention at San Francisco. (Mussolini declined.)

Racism

Both rural and urban nationalism contained a great deal of racism, but anti-Semitism was clearly stronger in the cities, where most Jews lived, than on the farms and in small towns. The American Farm Bureau Federation, as a case in point, appointed a Jew, Aaron Sapiro, as its general counsel in 1923. The most important sources of anti-Semitism in America were upper-middle-class Yankees and Polish and Irish immigrants; most of them were urban. The amount and intensity of racism in general but of anti-Semitism in particular that came forth in the arguments for immigration restriction was similar to what would soon be revealed in Germany. Madison Grant, author of the popular and virulently racist *The Passing of the Great Race* (1916), wrote, "The man of the old stock . . . is to-day being literally driven off the streets of New York City by the swarms of Polish Jews." Kenneth Roberts referred to East European Jews as "human parasites." Henry Ford published the anti-Semitic *Dearborn* (Michigan) *Independent* and had his dealers put copies of it in their new cars. Among other hate pieces, the *Independent* published a famous forgery, "The Protocols of the Elders of Zion," an alleged plan for Jewish conquest of the world.

The Klan

The Ku Klux Klan, most important hate organization of the decade, however, was overwhelmingly rural. During Reconstruction the Klan had come into being as a means to terrorize newly freed slaves. In 1915 a romantic history teacher at Lanier College, William J. Simmons, a man who worshipped at the shrine of the "lost cause," founded a new Ku Klux Klan. Simmons' purpose apparently was more to glorify the memory of past white supremacists than to preach hate, but he built more than he knew. It was Simmons who gave the organization its fantastic terminology. Simmons gave himself the title of Imperial Wizard. Local units were called Klaverns and other terms began with the letter K. Under Simmons the KKK was only an unimportant lodge, however. In 1920 it had only about 5,000 members, most of them in Georgia and Alabama. Then two professional fund-raisers, Mrs. Elizabeth Tyler and Edward Y. Clarke, took hold of the lodge, raised its initiation fee to $10, and began to high-pressure its growth. In two years it had grown to 100,000 members. At this point a Texas dentist, Hiram Wesley Evans, became Imperial Wizard and changed the nature of the Klan. It went into politics and quickly demonstrated its strength. A Klan-supported politician in Texas defeated the incumbent in the 1922 Democratic primary. The following year, when the governor of Oklahoma, J. C. "Our Jack" Walton, opposed the Klan and declared martial law in an effort to suppress it, the Klan was active in bringing about his successful impeachment.

The Klan was different things in different parts of the country. In the South it was primarily anti-black; in the Midwest and Far West it was primarily anti-Catholic; in the East, although it was never very strong east of Pennsylvania, it was primarily anti-Semitic. Everywhere it opposed the immigrant and immigration as a national policy, persecuted bootleggers and preached the dry gospel, railed against divorce, and tried to enforce monogamy. In general, it upheld what rural, old-fashioned, white, Anglo-Saxon Protestants held to be "the American way of life." Everywhere its strength was its conspiratorial secrecy (members wore white masked hoods and gowns at meetings and were supposed never to reveal membership), its working as a bloc in politics, and its terror devices. Klansmen several times beat people horribly and killed upon a few occasions. Usually it found it necessary only to burn a cross conspicuously or conduct a masked parade to intimidate its victims.

Politically, the Klan was bipartisan. In Oregon it moved into the Democratic party, elected a Democratic governor by a huge plurality, and in a state initiative brought passage of a law designed to abolish parochial schools by requiring that all school-age children attend public schools. In 1925 in *Pierce* v. *Society of Sisters,* the Supreme Court found the Oregon law unconstitutional. In Indiana the Klan was primarily Republican, but it had strength in the Democratic party as well.

The Klan reached its heights and started its downfall in Indiana. Both its rise and its decline there were due to the extraordinary activities of D. C. Stephenson, leader of the Klan in the entire Midwest. Through rallies that were masterpieces of showmanship—Stephenson liked to arrive at rallies by airplane—and appeals to dark and latent prejudices easily exploited because of the rapid changes that were occurring in the half-urban and half-rural state, Stephenson built an Indiana organization of an estimated 350,000 members. In small towns practically all men of social consequence were members, and they became so bold they frequently marched with their white hoods thrown back. In 1923 and 1924 the Indiana Klan got control of the state legislature, both the United States Senators, and most of the congressional delegation. In the 1924 elections Stephenson had his friend Ed Jackson elected governor on the Republican ticket. But late in 1925 the Klan, at its height with an estimated national membership of 5,000,000, began to crumble.

One night in the summer of 1925 at a party in Indianapolis, Stephenson picked up a twenty-eight-year-old Sunday school teacher who worked as a secretary at the state house, plied her with bootleg liquor, got her on a Pullman bound for Chicago, and assaulted her. Humiliated, the girl took poison and became extremely ill. Stephenson and Klansmen friends got her off the train before it crossed the Illinois line—thus avoiding a federal offense—and got her to a hotel without undue notice. For several days they denied her medical aid for fear of discovery. A month later she died. Many Indiana politicians who had joined the Klan and cooperated with it only to save their political lives saw the chance to get off the Klan's hook. They saw to it that Stephenson was prosecuted for his crime, and in November, 1925, a jury found him guilty of manslaughter. The most powerful figure in the Klan had been found guilty of a sordid crime that violated the organization's principles, and he was lodged in the state prison of what had been the Klan's strongest state. Thereafter the KKK fell apart quickly, holding on longest in the South.

The Ku Klux Klan was the strongest terroristic, essentially fascistic, organization in the nation's history. Fascist organizations of the next decade never began to approach its strength, largely because they imported their unpopular ideas and methods whereas the Klan was entirely home-grown. Not all rural states succumbed to Klan rule, at least partly because state political leaders and newspaper editors fought it and exposed it for what it was. Although cooperating with the Klan might prevent political suicide, many Indiana politicians learned that going along with it could also mean political death. Speaking out on one's convictions proved not only the most honorable but the most expedient alternative in the long run.

The Election of 1928: The Tension's Climax

In the summer of 1927 President Coolidge issued a puzzling statement to the press: "I do not choose to run for President in 1928." Did he mean he would not run under any circumstances, would reluctantly accept a draft, or would look favorably upon a draft? He did not encourage the draft-Coolidge movement that developed, and the movement lost steam. Democrats and progressive Republicans in the Senate passed a resolution which stated it would be "unwise" and "unpatriotic" to depart from the two-term tradition. The poker-faced Coolidge may have been disappointed by the absence of a draft, but he later stated in his autobiography that he declined to seek the nomination because of the two-term tradition.

The Conventions' Choices

Although Senator Borah, former governor of Illinois Frank O. Lowden, and Vice-President Charles G. Dawes were talked of as Republican candidates, Herbert Hoover was the politically proper and logical man for the nomination. Popular with the country at large and seemingly "above" politics, Hoover was the symbol of prosperous Republicanism, of the businessman in government. The Kansas City convention nominated him on the first ballot and named Charles Curtis of Kansas, Republican majority leader in the Senate, as his running mate. The GOP platform pledged "vigorous enforcement" of the Eighteenth Amendment, praised the accomplishments of the Coolidge administrations, and promised action on the farm problem.

Several men contended for the Democratic nomination, but Governor Alfred E. Smith of New York, who had come close to nomination in 1924, was not to be denied. He not only had the delegates from Tammany Hall behind him at the Houston, Texas, convention (many of the New Yorkers pronounced the city

141

"Howston," the proper pronunciation of Houston Street in lower Manhattan), but those from practically all the states with big cities in them. He received the nomination on the first ballot. His nomination, however, did not sit well with the southern delegates because he was a wet, a Roman Catholic, and a New Yorker. To placate the southern delegates, Senator Joseph T. Robinson of Arkansas received the vice-presidential nomination, and the platform promised "an honest effort" to enforce prohibition. Smith said as president he would enforce the Eighteenth Amendment but that he would also work for the amendment's repeal. Using Dixie arguments, he declared prohibition was a matter for the states to decide. The Democratic platform differed little from the Republican. It urged enactment of a law prohibiting injunctions in labor disputes and was for public control of hydroelectric power, but it approved tariff protection and criticized the Republican party only for its lack of an agricultural program without out- lining one of its own.

Al Smith, 1928 Campaign Issue

The main issue of the campaign became the background and personality of the Democratic candidate. Smith was born in 1873 in a tenement in New York's lower east side, the son of Irish immigrant parents. When he was seven years old he became an altar boy at the parish church. At fifteen he had to quit school to help support the family, and at nineteen he went to work as a salesman and bookkeeper at the Fulton Street Fish Market. When he was old enough to vote he joined the local Tammany organization, a natural thing for any ambitious Irish boy from his neighborhood to do. Soon he was rewarded with an appointment as a process server, a routine task he performed for eight years. In 1903 he was elected to the state assembly. There his competence soon attracted attention; he was generally regarded as the best-informed man in the state on legislative mat- ters. In 1918 he was elected governor, but he was defeated in the Republican landslide in 1920. He won again in 1922, as he did also in 1924 and 1926. No previous New York governor had been elected four times. As legislator and gov- ernor, Smith was fair, efficient, and mildly progressive. He managed the bills that came from Hughes's investigation of life insurance companies, investigated the Triangle Shirtwaist Factory fire, and defended the assemblymen who had been elected in 1920 on the Socialist ticket. He was by no means a radical; he never went beyond the public opinion of his urban constituents.

In one way Al Smith was the personification of the American dream—the poor boy who rose above humble origins to a position of responsibility and acclaim. But the American dream route in politics had a rural setting, from a log cabin and one-room school to the courthouse and eventually the White House, not from a tenement and a fish market. And, very important, no Roman Catholic had ever before run for president on a major-party ticket.

Smith had to face powerful odds against him in 1928. Republican politicians basked in the decade's prosperity, and Smith could only promise that as president he would do nothing to upset the business cycle. He appointed John J. Raskob as his campaign manager. Raskob had been a Republican, had voted for Coolidge in 1924, had been a top official of General Motors, and had listed his occupation in

Who's Who in America as "capitalist." He was prominent in Roman Catholic lay organizations. Raskob's appointment and the generally conservative platform were attempts to leave the impression that Smith was "safe." On the other hand, Smith tried to capitalize upon what discontent there was with the GOP's record. He attempted to attract urban votes with his stand on prohibition, liberals with his speeches on electric power (for which he gained the endorsement of Senator Norris), and farmers with his support of McNary-Haugenism. Hoover, on the other hand, campaigned as a bone-dry and condemned government power projects and the McNary-Haugen bills as dangerous deviations from "rugged individualism" which would lead to a slave state. Hoover did not need to campaign hard. All that was necessary was to identify himself with prosperity and respectability. Hoover won easily with 444 electoral votes and 21,392,190 popular votes. Smith received only 87 electoral and 15,016,443 popular votes. Republicans won majorities in each house of Congress.

1928 Presidential Election Postmortem

After the election it was commonly said that Smith had lost the election because he was a Roman Catholic. How accurate was the assertion? Smith's religion, obviously, was a prominent feature of the campaign. A year before his nomination he had been asked by the editor of *The Atlantic Monthly* to write an article on the implications of a Catholic president. A Methodist bishop, James Cannon, Jr., of Virginia, mobilized Protestant opinion in the South against Smith. Thousands of scurrilous pamphlets and leaflets full of forebodings about the influence of the Pope in Washington if Smith should be elected were passed hand to hand and mailed anonymously. Responsible Republican officials did not circulate hate literature, but they did not actively try to prevent its circulation. An examination of a collection of such pamphlets in the Columbia University library —the so-called Book of Horrors—shows that the 1928 anti-Catholic literature repeated the same old discredited stories that had circulated as far back as the 1830's. It must be remembered that the Ku Klux Klan was not long dead. That it had faded in influence was apparent in the fact that a major party had nominated a Roman Catholic for president, but most of its members presumably did not discard their prejudices along with their white hoods.

Yet, did rural Protestant opposition to Smith exist because he was Catholic or because he was a symbol of an urban immigrant? Smith was almost the stereotype of the Irish urban politician. He wore a brown derby hat, gave campaign speeches to his "friends of the 'raddio' audience," and made his theme song "The Sidewalks of New York." His wet campaign intensified his rural opposition. Bishop Cannon said the issue of the campaign was "Shall Dry America elect a 'cocktail President?'" Whether Smith's opposition to prohibition provided religious bigots with a mask for prejudice or whether it only intensified their opposition to Smith cannot be determined, but obviously Smith's lower-class New York speech and mannerisms were inextricably entwined with rural Protestant opposition to him. Urban-rural division embraced the Catholic, prohibition, and immigrant issues. But it is doubtful if the Democrats could have won in 1928 with a Protestant candidate who was a combination Abraham Lincoln and Davy

Crockett. Smith undoubtedly suffered worse defeat than a Protestant, rural, and dry candidate would have—such a candidate would have carried the traditionally Democratic South—but prosperity gave Hoover a tremendous advantage.

An analysis of the election returns reveals that Smith polled a better vote in northern and eastern cities than had any Democratic presidential candidate in modern times. In 1924 Coolidge had beaten Davis by 1,300,000 votes in the nation's twelve largest cities; in 1928 Smith led slightly in these same cities. Democratic success in northern cities was a new phenomenon. Wilson in 1916, Cox, and Davis had been unable to carry the big urban counties of the North, but Smith's success in these counties was to build a new strength for the Democrats which in the 1930's and later was to be an important force. In the South the rural-urban division was the reverse. Hoover ran better in southern cities than in southern rural regions, with the exception of traditionally Republican areas of Appalachia. Given their gains in industrial cities and the depression that was soon to settle over America like a life-killing fog, the Democrats could take solace in the election results.

PART III

THE GREAT DEPRESSION
1929–1941

The Great Crash and the Hoover Administration

The sole function of government is to bring about a condition of affairs favorable to the beneficial development of private enterprise.

HERBERT HOOVER, 1931

Chapter Eight

Few presidents ever assumed office under such happy conditions as did Herbert Clark Hoover on March 4, 1929. There were no serious crises in the nation's foreign relations and none seemed to be on the horizon. At home the American people were enjoying unprecedented prosperity. Business was good. Industry was thriving. The skies over the cities were dark with the smoke of industrial prosperity. So confident of America's economic future were those who played the stock market that the price of speculative stocks went ever higher.

Not all Americans shared in the general prosperity, however. Agriculture generally had been depressed for most of a decade. There were a few sick industries, notably coal and textiles. Nebraska farmers or western Indiana coal miners and the retail businessmen dependent upon their trade could not agree with the dominant view that all was right with the world and that conditions would become even better. But these dissenters were a distinct minority. The United States dripped with optimism.

The figure of the new President himself evoked optimism and confidence. Hoover, born in a Quaker community in eastern Iowa in 1874, had been in the public eye for years. After graduating from Stanford University he had been a successful mining engineer and investor, making a fortune in foreign mining enterprises. He had first come to national attention early in the European war as director of Belgian relief and then as food administrator under Wilson after the United States entered the fighting. As Secretary of Commerce under Harding and Coolidge he had fostered the growth of trade associations and sought to increase sales of American products overseas. He seemed to be the epitome of the successful businessman-engineer in public office, an efficient but humane spokesman and symbol of the New Era. Even his appearance suggested prudence, solidity, stability. He wore high stiff collars years after most men had adopted less formal but more comfortable neckwear.

The Hoover who left the White House four years later was the same man. But by that time, the happy conditions which had surrounded his inauguration had disappeared and he had become an object of ridicule, scorn, and even hatred. There was a great deal of bitter irony in the situation. During the election campaign in 1928, Hoover had said that if the Republican policies of the preceding two administrations could only be continued, "we shall soon, with the help of God, be in sight of the day when poverty will be banished from this nation." There had been campaign talk of two chickens in every pot and two cars in every garage. But in 1932 and 1933 the shack towns which sprang up on the fringes of industrial cities were bitterly known as "Hoovervilles," and the newspapers under which homeless men slept on park benches were called "Hoover blankets."

The Wall Street Crash

When Hoover took office, the biggest stock market boom in the history of the United States was almost five years old. The boom got under way in the last half of 1924. The market skidded in early 1926 but recovered by the end of the year. The big bull market began in earnest in 1927 and soon got out of hand. The *Times* industrial index stood at 245 at the end of 1927 and at 331 at the end of 1928. In 1928 Radio Corporation of America rose from 85 to 420. The year 1929 saw an even wilder speculative market. By early September, the *Times* industrials had climbed to 452, an increase of about 85 per cent in twenty months. Radio reached a high of 505 on September 3; that is to say, if a person invested in Radio on January 1, 1928, and sold on September 3, 1929, he would have increased his capital by about 530 per cent.

Buying stocks on margin facilitated speculation. The market player who did not want to pay cash for the full amount of what he wanted to buy could put up margin, or a down payment, and borrow the balance from his broker, using the purchased stocks as collateral. The brokers, in turn, received the money from the so-called call money market, money provided mostly by bankers. The call market was a lucrative and safe investment. The interest rate was as high as 12 per cent, and the loan was relatively safe because the lender had only to demand more margin from the borrower if the value of the stocks used as collateral should fall. So advantageous were call money investments that money from all over the world poured into Wall Street, thereby stimulating margin buying and speculation. A few manufacturing corporations even invested in this fashion. In 1929 Standard Oil of New Jersey poured money into the call money market at an average of $69 million a day, thus lubricating stock speculation as well as automobiles.

The total of such brokers' loans is a rough indication of the volume of speculative stock buying. In 1926 brokers' loans amounted to about $2.5 billion. Just before the crash they totaled $6.63 billion, evidencing a very large—and, as it turned out, unhealthy—amount of speculation. Yet margin requirements were 45 and 50 per cent in 1929, which is not unusually low. Had the margin requirement been lower, we may assume the market would have been even wilder; but if the margin requirement had been as high as 75 per cent, it is not likely that the speculative bubble would have become so inflated.

The stock market began to behave erratically in September, 1929. But after each break in the market there was a recovery. Then on October 24—Black Thursday—came the beginning of the end. A few hours after the market opened there was a panic to sell and get out of danger. As more speculators wanted to sell rather than buy, the prices of stocks, of course, fell even lower. For some stocks there were no purchasers to be found at all, a phenomenon which, in its own way, indicated a crisis in financial capitalism. So many shares of stock traded hands—a new record of 12,894,650 during the day—that the ticker was hours behind the actual situation on the floor of the Exchange where the scene was one of panic and confusion.

At 1:00 p.m. on Black Thursday representatives of four big New York banks met in the office of Thomas W. Lamont of the J. P. Morgan firm. The bankers agreed to pool some of their resources, go into the market and buy, and thereby indicate to the panic-stricken speculators that they, the pillars of the financial community, were not alarmed. Lamont, in a model of understatement, told reporters after the meeting, "There has been a little distress selling on the Stock Exchange." At 1:30 Richard Whitney, vice-president of the Exchange and floor operator for the Morgan firm, jauntily walked to the post where United States Steel was traded, and ostentatiously placed an order for ten thousand shares at 205. The highest bid at that moment was 193½. The effect was electric. Whitney's action was taken to mean that the bankers had moved in to peg the market, that the bankers would not allow the market to hit rock bottom. The market became firmer and many issues made strong recoveries before the end of trading. The Times industrials came back enough so that there was only a twelve point loss for the day. On Friday and Saturday, trading was heavy but prices were steady. Asked for a comment on the economy, President Hoover said that "the fundamental business of the country, that is production and distribution of commodities, is on a sound and prosperous basis."

On these two fairly steady days the bankers who had shored up the market on Black Thursday quietly sold some of their recently acquired shares. When the market dropped precipitously again on Monday and Tuesday the twenty-eighth and twenty-ninth, no group of bankers again brought confidence with ostentatious buying. The prices went on down, down, down, and sometimes there were no purchasers at any price. The Times industrials fell ninety-two points in two days.

Thereafter, although there were occasional days when the market gained, the course was downward. Important business and political leaders issued statements on the soundness of the economy designed to be reassuring, but their incantations were without economic effect. (They were in time to have political effect: their statements were quoted against them later.) By mid-November, the stocks listed on the Stock Exchange had shrunk in their market value over 40 per cent, and prices continued to go down. A brief summary of stock prices indicates the extent of the wreckage. All the following prices were from the Dow-Jones index, in September, 1929, and January, 1933: thirty industrials dropped from $364.90 to $62.70, twenty public utilities fell from $141.90 to $28, twenty railroads declined from $182 to $28.10.

The New Era on Wall Street had been short lived.

The Course of the Economy, 1929–1933

Had the whole economy, apart from the stock market, been as sound as Hoover thought it was (in November, 1929, he said, "Any lack of confidence in the

economic future or the basic strength of business in the United States is foolish")
it is possible that the Wall Street catastrophe would not have seriously affected
most Americans. But the economy was not sound. There were several indications
before the market crash that there was economic difficulty ahead. The rate of increase of consumer spending slipped badly in 1929, well before the crash. Residential construction in 1929 lagged behind, off about $1 billion from 1928.
Business inventories increased from about $500 million in 1928 to about $1
billion in 1929. By mid-century such conditions as these would be red danger
flags, crying for some kind of remedial action. But in 1929 so optimistic was the
administration and so thoroughly ingrained was the laissez-faire ideology demanding a minimum of governmental "interference" in business that the administration
did not act.

One of the important ways in which the stock market crash widened out
into a general depression was through bank failures. Banks had many of their
assets in stocks which shrank in value after the crash. Furthermore, they held
devalued stock as collateral on loans. Many small banks in depressed areas had
failed in the 1920's, but after the crash bank failures became more frequent. In
the twelve months following July 1, 1929, 640 banks closed. The figure rose to
1,553 in the next year, and over $1 billion in deposits became inaccessible. In
the first ten months of 1932, 1,199 banks suspended operations.

Bank failures and the stock market crash reduced the total of purchasing
power and shattered economic optimism. The outlook for the economic future
being dark, people with capital were hesitant to invest in new or expanded ventures. And because there was less purchasing power to buy goods, manufacturers
decreased production to match the decreased effective demand. A cut in production involved putting labor on a shorter work week or laying off employees,
or both. Thus, a cut in production further reduced the total of purchasing power, which further brought a decrease in production, and so on, down and around
the vicious circle. The depression tended to snowball; the adjustments of business
to depressed conditions brought even worse conditions.

Any series of economic indices for the years 1929–1933 tell a dreary tale.
The New York *Times* "Weekly Index of Business Activity" reached its peak of
114.8 in late June, 1929, months before the crash. The index went down fairly
steadily until it reached its low of 63.7 in mid-March, 1933, the month that
Franklin D. Roosevelt became President. There was one slight gain during this
period. This index climbed—if that is the word—from 66.2 in early August, 1932,
to 73.8 in early January, 1933. Hoover and his defenders interpreted this slight
gain as self-justification, arguing that the economy was in the process of righting
itself when Roosevelt's election ruined everything by causing the business community to be fearful of the new administration's economic policies. The argument
cannot be proved or disproved, but it did not persuade many voters at the time or
many economists since then.

Other statistics tell a similar story. Gross national product (GNP, the total
of goods and services produced) fell from $104.4 billion, or $857 per capita, in
1929 to $74.2 billion, $590 per capita, in 1933. This was less GNP per capita than
there had been for the five years 1907 through 1911. (The above figures are all
in terms of 1929 dollars.) The total income from labor dropped from $51.1 billion
to $29.5 billion, while the total paid to salaried employees fell 40 per cent.

Business failures in 1932 were almost one-third more numerous than in 1929. Exports and imports declined by more than two-thirds. Farm prices, which were not good even in 1929, fell 61 per cent in those terrible four years. Total farm income fell from about $13 billion in 1929 to $5.5 billion in 1932. Dividends declined 57 per cent, but interest paid on long-term debts declined only 3.3 per cent.

The economic statistics most important in human terms were those on unemployment. The following figures are those issued by the Bureau of Labor Statistics of the Department of Labor, but they were not universally accepted. In 1929 there were 1,499,000 unemployed persons, constituting 3.1 per cent of the total civilian labor force. These figures rose in 1930 to 4,248,000 and 8.8 per cent, in 1931 to 7,911,000 and 16.1 per cent, and in 1932 to 11,901,000 and 24.0 per cent. The low came in 1933 when, according to BLS figures, there were 12,634,000 unemployed, constituting slightly over one-fourth of the labor force.

But other statisticians, using other definitions of employed and unemployed

THE STOCK MARKET, 1929–1936

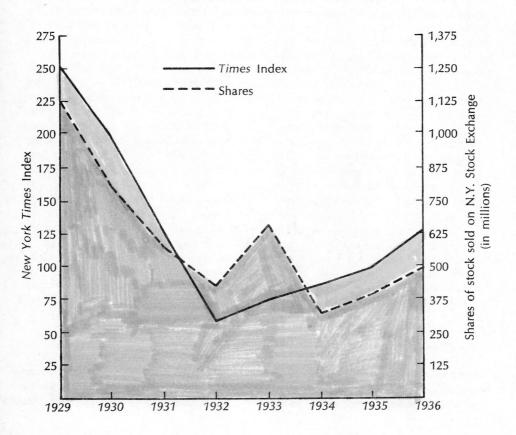

and other techniques, differed with the BLS mathematicians. The American Federation of Labor estimated there were 13,271,000 unemployed in 1933, the generally pro-business National Industrial Conference Board put the figure at 11,-842,000, and the Communist Labor Research Association claimed 16,138,000. We shall never know which, if any, of these estimates was accurate. Furthermore, even if we knew the total for certain, we would not know the answer to such pertinent questions as how many people were unemployed at one time or another during the Great Depression, how many people went how long without work, and how many people who were employed were working at occupations well below their capacity. We shall never know, for example, how many physicists were employed as dishwashers or how many teachers were selling encyclopedias—or trying to sell them.

The work of statisticians is extremely useful, but statistics cannot tell us how much pain and suffering there was in the nation as a direct result of the Great Depression. How much it hurt to be hungry, how much distress there was among parents who could not afford to clothe their children decently, how many personalities and bodies were warped as a result of poverty, and how much they were warped are questions beyond the ken of the statisticians. No one knows the answers to them.

But even a quick look through the newspapers of the early 1930's reveals some idea of the dimensions of misery resulting from the depression. Two stories from the New York *Times* in early 1932 bear repeating. An interview with the director of the nursing bureau of the New York City Department of Health summed up some of the observations of nurses who visited homes in the nation's largest and richest city. The nurses reported that due to doubling up to save rent, it was not at all unusual to find twelve or thirteen relatives living in a three-room apartment. They found that children who attended schools with free lunch programs were better fed than children not in such happy circumstances and that schools that served lunch had a lower absentee rate than those that did not. A quick survey of newspapers also reveals that it was not only unskilled workers and their families who were suffering. The *Times* of May 4, 1932, told the story of a forty-four-year-old unemployed civil engineer who in 1929 had earned $450 a month but who three years later was arrested for vagrancy when found sleeping in a Brooklyn vacant lot. For forty-six days the engineer had made the lot his home, living on handouts of food from neighboring housewives and children. A graduate of the University of Colorado with twenty years' experience in his profession, he had been unsuccessful in finding work of any kind.

Multiple stories such as these by thousands and the magnitude of the Great Depression will be seen. How large exactly was the mountain of misery we shall never know. We know only that the Great Depression was the greatest economic calamity in the history of the American people.

Why the Great Depression?

Why this economic desolation and decay had come about was a question that perplexed millions. Certain matters were obvious. The potential of a decent living for all still existed. The natural resources of the nation had not disappeared. The machinery for converting those resources to usable goods was unimpaired. The manpower and the brainpower to operate the machinery still existed. And the need for economic goods certainly existed. College students of the present generation often find it difficult to appreciate fully how badly people in the 1930's needed such basic goods as shoes, sweaters, and food. The resources, the means of production, and the need were there. Yet there was stagnation.

President Hoover interpreted the nation's economic difficulties as being only part of a world depression. The United States had been dragged down by the economic failure of Europe. The beauty of this interpretation for the Hoover administration was that it shifted responsibility for hard times away from Washington and from the American business civilization. Certainly there was a relationship between the American depression and the depressed economy of the western world, but one could have argued as well that the American experience dragged down Europe. Other conservatives argued that the stock market crash had caused the general depression and that the decision of the Federal Reserve Board in August, 1929, to raise the discount rate (the interest rate charged member banks for their loans from the Federal Reserve Banks) had caused the stock market crash. In other words, these people argued, governmental bungling had caused the depression, bungling in an area where, they felt, government should not have operated at all. At the other end of the political spectrum were the Marxists, who argued that such calamities as the Great Depression were an inherent and unavoidable feature of a capitalist economy.

There can be no certainty about the causes of the Great Depression, but most economists think along the following lines. They assume, first of all, that in a capitalist economy there must be expanding capital investment and a high level of consumer spending to maintain economic health. If the one declines, it should be compensated by an increase in the other. From 1919 until the depression, workers' productivity in American manufacturing increased about 43 per cent. That is to say, the volume of goods produced by any given number of man-hours of labor increased by about two-fifths. But wages and salaries did not increase appreciably and prices on the whole did not decrease. The increased productivity of labor, therefore, resulted in an increase in profits. Until 1929 these profits encouraged capital expansion. The market crash of October, 1929, brought a lack of confidence in the economy and a consequent decline in the rate of capital investment. But there was no compensating increase in consumer spending. Indeed, consumer spending declined along with capital investment.

The question arises, why was this economic dislocation of 1929 so much more serious than earlier and later downswings of the American economy? The answer seems to lie in certain deep-seated weaknesses in the economy throughout the 1920's.

Most important, there was a poor distribution of income during the supposedly palmy days of Republican prosperity. It was not a case of the rich getting richer while the poor got poorer, but it was a case of the rich getting tremendously richer while the poor got only slightly less poor. In 1929 the top one-twentieth of all receivers of personal income received about one-third of the total. With such a distribution of income, either a high level of investment or a very high level of luxury spending, or both, was necessary to keep the economy going. The spending of the very rich is much more erratic than the steady purchasing of the poor who necessarily spend all they receive for the necessities of life. After the crash, the spending and the investments of the rich declined and the whole economy collapsed. Had there been a compensating increase in the spending of the great masses of people (farmers and workers on low incomes) presumably the economy would have rolled along unscathed or only slightly damaged after 1929. But ordinary people could not spend more because they were already spending all, or nearly all, the money they received.

Although poor income distribution was probably the greatest weakness of the American economy, it had other faults. One weakness was the banking system. The failure of one bank naturally caused people to rush to withdraw their deposits from other banks. Bank runs became commonplace, endangering fairly sound banks as well as dubious ones. And when a bank failed, needless to say, its depositors were in no position to increase their spending and investments. Most economists also would agree that the complex structure of holding company pyramids made the economy of the 1920's unduly sensitive to business recessions. In the public utility field, for example, continued failure of an operating company to pay dividends meant default on the bonds of the holding companies stacked on top of the operating company. The situation was akin to what happens if one saws off one leg of a top-heavy stool.

Finally, another weakness was the inadequacy of even the supposedly best economic thought. Where economists today would have seen danger signals in abundance in the summer of 1929, the economists of that day saw only reasons for optimism. Even after the crash, the economists remained optimistically reassuring. In November, 1929, the Harvard Economic Society declared that "a serious depression . . . is outside the range of probability." At the end of the year, these Harvard professors expected a business recovery soon. In 1930, the widely respected Irving Fisher, professor of economics at Yale, wrote that the "outlook is bright" for the immediate future. The judgment of these foggy prophets was as widely trusted as the estimates of our economists today, perhaps more so.

The Hoover Administration and the Depression

As the depression deepened, the view grew among voters that Hoover was a "do-nothing" President, a kind of modern Nero. Certainly the Democratic party then and since did nothing to change this fairly common impression. And Hoover suffered in comparison with his successor because Roosevelt's pace was faster and his scope was broader. Yet the impression of Hoover as a "do-nothing" President was a false one. He did attempt to combat the depression. Indeed, Hoover's administration did more in its attempt to bring about recovery than had any previous administration, either Republican or Democratic, in earlier economic depressions. And it should be noted that Roosevelt continued some of Hoover's policies—the Reconstruction Finance Corporation was a notable example—although in an expanded form. Yet Hoover's policies did not succeed in effecting recovery. Neither he nor anyone else did enough fast enough to reverse the downward spiral from 1929 to 1933.

Hoover's economic philosophy, as well as that of most of his fellow-Republicans and huge sections of the Democratic party, greatly inhibited his attack on the depression. His most important inhibition was his conception of the role of the federal government in the economy. Hoover was not a follower of pure Adam Smith laissez-faire. He believed it proper for the federal government to stimulate business. In 1931 he said, "The sole function of government is to bring about a condition of affairs favorable to the beneficial development of private enterprise." But he held tight to the view that for the federal government to reform or reorganize the economy, even when the economy obviously did not function well, would mean inevitably a loss of individual freedom. He was so committed to the kind of relationship between business enterprise and the federal government he had promoted as Secretary of Commerce that even when the crash and the depression proved that relationship's inadequacies he had no alternative scheme. All he could do was work within his fundamental framework and hope for economic improvement. His political-economic philosophy failed its great pragmatic test.

He quite firmly believed that direct aid to poverty-stricken people was not a legitimate function of the federal government. All aid to the needy, he maintained steadfastly, was the responsibility of state and local government and of private charity. So far as the federal government's activities were concerned, he placed a higher value on the security of private property than on the welfare of human beings.

It is true, of course, that the welfare of human beings benefited from some of the Hoover policies. But individual welfare improved only indirectly. Hoover believed in a "trickle down" theory of federal aid. For example, the Hoover administration lent huge sums to banks and railroads, on whose condition the welfare of thousands of individuals was partially dependent. But Hoover stuck firmly to his conviction that federal aid directly to individuals would be a "dole" (a favorite smear word of that day) which would "injure the spiritual responses" of the American people. Some of Hoover's critics described his policies accurately, if inelegantly, when they charged that Hoover believed in "feeding the sparrows by feeding the horses."

Agriculture and the Tariff

During the election campaign of 1928 Hoover had recognized the need for bettering the condition of American agriculture and had promised a farm relief program and "limited" upward revision of the tariff. He mentioned these subjects in his inaugural address and soon thereafter called a special session of Congress, which met April 16, 1929, months before the crash, to consider these matters.

The Congress took months to write a tariff act because such distribution of federal largesse was inevitably accompanied by large-scale backstage bargaining, but after sharp but brief debate the national legislature passed an agricultural relief measure similar to the one the President had requested. Hoover signed the Agricultural Marketing Act on June 15. The Act created the Federal Farm Board and granted it fairly wide powers to supervise the marketing of agricultural commodities. Board members represented various agricultural interests. The major exception was cotton; most people in cotton production were Democrats. The chairman of the board was Alexander Legge, president of International

Harvester, whose appointment evoked criticism from agrarians. One magazine critical of the Hoover administration commented, "As a farm reliever Mr. Legge is an incomparable machinery manufacturer." Under the terms of the law the board had $500 million available on a revolving fund basis to buy agricultural surpluses, store them, and establish "stabilization corporations" and other agencies for marketing.

Unable to restrict production, but directed to buy farm surpluses, the stabilization corporations failed to solve the problem. Indeed, farm production was greater in 1932 than it had been when the act passed. The stabilization corporations soon owned mountains of commodities, which they tried to sell abroad. But when the financial crisis in Europe became severe in 1931, sales to Europe declined and the whole program foundered. If there had been no general economic decline, the Federal Farm Board scheme might have stabilized and relieved agriculture. But there was a general depression and the Hoover farm program was a thorough failure.

Over a year of bargaining and maneuvering was required to get a tariff bill enacted. The Hawley-Smoot Act of 1930 raised tariff barriers to new heights. The old Fordney-McCumber Tariff of 1922 had an average duty of 33 per cent; the new tariff's average came to 40 per cent.

The precise economic effects of the Hawley-Smoot Act are impossible to determine since there were other forces operating that tended to decrease international trade. Surely Franklin D. Roosevelt exaggerated for political advantage when he charged in 1932 that the new tariff was "one of the most important factors in the present world-wide depression." But surely Republican Senator James E. Watson of Indiana was even more wrong when he predicted in 1930 that if the Hawley-Smoot measure were passed, "within a year of this date we shall have regained the peak of prosperity." After the United States, one of the world's leading industrial and commercial powers, adopted a clear policy of economic nationalism with this tariff, other powers of the world followed suit. In 1932, Great Britain fully abandoned her free trade principles, and other countries raised their trade barriers. Indeed, 1930 was an inauspicious year to heighten tariff walls.

Politics and the Early Depression

Although Hoover publicly expressed confidence in the fundamental health of the economy just after the stock market crash, he was worried enough to call a series of conferences with business and labor leaders. In November, 1929, Hoover urged business leaders to maintain wages and expand their industrial construction. The business leaders agreed, contingent upon assurance from trade union officials that they would not strike or demand higher wages. A subsequent conference of trade unions assured the President on this point. That same month, Hoover telegraphed the nation's governors and mayors urging them to expand their public works programs.

In the first winter of the depression, industrialists did not appreciably cut wage rates, but they did not undertake any substantial amount of industrial construction. Labor honored its pledge. But in the spring and summer of 1930, industrial management seriously began to cut production, thereby reducing the national payroll, although they still did not reduce hourly wage rates importantly. The administration responded to this situation with an increase in its public works program. Federal public works increased from about $250 million in the last predepression year to about $725 million in Hoover's last year in office. State and local public works increased to a lesser degree. In the fall of 1930, Hoover created the President's Committee for Unemployment Relief which, with Colonel Arthur Woods of New York as chairman, sought to co-ordinate the relief activities of local agencies. Hoover was adamant in his conviction that relief for the unemployed was the responsibility of the states, counties, and municipalities rather than the federal government. Colonel Woods, unable to persuade the President to accept a bolder relief program, resigned the following April.

In August, 1931, Hoover appointed a new organization, the President's Organization on Unemployment Relief (POUR), with Walter S. Gifford, president of the American Telephone and Telegraph Company, as chairman. Its main effort was an advertising campaign that urged citizens to give to local community chests. In January, 1932, a Senate committee called Gifford to the witness stand and asked him if he knew the relief needs of rural districts and of towns too small to have a community chest. He admitted ignorance. When asked if he knew the total relief needs of the nation, he again admitted that he did not know. Congress, upon the warranted assumption that the Gifford committee was woefully inadequate for its task, refused Hoover's request to appropriate further funds for it.

By election time of 1930, the depression was not nearly as severe as it was soon to become, but the times were hard enough to put the Republican party at a bad disadvantage. Even before the elections, Hoover was confronted with a sometimes hostile Congress because a handful of progressive Republicans from the Midwest and the West frequently voted with the Democrats. The Senate nearly refused to confirm Hoover's appointment of Charles Evans Hughes as Chief Justice of the Supreme Court and did defeat his appointment of Judge John J. Parker of North Carolina to the nation's highest bench. After the 1930 elections the Republicans held the slimmest of margins in the Senate. There were forty-eight Republicans, forty-seven Democrats, and one Farmer-Laborite. Since the Republican Old Guard had been unsuccessful in purging such Republican progressives as Senator George Norris of Nebraska, Hoover had a hostile upper house on his hands. The Democrats had a majority of four in the new House of Representatives.

The Reconstruction Finance Corporation

The Hoover administration's most important antidepression measure was the establishment of the Reconstruction Finance Corporation in January, 1932. The RFC was a government-owned and chartered corporation, capitalized at $500 million, with authority to borrow three times that amount. Its purpose was to lend money to businesses which were in danger of collapse. Most of its funds during the Hoover administration went to support banks, railroads, and insurance companies, all institutions which would bring thousands of individuals down with them should they fail.

The way the RFC disbursed its funds caused political uproar. RFC officials issued statements during the agency's first few months calculated to leave the impression that it was aiding small business. In the summer of 1932, Speaker of the House John N. Garner of Texas pushed through legislation which required the RFC to report its loans to Congress. The reports made good ammunition for the Democratic party. A major political row involved Charles G. Dawes, the colorful former Vice-President who was the first president of RFC. In June, 1932, Dawes resigned from the RFC, announcing that he had to give full time to the affairs of the Central Republic Bank of Chicago. A few weeks later this bank received an RFC loan of $90 million. At that time the bank's deposits were only $95 million. The loan did not save it. The bank reorganized, and the RFC later had to resort to the courts to collect the loan. Dawes's successor, former Senator Atlee Pomerene of Ohio, authorized a $12 million loan to a Cleveland bank of which he was a director. The Democrats made a telling point when they charged that Hoover objected to federal relief to the poor but allowed the RFC to become "a rich man's dole."

Time and again during Hoover's last two years he opposed relief measures in Congress or vetoed them when they passed the House and Senate. These measures were generally popular, and with each veto Hoover's political stock sank lower. For example, Hoover vetoed a bill sponsored by Speaker Garner and Senator Robert F. Wagner of New York that appropriated $2 billion for a public works program; Hoover declared that "never before" had anyone made "so dangerous a suggestion." The President also vetoed a Wagner-sponsored bill that would have created a federal system of employment bureaus. Hoover's opposition to the bill of Senators Robert M. LaFollette, Jr., of Wisconsin and Edward P. Costigan of Colorado, which would have granted the states $375 million for poor relief, prevented its passage.

Hoover compromised his federal relief position ever so slightly when in July, 1932, he signed the Emergency Relief and Construction Act, a compromise measure submitted by Senator Wagner in an attempt to get something through that Hoover would approve. The law established a Reconstruction Finance Corporation fund of $300 million to be lent to the states for relief of the unemployed. It also appropriated $322.2 million for public works from general federal revenues. The states would have to repay the loans beginning in 1935, and no state would be permitted to borrow more than 15 per cent of the total loan fund. Governor Gifford Pinchot of Pennsylvania, in applying for the maximum loan of $45 million, reported that even if he could borrow 33 per cent more his state would have only enough to provide thirteen cents a day for a year to each of its unemployed workers. Pennsylvania actually received only about $11 million. In fact, by the end of 1932 the RFC had actually lent only one-tenth of the $300 million. The RFC had lent three times as much for Dawes's Chicago bank as for relief loans to the states. Actual expenditures for public works were even less.

The only real victory of progressives in either party was the enactment of the Norris-LaGuardia Anti-Injunction Act in March, 1932, sponsored by Senator Norris and Representative Fiorello LaGuardia of New York City. The act seriously inhibited the power of federal courts to issue injunctions in labor disputes and thereby rendered "yellow-dog" contracts ineffective. The "yellow-dog" was an agreement, frequently only oral, between employer and employee that the worker would not join a labor union. When trade union organizers tried to organize workers under such contracts, the employer was able to get an injunction from a federal court against all organizing efforts on the grounds that such efforts jeopardized an existing contract. There is evidence that Hoover did not really approve of the measure despite his signing of it. His Secretary of Labor, "Puddler Jim" Davis, worked behind the scenes to prevent its passage in Congress. That Hoover signed reluctantly the only important reform measure of his administration, a bill sponsored by two progressive Republicans, indicates a great deal about the confused but heated political struggles of the last two years of the Hoover administration.

Will There Be a Revolution?

As the depression became worse and worse in 1931 and 1932, and as people in desperate financial condition read of RFC loans to banks and presidential opposition to federal relief for individuals, the popular mood became understandably somewhat angry and ugly. Here and there, there were outbreaks of class violence.

The nation's farmers, in good times usually on the side of conservative political respectability, were perhaps the most violent part of the population during the early depression. At forced farm auctions, held by a creditor in order to pay off a farmer's debt, farmers sometimes terrorized prospective buyers from bidding, bought the property at a small fraction of its value, and returned it to the original owner. In at least one case, a mob of farmers beat a local judge who refused to stop issuing foreclosure orders.

In their desperation, in 1932 farmers in the western part of the Midwest organized the Farm Holiday Association. Milo Reno, a farmer president of the Iowa Farmers Union, was its leader. The idea of the movement was a strike against economic relations with urban people. The farmers would refuse to sell their products. They hoped this action would bring their urban opponents to heel and result in higher farm prices.

> Let's call a "Farmers Holiday"
> A Holiday let's hold
> We'll eat our wheat and ham and eggs
> And let them eat their gold.

The first "farmer's strike" was around Sioux City, Iowa, in August, 1932. The farmers blocked off the highways entering Sioux City with logs bristling with railroad spikes and turned back all shipments of food. They poured fresh milk, which would spoil soon anyway, into ditches. The farmers of the area were at that time getting two cents a quart for their milk and Sioux City consumers paid eight cents. The Farm Holiday idea spread in a sporadic fashion over the northern Great Plains, mostly in 1932 and early 1933, but there were a few farm strikes in the winter of 1933–34. Some governors refused to use the militia against the striking farmers.

The Farm Holiday movement had little economic effect. Here and there the price of fluid milk increased, but in general the tendency was to flood the unblockaded cities with goods and thus depress prices. Total livestock shipments to Iowa packing houses declined, but shipments to Chicago increased and the prices remained very low. Even had the Farm Holiday action been entirely successful and farm prices raised, there would have been a price problem when the products temporarily held back were released for sale.

The greatest effect of the Farm Holiday movement was to dramatize the plight of the farmers. Their "strikes" made headlines all over the country and helped to crystallize opposition to the already unpopular Hoover. When Hoover visited Des Moines during the 1932 campaign, distressed Iowa farmers staged a demonstration and parade against him, carrying signs which declared, "In Hoover we trusted; now we are busted," and "Hoover, Hyde [Hoover's Secretary of Agriculture], Hell and Hard Times. The Republican Four-H Club." Among the demonstrators at Des Moines was Republican Senator Smith W. Brookhart, who had campaigned for Hoover in 1928.

An even more dramatic and potentially explosive expression of widespread economic discontent was the march of World War I veterans on Washington in the summer of 1932. After the Armistice, Congress had passed lesiglation granting veterans "adjusted compensation certificates," a kind of bonus which was to be paid in 1945. A former army sergeant and unemployed cannery manager of Portland, Oregon, Walter W. Waters, spread the idea of a Bonus Expeditionary Force march on Washington to pressure Congress and the administration into paying off the certificates immediately. In May, 1932, the veterans started for Washington, riding freight cars, hiking, and living on handouts. Other unemployed veterans joined the BEF along the way, and by June there were about 15,000 bonus marchers in Washington, bivouacked in shacks and tents on Washington's Anacostia Flats. The marchers were unarmed, disciplined, and orderly; they made a vigorous effort to minimize the effectiveness of the small group of Communists who attached themselves to the movement. But the presence of so many desperate men in the nation's capital was potential dynamite. The superintendent of the Washington police did his best to be understanding and helpful with the BEF and to prevent an outbreak of violence.

Representative Wright Patman of Texas had introduced a bill embodying the BEF's demands. The bill passed the House on June 15. But the administration's opposition buttressed the opponents of a bonus in the Senate and the Senate defeated the Patman bill on June 17. Some of the marchers then left Washington but thousands of them, having no better place to go, remained in the Anacostia "Hooverville." President Hoover refused to receive a delegation of the veterans. He and his administration did nothing for the marchers other than to secure passage of a bill which would lend money to the veterans for transportation home—if they had a home—the loan to be deducted from the bonus payable in 1945.

Late in July, six weeks after the defeat of the Patman bill, the first outbreak of violence came. When the Washington police were clearing some veterans out of abandoned buildings, a policeman panicked and fired into a crowd of veterans. Two veterans were killed and others were wounded. At this point the administration moved with dispatch. Secretary of War Patrick J. Hurley ordered the army chief of staff, General Douglas MacArthur, to take action. MacArthur sent cavalry, infantry, and tanks into the Anacostia settlement. Two of Mac-Arthur's subordinate officers were Dwight D. Eisenhower and George S. Patton, Jr. The troops drove the veterans, some of whom had their wives and children with them, from the camp with bayonets and tear gas and then burned the tents and shacks. The bonus army straggled out of Washington. Recently discovered evidence reveals that MacArthur's vigorous attack on the marchers exceeded his orders. Hoover was upset but did not castigate his general.

MacArthur issued statements to the effect that the army's action had saved the capital from revolution, but the nation was hardly impressed. Instead, the nation was distraught and bitter that social and economic conditions had reached such a low point that the force of the United States government had been used against unarmed men and their families, men who had been victorious heroes only fourteen years earlier. Many who opposed the idea of a bonus were sickened by the inhuman efficiency with which the army dispersed the bonus marchers.

MacArthur clearly overestimated the danger to the nation's stability represented by the bonus army, but the question of how close the country was to a revolution was a moot point. Conservatives were aware that the situation was explosive and were fearful. When they contemplated that it was the farmers and the veterans, normally on the side of conservative social policies, who were creating the greatest violence, they had cause for concern. Yet the fear of conservatives was exaggerated. There was widespread discontent with the *status quo*, but there was little popular demand for a thorough overhaul of the economic and political structure, the abandonment of capitalism and of representative democracy. When the bonus marchers, assembled on the steps of the nation's Capitol on June 17, heard the news that the Senate had just defeated the bonus bill, they did not storm the Senate chamber in the traditional manner of European revolutionists at the barricades. Instead, they sang "America" and marched off quietly.

The depression prompted many people to revise their political-economic opinions and to reassess their old social values, but the extent of social revolt in 1932, aside from such exceptions as the bonus army and the farm strikes, was to turn the Republican party out of national power and install a Democratic Congress and administration. The American people seemed to agree with Thomas Jefferson, who had included this sentence in the Declaration of Independence: "Prudence, indeed, will dictate that Governments long established should not be changed for light and transient causes; and accordingly all experience hath shown, that mankind are more disposed to suffer, while evils are sufferable, than to right themselves by abolishing the forms to which they are accustomed." But there was a question in 1932 and early 1933 as to how long some evils were sufferable and what were light and transient causes.

The Early New Deal

Franklin D. Roosevelt is no crusader. He is no tribune of the people. He is no enemy of entrenched privilege. He is a pleasant man who, without any important qualifications for the office, would very much like to be President.

WALTER LIPPMANN, January 1932

Chapter Nine

In early July, 1932, the Democratic National Convention at Chicago nominated Governor Franklin Delano Roosevelt of New York for the presidency. The next day Governor Roosevelt captured the imagination of the American people. Instead of waiting to make an acceptance speech weeks later as was customary, he flew from Albany to Chicago in a Ford three-engine airplane. To deliver one's acceptance speech at the convention was unusual; to fly to the convention was in 1932 unprecedented and daringly dramatic.

The public was eager to hear the new nominee because it was almost a foregone conclusion that the Democratic candidate would defeat President Hoover, whom the Republicans had nominated in Philadelphia in mid-June. In April Roosevelt had created a generally favorable popular impression with a radio speech about the "forgotten man": the Hoover administration "has either forgotten or does not want to remember the infantry of our economic army." Roosevelt's 1932 acceptance speech seems a curious document to a later generation. On the one hand he promised greater economy in government and warned against extremism, either reaction or radicalism; on the other hand he criticized the Republican administration for "putting its head in the sand" and ignoring the "large number of destitute people in our midst who need food and clothing," deplored the pre-1929 "obeisance to Mammon . . . profits of speculation, the easy road without toil," and urged a "more equitable opportunity to share in the distribution of national wealth." But it was the climax of Roosevelt's speech which has lived:

I pledge you—I pledge myself to a new deal for the American people. Let us all here assembled constitute ourselves prophets of a new order of competence and of courage. This is more than a political campaign; it is a call to arms. Give me your help, not to win votes alone, but to win in this crusade to restore America to its own people.

The term "the New Deal" had been born, and the newly ordained prophets went forth in quest of disciples, which proved an easy task.

Roosevelt's Background

Fifty years old when nominated for the presidency, vigorous, possessed of a magic voice, confident, gay, warm, lucky, and clever, Franklin D. Roosevelt—or FDR as he was commonly called in the headlines—was to dominate the political scene more intensely and for a longer time than any previous president. He was a figure about whom it was difficult to be neutral or dispassionate. He evoked strong loyalties among a majority of citizens, but he evoked bitter animosity among a large minority. He was both well loved and well hated.

Roosevelt was born January 30, 1882, at Hyde Park, New York, to a family of wealthy landowners whose Dutch and English ancestors had settled the Hudson Valley in the seventeenth century. There was little about his father, James Roosevelt, to distinguish him from other Hudson squires other than that he was a Democrat, a distinct eccentricity in the circles in which he moved. Young FDR received his early education from private tutors at home and on European tours until he entered Groton in 1896. He went on to Harvard four years later. In his freshman year, he joined the Harvard Republican club, presumably because his fifth-cousin Theodore was the GOP vice-presidential candidate. Popular with his classmates and a good although not brilliant student, he finished his undergraduate course in three years, but he returned for a fourth year in order to serve as editor of *The Crimson*. In the fall of 1904 he entered Columbia University Law School and announced his engagement to Anna Eleanor Roosevelt, one of his distant cousins and a niece of the President of the United States. Theodore Roosevelt went to New York to give the bride away, her father having died when she was a small child. The couple had five children: a girl and four boys. FDR passed the bar examinations before his third year of law school was over, and he quit school at that point and worked for a Wall Street law firm. Most of his work there consisted of the preparation of briefs for cases involving corporations, an intellectual task he did not enjoy, but he delighted in the opportunities he had to appear in municipal court where he had his first real contact with ordinary people, with working men and immigrants.

Young FDR had an itch for politics. In 1910 he ran on the Democratic ticket for the New York State Senate from Hyde Park, campaigning vigorously from an automobile, something of a novelty in that slowly paced day. In the Democratic trend of that year he squeaked by his opponent to be the second Democrat elected from that district since the Civil War. He won re-election in 1912.

Early in 1912 FDR visited Governor Woodrow Wilson at Trenton and came away enthusiastic for the former Princeton president. He organized Wilson for president clubs in New York, thereby earning the opposition of Tammany Hall, which denied FDR the opportunity to be a delegate to the 1912 national convention. The thirty-year-old state senator campaigned for Wilson and was asked to be Assistant Secretary of the Treasury. FDR declined. But when Secretary of the Navy Josephus Daniels offered him the post of second in command of that department, young Roosevelt leaped at the chance. Theodore Roosevelt had been Assistant Secretary of the Navy under McKinley and had risen to the governorship of New York, the vice-presidency, and the presidency. Young FDR may have seen himself following in his distant cousin's footsteps.

As Daniels' assistant during the Wilson years of war and peace, FDR gained valuable administrative experience and built his contacts within the Democratic party. In 1920 the Democratic convention nominated him for the vice-presidency as James M. Cox's running mate in order to give balance to the ticket. Before he left Washington after Harding's electoral victory, he had impressed Supreme Court Justice Oliver Wendell Holmes as "a good fellow with rather a soft edge." The judgment seems valid for the young Roosevelt. But through personal tragedy he was soon to gain in maturity and internal strength, to harden the soft edge.

Polio struck Roosevelt in August, 1921, while he was vacationing at the family's summer place on Campobello Island off the coast of Maine. At first improperly diagnosed, the disease left Roosevelt paralyzed from the waist down. Although he had sufficient wealth, he apparently never considered retirement. He gamely fought his way back to an active and useful life, but thereafter he wore heavy steel braces on his legs and could not walk unaided. By 1924 he had recovered sufficiently to nominate Al Smith at the Democratic national convention with his famous "Happy Warrior" speech—and to demonstrate to the nation's Democrats that infantile paralysis, as it was then commonly called, had not knocked him out of politics.

In 1928 he proved his ability as a vote getter when he won election as governor of New York. Presidential candidate Al Smith lost his own state by 100,000 votes, but FDR won by 25,000. In 1930 he won re-election by a staggering 725,000 votes, unprecedented in New York's history. A humane and progressive governor as well as a popular one, FDR in 1931, through his political adviser James A. Farley, began to line up delegates for the 1932 convention.

When the Democrats met at Chicago, Roosevelt was clearly in the lead over other contenders for the nomination, the main ones being Al Smith, John N. Garner, and Governor Albert Ritchie of Maryland. The nominating and seconding speeches began in the stifling and sweltering auditorium the afternoon of Thursday, June 30. Orator after orator and demonstration after demonstration went on into the small hours of the morning. The first ballot began at 4:30 the next morning. Roosevelt received 661.25 votes to Smith's 201.75 and Garner's 90.25 and a scattering of "favorite sons" with lesser support. But under the rules of Democratic conventions of that time, FDR was about one hundred votes short of nomination because a two-thirds majority was necessary, a rule that in effect gave the South a veto power over nominations. Two other ballots that morning brought no real change. FDR gained only a little. The convention adjourned at 9:15 a.m. for a day of hotel-room bargaining. That evening the California delegation, controlled by the newspaper publisher William Randolph Hearst and the Texas delegation, supporters of Garner, swung to FDR, giving him the nomination. Garner's reward was the vice-presidential nomination. In 1936, the Democrats abolished their two-thirds rule.

The End of the Republican Era

Roosevelt and his political advisers realized that, having the political advantage over Hoover because of the depression, the best strategy was to keep the various factions and interests within the Democratic party as harmonious as possible, avoid words and actions that might alienate many voters, and let Hoover and his record be self-defeating. Roosevelt stuck to generalities usually and avoided a blueprint of what his New Deal would be. By the end of the campaign he had indicated in a rough way that he supported crop controls for agriculture, government regulation of stock exchanges, and cooperation of businessmen to combat the depression. He was silent on foreign policy and made no promises to organized labor.

The 1932 Presidential Campaign

The 1932 Roosevelt campaign makes the most sense when it is interpreted against the background of antagonistic interests and divisions within the Democratic party. During the course of the campaign, FDR displayed considerable agility as a broken-field runner on the gridiron of Democratic discord. Immediately after the convention, when Roosevelt was fearful he had alienated conservative Democrats, he ran toward the right and conducted a series of well-publicized conferences with important business leaders. When Senator Huey Long of Louisiana, a demagogic radical, objected strenuously (and profanely) to the direction of Roosevelt's campaign, FDR invited Long for lunch at Hyde Park, at which Roosevelt's patrician mother acquired a strong personal dislike for the Senator, and began to run to the left. The break toward the left sideline reached its peak on Roosevelt's swing through the West, culminating in his speech to the Commonwealth Club of San Francisco in late September. In this speech, one of his clearest statements of political philosophy, he spoke "of distributing wealth and products more equitably, of adapting existing economic organizations to the service of the people." And then Roosevelt ran to the right again, coming near to the right sideline in October in a speech at Pittsburgh in which he condemned the Hoover administration for failure to balance the budget, pledged himself to carry out his party's platform plank to reduce federal expenditures by 25 per cent, and called the Hoover spending policies "the most reckless and extravagant ... I have been able to discover ... of any peacetime Government anywhere, any time." This Pittsburgh speech was to haunt him in later days.

Hoover's campaign was in sharp contrast to his 1928 race against Al Smith. In 1928 Hoover never indulged in personal attacks; indeed, he never deigned even to speak his opponent's name in public addresses. But in 1932 Hoover's campaign speeches were bitter. He referred to prominent Democrats and progressive Republicans as "exponents of a social philosophy different from the traditional American one." And if the Republican protective tariff were altered, he warned, "The grass will grow in the streets of a hundred cities, a thousand towns; the weeds will overrun the fields of millions of farms...."

The voters, figuring that Hoover had not been conspicuously successful about grass in the streets, overwhelmingly repudiated their President. Hoover received 15,761,841 votes for 59 electoral votes, and Roosevelt received 472 electoral votes with 22,821,857 popular ballots. Hoover carried only six states. After the election, the Democrats had 59 Senate seats to 36 for the Republicans and one for the Farmer-Labor party, and 313 House seats to 117 for the Republicans and 5 for independents. The Socialist party's presidential candidate, Norman Thomas, received 884,781 votes, and 102,991 voters marked their ballots for the Communist nominee, William Z. Foster.

From Election Day to the Inauguration

The four months between Roosevelt's election and his inauguration were perhaps the longest four months for Americans in the present century. Throughout the 1920's, there had been a considerable movement for a constitutional amendment to reduce the time lag between elections and taking office. Until the Twentieth Amendment, ratified in February, 1933, the president was inaugurated on March 4, four months after his election, and the new Congress met in December the year after the election, thirteen months later, unless called into special session. The Lame Duck Amendment eliminated the ridiculous situation.

There were efforts during the interregnum to effect a degree of cooperation between the old and new administrations. Hoover and Roosevelt had conversations—very strained ones—and corresponded with one another. But Roosevelt legitimately feared that Hoover was trying to commit him to policies which might tie his hands when he became president, and Hoover legitimately was uneasy about adopting new policies which might be repudiated after March 4. Meanwhile, the economy continued downward. The international economic situation deteriorated badly, and American banks faced the worst crisis in their history.

Roosevelt's cabinet appointments offered something of a glimpse into what the New Deal would be, a curious mixture of tradition and unorthodoxy, of conservatism with experiment. The State Department went to Senator Cordell Hull of Tennessee, a hard-headed, sixty-one-year-old conservative who had championed the League of Nations, low tariff policies, and prohibition. The Secretary of the Treasury, William H. Woodin, was a charming, violin-playing industrial magnate, president of the American Car and Foundry Co., who had been a Republican until 1928. Henry Morgenthau succeeded him in December, 1933. The new Attorney General was Homer Cummins of Connecticut, a conservative who had been slated for a lesser post until Roosevelt's designated appointment, the western Democratic progressive Senator Thomas J. Walsh of Montana, died before inauguration. Senator Claude Swanson, an amiable but undistinguished Virginian, became Secretary of the Navy. Governor George Dern of Utah became Secretary of War, the politician James A. Farley became Postmaster General, and the conservative Daniel Roper of South Carolina became Secretary of Commerce. Roosevelt made three unorthodox appointments: Frances Perkins to Labor, Henry A. Wallace to Agriculture, and Harold Ickes to Interior. The appointment of Miss Perkins, a social worker who had served with Roosevelt in Albany, was the most unusual. She was not at first well received by the AFL leadership. Wallace and Ickes were each former Republican progressives, and Wallace's father had headed the Department of Agriculture under Harding and Coolidge. This was hardly a radical collection: three former Republicans (two progressive and one conservative) and three southern Democrats.

It is difficult today to understand fully how desperate was the nation's predicament on inauguration day, Saturday, March 4, 1933. The nation's banks, the very heart of American capitalism, had closed their doors, and business generally was at a standstill. Accepting a check was an act of faith; savings accounts were inaccessible; employers could not pay even their shrunken payrolls or receive accounts payable. The first "bank holiday" had begun just before the election when the governor of Nevada closed the banks of that state for twelve days to prevent the failure of a banking chain. The first major state to close its banks was Michigan, whose governor issued a "bank holiday" proclamation on February 10. In order to prevent further runs and failures, the governors of Indiana, Maryland, Arkansas, and Ohio took similar action before the end of the month. In the first three days of March, seventeen other states closed their banks. The flow of gold from the banking nerve center in New York both to banks in the interior and to foreign depositors was alarming, and the Federal Reserve System's gold reserves were falling dangerously fast. The gold reserve declined from about $1.4 billion in January to $400 million by March 3. The night before inauguration, Treasury officials, both old and new, worked together appealing to the governors of the states where banks were still open to close them immediately. The new governor of New York, Herbert M. Lehman, himself a banker, reluctantly took the step in the early morning hours of March 4, as did twenty-four other governors.

FDR at the Helm

The weather in Washington on inauguration day matched the grim national mood: rainy, gray, cold, and blustery. The atmosphere was not warmed by Hoover's chill attitude toward Roosevelt. In the limousine on the way to the ceremonies Hoover was aloof and quiet and looked as if he genuinely and firmly believed that the inauguration of the president-elect on the seat beside him meant the end of all that was good in American society. When Chief Justice Hughes read the presidential oath of office, Roosevelt surprised the country, listening on the radio, by repeating the entire oath rather than uttering the customary "I do." Then the new President turned and with an air of confidence but yet great seriousness, delivered his inaugural address. "This great Nation will endure as it has endured, will revive and will prosper. . . . Let me assert my firm belief that the only thing we have to fear is fear itself—nameless, unreasoning, unjustified terror which paralyzes needed efforts to convert retreat into advance." The "unscrupulous money changers" had failed and abdicated, Roosevelt declared. He hoped the "normal balance of executive and legislative authority" would be adequate to meet the problems of the economy's halt, but that if such conventional authority were inadequate he would ask Congress for "broad Executive power to wage a war against the emergency, as great as the power that would be given to me if we were in fact invaded by a foreign foe."

Roosevelt then called a special session of Congress to meet March 9, and the New Deal began. Executive orders and new legislation came with such rapidity and covered such a range of public affairs, particularly for the first few weeks of the new administration ("the hundred days") that the ordinary newspaper reader was more than a little bewildered. The citizen perceived that FDR provided action, a frontal attack on the depression that he had long hoped for, but the action came with such speed and against a background of such desperation that he was unable to see the New Deal in an organized and coherent fashion. Before the graduating classes of 1933 had received their diplomas, Congress had passed and the President had signed basic measures on banking and monetary matters and had created a host of new agencies generally known by their initials— "alphabet soup," FDR's critics called it—such as NRA, AAA, PWA, FDIC, and CCC. When these graduating classes had registered for the second semester of their senior year, the discredited Hoover had still been President and inactive despair had been the Washington mood.

It is necessary to organize a description of the early New Deal into its component parts—banking, industry, agriculture, and relief—for purposes of intellectual orderliness and clarity. The reader should remember that the citizen of 1933 was unable to see the New Deal as it unfolded with the organized hindsight afforded to a subsequent generation.

Banking and Stock Exchange Legislation

At 1:00 a.m. on Monday, March 6, Roosevelt issued an executive order declaring a national four-day bank holiday. For his statutory authority Roosevelt stretched a point and used the long-forgotten Trading-with-the-Enemy Act of 1917. While the new Congress made its way to Washington, Treasury Department officials hurriedly wrote a banking bill to be enacted as soon as possible. They finished their draft at 2:00 a.m. the day Congress convened. Most members of Congress had little more than a rough idea of the bill's provisions, but they pushed the Emergency Banking Act of 1933 with unprecedented speed. The House allowed only forty minutes for debate on the bill, but even so there were cries of "Vote, vote." Such was the bipartisan panic over the banking crisis that during this forty minutes the Republican floor leader of the House Bertrand H. Snell said, "The house is burning down, and the President of the United States says this is the way to put out the fire." The Senate took only a little more time. At nine that evening, Roosevelt signed the measure into law, only nineteen hours after its drafting had been completed.

The Emergency Banking Act

The Emergency Banking Act granted the President authority for the banking orders he had already issued, established a means to help banks in distress, and provided a scheme for the reopening of the closed banks. The Act permitted the Reconstruction Finance Corporation, begun under the Hoover administration, to buy the preferred stock of banks and empowered the Federal Reserve Banks to lend money to state-chartered banks, which were not members of the Federal Reserve. The Act authorized the issue of additional Federal Reserve bank notes with commercial "paper" for support. The Act divided the closed banks into four categories. Those that government examiners thought to be fully sound were to resume normal operations. By March 15 half of the nation's banks, which held 90 per cent of the nation's deposits, were open for regular business. A second category, about one-fourth of the total, were authorized to pay out a fraction of their deposits. The third group of banks, in worse condition, were allowed to reopen under the supervision of "Conservators" but could not pay out old deposits. They were allowed to accept new deposits, in effect to begin operations anew. The fourth category, about one thousand banks in all, were in such poor condition they were not allowed to reopen at all.

When the banks began to reopen, much of the fear and panic began to subside. Business was not yet as usual, but the economic heart of the economy had begun to beat again. On Sunday evening, March 12, only eight days after inauguration, Roosevelt addressed the country in the first of his radio "fireside chats." He explained the government's banking program in laymen's terms, and the confidence of his voice was contagious. The worst had ended.

The measures against the banking crisis in Roosevelt's first few days in the White House were very much a one-man show. Such was the crisis that he could have successfully put through almost any kind of banking program, and there were several alternatives. He conceivably could have nationalized American banking; he could have done nothing, allowed the banks to wallow in their own failure. The alternative Roosevelt chose was a middle way and essentially a conservative one since it preserved the essence of capitalism, private investment for profit. Raymond Moley, one of Roosevelt's advisers whose economic conservatism later prompted him to leave Washington and become an opponent of the administration, wrote in his *After Seven Years*, a book generally critical of Roosevelt, that FDR was

> intent upon rallying the confidence, first, of the conservative business and banking leaders of the country and, then, through them, of the public generally. . . . If ever there was a moment when things hung in the balance, it was on March 5, 1933—when unorthodoxy would have drained the last remaining strength of the capitalistic system. Capitalism was saved in eight days. . . .[1]

In time, capitalism's savior was to draw the hostility of the capitalists, but they were grateful recipients of his relief in March, 1933.

Regulation of Banking and Securities Trading

Capitalists, particularly bankers and stock market speculators, had never been more unpopular with the American public than they were in the early 1930's, and the headlines about the revelations of the so-called Pecora investigation were important in shaping this public opinion. The Senate Committee on Banking and Currency had begun an investigation of Wall Street practices in April, 1932, while Hoover still was President. In January, 1933, Ferdinand Pecora, a former Roosevelt Republican then a Democrat and a Sicilian immigrant who had become an assistant district attorney in Manhattan, became chief counsel for the committee. Pecora's research and sharp questioning of important financial figures brought sensational results. Among the disclosures were that the House of Morgan had maintained a "preferred list," friends of the firm who were occasionally offered an opportunity to buy stocks well below the market price; that there had been stock market pools and other devices to rig the market; that commercial banks had engaged in dubious financial practices to advance the interests of their affiliated investment firms; and that several prominent financiers had employed deception in order to reduce substantially their federal income

[1] Raymond Moley, *After Seven Years* (New York: Harper and Brothers, 1939), p. 155.

taxes or even to avoid payment of them altogether. The list of prominent persons who had profited from the "preferred list" scheme was shocking. Among the recipients of these favors in 1929 were: Calvin Coolidge; Newton D. Baker, Wilson's Secretary of War; John W. Davis, Democratic presidential candidate in 1924; Bernard Baruch; Owen J. Roberts, whom Hoover appointed to the Supreme Court; William H. Woodin; John J. Raskob and William G. McAdoo, both prominent conservative Democrats; General John J. Pershing; and Charles A. Lindbergh. And the fact that J. P. Morgan had paid no federal income tax whatsoever in 1930, 1931, and 1932 dismayed less wealthy persons who had sent checks to the Collector of Internal Revenue. The wave of public resentment against bankers and Wall Street that grew from the Pecora investigation—it continued until June, 1934—expressed itself in a modification of tax law, a new banking act, and two pieces of legislation regulating the activities of the stock market.

The plugging of several income tax loopholes was a relatively simple matter —a series of amendments to the Revenue Act of 1934 called a halt to the tax deception devices the Pecora committee had revealed—but legislation to cope with banking malpractices was somewhat more complicated. The Glass-Steagall Banking Act of June, 1933, increased the powers of the Federal Reserve Banks to regulate the activities of the member banks, greatly inhibited member banks' opportunity to provide credit for speculation, called for all commercial member banks to divorce themselves utterly from any affiliated investment companies, and created the Federal Deposit Insurance Corporation (FDIC). The FDIC guaranteed depositors' accounts up to $2,500. (This guarantee was raised to $5,000 in 1935, and to $20,000 during the Nixon administration.) Although the principle of government guarantee of deposits was an obvious method of promoting public confidence and lessening the likelihood of bank "runs," the eastern bankers who controlled the American Bankers Association used their organization to oppose the bill, which was carried only by the insistence of the South and the West. The FDIC proved very effective: all the bank failures of the rest of the 1930's amounted to less than 8 per cent of the failures of 1933.

In May, 1933, Congress enacted the Truth-in-Securities Act which required that investors in new stock issues be fully apprised of the issuing company's financial condition, but the Act did not establish any regulatory body to police the exchange of stocks. The situation was remedied by the Securities Exchange Act of June, 1934, which established the Securities Exchange Commission and which extended regulation not only to new issues but to all securities traded. Most Wall Street leaders fought the bill vigorously, but the overwhelming vote for passage in both the House and the Senate indicated how far the mighty had fallen in public trust. Characteristically, Roosevelt, having won a round with Wall Street, then appointed Joseph P. Kennedy, a Boston millionaire who had himself been a securities manipulator, as chairman of the new SEC. Kennedy, however, turned out to be somewhat firmer than warm New Dealers had feared, although his successors, James M. Landis (1935) and Professor William O. Douglas of Yale (1937), strengthened the Commission. As with much other New Deal legislation, businessmen not only learned to live with the new law but thrived under it, thereby wrecking their own original pessimistic predictions of ruin before the law was passed.

Four Strands of New Deal Thought

The immediate banking crisis over, the Democratic party, through its firm control of the Congress and the administration, was ready to move on to the larger problem of bringing about economic recovery and providing relief. But what was the Democratic party? Certainly it was not a cohesive organization representing a particular political-economic point of view. It was a coalition of various regional economic and political interests, interests whose desires were sometimes, but not always, in conflict with one another. Within the party in 1933 can be seen four main economic positions with many subclassifications. First, there was an agrarian interest, stronger on the Hill than in the administration, that believed recovery lay in the direction of monetary inflation. Some nonagrarians also wanted a degree of inflation. This was an old and honorable tradition in the Democratic party, dating back to the days of William Jennings Bryan and earlier. Second, there was a small but influential group of economic conservatives, whose Democratic godfather may be said to be Grover Cleveland, and whose greatest concern was economy in government and a balanced budget. Third, there was a group to whom liberalism meant restoring industrial competition. The hero of this group was Louis D. Brandeis, and the early days of the Wilson administration had been its period of glory. Finally, there was a group whose intellectual debt was to Herbert Croly, who saw the federal government playing a strong and positive role in the economy. Within this group were some who were essentially conservative—Raymond Moley, for example—and who were seeking a collaboration between government and business in industrial planning in which the business community would play the paramount role. Rexford Tugwell, another industrial planner, would have had government be paramount. Others, often considered radical but certainly not radical in the sense that they rejected capitalism, were thinking along the lines of the British economist John Maynard Keynes, even though they by no means disapproved of government-business collaboration. To summarize Keynes briefly leads to oversimplification, but in essence Keynes argued that governments should play the role of stimulator and regulator in capitalist national economies, that they should stimulate the economy during depression by deficit government spending and that they should slow down dangerous booms by a government fiscal surplus. Keynes's direct influence in the New Deal, however, has often been overstressed. His great work, *The General Theory of Employment, Interest and Money,* was not published until 1936, after the New Deal had already adopted "Keynesian" measures. Some of the "Keynesians" in the New Deal, for example, Marriner S. Eccles of the Treasury Department and later the Federal Reserve Board, had not even heard of Keynes until after they had arrived at conclusions similar to his on their own.

It is in the nature of things in American politics that any president must play the role of conciliator and leader of the various factions and power groups within his party and the nation. The success of a president depends upon his ability to keep his coalition harmonious and yet move ahead. FDR proved remarkably successful in this respect, first yielding to this pressure, then to that pressure, and then, through his power to shape public opinion, aiding still another group to increase its pressure. Roosevelt was a most adroit political broker and manipulator. The New Deal will not be understood if one is looking for a consistent economic philosophy or a logical development of a grand plan. But the New Deal administration was willing to experiment, and it accepted the idea of using the power of the federal government to help the economy crawl and scratch its way back to normal health while reforming glaring wrongs and providing relief along the way.

During the so-called First New Deal (until early 1935), the administration had something for all four main economic philosophies within the coalition. For the Bryan tradition, there was inflation; for the Cleveland tradition, there was an effort to balance the budget (an effort not abandoned, and then only reluctantly, until the winter of 1933–34); for those concerned about Wall Street there was the banking law and the SEC; for the planners of various kinds there were, among other things, the National Industrial Recovery Act and the Tennessee Valley Authority.

Monetary Manipulation

At least as far back as the late eighteenth century, American farmers had occasionally demanded monetary inflation with great political vigor. In the late nineteenth century, they had been at the forefront of the greenback and free silver movements, both of them inflationary proposals which had the alleviation of debtors' burdens and higher prices in view. In 1933 with heavy Democratic majorities in each house of the Congress, the Bryanite agrarian wing of the party was determined to get an inflationary monetary policy.

Roosevelt was prepared to go part way with the Bryanites, for certainly the prices of early 1933 indicated a severe deflation. Through a series of executive orders and laws in March and April, 1933, the United States in effect abandoned the gold standard. On March 6 Roosevelt prohibited the redemption of currency in gold coin, and by the end of April gold had been nationalized and its export prohibited without the consent of the Treasury. Subsequently, Congress by joint resolution declared void all clauses in either public or private contracts that required payment in gold. (The Supreme Court upheld the validity of this action in the Gold Clause cases of 1935.) With this tacit abandoning of the gold standard, the value of the dollar fell to eighty-five cents on foreign exchanges, thereby making it 15 per cent easier for foreigners to buy American products, and domestic wholesale prices increased. A degree of inflation, in other words, proved advantageous for the American economy.

Inflation versus Stabilization

In the spring of 1933 FDR had to come to a decision: on the one hand, further inflation seemed salutary at the moment and inflationists had large majorities in Congress; on the other hand, FDR had pledged support of the World Economic Conference, to meet at London in June to seek international agreements on monetary stabilization, lowering of tariffs, and encouragement of international trade. Roosevelt was in the kind of position he did not like: he had two mutually exclusive alternatives before him. He could not choose both inflation, even controlled inflation, and support of the Conference.

The inflationists in Congress were impatient with the President. In April Senator Burton K. Wheeler of Montana proposed the old 1896 Democratic plank of free and unlimited coinage of silver at the ratio of sixteen to one, and the Senate defeated his proposal by only ten votes. Senator Elbert D. Thomas of Utah then introduced a broad amendment to the Emergency Farm Relief bill (the first Agricultural Adjustment Act). Through pressure from the White House, the inflationary schemes were only made available for the President's use, rather than made mandatory for him. When this measure passed, the President was authorized to pursue any or all of six inflationary schemes: (1) issue $3 billion in fiat "greenbacks"; (2) adopt bimetallism, the President being free to fix the ratio of gold to silver; (3) reduce the weight of the gold dollar by as much as 50 per cent; (4) persuade the Federal Reserve Banks to buy government bonds in the open market up to $3 billion in order to increase the lending power of banks; (5) accept, for a period of six months, silver at not more than fifty cents an ounce in payment of debts from foreign governments.

Roosevelt eventually decided in favor of the United States "going it alone" instead of cooperating with other powers in seeking to stabilize currencies. His radio message to the Conference, to use his own words, "fell upon it like a bombshell." The American delegation was deeply embarrassed, but John Maynard Keynes, in disagreement with his own government, declared that Roosevelt was "magnificently right."

Manipulating the Price of Gold

But after the Conference "bombshell" Roosevelt refrained from further inflationary actions until it could be seen how far the dollar would decline in international exchange of its own accord and how far the upward turn of the domestic economy would go. Economic health did improve markedly during June and July, although the improvement was by no means solely attributable to monetary manipulation. In the fall, however, the business index fell sharply—sometimes referred to as "the first Roosevelt depression"—and FDR resolved to move ahead with further inflationary measures. In October he ordered the Reconstruction Finance Corporation to begin buying gold at a price above the world market. The first RFC purchases were at $31.36 an ounce when the world price was $29.80, which meant that the dollar was worth seventy-two cents in international exchanges. The price paid for gold kept rising and the value of the dollar kept declining until the end of January, 1934. On January 15 Roosevelt asked for the Gold Reserve Act, which became effective January 31, and which authorized the President to fix the gold content of the dollar between fifty and sixty cents. Roosevelt fixed the price of gold at an even $35 an ounce. When Roosevelt took office the price had been $20.67. In other words, the dollar had been devaluated roughly 40 per cent.

The whole gold price manipulation left the United States in an odd status so far as the gold standard was concerned. There was no unalterably fixed gold content to the dollar, no gold was coined, one could not demand gold in exchange for currency, and gold could not be exported without permission. Yet gold was available for foreign payments, the federal government continued to buy and store it at Fort Knox, Kentucky, and the dollar had at least a theoretical gold content. The arrangement was certainly not the conventional gold standard, but it was not altogether on a paper basis either.

To assess the Roosevelt gold policy is a difficult task. This much is clear: prices, although they did rise, did not increase to the point desired. Certainly there was no economic magic in such manipulation. The decision to manipulate the dollar rather than to cooperate with other world powers in currency stabilization is also difficult to assess. Some experts have gone so far as to say that the London Conference "bombshell" laid the foundations for economic nationalism that ended in World War II; others point out that a managed money system can be used either to further world trade or to promote national self-containment, and that United States policy promoted international commerce. One further effect was that with the banking legislation and the control of stock purchase margin requirements, the new monetary policy tended to shift the locus of power over monetary policy from Wall Street to Washington.

Silver

The silver fiasco remains to be explained. Silver and gold had, over the course of decades of political-economic conflict, come to be symbols for more than they actually were. In general, conservatives tended to equate an orthodox gold standard with all that was desirable in western civilization, and agrarians thought of gold as the rich man's metal and of silver as the poor man's saviour. The Congressmen from the western silver states, of course, had an obvious economic interest in providing a better market for silver, which had declined from $1.12 an ounce in 1919 to twenty-nine cents in 1931. In early 1934 despite FDR's objections, the silver steamroller began to move in Congress, well supported by agrarian interests generally. In March a silver-purchase bill introduced by Martin Dies of Texas passed the House by an overwhelming majority, and the Senate Agriculture Committee gave a version of the Dies bill unanimous endorsement. Since Roosevelt had failed to use the silver powers granted him by the Thomas Amendment to the Emergency Farm Relief bill, the silverites did not trust him with another permissive piece of legislation. Finally, FDR capitulated in May and asked Congress for silver legislation that would grant the executive a little discretion. The measure passed in June.

The Silver Purchase Act of 1934 enjoined the Treasury to purchase silver at home or abroad until its supply of silver equaled one-fourth the value of all its metal or until the market price of silver reached $1.29 and to put silver certificates, redeemable in silver dollars upon demand, into circulation. The silver purchase program was a vast handout to a special interest group, the western silver mine operators, but, contrary to the expectations of agrarians, it had no significant effect upon prices in general. The goal was to raise prices to the 1926 level, but despite all of the many New Deal measures, prices did not reach that level until after America entered World War II.

Budget Balancing and Relief Spending

When FDR entered the White House, he held quite orthodox and un-Keynesian views about budget balancing and governmental economy. When he criticized Hoover's deficit in his 1932 campaign speech at Pittsburgh, he was not cynically exploiting the situation for political advantage; he was genuinely alarmed by the slowly growing national debt. At the same time, however, Roosevelt realized that federal relief had to be increased. Throughout 1933 he was torn between a desire for a balanced budget and the necessity for more relief.

His first week in office FDR sent a message to Congress urging greater governmental economy, to be accomplished through a cut in federal salaries and veterans' pensions. Congress, sensitive to the powerful veterans' lobby, was hesitant, but Roosevelt insisted and the Economy Act became law on March 20. FDR sweetened the medicine with a proposal to amend the Volstead Act to permit the manufacture and sale of beer with an alcoholic content of 3.2 per cent, thereby increasing federal revenues with a beer tax and soothing the boys in the nation's American Legion halls. This light beer became legal before the end of the month. (In February, 1933, the Lame Duck Congress had submitted the Twenty-first Amendment to special state conventions, and the required number of states had ratified it, eliminating the Eighteenth Amendment by December 5, 1933.) With such measures, federal spending at first actually decreased; the deficit for the first five months of the New Deal's first year was approximately 25 per cent less than the deficit for the corresponding five months of Hoover's last year.

The strongest voice for orthodox economy within the administration was that of the Director of the Bureau of the Budget, Lewis W. Douglas, from an important Arizona copper-mining family. Roosevelt leaned heavily on Douglas in the first months of his administration, much to the annoyance of less orthodox New Dealers whose emphasis was relief and recovery rather than economy. At the opposite pole from Douglas was a small group within the administration, of which Marriner S. Eccles was later to be the chief spokesman, which advocated deficit spending as a positive good under the circumstances. Big spending would, they argued, not only prime the economic pump, but would bring a degree of inflation ("reflation," Eccles called it) desirable at that time by expanding bank credit.

Roosevelt never fully accepted this Keynesian idea (he was to call for a reduction of spending and deficit in 1937) but he gradually abandoned the emphasis on a balanced budget in favor of greater relief spending. In the summer of 1934, Douglas, tired of rather unsuccessfully inhibiting federal spending, gave up the task as hopeless and resigned, leaving Treasury Secretary Morgenthau as the primary spending brake.

After the first few months of the New Deal, the gross federal debt began to climb. (See graph on page 178.) During World War II military expenditures drove the figure beyond the wildest fears of the budget balancers (in 1945 a $258,682,187 total, with a per capita of $1,848.60), but they did not complain as much about the enormous debt brought about for bombs and battleships as they had about the smaller debt incurred for relief and civilian public works.

One cannot avoid the conclusion that the political debate over the federal debt had more to do with how the money was spent than the fact it was spent. In the worst years of the Great Depression, only a fairly small but extremely vocal minority of citizens opposed the principle of great federal spending for relief of the poverty stricken.

Relief Measures

The first significant New Deal relief measure, and one that evoked relatively little opposition, was the act of March 31, 1933, creating the Civilian Conservation Corps (CCC). The CCC with an initial appropriation of $300 million quickly took two hundred and fifty thousand young men from relief families and put them to work under direction of the War Department at soil conservation and reforestation projects. The young men in "the C's" received board and room at the work camps and $30 a month, of which $25 automatically went home to their families. By 1940, when the CCC came to an end, more than 2,225,000 young men had worked in the program, and their labors had significantly improved the condition of the countryside.

The Federal Emergency Relief Administration came into being in May, 1933. FERA granted relief to the needy indirectly through the states, one-half of its $500 million being used to match state relief expenditures for the previous three months at a one to three ratio. Roosevelt brought in Harry Hopkins, a New York social worker, to head FERA, and he brought imagination to his task. Hopkins greatly preferred work relief to cash relief and persuaded the state relief agencies he coordinated to inaugurate work relief programs.

In the fall of 1933 the administration abandoned FERA for the Civil Works Administration (CWA), which had a strange origin. Title II of the National Industrial Recovery Act of June, 1933, had created the Public Works Administration (PWA) with a huge appropriation of $3.3 billion. FDR placed Interior Secretary Harold Ickes in charge of PWA, and so careful was "Honest Harold" that no money be wasted that he spent it very slowly and without immediate economic effect. In November Roosevelt created CWA, put Hopkins in charge, and transferred $400 million from PWA. Within two months CWA had four million people busily building and repairing schools, highways, sewer systems, and airports. The goal of CWA had been to provide work relief fast, and that it did. Within two months, more people were on CWA than there had been in the armed services during World War I, and they received a higher average wage. But Hopkins' boldly unorthodox methods—jobs for three thousand writers and artists, for example—aroused considerable opposition, and in the late winter of 1933–34 Roosevelt closed out CWA. Congress then reinvigorated FERA with a $500 million appropriation. One can fairly conclude that the New Deal's relief activities in 1933 and 1934 were a great help to the needy, although far below what was necessary for a decent standard of living, and that the program was erratic. The PWA, however, under Ickes' direction slowly grew into a major achievement. In its six years of existence it helped in the construction of thousands of school buildings and gymnasiums, dams, bridges, postoffices, and courthouses, creating about four million man-hours of work.

There was aid for the middle classes also in the form of mortgage relief.

Mortgages contracted before the crash, of course, were not scaled down to meet the new economic conditions and worked a considerable hardship on home owner-debtors. In June, 1933, Congress created the Home Owners Loan Corporation, which in time bought up approximately one-sixth of the total urban home mortgage debt and refinanced the loans at lower interest rates on long terms. The following June, Congress established the Federal Housing Administration (FHA) to stimulate the all-but-idle residential construction industry. The FHA, instead of lending money for mortgages directly, guaranteed mortgages contracted by the usual lending agencies. This agency revolutionized home financing and made home ownership feasible for many families by lowering down-payment requirements and setting up an amortized long-term mortgage system that was rare before the depression. Most lending institutions at first resented this "intrusion" into their domain, but they soon learned that the different mortgage practices opened up a vast new lending market.

PUBLIC DEBT OF THE FEDERAL GOVERNMENT, 1929–1939
(In thousands of dollars)

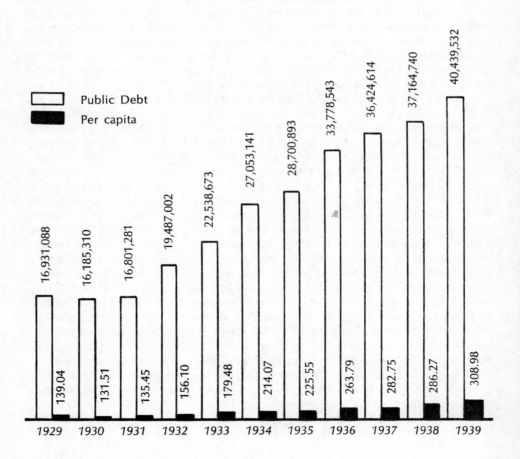

Public Debt
Per capita

1929	1930	1931	1932	1933	1934	1935	1936	1937	1938	1939
16,931,088	16,185,310	16,801,281	19,487,002	22,538,673	27,053,141	28,700,893	33,778,543	36,424,614	37,164,740	40,439,532
139.04	131.51	135.45	156.10	179.48	214.07	225.55	263.79	282.75	286.27	308.98

The New Deal expanded considerably the scope of the Reconstruction Finance Corporation's activities, and its loans and stock purchases can be considered as a kind of relief to business, although some of its funds were lent for projects that aroused business opposition. An RFC report of 1941 revealed that the powerful economic engine had lent over $15.7 billion since its establishment in 1932, much of it to railroads, banks, and insurance companies.

The NRA: Experiment in Business-Government Planning

The irrationality of the whole industrial depression appalled many logical minds. After all, such prerequisites for economic health as a vast industrial plant, an efficient transportation and distribution system, and an abundance of competent manpower still existed. There had been no war or physical calamity to wreck the material foundation for a thriving economy. Many people concluded that some kind of planning was necessary to make the economic wheels resume their turning. Some of the more imaginative businessmen began to think in terms of planning. Naturally, they believed such planning should be done by businessmen cooperating through trade associations. In 1931 Gerard Swope, president of General Electric, and the United States Chamber of Commerce each came forward with plans for "industrial self-government." Such plans, however, required at least the consent of the federal government, for they ran afoul of the antitrust laws. Before the 1932 elections, Roosevelt had indicated interest in such schemes, and on June 16, 1933, when he signed the National Industrial Recovery Act creating the National Recovery Administration (NRA), these ideas came to fruition in modified form.

But the legislative origin of NRA was somewhat different. In December, 1932, Senator Hugo L. Black of Alabama had introduced an AFL-sponsored bill to prohibit interstate shipment of goods produced by labor working more than thirty hours a week. The idea was to spread the available employment. On April 6, 1933, the Black bill passed the Senate. FDR disapproved of the bill and rushed Labor Secretary Frances Perkins to the House labor committee to head it off. Secretary Perkins urged minimum wages and government control of production. Business objected, and the administration worked the rest of April and early May on drafting a bill. Administration spokesmen presented the draft of the measure to the convention of the United States Chamber of Commerce in early May, and that group was enthusiastic for the central idea but wary of the labor provisions.

The final bill had within it something from each of several schools of economic thought. For business, there was a section providing for codes of fair competition and exemption from the antitrust laws; for the national planners, there was a scheme of government licensing of business through government approval of the codes written by industry; for labor, there were minimum wages, maximum hours, and Section 7a, which promised collective bargaining; for the advocates of a large public works program, there was the whole of Title II, which established the Public Works Administration. Still, the bill had rough sailing in Congress, and the Senate adopted the conference report on it by only a seven-vote margin. The Act was to be in effect for only two years. It could, of course, be renewed.

NRA proved to be far less than a success. In the first place, industries could not write the codes quickly, and while the codes were in preparation many businesses practiced a kind of "chiseling in advance" by expanding production to the limit while there was no floor under wages, so that they could build up inventories to be sold after the codes became effective and brought higher prices. To head this off, the NRA asked all employers in late July, 1933, to accept the President's Re-employment Agreement (PRA), commonly called the Blanket Code, which established minimum wages and maximum hours. But much damage had already been done. Industrial production in July rose slightly higher than the 1923–25 average, only to fall roughly 35 per cent by October as PRA became effective and inventories were built. Inventory building during the summer was a major factor in the "first Roosevelt depression" in the fall of 1933. In the second place, the writing of the codes fell mostly to the bigger businesses within each industry. Labor's role in code writing was small except for the clothing industry, where there were large unions and small entrepreneurs. Consumers never had more than token representation in the drafting of codes. In the third place, there was confusion in the administration of the Act. There was constant conflict among the NRA administrators, the chief of whom was General Hugh S. Johnson, a blustering probusiness ex-cavalryman whom FDR eventually eased out. Some of the administrators believed in giving business its head, some became ineffectually concerned about protecting the consumer, and some conceived their role as business regulators. In the fourth place, the labor provisions and interpretations of those provisions proved quite inadequate from labor's point of view. By early 1935 labor leaders were saying that NRA stood for "National Run-Around." In the fifth place, small businessmen complained of the red tape inherent in the NRA and of domination by big business. As the economic historian Broadus Mitchell has put it, "A code was something between a charter of a medieval guild and the agreement of a modern cartel," but small businessmen— and trade unionists, too—saw their codes as closer to a cartel agreement than to a guild charter.

The President was understandably distressed when a unanimous Supreme Court declared NRA unconstitutional in the Schechter case on May 25, 1935, less than a month before the statute was due to expire. It is true that immediately after NRA died unemployment increased, hours of work increased, and wages decreased. Yet few deeply mourned the passing of the experiment which, as some intellectuals noted, had similarities to European syndicalism. As will be described more fully in chapter eleven, many industries continued to practice the anti-competitive devices NRA had sanctioned even after the Schechter decision. NRA had brought a psychological lift and a sense of national solidarity in the summer of 1933. By 1935 the immediate economic crisis had passed. The first flush of NRA-inspired confidence and feeling of purpose had helped, but it had not brought recovery. Greater institutional changes and vastly greater federal spending proved necessary to bring recovery.

The First New Deal and Agriculture

Agriculture received legislative attention from the very beginning of the New Deal. Two problems confronted agriculture: farm mortgages, which were rapidly being foreclosed and provoking violence in the Corn Belt; and the more general problem of raising farm prices to an equitable ratio with the prices farmers had to pay for industrial goods.

Roosevelt began the attack on the mortgage problem in late March, 1933, by consolidating all of the existing federal farm credit agencies into the Farm Credit Administration, and in May and June, Congress enacted the Emergency Farm Mortgage Act and the Farm Credit Act. With this legislation the FCA in time refinanced one-fifth of the total farm mortgage indebtedness. The agricultural bloc demanded further relief, which Congress provided in June, 1934, with the Frazier-Lemke Farm Bankruptcy Act. This unusual law enabled a farmer who had lost his farm through foreclosure to buy it back at a figure determined by a federal district court, the payment to extend over six years at just 1 per cent interest. In 1935 the Supreme Court found the Frazier-Lemke law unconstitutional, but the next year a revised version of the law passed Congress and was later upheld in the courts.

The first week of the new administration Agriculture Secretary Henry A. Wallace began a series of conferences with farm leaders on the general problem of raising farm prices. From these meetings came the Agricultural Adjustment Act (AAA) of May 12, 1933. The AAA was not a new idea; it was the culmination of farm measures and proposals that went as far back as the Populists. The purpose of AAA was to bring about a balance between the production and consumption of farm products so that farm income would have the same relative purchasing power—"parity"—that existed from 1909 to 1914. The law empowered the Secretary of Agriculture to use several methods to achieve that goal. For seven basic farm products (wheat, cotton, corn, hogs, tobacco, milk, and rice— later amended to include beef and sugar), AAA could enter into agreements with individual farmers by which the AAA would pay the farmer to limit his production by taking some acres out of cultivation. The AAA also was empowered to buy up agricultural surplus, or to lend money to farmers and accept their crops as collateral, until prices rose. This method was put to work in the fall of 1933. Finally, AAA granted the Secretary power to subsidize agricultural exports. The whole program was financed from revenues acquired from a special tax on food and fiber processors, who, of course, passed the tax on to the consumer.

AAA got off to a bad start so far as public relations were concerned. Alarmed by reports of a bountiful crop of cotton already planted and a redundancy of baby pigs, the AAA had about one-fourth of the cotton acres plowed under and over six million young pigs slaughtered. Coming at a time when thousands were hungry and in rags, besides traditional opposition to waste, there was a loud public outcry. The Socialist Norman Thomas pointedly suggested that Wallace was trying to solve the paradox of poverty in the midst of plenty by eliminating the plenty. The later prevention of production by letting land lie fallow was far greater than the destruction of 1933, but it was not so dramatic as the killing of baby pigs and evoked far less opposition.

Crop restriction, plus serious droughts in the Midwest in 1933 and 1934, brought some of the effects desired before the Supreme Court declared the law unconstitutional in 1936. The price of cotton, wheat, and corn approximately doubled from 1932 to 1935, total farm income rose from $4.5 billion to $6.9

billion, and total farm mortgage indebtedness declined. Farmers complained about the program at times, but in AAA referendums they voted overwhelmingly to continue the program. Perhaps they were chagrined that agriculture had become a subsidized industry, although industrialists had never shown much embarrassment about the government subsidies they received.

Not all farm people benefited from AAA by any means. Cotton tenant farmers directly suffered from the program. Benefit payments went to the landlord rather than the tenant, and the landlord, having cash in his pocket at last, bought tractors and other equipment which diminished the demand for tenant labor. This feature of AAA, plus the dust storms, displaced thousands of southern tenant farmers. John Steinbeck later publicized the plight of these people in his *The Grapes of Wrath* (1939).

An Assessment of the Early New Deal

By the winter of 1934–35 (the New Deal was to change its emphasis, implicitly, in the spring) an objective judge of national events would have had to say that the administration had done a great deal to improve the economy but that there was still a long way to go. Unemployment had decreased by about 1.7 million since 1933. The physical volume of industrial production was up about twelve index points from 1932. Farm problems were not as acute. Most of all, the banking system had been stabilized and the sense of panic that characterized February and March, 1933, had vanished. Yet about eleven million workers remained without jobs, and the relief situation, although improved, still left millions of people in desperate and deplorable condition. The effectiveness of the monetary manipulation program had been dubious, and the silver purchase program was an enormous boondoggle. Organized labor and workers who wanted to become organized were justifiably distressed with the New Deal's labor policies.

In sum, recovery had not been achieved, relief had improved only a little, and reform had largely concentrated on financial institutions. Yet, in the congressional elections of 1934, the electorate returned even greater Democratic majorities, perhaps because the Republicans presented no attractive alternatives. The Democratic share of the popular vote increased slightly, an unprecedented development for a majority party in an off-year election. GOP representation in the House shrank from 117 to 103, and the Republicans lost 26 of the 35 contested Senate seats. After the elections the Republicans had only seven governorships left.

The Later New Deal

We affirm our unalterable conviction that . . . the fate of the nation will depend, not so much on the wisdom and power of Government, as on the character and virtue, self-reliance, industry and thrift of the people. . . .

<small>REPUBLICAN PLATFORM OF 1936</small>

The issue in this election is plain. The American people are called upon to choose between a Republican administration that has and would again regiment them in the service of privileged groups and a Democratic administration dedicated to the establishment of equal economic opportunity for all our people.

<small>DEMOCRATIC PLATFORM OF 1936</small>

Chapter Ten

For the first several months of the first Roosevelt administration, the usual political tugging and hauling between political parties and amongst economic interest groups was considerably subdued. The business community, with some important exceptions, had supported Hoover in 1932, but Roosevelt did not alarm most businessmen at the beginning of his first term. So great was the sense of urgency arising from the economic calamity and so discredited was conventional business leadership that Roosevelt enjoyed at first an unusual degree of unanimity. The Democratic party was as united as ever it can be, the Republicans were in a bewildered daze, and most of the nation's press gave the administration at least critical support. The New York *Daily News*, the nation's most widely circulated tabloid and usually Republican, even sponsored a campaign to raise funds for a White House swimming pool.

But this unity, bred of crisis, was not to last long. As FDR put it, "Now that these people are coming out of their storm cellars they forget that there ever was a storm." After the banking crisis was past, after the economy stopped its downward skid, and after the Republicans began to recover from their depression shell shock, criticism of Roosevelt and his associates started becoming sharp. The Roosevelt haters came into being. By 1935 the vehemence of their almost hysterical attacks on "that man in the White House" was greater than that against any American president since Andrew Johnson.

"Polarized Politics"

The formation of the American Liberty League in August, 1934, symbolized the new conservative opposition to the New Deal. Fronting for the Liberty League was a group of conservative Democrats who had dominated their party in the 1920's but who had been pushed aside by the Roosevelt forces: Al Smith; Jouett Shouse, former director of the national committee; John J. Raskob, millionaire former chairman of the national committee; John W. Davis, Democratic presidential candidate in 1924; and Bainbridge Colby, once Wilson's Secretary of State.

Behind these Democrats was an impressive array of rich and powerful business-men who usually voted Republican. Most of these tycoons were of the DuPont family or in businesses in which the DuPonts had a large interest, such as General Motors. The League was ostensibly a nonpartisan organization, but it required no particular political insight to perceive that it was primarily an anti-Roosevelt organization. Its millions of dollars were devoted to propaganda, mostly in a long series of pamphlets, which attacked the New Deal as a violator of the Consti-tution, state rights, and "free enterprise." But despite its great energy, the voters ignored its arguments in the 1934 congressional elections.

But the voters, or large numbers of them, displayed a mood in 1934 and 1935 that seriously disturbed Roosevelt. They returned a heavier Democratic majority to Congress, but they did so partly because the Republicans had not provided what they considered acceptable alternatives. Large numbers of voters were attracted to ideas and leaders more radical than the New Deal had been. All over the country people were responding to a variety of left-of-center but non-Communist political leaders, and, if some of their notions were strange indeed and some of the leaders were demagogues, fanatics, or crackpots, the basic dissatisfaction with the Roosevelt administration was still apparent.

Radical Reformists

The novelist Upton Sinclair, who had been a Socialist most of his life except during World War I, led a radical movement in California that momen-tarily won control of the state Democratic party. In 1933 he published I, Governor of California and How I Ended Poverty. The next year he entered the Democratic primary for governor and won a clear majority in a field of nine candidates. The McAdoo machine's candidate was George Creel, Wilson's wartime propaganda chief, who received 288,106 votes to Sinclair's 436,200. Sinclair's EPIC program (End Poverty in California) included a $50 a month pension for poverty-stricken people over age sixty and a "production for use" system for the state's un-employed in some ways similar to cooperatives and in some ways similar to state socialism. The campaign against Sinclair in the fall was bitter and dirty. FDR refused to support Sinclair, even though he was the Democratic candidate, and the Socialist party repudiated him. The state's newspapers were solidly against Sinclair, and prominent Hollywood figures contributed a big campaign chest to his Republican opponent who won the election by 260,000 votes. A middle-road candidate received over 300,000 votes. EPIC collapsed as quickly after the election as it had grown; by 1936 it was almost extinct.

California was also the home base of the Old Age Revolving Pension, or the Townsend Plan. Francis E. Townsend of Long Beach, a retired physician, urged that the government pay a pension of $200 each month to all unemployed people over sixty and that the pensioners be required to spend the entire sum within a month in order to be eligible to receive the next $200. Dr. Townsend was not as clear with his arithmetic about the scheme's financing as he was in his exposition of the benefits that would flow from the Plan, but the necessary funds, he explained, were to come from a 2 per cent tax upon all financial transactions. The Townsend Plan was very popular among the indigent aged, who formed Townsend Clubs all over the country and pressured their Congressmen.

From Louisiana came Senator Huey Long and his Share Our Wealth plan with its slogan "Every Man a King." Long, the "Kingfish," was from poverty-stricken northern Louisiana, and he had long been the champion of the "wool hat boys" in that state's politics. A vulgar corruptionist and a demagogue he surely was, but he used his political machine to get for the poor of his state many of the things they needed: better schools, highways, and hospitals. After he moved from the governor's mansion to the United States Senate in 1930, he increasingly became a national figure. He supported FDR strongly in 1932 but turned against him in 1933 to organize the Share Our Wealth society. He promised every family a $5,000 homestead and a $2,500 annual income, the funds to come from confiscation of great fortunes. There was about Long and many of his followers much that was illiberal and anti-democratic—anti-Semitism, contempt for civil liberty, disregard for democratic political process—but it is significant that a demagogue in the 1930's gained his popularity with economic radicalism. After Long was assassinated in September, 1935, the Reverend Gerald L. K. Smith of Kansas became the movement's leader. Smith emphasized the fascist aspect of the movement and subdued economic unorthodoxy; the movement soon shrank to political insignificance.

Similar to Long in some respects was a Roman Catholic priest, the Reverend Charles E. Coughlin, who ranted each Sunday from his radio station in Royal Oak, Michigan, a Detroit suburb. Father Coughlin capitalized upon agrarian suspicion of "international bankers" to build up his National Union for Social Justice, although most of his radio listeners were in big eastern cities. He first supported the New Deal and then turned against it with most extreme language. As did the Long movement, he later became primarily anti-democratic and anti-Semitic.

Respectable Dissenters

Besides these groups that Theodore Roosevelt would have called the "lunatic fringe," there were more respectable political developments that threatened to undermine the Roosevelt camp. In the upper Mississippi Valley, the LaFollette Progressives in Wisconsin and the Farmer-Labor party in Minnesota made overtures to labor and farm groups in neighboring states with a view to forming a new national party if the New Deal did not move in the directions it wanted. Organized labor in 1934 had become thoroughly disgruntled with the President and had begun to try to get what it wanted through sympathetic Congressmen such as Senators Wagner and LaFollette.

Under the circumstances, there was only one thing for Roosevelt or any other politically sensitive chief executive to do: move to the left and urge reform measures. With the political right having shifted to powerful attack and with large numbers of farmers, laborers, and the down-and-out increasingly flirting with political leaders to Roosevelt's left, pursuing the old direction or standing still would have been political suicide. Facing political reality, Roosevelt urged action upon the Congress elected in November, 1934. The first session of that Congress enacted a very large and important body of reform legislation that significantly altered the American economic and political structure, and this second New Deal took the steam out of the left-of-FDR movements.

Fundamental Reforms: Progressivism's High Tide

Many, many reforms were enacted by the Seventy-Fourth Congress, and among this legislation the two most far-reaching were the National Labor Relations Act and the Social Security Act.

The Wagner Act

The legislative history of the labor measure, generally called the Wagner Act, was a curious one. Despite the adulation which the labor movement came to have for Roosevelt, the Wagner Act, which did more for trade unionism than any other federal law at any time, was not Roosevelt's idea. Indeed, he did not state his support of the law until its passage was practically assured. All through 1934 Senator Wagner had worked fruitlessly for legislation more favorable to trade union growth than Section 7a of NRA. In February, 1935, he reintroduced his measure into the new Congress and successfully resisted efforts of a few Senators to amend the essential features of the bill. On May 16, 1935, eleven days before the Supreme Court declared NRA unconstitutional, the Senate passed the bill sixty-three to twelve. Still Roosevelt kept silent. On May 24, three days before NRA went down, at last FDR announced his support. Less than a month later the House, over the practically unanimous opposition of business, passed the bill without even a roll call.

The new labor law declared that employees engaged in interstate commerce had the "right" to join or form labor unions and to bargain collectively with their employers through representatives of their own choosing. A union which won majority support from the workers in any plant, company, or industry in a secret-ballot election conducted by the National Labor Relations Board, which was established by the law, became the sole bargaining agent of the employees. The law required employers to recognize and bargain with the union in good faith. The law also, in a list of "unfair practices," prohibited employers from interfering with employees in the practice of their union rights, from aiding or financing a company union, and from discriminating against employees as a means to defeat a union. The passage of the Wagner Act coincided with a great wave of labor militancy, and with this law behind them workers soon became organized in American industry as they had never been before.

The Social Security Act

The idea behind the Social Security Act of August 14, 1935, went back several years. The Bull Moose platform of 1912 had advocated old-age pensions, and by the time Congress passed the Act of 1935 about half of the states had enacted old-age pension or unemployment compensation laws, although few of them were adequate. In 1934 two separate social security bills were before Congress, and FDR asked for a special Committee on Economic Security to study the problem and formulate a plan. The committee reported the following January, and their proposed bill moved easily through both houses, delayed only by disagreements over details. Senator Wagner sponsored the bill in the Senate;

Congressmen David J. Lewis of Maryland and Robert L. Doughton of North Carolina were its co-sponsors in the House. Though businessmen growled that Social Security was the opening wedge of socialism and the end of American self-reliance, only thirty-three Representatives and six Senators voted against the bill.

The Social Security law was one of the most complicated ever passed by Congress. Old-age pensions under the law were to be administered by the federal government. All employers and employees except those in certain categories (public employees, domestic servants, farm and casual workers, and employees of educational, philanthropic, and religious institutions) were required to pay a payroll tax of 1 per cent on all wages under $3,000 a year, the tax to be increased gradually until it reached 3 per cent in 1949. The revenues thus gained would go into a reserve fund from which, beginning in 1942, retired workers over sixty-five years old would receive monthly payments of from $10 to $85, depending upon how much they and their employers had contributed. For people already retired and sixty-five, the federal government would share the cost of pensions with the states, the federal contribution being limited to $15 per month.

The other main part of the law had to do with unemployment compensation. Here the scheme involved federal-state cooperation. A federal unemployment tax was placed upon all employers except those in certain categories. Employers, however, would be allowed a credit up to 90 per cent of the tax for contributions made to state unemployment compensation funds. This was the lever Congress used to encourage the passing of state funds; within two years all of the states had established such programs. The federal law required minimum standards of the states, but the states varied widely in the adequacy of their unemployment programs. Other parts of the Social Security Act provided funds to be granted to the states on a matching basis for the blind, for occupational training of those who were otherwise physically handicapped, and for indigent dependent children.

Although the law was one that a majority of the public clearly wanted, it drew a great deal of criticism about its details. Employers objected to its costs. The unemployed objected that to get unemployment benefits one had first to get a job and then lose it. Others were dissatisfied that there were so many employees in the exempted categories. Some economists warned that the growth of a large reserve fund, taken from active circulation, would be deflationary. But the proponents of the law argued that at last social security was recognized as a legitimate function of the federal government and that the law could be improved in the future. And it was. A 1939 amendment to the law moved the beginning date for old-age pensions forward to 1940, and since then the law has been amended several times to extend the coverage and increase the amount of the payments.

A New Taxation Policy

Another indication of the New Deal's new direction was a changed emphasis in taxation policy. On June 19, 1935, FDR urged Congress in a special message to revise the federal tax system with a view to accelerating progressive income taxation and "encouraging a wider distribution of wealth." Congress quickly responded with a new tax law that sharply increased inheritance taxes, imposed a new surtax on net incomes over $50,000, and initiated a graduated net income tax on corporations.

The Banking Act of 1935

The Banking Act of 1935 was, in the words of the *Federal Reserve Bulletin*, "the most fundamental revision of the Federal Reserve Act since its adoption . . . in 1913." The banking measures of 1933 had been taken primarily with a view to getting the banks open and functioning again; the law of 1935 was a reform measure designed to centralize control of national banking in Washington. The 1935 law was the idea of Marriner S. Eccles, a maverick Utah banker who had become chairman of the Federal Reserve Board. Eccles argued that centralized control of the Federal Reserve's monetary powers was necessary in order to make the supply of money compensatory to fluctuations in the business cycle, a necessary weapon in the federal arsenal in the battle for economic stability. Eccles did not get from Congress all he wanted, but the law did give the Federal Reserve Board increased authority, including power to fix the discount rate directly, to set reserve requirements for member banks, and to control the System's open market operations. The law also extended the classifications of commercial paper against which Federal Reserve notes could be issued.

The Public Utility Holding Company Act

Actions of both the Congress and the President in 1935 had great effects upon powerful public utility companies. Public utility holding company empires, such as the one Samuel Insull built in the 1920's, had been under public attack since some of them collapsed with the depression. In 1935 a demand came for a "death sentence" for holding companies in this field. The companies lobbied intensively, but their effect was mitigated by an investigation led by Senator Hugo Black of Alabama which brought forth the information that the flood of telegrams that had besieged Congressmen had emanated from lobbyists rather than their ostensible senders. The law finally passed in August, 1935, contained a modified "death sentence." The law required the Securities Exchange Commission to limit each holding company to a single integrated system. In other words, holding companies above the first level were illegal. The SEC also received complete powers to supervise the financial activities of these holding companies. The public utilities fought back with a vengeance in the courts after they had lost in Congress, but in 1938 the Supreme Court upheld the constitutionality of the law.

Rural Electrification Authority

On May 11, 1935, Roosevelt established the Rural Electrification Authority (REA) and granted it $100 million from already appropriated funds. At that time, only one-tenth of the nation's farm families had electricity, necessary not only for a modern home but for the new farming technology. The next year, Congress passed the Rural Electrification Act, which encouraged farmers without electric power to form themselves into cooperatives and with low-interest REA loans to acquire the necessary generating and distributing facilities. Where sufficient electric generating power already existed in private companies, the REA co-operatives were to buy their power at wholesale rates and distribute it to their members. The private companies became alive. They went about building power lines to remote rural areas as they never had before. Between the co-ops and the new efforts of the private companies, America's farms rather quickly became electrified. Although city people paid little attention to this movement and most historians have slighted the subject, the REA did perhaps more than any other New Deal measure to raise the living standard and ease the physical work burden of a large number of people.

Expanding Federal Relief

The Works Progress Administration (WPA), created by executive order on May 6, 1935, under authorization of the Emergency Relief Appropriation Act of April 8, 1935, was the biggest, most ambitious, and generally most successful relief program the federal government has ever undertaken. Since the idea behind WPA was to put the unemployed to work on public works programs in unprecedented numbers, the administration denied that WPA was a relief measure. Indeed, FDR had said in January that the federal government "must and shall quit this business of relief." But the public quite properly identified WPA with relief, and its administrators ran the program with an eye toward relieving distress among the unemployed. What Roosevelt had in mind with his somewhat Hooverian statement was a distinction between the federal government's giving direct payments to the poverty stricken and employing them for useful work. WPA shifted to the state and local governments responsibility for relief to "unemployables" and endeavored to hire the "employables" on its projects. Actually, as the record of industry would show during World War II, thousands of the "unemployables" handed back to the states were capable of gainful employment.

By 1941 over eight million different persons, almost one-fifth of the labor force, had been on WPA. The average number on the monthly payroll from 1935 to 1941 was 2,112,000. Their wages depended upon their degree of skill and their geographic region. The average monthly wage of all classifications was $52.14 in 1936. In its first six years, the total WPA expenditure was $11.4 billion. Because of their poverty, the receivers of this money spent it quickly, and the stimulation to the economy in general was direct and fast.

Most of the money went for construction and conservation projects—highways, streets, levees, airports, schools, hospitals, and other public buildings. About one-fifth of it went for various kinds of community service programs which employed people with all kinds of skills—musicians, actors, dentists, historians, and painters. Secretary of Interior Ickes, who was chief of the WPA planning division, concentrated on permanent and material public works; WPA Administrator Harry Hopkins, who was the more powerful figure in WPA, operated on the assumption that painters and actors had to eat even if they could not build bridges and dams.

WPA became one of the major targets of New Deal critics. Some of the charges were true, others were false, and still others depended upon one's basic assumptions. One charge was that too many of the WPA construction projects were of peripheral utility. The answer to this was that if WPA administrators had undertaken projects conventionally in the domain of private enterprise the outcry against "socialism" would have been even greater. Many people objected to the projects that employed artists, writers, and actors. Congress in 1939 eliminated the WPA Federal Theater Project altogether. A very widespread and heated charge was that WPA laborers loafed on the job. Others replied just as heatedly that, although some did shirk, most WPA workers gave more than full value for the wages they received. The most serious charge was that the Democratic administration used WPA for its partisan advantage. This charge is difficult to assess. Certainly it is true that most WPA employees supported the Democratic party, but most of them came from classes of society that usually supported that party and, furthermore, they probably felt that the Democratic party had done more for them in their struggle with the depression than had the Republicans. There were some real cases of local WPA officers using their power for corrupt political purposes in Pennsylvania, Kentucky, and Tennessee. Congress responded with the Hatch Act of 1939, which prohibited political activity for all employees of the federal executive branch below the policy-making level and made it unlawful for anyone to coerce a voter to influence his vote in any federal election. All things considered, one could build a better case against WPA for its failure to end economic distress among the depression's victims. Still, the record of WPA was remarkable in that it provided at least some income to millions who would otherwise have been destitute and, by employing thousands of skilled workers of hand and brain, helped to preserve skills for a later day.

Two other congressional actions of 1935 expanded relief for young people. Congress doubled the appropriation for CCC, inaugurated in 1933. In August, 1935, there were a half-million young men in the one thousand five hundred CCC camps over the country. When the program ended in 1940, there had been over 2,250,000 members in the Corps at some time or another. The National Youth Administration (NYA) came into being under the same act that had provided for WPA. The main purpose of NYA was to provide part-time employment for high school and college students, enabling them to continue their studies and remain off the labor market, but there was a smaller out-of-school NYA program for people age eighteen to twenty-five. In June, 1940, the average monthly wage of the over 200,000 high school NYA students was $4.74; the average for the 100,000 college undergraduates was $12.68, and the average for the 1,655 graduate students was $21.72. The selection of students for NYA jobs was on the basis of need, and the schools, rather than the federal government, directly controlled selection. In colleges and universities the faculty officer who administered the student loan system usually was in charge of NYA. NYA students as a rule worked in libraries and laboratories, did clerical work, and assisted faculty members in research. Some research projects, such as the Lorge-Thorndike *Semantic Count of English Words,* highly important in the teaching of reading and in compiling dictionaries, could not have been completed without the large quantities of skilled manpower that NYA made available.

One final reform measure. The Resettlement Administration, headed by

Rexford Tugwell and created by FDR's executive order in April, 1935, was a Department of Agriculture unit whose functions were both relief and reform. RA consolidated all the various rural relief activities previously handled in the Department. The biggest part of its job was to continue and expand the program, begun the previous year, of buying up submarginal land and resettling the destitute families on this poor land in more promising areas. RA managed to remove about nine million acres of submarginal land from cultivation and move the families. It also built three "greenbelt" towns near Washington, Milwaukee, and Cincinnati as experiments in suburban planning. The very nature of RA's work involved government planning and paternalism, and it drew a considerable amount of fire from administration critics. In 1937, the White House consolidated RA into the new Farm Security Administration.

The Election of 1936: A Champion Political Coalition

As November, 1936, approached, both parties regarded the presidential election as a political showdown. The public would have its first chance to express itself directly about Franklin D. Roosevelt, whose renomination was a foregone conclusion. Roosevelt and the New Dealers would see how politically wise their shift to the left had been. Republicans and old-line conservative Democrats would see how effective their increasingly bitter attacks on FDR had been.

The Republican party did not have an obvious candidate. Ex-President Hoover had his supporters, but the voters seemed to have spoken clearly about him in 1932 when he ran against the same man. Senator Arthur H. Vandenberg of Michigan, who had won in 1934 despite the Democratic landslide, looked promising but he did not seek the nomination. Old Senator William E. Borah of Idaho was willing enough, but he was too unorthodox for most members of his party. The Cleveland Republican convention decided on Alfred M. Landon, governor of Kansas who had also survived the 1934 elections. Landon had attracted attention for balancing the Kansas budget and had the support of the Hearst newspapers, which in 1932 had supported FDR. Landon had done nothing recently to disturb seriously the more dyed-in-the-wool conservatives in his party, and the more liberal Republicans were gratified that he had supported Theodore Roosevelt in 1912. He was a man of little flair and color, but the nomination of Colonel Frank Knox, publisher of the Chicago Daily News, for the vice-presidency lent glamour to the ticket.

The Republicans also had difficulty in writing their platform. The problem was how to denounce the New Deal as a whole and yet appear sympathetic to those parts of it that seemed popular. Their platform criticized the Roosevelt administration for being bureaucratic and appealing to class prejudice, but it asserted that the Republicans supported labor's right to organize, aid to the unemployed, regulation of business, and subsidies to farmers. The Republicans promised, if elected, to repeal the Reciprocal Trade Agreements Act and to balance the federal budget.

Even the more conservative Democrats had little alternative in their convention at Philadelphia but to renominate FDR and endorse his administration

> *Today for the first time in seven years the banker, the storekeeper, the small factory owner, the industrialist, can all sit back and enjoy the company of their own ledgers. They are in the black. That is where we want them to be; that is where our policies aim that they shall be; that is where we intend them to be in the days to come.*
>
> *Some of these people really forget how sick they were. But I know how sick they were. I have their fever charts. I know how the knees of all our rugged individualists were trembling four years ago and how their hearts fluttered. They came to Washington in great numbers. Washington did not look like a dangerous bureaucracy to them then. No, it looked like an emergency hospital. And all of these distinguished patients wanted two things—a quick hypodermic to end the pain and they wanted a course of treatment to cure the disease. They wanted them in a hurry, and we gave them both. And now, my friends, most of the patients seem to be doing very nicely. Some of them are even well enough to throw their crutches at the doctor.*
>
> PRESIDENT ROOSEVELT, campaign speech, Chicago, October 14, 1936.

Both Roosevelt and Garner were nominated amid huge demonstrations on the first ballot. The platform was a reaffirmation of the ideas of the later New Deal. As he had done in 1932, Roosevelt went to the convention to accept the nomination, and in his speech he condemned "economic royalists" who would bring the American people into "industrial dictatorship." In his conclusion he became a little mystical, but his thought was widely acclaimed: "There is a mysterious cycle in human events. To some generations much is given. Of other generations much is expected. This generation of Americans has a rendezvous with destiny."

Both Roosevelt and Landon campaigned hard. Landon seemed unable to excite people's imagination, but he did a good job of what a later generation of advertising men would call "projecting an image" of a sincere, hard-headed, homespun, flexible conservative. Roosevelt met the attacks of his critics by asserting that, instead of being the opponent of capitalism that his opponents charged he was, he was that economic system's saviour.

The flood of Roosevelt votes in November was bigger than almost anyone expected. Roosevelt received 27,476,673 popular and 523 electoral votes; Landon received only 16,679,583 popular votes with just 8 commitments in the electoral college. Landon lost his own state and carried only traditionally Republican Maine and Vermont. He received less than 40 per cent of the popular vote.

An analysis of the campaign and the vote reveals several significant developments. Important for later political history was labor's role in the Roosevelt victory. John L. Lewis and Sidney Hillman, leaders of the newly formed CIO, and George L. Berry of the AFL Pressmen's Union formed Labor's Non-Partisan League in the spring of 1936. Compatible with the Gompers tradition of rewarding political friends and punishing enemies, the League participated actively in several congressional races. But the League also supported Roosevelt with campaign speeches and financial contributions (about $1 million) to a far greater extent than organized labor had ever before supported a presidential candidate, far greater than the AFL's aid to LaFollette in 1924.

Another development with long-term significance was a shift in the black vote. Traditionally, Negroes who voted, which meant northern and western Negroes, had favored the Republican party, the Grand Old Party of the Great Emancipator. But in 1936 a majority of the black vote went to Roosevelt and the Democratic party.

Interesting also was the degree to which the Roosevelt and Landon votes reflected social-economic class. Traditionally, both major parties received support from all income groups. In 1936, certainly, many people with lower incomes voted Republican and some of the rich voted Democratic. But the vote in 1936 indicated more of a "horizontal" division than there had been previously. The story of the *Literary Digest* pre-election poll was revealing. That magazine, which died soon after the election, conducted a post card straw vote from mailing lists drawn from telephone directories and automobile registration records. Upon this kind of a sampling the magazine predicted that Landon would win. People who did not have the money for telephones and autos drastically upset the prediction. Nor did newspaper support make any difference. In 1936 an overwhelming majority of the nation's metropolitan dailies not only supported Landon but attacked Roosevelt with fury. The voters ignored the editorials.

Roosevelt's 1935–36 program had well undercut the upsurge of the political left. In June, 1936, the followers of the late Huey Long, Father Coughlin, and Dr. Townsend formed the Union party, whose symbol was the Liberty Bell. The organization nominated a relatively little-known Republican Congressman from North Dakota, William Lemke—"Liberty Bell Bill"—and Father Coughlin predicted that he would receive twelve million votes. Roosevelt strategists feared Lemke might run well. But on election day he received only 892,000 votes, less than Debs received in 1912 or 1920 and far less than LaFollette in 1924. Norman Thomas, running again on the Socialist ticket, lost ground with 187,000 votes; the Communist nominee, Earl Browder, received only 80,000.

Roosevelt's victory was unprecedented in the history of modern politics. Not since James Monroe, before the days of modern political parties, had a candidate received such an endorsement. Nor has any presidential candidate since 1936 won by such a margin in the electoral college. If any presidential election could be regarded as a mandate, it seemed in November, 1936, that the electorate had given the signal for another four years of the later New Deal. Roosevelt had overwhelming Democratic support in Congress—328 House seats and 77 in the Senate. But no sooner had this champion political coalition been formed than it began to come apart at the seams.

The deterioration of the Democratic coalition was the most important political development of the next four years. The battle over the Supreme Court, the "recession" of 1937–38, and the intrusion of foreign affairs into domestic politics seriously divided and weakened the Roosevelt camp.

The Supreme Court Fight

Roosevelt said nothing in his second inaugural address of January 20, 1937— the first inauguration on this date provided by the Twentieth, or Lame Duck,

Amendment—to indicate that he planned any action concerning the Supreme Court. His second inaugural, one of his most widely quoted speeches, called for a continuation of the New Deal to meet the problem of poverty: "... here is the challenge to our democracy: In this nation I see tens of millions ... who at this very moment are denied the greater part of what the very lowest standards of today call the necessities of life. ... I see one-third of a nation ill-housed, ill-clad, ill-nourished." But the second term was to have fewer benefits for the "one-third of a nation" than the six months from March through August, 1935.

On February 5, 1937, less than three weeks after the second inauguration, FDR sent a message to Congress calling for the reorganization of the federal judiciary. The message triggered a political and constitutional crisis. To understand the uproar over the judiciary reorganization bill one must known the background of the relations between the New Deal and the Supreme Court.

The Nine Old Men and Their Decisions

Roosevelt had made no appointment to the Court. Clearly, the Supreme Court's political complexion was far more conservative than the executive, the Congress, and the mood of the electorate. Four of the nine justices were confirmed conservatives who found their social philosophy in Herbert Spencer and their legal philosophy in John Marshall's sanctity of contract cases. They would not have been out of place on the late nineteenth-century bench. The four were Willis Van Devanter, appointed by President Taft in 1911; James C. McReynolds, appointed by President Wilson in 1914; and George Sutherland and Pierce Butler, each appointed by President Harding in 1922. At the other end of the Court was a group of three progressives: Louis D. Brandeis, appointed by Wilson; Harlan F. Stone, appointed by Coolidge; and Benjamin N. Cardozo, appointed by Hoover. In between these two groups were two other Hoover appointments: Chief Justice Charles Evans Hughes and Owen J. Roberts. Six of the justices were over seventy years old.

The Supreme Court had begun to thwart the legislative and executive branches early in 1935. In the "hot oil" cases, decided in January, 1935, the Court held Section 9c of the NIRA unconstitutional on the grounds that it bestowed an undue amount of legislative power upon the President in the regulation of the oil industry. Only Cardozo dissented. On February 18, the Court ruled in the gold-clause cases. It agreed with Congress and the President that clauses in private contracts that called for payment in gold need not be honored, but it ruled that gold clauses in government bonds must continue in force. On May 6 the Court struck down the Railroad Retirement Act of 1934 by a five to four decision on the grounds that a compulsory retirement and pension system denied due process of law "by taking the property of one and bestowing it upon another."

Then on May 27, 1935, "Black Monday," the Court unanimously struck down three actions. It found the Frazier-Lemke Farm Mortgage Act unconstitutional. It ruled that Roosevelt had acted illegally in removing William E. Humphrey from the Federal Trade Commission because independent regulatory commissions were responsible to Congress rather than to the president. And, most important, the Court declared all of NIRA unconstitutional in *Schechter* v. *United States*. The Court found two faults with NIRA: the law conferred too much legislative power to the executive branch and went too far in its assumption of what constituted interstate commerce. FDR retorted that the Court's view of interstate commerce was a "horse-and-buggy definition."

In 1936 the Court went even farther. On January 6, the Supreme Court in *Butler* v. *United States* invalidated AAA. The Hoosac Mills Corporation had refused to pay the AAA's processor's tax, and the government had brought suit against Butler *et al.*, receivers of the company. The Court held six to three that agricultural production was not interstate commerce and that the processing tax was a device for unconstitutional regulation of agricultural production. In *Ashton* v. *Cameron Co. Water District* the justices by a five to four vote struck down the Municipal Bankruptcy Act of 1934 as an invasion of state sovereignty. In *Carter* v. *Carter Coal Company* a majority of five invalidated the Guffey-Snyder Coal Conservation Act, which Congress enacted after the Court had defeated NIRA in an effort to rewrite NRA benefits for the coal industry. The majority opinion in the Carter case, written by Justice Sutherland, had such a narrow view of the commerce clause of the constitution that FDR's "horse-and-buggy" comment fitted it well. Then came the Tipaldo case, in which by another five to four division the Court nullified a New York state law regulating the hours and wages of women workers. The decision, written by Justice Butler, reasserted the old doctrine that such state laws ran counter to the freedom of contract provisions of the Fourteenth Amendment, previously stated in the 1909 Lochner case and *Adkins* v. *Children's Hospital* (1923).

These decisions against New Deal measures brought a considerable demand that something be done to change the situation. From Capitol Hill came a flurry of proposals to curb the Court's powers. The newspaper columnists Drew Pearson and Robert Allen in 1936 published *Nine Old Men,* a popular attack upon the Court conservatives. Yet throughout 1936 Roosevelt made no overt move, although he and millions of others were concerned about what the Court might do when the Wagner Act and the Social Security Act came before it for review.

The Federal Judiciary Reorganization Bill

FDR's effect was electric when he proposed his Federal Judiciary Reorganization bill in February, 1937. The proposal was both ingenious and naïve—ingenious in the way that FDR seemed to obscure the proposal's real intention and naïve in the assumption that the public would not see through the ingenuity. Roosevelt proposed that Congress empower him to appoint a new federal judge, at any level in the system, whenever any incumbent judge should fail to retire within six months after becoming seventy years old. No more than fifty additional judges might be appointed, and as many as six of these might be to the Supreme Court. In making his proposal, FDR put his emphasis upon supposedly crowded court dockets, the alleged result of aged and infirm jurists. No special perspicacity was necessary to see that behind the reform was a desire to appoint enough new justices to override the four Supreme Court standpatters.

There was a great deal of hogwash as well as some good sense in the national debate that followed. Many of the President's supporters saw nothing wrong about altering the traditional division of powers among the government's three branches and failed to see that in some circumstances a Supreme Court could resist an executive and a Congress in such a way that those who call themselves liberals would applaud. Many of the President's opponents used a constitutional shield to obscure their opposition to the New Deal and exploited the rather popular conception of the Constitution that confused that document with Holy Writ and saw the Supreme Court as a collection of reincarnated Biblical prophets.

Reaction to the "Court-Packing" Proposal

What happened in the struggle over the "court-packing" bill is fairly clear; how to interpret what happened is something else. Immediately the nation's press came out in overwhelming opposition to FDR. Then a group of Senate Democrats, most of them conservatives, met at the home of Senator Millard Tydings of Maryland and planned their strategy. Among the Senators at the meeting were Walter George of Georgia, Frederick Van Nuys of Indiana, Harry F. Byrd of Virginia, and Burton K. Wheeler of Montana, who was then regarded as an extreme liberal and had been LaFollette's running mate in 1924. Wheeler's position was a strange one. His opposition to FDR's proposal was strong, but he had sponsored an even more radical proposal: an amendment to the Constitution which would have empowered Congress to override with a two-thirds vote any Supreme Court decision that declared a law of Congress unconstitutional. Wheeler assumed leadership in the Senate fight against the bill. These Democrats met for lunch with a group of Republicans a few days later, and the Republicans agreed as a matter of tactics to stay in the background.

The Senate Committee on the Judiciary opened hearings on the bill on March 10, and a parade of witnesses provided good headlines. Later in the month, Chief Justice Hughes addressed a public letter to Wheeler in which he stated, "The Supreme Court is fully abreast of its work. . . . There is no congestion of cases upon our calendar." Then on March 29 the Court announced its decision in West Coast Hotel v. Parrish in which by a five to four vote it upheld the state of Washington's minimum wage law and reversed itself on the Tipaldo case. At the time most people interpreted the change in the Court's opinion, made possible by the change in Justice Roberts' view of the matter, as a strategic retreat in the fight. Actually, Roberts had decided to uphold the Washington law shortly before Christmas, 1936, almost two months before FDR let fly with his Court bomb. Hughes had postponed the decision until the return of Justice Stone, who had been ill. On April 12 the Court upheld the Wagner Act with three decisions: National Labor Relations Board v. Jones and Laughlin Steel Co. (the most important), NLRB v. Fruehauf Trailer Co., and NLRB v. Friedman-Harry Marks Clothing Co. With these developments, widely interpreted as a capitulation by the Court, the strength of the President's forces waned, although he insisted on a showdown. In late May the Court upheld the validity of the Social Security Act in two cases.

On May 18 the Senate Judiciary Committee voted to reject FDR's court plan, although its report, signed by seven Democrats and three Republicans against eight Democratic dissenting committee members, did not appear until the next month. The report stigmatized FDR's proposal as "a needless, futile, and utterly dangerous abandonment of constitutional principle." Also on May 18 Justice Van Devanter informed the President of his desire to retire the following month.

Both Van Devanter and Sutherland had wanted to retire before the whole struggle began but had been deterred from doing so because of the failure of Congress to keep its pledge to retired Justice Oliver Wendell Holmes. When Holmes stepped down from the Court in 1932, Congress had agreed to continue the salaries of judges who retired after reaching seventy years of age if they had served for ten years. But Congress had later reduced the pay. After FDR made his proposal, opponents of his plan rushed through another retirement bill in the hope of heading off a more drastic measure. Senator Borah then prevailed upon his friend Van Devanter to retire.

Van Devanter's retirement filled FDR with consternation despite the opportunity it afforded him to make his first Court appointment. Before the Court fight began, FDR had promised the first appointment to Senator Joseph T. Robinson, the Senate Democratic majority leader who was then fighting a strenuous but losing battle for the Roosevelt proposal. But Robinson was sixty-five years old, hardly a specimen of the "younger blood" Roosevelt said the Court needed, and Robinson was an old-style Arkansas conservative. As Senate majority leader, Robinson continued the fight on into the hot Washington summer. Roosevelt refused a compromise, and he and Farley used their patronage powers to try to force Senators into line.

Then, on July 13, Senator Robinson died of a heart attack. His death got Roosevelt off the hook of his Court appointment, but Robinson's friends in the Senate—and they were many among the conservative Democrats—regarded his death as the result of overwork for a cause they did not like. On the train coming back from the Robinson funeral in Arkansas, the southern conservative Democrats mapped their strategy. Upon their return to Washington, Vice-President Garner, who opposed the Court measure, and the new Senate majority leader, Alben W. Barkley of Kentucky, told the President that he did not have the votes for his Court plan and that he had better compromise. Roosevelt relented. The result was the Judicial Procedure Reform Act of August 27, 1937, which expedited the movement through the federal court structure of cases involving the constitutionality of federal laws and which inhibited the power of federal judges to stay the execution of federal laws with injunctions.

These were the main facts of the Court fight. How to interpret them? Many have argued that Roosevelt lost the battle but won the war, pointing out that after March, 1937, the Supreme Court's decisions were compatible with New Deal intentions. Certainly, it is true that thereafter the Court was in harmony with Congress and the executive. But if Roosevelt won the war he lost his army in the process. Roosevelt lost his magic with the big Democratic congressional majorities after his defeat in the Court battle. The cooperation of White House and Capitol Hill that had characterized the reform wave of 1935–36 was gone, never again to be revived behind a reform program.

The Elections of 1938

The battle over Roosevelt's Court proposal was not the only matter to disrupt the Democratic coalition. Foreign affairs began to intrude increasingly upon domestic policies, and the natural alliances of domestic issues did not necessarily transfer to questions of foreign policy.

One foreign matter that tended to disrupt the Democratic party was the Spanish revolution. In 1931 a democratic movement had overthrown the Spanish monarchy. In July, 1936, General Francisco Franco led a revolt against the Spanish republic, supported by the army, the Roman Catholic church, the large land-holders, and most of the businessmen. In some respects the Franco movement was similar to German and Italian fascism, yet it was in other respects more like preindustrial reaction. The German and Italian fascists supported Franco and used the Spanish battlefields as testing grounds for their troops and the new military equipment and techniques. The republican government—generally called the "Loyalists"—moved increasingly to the left and accepted the support of the Comintern. The civil war became a conflict between fascist and communist. Many were the views in America as to what course the federal government should pursue in the Spanish conflict, but in general the liberals who had worked for Roosevelt and the New Deal sympathized with the Loyalists and American Roman Catholics supported the pro-Franco position of the Spanish church. Roman Catholics constituted a considerable part of the leadership and the rank-and-file in the big urban political machines in the Democratic party. The tensions between the liberals and the city machines seldom came out into the open over the Spanish question, but the Franco revolution added still another factor to the precarious balance of forces which is the Democratic party.

The threat of general European war and anxiety over American neutrality in the event of war similarly created problems for the political coalition that mid-nineteenth century politicians had called the Democracy. In October, 1937, Roosevelt delivered a speech at Chicago in which he advocated a "quarantine" of aggressor nations. The speech was definitely unpopular. In December, 1937, Democrats in the House became sharply divided over an amendment to the Constitution offered by Representative Louis Ludlow, Democrat of Indiana. An idea greatly like the one the Socialists had advocated in 1916 and that Bryan and LaFollette had come to favor in early 1917, the Ludlow amendment would have required a majority vote in a national referendum before a declaration of war could be made, except in the case of an invasion of the United States or its territories. Roosevelt strongly urged the resolution's defeat, and it was defeated but only by a margin of twenty-one votes. A majority of House Democrats from the Midwest and the West voted for the Ludlow amendment; a majority of Democrats from the East and the South voted against it. Three-fourths of the Republican votes were in favor of the measure.

The Wagner-Van Nuys antilynching bill pointed up the North-South division among the Democrats. The bill proposed to make lynching a federal crime and to allow the families of lynching victims to sue the county in which the crime had occurred. The bill had strong support in the North, but southern Senators defeated it by threatening a filibuster. Roosevelt, to the dismay of northern liberals, said nothing in support of the measure.

Roosevelt himself further disrupted the party with his so-called purge attempts in the Democratic primaries of 1938. On June 24, 1938, he declared in one of his radio "fireside chats" that he would use his influence to defeat some Democratic conservatives in the primaries. "Never before," he said, "have we had so many Copperheads." The results of the "purge" were disastrous from FDR's point of view. In the contests in which the President publicly expressed his preference, only two of his choices won: James H. Fay beat John O'Connor for a House seat in New York City and Barkley, the incumbent, defeated A. B. "Happy" Chandler for the Senatorial nomination in Kentucky. But Senator Tydings won over FDR's opposition in Maryland; Roosevelt's choice came in third in Georgia where Walter F. George, whom the President had marked for defeat, won re-election; in South Carolina it was probably only FDR's opposition to Ellison D. "Cotton Ed" Smith that enabled that ancient reactionary to win. Roosevelt's favorite in South Carolina, Governor Olin D. Johnston, hardly met most people's standards of what constituted a liberal. When one considers that Claude Pepper in Florida and Lister Hill in Alabama, both considered southern liberals, had already won their primaries before Roosevelt announced his "purge" plan, it is clear that FDR did not do southern liberals any favor.

With the Democratic party at war with itself, it was no surprise when the Republicans regained a great deal of lost ground in the general elections in November. In the new Congress the GOP had eighty more House seats than it had in the Congress elected in 1936, and it picked up eight seats in the Senate. The Republicans also regained power in a number of state governments in what before the depression had been heavily Republican territory. For decades after the 1938 elections, Congress was governed by a tacit alliance of Democratic and Republican conservatives. Ironically, Roosevelt contributed to the making of that alliance.

The "Recession" of 1937–1938

The downswing in the business cycle that came in the fall of 1937 considerably embarrassed the Roosevelt administration, which tried to reduce the sting of the depression within a depression by calling it only a "recession." Until September, 1937, the New Deal had brought about a fairly steady improvement of the nation's economic condition, as the table on page 202 indicates. That the New Deal had by no means ended the Great Depression, even though some of these statistics show a return to 1929 levels, can be seen in the persistent problem of unemployment. The volume of unemployment had declined—from roughly 12,500,000 in 1933 to 7,250,000 in 1937—but no economy with roughly 14 per cent of its civilian labor force without jobs could be called healthy.

Nevertheless, some people feared that the recovery trend might become a runaway inflationary boom. Early in 1937 the Federal Reserve Board raised its reserve requirements by 50 per cent and began to buy government bonds on a large scale. Roosevelt, in his budget message of January, heeded the loud cry

THE NATION'S ECONOMY, 1929–1937
(100 is 1935–1939 average)

	Physical Volume of Industrial Production	Factory Employment	Payrolls	Wholesale Prices
1929	110	108.3	127.5	118.2
1932	58	67.8	54.0	80.4
1933	69	74.9	57.9	81.8
1934	75	87.6	74.5	93.0
1935	87	93.2	85.6	99.3
1936	103	101.0	99.1	100.3
1937	113	110.9	118.3	107.1

against deficit financing and the growing national debt and announced that it was time for a cutback in federal spending. Secretary Morgenthau called for a reduction in expenditures for agriculture, public works, and relief. The new budget was significantly lower. The federal deficit for the fiscal year 1936 (July 1, 1935, to June 30, 1936) had been $4.3 billion; for fiscal 1937 the deficit was reduced to $2.7 billion and for fiscal 1938 down to only $740 million. The reduction in deficit had been accomplished by cutting back sharply on WPA, reducing farm subsidies, and stopping future commitments for RFC and PWA.

The restriction of credit, the reduction in federal spending, and other factors, such as the decrease in purchasing power brought by the new social security taxes, had a quick effect. But the effect was not what holders of orthodox economic views had predicted if only "that man" would give business a "breathing spell" and balance the budget. There was instead the "recession." Unemployment in 1938, according to Bureau of Labor Statistics estimates, was 2,637,000 greater than in 1937. Every other important economic indicator showed trouble. Farm prices, for example, fell from 15 to 20 per cent.

During the winter of 1937–38, there were sharp struggles within the administration about what course to pursue to combat the economic decline. Morgenthau argued for continued economy. Others argued that business had declared a "strike of capital" and that an antimonopoly program should be undertaken. The few Keynesian economists in the administration called for a vast injection of federal financial plasma into the ailing body economic. Roosevelt remained undecided until August, 1938, when he announced an easing of credit restrictions, asked Congress for increased appropriations for relief and agriculture, and embarked upon an antitrust policy that was the reverse of the NRA.

Congress responded. WPA expenditures for the last six months of 1938 were roughly 50 per cent greater than they had been the last six months of 1937. Agricultural subsidies increased almost fourfold. Military and naval spending increased sharply, although the amounts spent were small in comparison with what they would be in just a few years. These actions succeeded in reversing the direction of the economy. The economic indicators for 1939 were almost as high as they had been for 1937. Average unemployment in 1939 was better than one million less than in 1938.

The antitrust drive was doubleheaded. Congress provided the Antitrust Division of the Department of Justice an increased appropriation, and Roosevelt appointed Thurman Arnold of the Yale Law School to be head of the Division. Arnold began nearly a hundred new antitrust suits, although by the time the cases could reach their climax, defense and war considerations had changed the administration's antitrust policy once more. The other part of the antitrust program was the Temporary National Economic Committee, created by Congress in June, 1938. The TNEC conducted hearings for several months and launched many special research projects to study how concentrated economic power was in America and how that concentration had been achieved. Never before or since has there been such a thorough study of American monopoly and its methods, and the TNEC hearings and research monographs, which run several feet on the library shelves, constitute a gold mine of information about the operation of the American economy in the late 1930's. The TNEC's final recommendation in the spring of 1941 contained nothing startling; by then defense and foreign policy matters had long before supplanted the reform impulse.

The Death of the New Deal

To say precisely when the New Deal died is impossible, for it did so without announcement and without drama. Reform did not die of a heart attack; it died of a slow smothering. Certainly, when Roosevelt said after the United States entered the war, referring to himself, that "Dr. Win-the-War" had replaced "Dr. New Deal" he only recognized a change that had occurred long before. Perhaps recognition of the death of the New Deal came in FDR's message to Congress of January 4, 1939, when he said, "We have now passed the period of internal conflict in the launching of our program of social reform. Our full energies may now be released to invigorate the processes of recovery in order to preserve our reforms." Perhaps its death could be dated even earlier.

Indeed, after the 1936 elections the Fair Labor Standards Act of 1938 was the only important reform measure enacted, the only new departure that directly benefited large numbers of ordinary people. The idea of this measure was by no means altogether new, since in 1936 the Walsh-Healy Government Contracts Act had become law. The Walsh-Healy law required all employers who had contracts with the federal government of $10,000 or more to pay at least the prevailing wages of their locality, to provide an eight-hour day and a forty-hour week, and not to hire boys under sixteen and girls under eighteen years of age. Thereafter, the movement to spread a "floor under wages and a ceiling over hours" bogged down. In 1937 an FDR-sponsored wage-hours bill passed the Senate but failed to get through the House. Southern communities regarded low wages as their best lure in persuading northern businesses to move south, some northern businessmen wanted to continue paying low wages to at least some of their employees, and farmers everywhere who employed much labor opposed any increase in their business costs. The wage-hours bill finally got through Congress in the spring of 1938, but only after exempting sailors, domestic employees, and agricultural workers from its provisions. The new law applied to employees engaged in interstate commerce or in production of goods destined for such interstate movement. The minimum wage under the law was twenty-five cents an hour, to be increased gradually until reaching forty cents in 1945. Maximum hours were forty-four, to be reduced by 1940 to forty hours. Employees were to be paid time-and-a-half for all work over the maximum hours. The Act also forbade employment of children under sixteen years of age and under eighteen in certain dangerous industries. These minimums were modest enough; a worker might still receive only $10 for forty hours' work. But when the law went into effect its outcome was to increase wages for roughly 350,000 employees and to reduce the workweek of about one million people.

The New AAA and the National Housing Act

Two other laws of the first half of Roosevelt's second term deserve mention: the new AAA and the Wagner-Steagall National Housing Act of 1937. Neither of these measures in any significant way began programs that had not already been pursued earlier in the New Deal. When the Supreme Court invalidated the first AAA in January, 1936, Congress responded the following month with the Soil Conservation and Domestic Allotment Act. This law made soil conservation rather than crop restriction its ostensible purpose and circumvented the Court's objection to the AAA processing tax by paying benefits to farmers from regular federal revenues. In February, 1938, a new, permanent Agricultural Adjustment Act became law.

The new AAA retained the soil-conservation and benefit-payment aspects of the earlier programs. If the growers of five basic crops—cotton, tobacco, rice, wheat, and corn—so voted by a two-thirds majority in a referendum, marketing quotas would be enforced. Farmers who sold more than their established quota of these crops were subject to heavy fines. The Act also authorized the Commodity Credit Corporation to make storage loans of up to 75 per cent of the parity price—later increased to 85 per cent. In other words, if the market price of one of the five basic commodities should fall below 75 per cent of parity, the farmer had the option of storing his crop and receiving a loan from the government. Agriculture Secretary Wallace called this feature of the Act the "ever-normal granary," the idea being that a surplus in abundant years would be stored for lean years. The trouble in practice was that, for most crops in most years, there was only surplus. The new AAA also provided federal crop insurance for wheat-growers, the premiums and the benefits to be paid either in wheat or its cash equivalent.

Most of the Act was only a new device for subsidies to commercial farmers who took the option of participating in the program. But there was one new feature which worked for the direct benefit of urban families. The Act empowered the Surplus Marketing Administration to purchase food surpluses and distribute them to families on relief or on WPA and to school lunch programs. Under this arrangement a food stamp plan developed. Relief families received food stamps entitling them to a half-dollar's worth of surplus food for every dollar they spent for food in the usual way. The return of prosperity, which came only when defense and war contracts stimulated industry, ended the food stamp plan.

The National Housing Act of 1937 provided for the continuation and expansion of urban slum clearance and public housing that had begun under PWA.

Under this Act the United States Housing Authority could lend local housing authorities up to 100 per cent of the cost of new public-housing apartments which were reserved for families with low incomes. Private real estate interests prevented an expansion of USHA activities in 1939. New housing under the law was only a beginning of a solution to the enormous slum and housing problem that confronted, and still confronts, the nation's poor, but it was a necessary step toward a vital goal.

But despite such laws, after 1937 the New Deal was on the wane and on the defensive. In 1939 and 1940 the conservative congressional alliance of southern Democrats and northern Republicans attempted to pass crippling amendments to the nation's labor law, which were defeated only by all-out efforts in labor's camp. The Miller-Tydings Act of 1937 amended the antitrust laws to make manufacturers' price maintenance agreements legal. Under such agreements, euphemistically known as "fair trade," manufacturers determined the price retailers must charge for their products.

The New Deal: An Appraisal

What can one say of the New Deal to summarize it? This much seems clear: it relieved economic distress, although it by no means eliminated poverty; it improved the nation's economic condition, although it was the war rather than the New Deal that brought a return of prosperity (there still were 7,600,000 unemployed in January, 1941); it brought vitally needed social-economic reforms that brought to fruition some of the demands of progressives of the previous half-century. What were the motives of Roosevelt and the other New Dealers? The motives of human beings are complex, but most people would agree that the New Dealers wanted to provide relief and bring about recovery, that they were ever sensitive to political advantage, and that most of what they did was tempered by humanitarian considerations. Did the New Deal "save capitalism" from failure as many historians have written and as Roosevelt himself so confidently assumed? To know really the answer to the question, one must know what would have happened if there had been no New Deal. In a sense, capitalism had failed before Roosevelt took office. The question was: Would it be rebuilt or would it be scrapped for some other economic arrangement? It was in fact rebuilt. The capitalism that emerged from the New Deal years was not a duplicate of the predepression model. The federal government had assumed a larger role in the operation of the economy and had acquired new powers to regulate it, and organized labor and organized agriculture were stronger than they had been before 1933. But the new model was unmistakably still capitalism; production for profit rather than production for use was still the economic order of things.

Economic Change
in a Time of Trouble

I see millions lacking the means to buy the products
of farm and factory and by their poverty
denying work and productiveness to many other millions.
I see one-third of a nation ill-housed, ill-clad, ill-nourished.

FRANKLIN D. ROOSEVELT,
Second Inaugural Address, 1937

Chapter Eleven

Important for the economy as were the political events in Washington in the 1930's, one cannot grasp all the important economic changes of the period by focusing on Washington alone. In areas of activity not related to the nation's capital, or only indirectly related to it, there were many economic developments which affected the way Americans lived. Perhaps the most significant of these were the growth in the strength of the labor movement, the social and economic experiment of the Tennessee Valley Authority, the continuing technological revolution, basic changes in the economics of agriculture, and a continuing tendency toward industrial and financial monopoly.

Organized Labor, 1929–1935

In the last year of prosperity organized labor was weaker than it had been during World War I. In 1929 the AFL had only 2.77 million members. Its poor condition was partly the result of employer and government opposition, but much of the responsibility for the decline must be put upon its undistinguished leadership, which was lacking in militance, vigor, and imagination.

The early depression worked hardship even on craft unions. Unemployment and partial employment made it difficult or impossible for members to pay their dues. Some employers took advantage of growing unemployment and resulting competition for jobs to weaken the unions. Others who had no quarrel with the unions in their shops were in difficulty when their competitors broke unions and lowered their labor costs. By 1933 AFL membership had declined to 2.3 million.

Section 7a of NIRA, which declared "employees shall have the right to organize and bargain collectively through representatives of their own choosing," stimulated labor organization. Using such slogans as "The President wants you to join the Union," trade unions increased their membership but were soon to find that Section 7a was not the boon labor leaders at first thought it would be.

A few employers, such as Henry Ford, chose to stay outside of NRA altogether rather than to give an inch toward unionism. More employers circumvented the spirit but not the letter of the law by resorting to "company unions." A company union is not a bona fide labor organization; it is by definition dominated by and dependent on the employer. By 1935 there were 593 company unions, of which almost two-thirds had been founded after passage of NRA. These "phony unions" had 2,500,000 members.

The administration of Section 7a also vitiated the law. The National Labor Board, of which Senator Wagner was chairman, tried to give the NRA labor provision real substance, but the NLB had little actual power, and NRA administrators and the President himself on important occasions made administrative decisions contrary to NLB's wishes. When Roosevelt abolished NLB in July, 1934, and established a new National Labor Relations Board, the new board was only slightly more effective.

The auto industry illustrated the frustrations that labor organizations found under NRA. This relatively new industry was traditionally "open shop." Craft unions had made a few efforts to organize skilled workers in the industry and there had been sporadic attempts to organize the mass of the unskilled, but company opposition and employee disinterest had prevented any real results. In March, 1934, however, two thousand workers at Fisher Body voted for a strike to achieve union recognition, a 20 per cent wage increase, and a thirty-hour week. Labor unrest was considerable, and a strike threatened to spread and tie up the industry. Since auto production was a vital part of the economy, the administration in Washington was eager to prevent an interruption of production. The day before the strike was to begin FDR got a postponement and persuaded management and labor to accept a "compromise" which fell far short of granting the union what it wanted. Instead of majority representation by a union within a company, Roosevelt forced through a plan that called for proportional representation and circumvented the NLB by creating a special Automobile Labor Board. Proportional representation made real unionism impossible. Under this arrangement any number of unions, including company unions and all kinds of splinter organizations, could represent its members in collective bargaining, and management, confronted with divided opposition, could play off one group against another. Before the Supreme Court killed NRA in May, 1935, Roosevelt had created special labor boards for textiles and steel as well as automobiles.

The Wagner Act of July, 1935, eliminated most of the legal roadblocks to a vigorous labor movement, and soon there were startling developments within the labor movement. The combination of the Wagner Act and the new CIO vastly altered labor-management relations. Until the New Deal, Big Business had stood almost alone in the industrial sector of the American economy. Early in the Roosevelt first term, Big Government had come into being. After 1936–37 Big Business was to be confronted by Big Labor.

Labor's Civil War

For several years there had been conflict within the AFL between the leaders of a handful of industrial unions and the main body of the leadership. In 1935 the conflict came to a head and resulted in a split into CIO and AFL.

Advocates of industrial unionism argued that only within industrial unions

—that is, "vertical" unions embracing all of the workers of an industry no matter what their craft or degree of skill—could the mass production and basic industries such as steel and auto be recognized. Craft unionists were not interested in unionizing the unskilled workers in such industries. Furthermore, they identified industrial unionism with economic radicalism and pointed with alarm to the old IWW, even though the AFL had long contained the industrially organized United Mine Workers whose president, John L. Lewis, was usually a Republican. But the industrial *versus* craft union argument was only part of the conflict which led to the founding of the CIO, although it was a central part. In general, the leaders of the industrial unions in the AFL were more interested in political action than the more conservative leaders who dominated the AFL executive board. Further, the industrial unionists were far more militant. The record of craft and industrial unions under NRA demonstrated that. From June, 1933, to May, 1935, craft union membership grew by 13 per cent; the few industrial unions then in existence increased their membership by 132 per cent. Lewis' UMW grew from about sixty thousand to about five hundred thousand. The International Ladies' Garment Workers Union (ILGWU) increased fourfold, and the United Textile Workers trebled its membership.

The progressive yeast that was working in the minds of millions of Americans and the upturn of business that came in 1933 and 1934 led thousands of workers in basic industries to try to organize themselves. They received "federal charters" from the AFL. They were not component national or international unions, such as the printers or the painters; they were only local unions affiliated loosely with the AFL. Membership in such "federal locals" increased from 10,396 in 1933 to 111,489 in 1935. The conservative craft unionists who controlled the AFL proposed to divide these members up among the various craft unions; the industrial unionists proposed to make the "federal locals" the nuclei of industrial organizations in each basic industry.

At the San Francisco convention of the AFL in 1934, Lewis, with great parliamentary skill, guided through a resolution which called for an organizing campaign in steel and the granting of provisional charters to industrial unions in auto, cement, and aluminum. But during the next year the AFL hierarchy did practically nothing to put the resolution into action. John L. Lewis was furious, and a furious John L. Lewis was something dramatic to behold.

Built like a bear with the mane and head of a lion, John Llewellyn Lewis had been born of Welsh parents in Iowa in 1880. The father had been a victim of coal operators' blacklists; the son began to work in the mines at the age of twelve. Young Lewis married a schoolteacher, who gave him the education he had been denied in his coal-mining community. At the age of thirty-nine, in 1919, he became president of the miners. An ardent admirer of Shakespeare, he had a roaring voice and a tongue spiced with Elizabethan rhetoric.

At the 1935 AFL convention at Atlantic City, Lewis told the delegates, "At San Francisco they [the AFL old guard leadership] seduced me with fair words. Now, of course, having learned that I was seduced, I am enraged and ready to rend my seducers limb from limb." He introduced a resolution condemning the AFL leadership and denying craft unions the power to organize basic industry. His resolution was defeated by a two to one vote, but during the roll call there was an incident which revealed how deeply and passionately labor felt about the matter. William L. Hutcheson, politically conservative president of the carpenters' union who was a member of the Liberty League, called Lewis an unprintable name. Lewis replied with a fist to Hutcheson's face, and the two men brawled briefly.

Three weeks later, November 10, 1935, Lewis and leaders of seven other AFL unions met again at Atlantic City and formed the Committee for Industrial Organization. William Green charged them with dual unionism and urged them to disband, but in January they again demanded charters for industrial unions from the AFL executive board. The board ordered the CIO to dissolve, and when it refused to do so, suspended the CIO unions from the AFL. The 1937 AFL convention expelled them altogether. The ten expelled CIO unions were: the UMW; Sidney Hillman's Amalgamated Clothing Workers; the Oil Field, Gas Well, and Refinery Workers; Mine, Mill, and Smelter Workers; United Textile Workers; United Auto Workers; United Rubber Workers; the glass workers; Amalgamated Iron and Steel Workers; and David Dubinsky's ILGWU. After their final expulsion from the AFL, the CIO unions reorganized as the Congress of Industrial Organizations.

The CIO's Victories

The CIO was particularly eager to organize the steel industry. Lewis, the CIO president, wanted organized allies in steel since that industry was so closely related to coal. In early 1936 the CIO reached an agreement with the weak and ineffective Amalgamated Iron and Steel Workers and established the Steel Workers Organizing Committee (SWOC). CIO put $500,000, mostly from the UMW, and many of its best organizers into the campaign to unionize steel workers. SWOC worked largely within the company unions, where there was considerable dissatisfaction.

The UAW and the Sit-Down

The plan was to postpone organizing other industries until the CIO succeeded in steel, but the auto workers would not wait. In the fall of 1936 the UAW had only thirty thousand members and no contracts; a year later, it had about four hundred thousand members and contracts with 381 companies. The sit-down strike was the weapon. In December, 1936, employees of the Fisher Body plant in Cleveland sat down at their jobs, declared themselves on strike, refused to leave the plant, and presented their demands to management. Their idea spread quickly. In January, 1937, when General Motors officials refused to bargain, UAW began a sit-down against that firm, the largest of the industry. There was little that management could do to break a sit-down strike. Any efforts to bring in strikebreakers or to clear out the strikers with police or company guards would result in a pitched battle that would endanger the company's machinery. GM made one effort to dislodge the strikers from a Chevrolet plant in Michigan, but the Chevrolet local president, a young man named Walter Reuther, proved an able battle tactician and the company police gave up the fight. GM, unable to defeat the UAW and eager for the profits the optimistic economic outlook promised—the "recession" did not begin until the fall of 1937—had no alternative but to surrender. The UAW got almost all it asked. A strike against Chrysler brought quick results; Chrysler signed a contract with the UAW in April.

Of the important auto firms only the Ford Motor Company was able to resist the UAW. Henry Ford, the founder of the business, still directed it, and the Ford family controlled almost all of its stock. The company was one of the few giant family firms left in America. Ford had an effective antiunion organization in what was called the Ford Service Organization, headed by an ex-boxer named Harry Bennett. Using labor spies and violence when he thought necessary, Ford was able to hold off the UAW until 1941, when, after a strike, he too capitulated.

The wave of sit-down strikes in auto in the winter of 1936–37 presents some interesting insights into the social psychology of American workers during the depression. The auto workers were militant. They would not take no for an answer, and they were ready to fight. Morale was superb among the strikers. But—and this attitude confounded Marxist revolutionaries—the sit-down strikers were not the least interested in social revolution. They did not present demands for a labor owned and controlled industry, and they were careful not to damage industrial property during the sit-downs. Their demands were only for a union contract. If ever in America's recent history there was what Marxists call a "revolutionary movement" it was in Detroit in early 1937—even young girls working at soda fountains, excited by the UAW's success, took keys by force from their drug store managers, locked the doors, and declared a sit-down—but the goals of this wave of labor excitement were the traditional ones of the labor movement.

Organizing Steel and Other Basic Industries

Unionism's successes in auto put a new light upon the SWOC campaign. In March, 1937, the month after GM signed with UAW, officials of the Carnegie-Illinois Steel Company, the largest of the firms in the huge United States Steel holding company, agreed to a contract with SWOC without a strike. The contract gave union recognition, a forty-hour week, a 10 per cent wage increase, seniority rights, and paid vacations. Other United States Steel subsidiaries and many independent firms quickly followed suit. Here, indeed, was a turning point in American industrial history. Within two months, two of the nation's largest aggregations of capital, General Motors and United States Steel, long vigorous opponents of unionism, had surrendered to the CIO.

The four companies of "Little Steel"—Republic, Inland, Bethlehem, and Youngstown Sheet and Tube—led by Tom Girdler of Republic, fought on against the CIO in the old-fashioned manner. SWOC began a conventional strike in May, 1937. Inland agreed to unionize, but the others resisted. On Memorial Day at the Republic plant in South Chicago, police killed ten pickets and wounded many others. The strike was lost. Eventually, in 1941, when again a bright economic future made management want industrial peace and uninterrupted production, "Little Steel" bowed to the law as interpreted by the Wagner Act's National Labor Relations Board and signed contracts with SWOC.

The CIO went on to organize most other basic industries. By Pearl Harbor the CIO had about five million members. But the growth of the CIO had not weakened the AFL. Significantly, when presented with competition, the AFL began to expand as it had not done since World War I. By the end of 1941, about four and a half million workers belonged to AFL unions. About another million were in independent unions. Trade union membership had grown roughly three and one-half times since 1933.

Labor-Employer Relationships

The trade unions had achieved their new status only through their own efforts. The Wagner Act had been a tremendous boon, but it had not been the gift of the Roosevelt administration. And employers had fought the unions tooth and nail until they came to the conclusion that further resistance would cost them more in profits than it was worth. Eventually, most big employers not only learned to live with the unions but to welcome the production stability they usually offered. But at first they almost universally regarded unions as dangerous intruders into what they considered their exclusive right to determine all corporate policy, including labor policy. A special investigation by a Senate committee headed by Robert M. LaFollette, Jr., revealed the lengths to which many employers went to defeat unions. Many of the important and respected firms of the nation employed the services of so-called industrial detective agencies for antiunion espionage. Labor spies sought the position of recording secretary of locals in order to get lists of names and other union records; spies also acted as *agents provocateurs,* and the amount of union violence and crime that was actually employer-inspired will never be accurately known. An NLRB member estimated that, in the 1930's, employers spent $80 million a year for labor spy services. A few employers also spent large amounts of money for firearms, ammunition, and tear gas.

One of the most effective weapons against unions was the ancient charge that unionism was economic radicalism and that trade union leaders were foreign-inspired subversives whose purpose was to destroy the republic. This charge in various forms was common, especially against the CIO. Until the late 1940's, there were enough Communists in the leadership of certain CIO unions to give sting to the accusation. In the great wave of unionization, workers in basic industry had clamored for organization to such an extent that the existing supply of organizers was inadequate. Into the vacuum rushed Communist functionaries. Established CIO leaders were usually able to keep them out of fields in which they were directly interested. A few Communists managed even to infiltrate national CIO headquarters, although they were never strong enough to determine policy.

The Tennessee Valley Authority

Even before the depression the area of the upper Tennessee Valley and its tributaries was a poor land with poor people. The land was hilly to mountainous, the soil was poor to ordinary, and investment capital was nonexistent to scarce. With the depression, bad conditions only became worse. But the Tennessee

Valley Authority (TVA) provided economic stimulation and capital improvement that boosted the region's economy, saved soil from erosion, and prevented floods downstream; and most important, it enormously bolstered the nation's supply of electrical energy.

Harnessing the Tennessee River had been a political issue long before TVA. The National Defense Act of 1916, among other things, authorized the President to construct a plant for the manufacture of nitrates by the use of water power. In late 1917, President Wilson designated Muscle Shoals on the Tennessee River in northern Alabama as the site. The war ended before the plants there could become productive, but in the early 1920's work on Wilson Dam was completed. In the first month of the Harding administration in 1921, the Secretary of War invited proposals from private business for acquisition of the facilities. Henry Ford submitted a complicated plan that would have cost him millions of dollars but would also have profited him enormously. The Harding and Coolidge administrations were enthusiastic about Ford's plan, as were southern agricultural interests which wanted the fertilizer the plants could produce. The House of Representatives accepted the Ford scheme in March, 1924, but George W. Norris of Nebraska, chairman of the Agriculture and Forestry Committee, blocked the bill in the Senate. Norris had conceived the idea that was the kernel of TVA: a vast hydroelectric and water control system operated by the federal government. Norris' idea was at first unpopular, and it was only by parliamentary maneuvering and threatening to filibuster that Norris succeeded in 1925 in preventing Wilson Dam from being turned over to private interests. In 1928, however, Norris got a bill through Congress which called for the government's operation of the dam and nitrate plants and the building of a new dam upstream to insure a steady supply of adequate water for Wilson Dam. Coolidge killed the bill with a pocket veto. Norris got another Muscle Shoals bill through Congress in February, 1931. Hoover vetoed the bill on conventional private enterprise grounds.

Between his election and first inauguration, Franklin D. Roosevelt visited the Tennessee Valley with Senator Norris. FDR agreed with Norris and even expanded on the Senator's vision. On April 10, 1933, FDR asked Congress to create the TVA.

> It is clear that the Muscle Shoals development is but a small part of the potential public usefulness of the entire Tennessee River. Such use ... transcends mere power development: it enters the wide fields of flood control, soil erosion, afforestation, elimination from agricultural use of marginal lands, and distribution and diversification of industry. In short, this power development of war days leads logically to national planning for a complete river watershed. . . .

He signed the TVA bill into law on May 18. In 1935, Congress amended the TVA act to clarify and expand its powers to generate and market electric energy.

In the next twenty years, TVA became one of the biggest engineering projects and social experiments in the history of the world. Its activities extend over forty thousand square miles—about the area of England and Scotland—and over parts or all of seven states: Virginia, North Carolina, Georgia, Alabama, Mississippi, Tennessee, and Kentucky. It built twenty new dams and improved five others. It built locks and provided a navigable channel for over six hundred miles. It produced thousands of tons of fertilizer and taught the farmers of the region how to use it and to farm better. It produced billions of kilowatt hours of electrical energy, used not only for the convenience of the inhabitants of the valley but for the powering of the aluminum industry and the manufacture of the atom bomb during World War II. Its reservoirs provided excellent recreation facilities. It saved untold millions of dollars in flood control; it well protected the valley itself from flood, and by holding back flood waters until the worst was over along the Ohio and the Mississippi, it helped to limit floods for hundreds of miles downstream.

Opposition from Private Power Companies

TVA brought about these achievements only over the spirited opposition of private electric power companies. The statutes provided that TVA's primary function was water control but that it could sell its "surplus" electric power, giving preference to publicly owned power-distribution systems and electric cooperatives. It also could transmit its own power and retail it to farms and villages that could not buy power privately at reasonable rates. Very important, TVA could also regulate the retail rates for the electricity it generated and sold wholesale.

TVA early announced that it had no intention of duplicating already existing privately owned transmission systems and began to attempt to purchase some facilities from private companies in the area. In 1934 it made two contracts to purchase parts of the holdings of Commonwealth and Southern Corporation and of National Power and Light Company, both holding companies. TVA and these companies also agreed to grant one another special territorial guarantees. TVA would stay out of the private companies' areas; the private firms would stay out of TVA's territory. The agreement on spheres of influence was to expire in five years or when the power house at the new Norris Dam was completed, which-ever was earlier. At this point, a small minority of stockholders of Alabama Power Company, a Commonwealth and Southern subsidiary, sued to prevent the com-pany from carrying out the contract for sale of part of its property. They argued that it was unconstitutional for TVA to sell power generated at Wilson Dam. A judge of the federal district court in Birmingham agreed and voided the contract. The Supreme Court in this case, *Ashwander* v. *TVA*, upheld the constitutionality of the contract in February, 1936, but the case pertained only to power generated at Wilson Dam, and the Court's opinion did not clearly indicate the constitutional boundaries of TVA's power activities. Nineteen power companies, led by Wendell L. Willkie, president of Commonwealth and Southern, thereupon sued to block the sale of power from other dams. In January, 1939, the Supreme Court again upheld TVA. Without a legal leg left to stand on, Willkie was ready to sell the Commonwealth and Southern holdings in the TVA area. In August, 1939, he sold the entire Tennessee Electric Power Company to TVA and got his price of $78.6 million.

Another bone of contention between TVA and private power companies was the so-called yardstick concept of electricity rates. The yardstick idea was that federally operated electric operations furnished a guide by which to compare the rates charged by private firms. The charges, countercharges, and general confusion over the term were fantastic. Actually, to compare TVA's rates with those of private companies was extremely difficult or even impossible because TVA was a multipurpose organization. Arbitrary accounting was involved in determining what should be considered as a cost of electricity generation and transmission and what should be a cost of water control. The privately owned utilities wildly charged that since TVA paid no taxes and they did, it was unfair to compare their rates with TVA's. They conducted a broad-scale advertising campaign to sell this idea to the public, the cost of which they included in determining their costs, an accounting procedure not designed to save the consumer's money. TVA of course paid no taxes to state and local governments. But authorities did recognize that the existence of large amounts of tax-free property in a local district would create important revenue and social problems, and it paid millions of dollars to local governments in lieu of taxes. The private firms, nevertheless, asserted that TVA's consumers were subsidized by American taxpayers in general. Whatever the merits of the whole complicated argument, the entire nation's average electric rate dropped 23 per cent in the seven years after TVA's establishment whereas they had dropped only 2 per cent in the previous seven years—and the privately owned utilities still made profits.

An Evaluation of TVA

TVA has a significance in political and social theory apart from its relationship with capitalist enterprise. Wise men have long been concerned about a conflict between efficiency and democracy. Centralized power, often necessary to accomplish a huge and complicated task efficiently, runs the danger of becoming autocratic or bureaucratic, whether the centralized power be in a government, a business, a union, a university administration, or anything else. Defenders of TVA have asserted that TVA represents a solution to the dilemma in that it divorces the central authority (the federal government at Washington) from the administrators of the job of generating and distributing electric energy (TVA officials, cooperatives, municipalities, and the private electric companies that buy TVA electricity wholesale). If there has been a great deal of mystic vapor written about "grass roots democracy," it is still true that there is a serious problem in centralization and that TVA avoided at least some of the bureaucratic bogs that characterize centralized power.

In 1937 Roosevelt asked Congress to consider the establishment of other "valley authorities." Congress failed to do anything important on the subject, and the President did not insist. There have been no further TVA's. The federal government's hydroelectric activities, however, already begun at Boulder Canyon on the Colorado River near Las Vegas, Nevada, continued without the unified regional concept that characterized TVA. The Boulder Canyon project, with its canal to the arid Imperial Valley of California, was completed in 1936. The federal government also built Bonneville and Grand Coulee dams on the Columbia and the earthen Fort Peck Dam, primarily for flood control, on the Missouri.

Technological Change, 1929–1940

The Great Depression did not appreciably slow down the long-term trend toward greater technological efficiency in industry. Indeed, increased productivity of labor through technological innovations complicated the problem of unemployment. By the end of the decade fewer workers could manufacture more products than they could in 1929. In 1939 there were almost one million fewer employees in nonagricultural establishments than there had been in 1929, but the physical volume of what they produced was almost as high as it had been the year of the great crash.

New Products

New industrial products in the 1930's wrought changes in the national economy. Engineers during the decade developed a new process of electric welding that made possible the fabrication of steel alloys that had theretofore been impossible or too expensive for most purposes. There was also a great increase in the use of aluminum, of which the Aluminum Corporation of America, Alcoa, had a monopoly until World War II. At first used mostly for kitchen utensils, aluminum came to be used as the basic metal in a great many products in which its lightness was a distinct advantage. The first all-aluminum railroad car was built in 1931, and many truck trailers were made of aluminum. Aircraft of aluminum almost entirely displaced the older wood and fabric craft of the 1920's. By the mid-1930's the DuPont Corporation had developed nylon, a new synthetic fiber far superior for most purposes to the older synthetic rayon, but problems of modifying knitting equipment and of dyeing the new material delayed its introduction on the market until the fall of 1939.

Revolution in Farming

Technological change in agriculture, stimulated by the AAA's acreage restrictions and the money it paid farmers to keep some of their land out of production, amounted almost to a farming revolution. Horses and mules still provided the power on most American farms at the beginning of the depression. Few farmers found the heavy and expensive tractors, which had steel-rimmed wheels with lugs or cleats for traction, economically feasible. About 1930 farm implement manufacturers replaced the steel rims with low-pressure pneumatic tires which increased the efficiency of the tractor about 25 per cent and, by reducing the size of the engine, made it possible significantly to reduce a tractor's cost. By 1940 the tractor had practically eliminated the horse and mule from the farms that produced most of the nation's food and fiber.

Agricultural scientists, many of them in the state universities and the state agricultural experiment stations, developed new plant strains that increased yields per acre and resistance to disease. Thatcher wheat largely displaced other hard red spring wheat varieties in the late 1930's and increased national production by millions of bushels. Even more dramatic were the results of hybrid corn culture. In 1933 hybrid corn was rare; by 1939 it constituted about one-fourth of the national corn acreage.

Communication and Transportation Advances

Communications and transportation underwent important changes during the 1930's. Scientists and engineers in the communication industry made advances in the 1930's which made possible a communications revolution during and after World War II. The Radio Corporation of America, for example, in 1935 built a television transmitter atop New York's Empire State Building and announced the inauguration of a vast television research program. On April 30, 1939, RCA and the National Broadcasting Company made the first television broadcast to the public from the New York World's Fair. President Roosevelt was on camera during the broadcast. Only a few hundred people in New York City had television receivers, however, and television did not become a major communications medium until the late 1940's. Another electronic development of the 1930's that was to affect television years later was the coaxial cable. In 1936 engineers of the American Telegraph and Telephone Company installed the first coaxial cable from New York to Philadelphia, thereby making it possible for long-distance telephone wires to transmit hundreds of messages simultaneously. E. F. W. Alexanderson perfected frequency modulation radio, FM, which eliminated the static inherent in regular amplitude modulation, or AM, radio broadcasting in 1933. The major radio broadcasting networks, however, were uninterested in the new system because it required special radio receivers, which the public was not likely to buy during the depression, and because the broadcasting range of an FM transmitter was limited by the earth's curvature. FM radio broadcasting did not become significant until after World War II.

Some of the most startling technological innovations in the 1930's were in transportation. Commercial aviation at the beginning of the decade was in its infancy, inefficient and irregular despite the handsome subsidies commercial airlines received from the federal government through fat air mail contracts. Although air service was available between most major cities, travelers shunned flying because of the danger and the risk of being grounded by poor weather. Commercial aviation could not be successful until it had better, more dependable aircraft, adequate airfields, and improved night- and blind-flying electronic equipment. During the decade a vast network of beacons and radio directional signals made bad visibility flying relatively safe, the federal government undertook airfield construction and modernization as part of its public works program, and, in 1936, the Douglas Aircraft Company began to sell the famous DC-3. The DC-3, a single-wing, aluminum, twin-engined craft with a distinctive bump on its nose, became to aviation what the Model T Ford had been to automobiles. It carried a payload of nine thousand pounds, and accommodations for twenty-one passengers, and cruised at 180 miles per hour. As the C-47, it was the workhorse of the armed forces during World War II, and even twenty-five years after its introduction it was still the most economical plane to use for short-haul commercial flying. By 1940 plane travel was no longer the novelty it had been only a few years earlier. But flying was still more expensive than rail travel, and most people associated air travel with glamour and opulence. The air lines did little to counteract this impression; they even employed attractive waitresses, dressed them in chic uniforms, and called them stewardesses. Not until after the war with the introduction of "air coach" or economy flights, did the airplane become a civilian mass transportation device.

Cars and trucks became more reliable, faster, and cheaper during the thirties, and roads improved. However, the first four-lane, no intersection, "super highway" of important length was not opened for traffic until October, 1940, when the Pennsylvania Turnpike, a toll road which then connected a point east of Pittsburgh to the Harrisburg vicinity, went into operation. The Turnpike set new standards of highway construction; it had no grades of over three and no curves of over six degrees. Better engines, including the new Diesel engine, enabled trucks to haul economically a larger proportion of the nation's freight. Trucks had a ready business in the areas not served frequently by railroads and required relatively little capital investment. In 1940 the states issued licenses for over four million trucks.

Motor and air transport inevitably had a serious impact upon the older means of public transportation. In city after city during the depression streetcar companies changed to buses, and the urban bus lines in turn limited their service as the privately owned automobile decreased passenger demand. Railroads were also caught in a technological and economic bind. Already hard hit in their operations because of the general decline of the economy, they faced stiff competition from the trucking industry. As natural gas and fuel oil, carried to the consumer by pipeline, increasingly displaced coal for space heating, the railroads lost one of their most important cargoes. Competition from automobiles, intercity buses, and, to a lesser extent, commercial airlines ate into railroad revenues from passenger traffic. Some railroads, particularly the western systems, tried to compete with their new passenger competition by special excursion fares and faster, more comfortable trains. Some of the new and fast express trains, notably the Burlington's Zephyr, captured the public imagination for a while in the mid-1930's, but in general, railroad management displayed little initiative in its passenger operations. Some railroad officials appeared to abandon hope for profitable passenger traffic and actually to discourage rail travel. Their primary answer to declining revenues was to petition the Interstate Commerce Commission and the state regulatory bodies for permission to increase fares and cut operations. Wartime stimulation of passenger traffic only postponed the process of the railroads' pricing themselves out of the market.

Agriculture

A discussion of the AAA programs, important as they were, omits some vital developments on the nation's farms in the 1930's. Perhaps the most important fact about agriculture during the Roosevelt era was the continuing trend toward bigness, bigness both in acreage and in capitalization, a drift toward concentration, due to several factors, that had been in process for decades.

The drop in farm prices that came in the early 1920's quickened the agricultural concentration movement and the tragic further decline of prices after

1929 moved it even faster. When farm prices were low, inefficient farm units could not meet their costs of production, and, generally, big farms were more efficient than small ones. Big or small, the technologically improved and scientifically farmed agricultural unit was the more efficient one, and it took capital to make innovations. The reasons for lower farm prices were many, including nonagricultural technological advance. Synthetic fibers, for example, such as rayon and nylon, reduced the market for cotton and depressed its price. The only way out for the cotton farmer, then, was to increase his efficiency of production, which he did with the tractor and, beginning in the late 1930's, the mechanical cotton picker. The cotton farmer who could not raise the capital for such equipment inevitably fell by the wayside.

Even the weather during the depression decade hastened concentration. Beginning in 1931, western farmers were plagued with a series of droughts. Then came the grasshoppers, which left a path of ruin in their wake. They even ate the paint off houses. Successive droughts and the steady winds that are characteristic on the Great Plains resulted in dust storms. The first serious dust storms began in 1933. A particularly hard-hit area in western Kansas, Oklahoma, and Texas, and eastern New Mexico and Colorado came to be called the "Dust Bowl," but wind erosion was a serious problem as far north as North Dakota. One of the worst dust storms came in May, 1934. The vital top soil of hundreds of farms was literally gone with the wind. Huge clouds of dust obscured the sun as far east as the Appalachians; nearer to the Great Plains the flying grit made breathing difficult, worked its way into automobile engines and other machinery, and was the despair of house-cleaning wives. (Pare Lorentz in 1936 made a great documentary film of this storm entitled "The Plow That Broke the Plains" and followed it a year later with another on water erosion entitled "The River.") Farmers with low capital and credit were wiped out for good, as were even some who had big investments. One economic effect of the dust storms was to reduce the number of farm units and give greater advantage to the well capitalized and efficient farmer outside the dust center.

Farm owners who were unable to compete frequently became tenants, and those who were tenants found their chances of becoming owner-operators diminishing. Throughout the 1930's there was an increase in the proportion of the national agricultural product that came from tenant-operated farms and from big farms that hired large numbers of wage laborers. In 1935 over two-fifths of all the farms in the United States were tenant operated; 47 per cent of all the national farm acreage was tended by tenants or wage laborers. The old American concept of the "agricultural ladder," in which the farm laborer became a tenant and eventually an owner, no longer reflected reality.

Farm tenancy was especially grim in the South. In 1934 the average net income of sharecroppers in seven cotton states, including their "sow belly" and molasses "furnish," was only $312, or $71 per capita. In the lower Mississippi delta, where the land was richest, the tenants were poorest. They averaged only $38 a year per capita. Their living conditions were indicated by the average value of their shacks. North Carolina's tenant shacks were the best in the seven cotton states surveyed, and their average value was only $417. In Alabama the figure was $194. At the other end of the agricultural scale were the well-capitalized Associated Farmers of California, about one-fifteenth of that state's farmers, whose holdings were so vast that they employed most of the 350,000 farm migrants who trekked to the Golden State.

The weight of the evidence indicated that, for agriculture in general and excepting only a few special crop raisers, the family-sized and family-operated and owned farm was doomed. Farming had become a business, subject to the same tendencies toward concentration that affected industry. But ideas die hard, and the farmer himself, the public in general, and the federal government continued to think of agriculture as a family enterprise.

Business and Economic Power in the Depression

According to classical economic theory, when there is a downswing in the business cycle in a capitalist economy and the demand for goods and services decreases, competition among those who sell goods and services causes them to lower prices until supply and demand are again in balance. The theory did not describe the facts during the Great Depression. Lack of competition, the power of businessmen in monopolistic or oligopolistic industries to maintain prices, prevented smooth functioning of the theoretical economic model. Instead of reducing prices, most industries reduced production, thereby causing unemployment which further depreciated demand. Indeed, there was a strong correlation between the degree of concentration in an industry and its degree of price maintenance. In industries where there was a great deal of competition prices fell during the depression, but in only a few of the industries where monopoly or near-monopoly conditions prevailed was there an important lowering of prices. For example, agriculture, which was in general characterized by a multitude of producers without power over the market, saw its prices fall 86 per cent from 1929 to 1933, while its production declined only 6 per cent. On the other hand, the prices for twenty leading agricultural implements, which are made by an oligopolistic industry, declined only 6 per cent between 1929 and 1934 while production and employment fell 80 per cent.

But officers of companies in oligopolistic industries were not averse to increasing prices when it appeared the market would accept a rise in prices. The economy improved in the first Roosevelt term of office, and in the spring of 1937 industrial production was nearly as high as it had been in 1929, although, because of increased productivity per man-hour and growth of the labor force, unemployment remained serious. Industry increased its prices to such an extent that economists warned that there would be serious consequences unless wages and mass purchasing power kept pace. Leon Henderson, then an economist for the WPA, even predicted that, because of too rapidly rising prices, there would be a major business recession within six months. He proved to be right. The recession of 1937–38 began in October.

The NRA and Trade Associations

The degree of concentration of economic power into the hands of a relatively few businessmen increased during the New Deal years despite the supposed antibusiness attitude of the federal administration. Part of the increased power came from the continuing growth of the large companies within an industry. For example, between 1928 and 1938 the control of the twenty biggest oil companies over crude oil production increased from 46 to 53 per cent, over refining capacity from 66 to 76 per cent, and over gasoline production from 71 to 84 per cent. The percentage of the nation's total copper production controlled by the sixteen largest copper companies increased from 81.4 in 1929 to 87.5 in 1937. But more important than the trend toward bigness in business firms during the 1930's was a great increase in the number and power of trade associations, organizations formed by businessmen within the same industry; the National Recovery Administration played a major role in the stimulation of these groups. NRA gave the activities of these associations legality and power. The code authority in steel was the board of directors of the Iron and Steel Institute, and the officers of the Distilled Spirits Institute became the regulators of the NRA code for their industry. Existing trade associations were the dominant power in the writing of the NRA codes or their administration, or both; in industries without a trade association the NRA frequently called one into being. The Supreme Court's opinion in the Schechter case in May, 1935, killed the NRA, but it did not kill the trade associations, which continued to function as always. After the death of NRA, industries accused in antitrust actions frequently made the defense that they were only following practices that had been sanctioned or even required under their NRA code.

Fair Trade Laws

Government, both state and federal, also helped to eliminate price competition with so-called fair trade laws. In a 1922 case the Supreme Court found agreements between a manufacturer and a retailer in which the retailer agreed to charge consumers a price fixed by the manufacturer illegal under the antitrust laws. Such agreements were called "resale price maintenance" agreements. In 1931 California passed the first of the state "fair trade" laws to permit such agreements. Only a few other states followed suit until after the end of NRA, when business pressure groups lobbied such laws through state legislatures at a feverish rate. By 1939 only six states remained without "fair trade" laws. In most of the states the bills went through the legislature without much public debate and without becoming an issue before the public. Only three legislatures of the first thirty-two to pass such laws conducted public hearings at all, and in one of these the hearings came only after the bill was passed. Evidence that these state laws were the result of a concerted lobby is seen in the fact that one of the original bill drafts contained a stenographic error that made nonsense of an important provision. The stenographic error went through the legislature of that state and ten others before it was caught and corrected.

The Supreme Court in a case involving the Illinois law ruled that a state could constitutionally sanction resale price maintenance contracts when the products were specifically designated. Then in 1937, Congress passed a federal "fair trade" law, the Miller-Tydings Act. The Act, which was passed as a rider to a District of Columbia appropriations bill so that Roosevelt would be in no position to veto it, amended Section I of the Sherman Antitrust Act to exempt from prosecution parties to a resale maintenance agreement in states where such arrangements were sanctioned by "fair trade" laws. In other words, in most states manufacturers could control the prices of their products even after they had yielded control of them to jobbers, wholesalers, and retailers. Should a retailer violate the agreement and sell below the established price, he ran the risk of having the manufacturer shut off his source of supply. The Temporary National Economic Committee recommended that the Miller-Tydings measure be repealed and the Antitrust Division of the Department of Justice supported repeal, arguing that "fair trade" laws were a cloak for many conspiracies in restraint of trade. Congress did not act.

A Collectivized Economy

By the late 1930's it appeared to many that power had become centralized or, to use a popular term of the decade, "collectivized." No single economic institution—government, business, labor, or agriculture—controlled the whole economy, and no single branch or agency of government, no individual corporation, no union, no farm organization controlled all its sector of the economy. Nevertheless, centripetal forces operated to build clusters of economic might with powerful leverage. This was no new trend. It had existed for a long time, particularly in financial and industrial ownership and management, and it probably was inherent in an industrial society. In the 1930's the trend was only accentuated with the further development of industrial and financial concentration of power, with the extension of the federal government's economic role, and with the growth of labor unions.

The industrial employee most likely worked for a giant corporation. One per cent of the nation's employers accounted for 48 per cent of all employment, and 5 per cent of the employers had 70 per cent of the workers on their payrolls. The "blue collar" worker, especially in basic industry, was likely to be a member of a large labor union. The "white collar" worker and the business executive more often than not were cogs in a vast corporation's intricate personnel system. The small businessman was sensitive to the policies and activities of the corporate mammoths. Even the farmer, the supposedly independent "sturdy yeoman," was likely to receive benefit checks from the AAA and belong to a powerful farm organization such as the American Farm Bureau. He might even be a wage employee of one of the agricultural corporations that operated "factories in the fields." And no matter how the individual made his living he, as a consumer, bought the products of the huge industrial combinations. Individuals, economically at least, were atoms of the mass.

Society and the Great Depression

The persons who are killing blacks in northern Alabama
are the white workers—sharecroppers, trade unionists,
and artisans. The capitalists are against mob law and
violence and would listen to justice in the long run
because industrial peace increases their profits.

W. E. B. DuBois, 1931

Chapter Twelve

The Great Depression was so severe and so long—over a decade—that it seriously affected the essential structure of American society and reshaped significantly the basic institutions of social life. No social institution, such as the family or the school, can go without change for any period of years, and when the basic economic environment worsens as it did during those years, the changes in institutions become marked. The Americas of 1929 and 1941 were quite different.

Poverty, economic insecurity, and the bleak prospect for the economic future colored society in most of its noneconomic aspects. The fundamental assumptions people made about society and their role in it, the way they educated their young, what they did in their leisure time, how healthy they were, even how many they were and where they were, were all affected fundamentally and profoundly by the overriding, omnipresent, dismal economic situation. For that matter, for many people the depression's effects continued long after the hard times were over. There is an invisible scar inflicted by the depression in the psyche of many whose personalities were formed during the 1930's. Part of the different values and assumptions of generations—the "generation gap"—can be explained by one generation's maturing in hard times and the next's growing up when times were flush, even if the living was not always easy.

Population, Health, and the Family

A declining death rate and increased longevity coming at the same time as a declining birth rate had important effects on the age mix of the population. (In 1933 there were only 6.5 births per 1,000 population, and over the decade the figure was about 18; in 1915 the rate had been 25 per 1,000.) The average age increased; there was an increasing number of old people and a decreasing number of young ones. People over forty had great difficulty in finding remunerative employment, and it appeared at the time that within a generation a relatively small, economically productive group of young people would support the rest of the population. And if the population became stable, as many demographers predicted, there would be troubling ramifications for the economic market.

The declining death rate was due primarily to advances in medical treatment. Nutritionists' discovery of the importance of vitamins to health led to an improvement of the diet, and the biochemists' ability to synthesize vitamins led to their sale across drugstore counters. The discovery that nicotinic acid was a cure for pellagra was a boon to poor southerners. In the mid-1930's doctors began to use sulfa drugs extensively. Research on sulfa drugs had been started in Germany and perfected and applied to more uses by physicians at The Johns Hopkins University.

The advantages of good medical care, however, did not extend to all parts of the population. The poor spent far less for medication than the economically comfortable. President Hoover's Committee on the Costs of Medical Care reported in 1932 that the total medical bill of the nation amounted to $30 per person per year. Those with incomes of between $1,200 and $2,000 spent only $13 and those who received less than $1,000 only $9. Even in 1929 about half of the population had incomes under $2,000 a year. A 1936 survey by the Federal Public Health Service indicated that the duration of illness among low-income families was longer than among the rest of the population. Nor was hospital service readily available to all. Eighteen million people lived in counties with no hospital facilities. The problem was not a shortage of doctor services; in 1932 the average doctor was idle at least one-third of his time.

Americans, ever among the most restless people of the world, continued during the depression to migrate from one part of the country to another in their quest for economic betterment. Curiously, however, the migration patterns during the 1930's were consistent with those of the previous ten years and would continue in the postwar decades. The areas that lost population, either relatively or absolutely, were rural New York and New England, the Appalachian areas generally, especially the southern Appalachians, and the Great Plains. The West Coast states (especially California), Arizona, and Florida had the greatest rates of growth.

The urban movement, an almost steady trend since the country's beginnings, continued during the depression although the movement from city to suburb muddied the statistical picture. Many cities grew only slightly or actually decreased between 1930 and 1940, but when one included the suburban population as part of the urban group, the census figures indicated no reversal of the long-term urban trend.

Families are among the slowest of social institutions to change in structure or pattern, but clearly there were some significant changes in the American family during the depression even if they were only temporary. Some of the effects of hard times become clear in the social statistics. Particularly early in the depression, couples deferred marriage in the hope of an economic upturn. The number of marriages per thousand population dropped markedly from 1929 to the end of Hoover's presidential term and then returned for the rest of the decade to about what it had been. There was a slight tendency, however, for people not to marry as young. Since the late nineteenth century the median age for marriage had declined, both for men and women. (In 1890 the median age for men was 26.1 years; in other words, half the men were older than that when they married.) The median age at time of marriage dropped only slightly between

1930 and 1940, but with peace and affluence after the war the trend toward more youthful marriages quickened.

The divorce rate declined during the depression years, but one should not conclude this decline indicated greater marital bliss. Since the incidence of desertion, the "poor man's divorce," increased during the 1930's, it is probable that the decline in the divorce rate reveals nothing more than less money around to pay lawyers, court costs, and alimony.

As America became industrialized and urbanized, there had been a trend away from the extended family (the norm in agricultural societies of the Western world) toward the nuclear family. (These are sociological terms, convenient despite their lack of common usage: a nuclear family consists of husband, wife, and children, if any; an extended one consists of a nuclear family plus other relatives in the same household.) During the depression, in order to cut costs, nuclear families frequently doubled up with relatives—back to the grandparents or in with a brother's or sister's family—until things got better. Decades later, as baby sitters became hard to get, and as people felt lonely in a fragmented and anonymous society, there was speculation, often romantic and nostalgic, about going back to the extended family organization. There may be merit in the idea, but it did not appeal to those who were forced into it by economic necessity during the 1930's; when prosperity returned, the nuclear families pulled out and established their own households as soon as they could.

"Melting Pot" or "A Nation of Nations"?

European immigration during the 1930's shrank to numerically insignificant proportions. The restrictive immigration laws had an effect, but most countries did not exhaust their immigration quotas. In the 1920's 2,477,564 European immigrants had come to the United States (more than in the 1870's), but during the 1930's the number declined to 348,289 (fewer than in any decade since the 1820's). The limited economic opportunities of depression America did not attract immigrants. Further, some of the European nations were less hard hit by the depression than the United States, and some, Sweden for example, had welfare-state features that offered the ordinary worker far more security than he could then obtain in the New World. Indeed, from 1931 to 1936, the number of people abandoning American life for the Old World was greater than the number of immigrants.

Although immigrants were relatively few in numbers compared to the years before World War I, refugees from Nazism and fascism, both Jewish and Gentile, were culturally important. A remarkable number of the refugees were intellectuals and artists, and their cultural contribution to America was rich beyond all measurement. Among the physicists were Albert Einstein and Enrico Fermi, whose fame among laymen became great when they helped to develop the atom bomb during World War II, but who were deservedly respected by scientists long before the war. Other refugee figures of prominence were the novelist Thomas Mann; the composers Kurt Weill, Arnold Schoenberg, and Paul Hindemith; the painters Piet Mondrian, George Grosz, and Hans Hoffman; the architects Walter Gropius and Ludwig Mies van der Rohe; and the conductor Arturo Toscanini.

The reduced size of the immigration stream and the change in its nature from poorly educated peasant or proletarian to intellectually sophisticated cosmopolite helped to bring about a partial change in attitude toward immigrants. Most Americans of all shades of political opinion had either been skeptical of the wholesomeness of mass immigration or believed that the new immigrant should become assimilated as soon as possible, or both. The goal was for the immigrant to lose all trace of his "foreignness," to adjust to his new nation by becoming indistinguishable from his fellow-citizens. Early in the twentieth century, a few liberal intellectuals had begun to doubt the desirability of this "melting pot" goal and to argue the virtues of "cultural pluralism." They saw much that was valuable in the culture of immigrants and believed it should be preserved. They also denied the validity of the stereotyped impressions of immigrants. During the 1920's "cultural pluralism" as a socially desirable attribute gained considerable ground, and toleration of minority groups and their ways of living came to be one of the commonest tenets of the liberal creed. By the end of the 1930's in the overwhelming majority of educated circles, to express a hostile sentiment toward a minority group, especially an anti-Semitic or anti-Negro slur, was to place oneself beyond the pale of respectability.

But there were many prejudiced people. In earlier periods of national stress, such as the late 1880's and the 1890's, there had been an upsurge of nativism; not surprisingly, that kind of prejudice came to the fore again in the 1930's. The organized nativist movements of the depression had fascist overtones or were outright fascist, and most of them were vigorously opposed to Jews and blacks. Identification of the hate organizations with European fascism, which became increasingly unpopular after it began to threaten world peace, hampered their growth in the United States. White European minority groups suffered far more from personal and social discrimination, sometimes subtle and disguised, sometimes not, than they did from organized and blatant hate groups such as the German-American Bund or the Silver Shirts.

The once scorned "new immigrants" increasingly expressed themselves in politics during the 1930's in the urban areas where they were most numerous, just as earlier immigrant groups, such as the Irish and Germans, had become politically mature. A perusal of the Congressional Directory revealed a sprinkling of Italian and Slavic names among the members of the House of Representatives. In New York State, where minorities were a majority, nationality bloc politics became more complicated. Both major parties there endeavored to present a "balanced ticket" to appeal to Anglo-Saxon, Irish, Jewish, and Italian voters. No small part of the phenomenal political success of Fiorello LaGuardia, the vigorous and efficient reformer who became mayor of New York City in 1934, was that he had an Italian father and a Jewish mother and could speak many of the languages used in America's greatest city.

Ethnic politics came even to the Southwest during the decade when Mexican-Americans for the first time in the century began to be elected to important offices. For example, Dennis Chavez of New Mexico served two terms in the House before he moved to the Senate in 1935.

One could not say, however, that the Mexican-Americans reached anything like the level of acceptance that European ethnic groups did, especially in the area from Texas to California where they were the most numerous. Nor were the situations precisely analogous. The Italian-Americans, for example, immigrated after Anglo-American culture had been well established for years. There was Mexican immigration across the border into the southwestern states, of course, but there had been Mexicans in that area before the Treaty of Guadaloupe Hidalgo in 1848. In some ways the southwestern Mexican-Americans were more analogous to the French population of Canada than to immigrant groups that came after the foundation of the republic. The number of Mexican-Americans born in Mexico declined during the 1930's by about half, partly because of the depression and partly because the Immigration Service applied strictly the law's provision that those who might become public charges could be denied entry. The immigration quota laws did not apply otherwise to inhabitants of the Americas. The big influx of immigrants from south of the border came during and after World War II.

The Depression and Black Americans

The depression's economic effects upon blacks were disastrous. Even during periods of prosperity blacks had by no means fully shared the benefits of good times; with hard times came more than their fair share of economic want. An old saying that they "were the first to be fired and the last to be hired" accurately described the situation. In both the South and North, jobs that had once been reserved mostly for blacks, menial, dirty, back-breaking jobs, came to be filled by whites as the whites' chances of finding better employment diminished.

Lessened economic opportunity in industry slowed down the southern black migration to the North. The net migration of Negroes out of the South during the 1930's was an estimated 317,000, about half the figure for the 1920's. The southern Negro knew that his chances of finding a decent job in the North were remote, but he figured that he would not be any worse off economically, that he stood a better chance of getting relief, and that his children's education was likely to be better. Therefore, undoubtedly, more southern Negroes would have left Dixie if they had had the money for train or bus tickets. One migration statistic foreshadowed a development that was to become major in the next decade: between 1930 and 1940 the black population of California increased 53 per cent.

The Effect of the New Deal on Blacks

The economic impact of New Deal legislation on black Americans was complicated. On the one hand, some New Deal legislation actually decreased black earnings. The NRA codes in the steel, tobacco, and laundry industries provided lower minimum wages for blacks than for whites, and in industries where there was no discrimination in the minimum wage employers frequently fired blacks rather than pay them what the employer considered "white man's wages." The AAA's acreage restrictions program created a crisis for sharecroppers, as has already been described, and blacks constituted a large proportion of sharecroppers. Incidentally, some white and black sharecroppers, seeing no discrimination in their common calamity, organized the biracial Southern Tenant Farmers Union which stirred large southern landowners to a frenzy of reaction. On the other hand, in the administration of federal relief, New Deal Washington consistently avoided discrimination, although at local levels, particularly in the South, officials sometimes undermined Washington's policy. NYA did not discriminate in selection, nor did CCC, although it segregated blacks in its camps.

But if the economic balance sheet is not clear, the New Deal's political impact on blacks is: the New Deal successfully shifted the bulk of the black vote from the Republicans to the Democrats. Black political leaders began to desert their historic affiliation with the party of Lincoln in 1928, when the GOP, in its attempt to get the votes of southern whites, ignored its southern Negro leaders to concentrate on their Republican "lily-white" rivals. During his administration, Hoover lost the support of many blacks, just as he lost the support of whites, because his depression policies were inadequate to halt its course or to ameliorate its hardship. In the congressional elections of 1934, the shift in the black vote became apparent. In 1928 Oscar De Priest, a Republican alderman in Chicago and a political crony of the incredible Mayor William Hale "Big Bill" Thompson, became the first black to be elected to Congress since Reconstruction and the first ever from a northern state. In 1934 the voters in his district, the heavily black South Side, replaced him with a black Democrat, Arthur W. Mitchell, who as late as 1930 had been a registered Republican. In 1936 and since, the overwhelming proportion of the black vote—as well as it can be identified—has gone to Democratic presidential candidates. In some northern states, the black vote became so important as to be almost a balance of power between the two parties, and the growth of black leverage within the Democratic party served to further complicate that party's intricate relationship between North and South, agriculture and industry, liberalism and conservatism.

Many militant blacks, however, were not altogether happy about the Democratic party or even about Roosevelt himself; they considered the Democrats only the better alternative. As late as 1940 only three southern states—North Carolina, Florida, and Louisiana—had repealed their poll tax laws, and it was Democratic politicians and economic interests within their party that blocked repeal efforts. FDR never asked Congress for a federal law against lynching and did not use his position to further the Wagner-Van Nuys antilynching bill. The ambivalence, frustration, and occasional exasperation black militants felt toward Roosevelt was best dramatized in the "March on Washington" movement.

Defense Contracts and Discrimination

As defense contracts in 1940 began to improve employment and wages, blacks noted with bitterness that employers were pursuing a rather consistent policy of hiring and wage discrimination against them. In January, 1941, A. Philip Randolph, militant president of the Brotherhood of Sleeping Car Porters, proposed the idea of fifty thousand to one hundred thousand blacks going to Washington to demand from their government that it do something to prevent color discrimination in defense industries. After all, less than a month before Randolph announced his idea the President, in urging aid for Nazi-beleaguered England, had referred to the United States as an "arsenal of democracy"; Randolph was only urging that blacks be democratically allowed to enter the arsenal. The "March on Washington" idea became popular; by June blacks all over the nation by the thousands were getting ready to go to the nation's capital as Coxey's Army and the Bonus Marchers had gone before. Official Washington was in a panic. "What will they think in Berlin?" was a common question, and what would they think in Dixie if he capitulated must have been another question in Roosevelt's mind. Mrs. Roosevelt and Mayor LaGuardia met with Randolph and argued that his March would do no good and might cause adverse reaction. Randolph refused to call it off. The President called Randolph to several meetings at the White House, but Randolph would not relent. On June 25 FDR capitulated and issued Executive Order 8802 in which he said "there shall be no discrimination in the employment of workers in defense industries or Government because of race, creed, color, or national origin. . . . And it is the duty of employers and of labor organizations . . . to provide for the full and equitable participation of all workers in defense industries, without discrmination. . . ." The order also created a Committee on Fair Employment Practices to police against discrimination.

Randolph was wise in insisting that labor organizations be included in the President's order. Most labor unions discriminated against blacks until the mid-1930's. With a few exceptions, unions until then were only for skilled workers, and not many blacks were in that category. When they did have skills, the unions frequently refused to admit them to membership, which meant that in the few closed shop industries employment was impossible. On the other hand union men argued that all too often employers used blacks as strikebreakers. Racial discrimination in the CIO's industrial unions, however, would be economically disadvantageous, and most of the CIO leaders were vigorous opponents of discrimination. Many black workers were at first skeptical of the CIO; they found it hard to believe that a union could, first, be effective in unskilled industries and, second, would not invoke some kind of Jim Crow. When the CIO's practices reassured black employees, they rallied to it strongly. Most of the AFL unions, by one device or another, continued discrimination.

Perhaps the most important development concerning blacks in the 1930's was an important growth in the numbers of Americans, both black and white, who refused to accept the *status quo* in racial relations. There had, of course, long been militants in both races; they only became more numerous and more vocal during a decade that saw widespread criticism and reaffirmation of democracy. Time and again during the 1930's there were incidents, some major and some not, that outraged many people's sense of fairness and decency, which in an earlier time might have passed almost without notice. For example, at the 1936 Olympic Games in Berlin, Nazi track officials grossly handicapped the great black sprinter from The Ohio State University, Jesse Owens, and after Owens won despite unfair officiating Hitler refused personally to give him his award, as he did with "Aryan" athletes. The whole affair was in the newspapers for several days. To show their disapproval, some of the other winning American athletes refused to accept their trophies from the Nazi chief. In 1939 the Daughters of the American Revolution refused to rent their Washington auditorium, called Constitution Hall, for a concert by Marian Anderson, the world renowned contralto, because she was black. The outcry was loud, and Interior Secretary Ickes, once president of the Chicago chapter of the National Association for the Advancement of Colored People, arranged for Miss Anderson to give her famous concert from the steps of the Lincoln Memorial. The heightened militancy of blacks and the sharper pangs of conscience among whites helped to prepare the way for the advances toward equality that came after the war.

The Erosion of Social Assumptions

It is extremely difficult to say with any certainty how popular assumptions about society and widespread social values changed during the Great Depression. The vast bulk of people seldom reflect deeply upon what makes a society operate or fail to operate properly and are largely inarticulate about what they do believe. Articulate intellectuals often fail to examine and make explicit their social assumptions, and even when they do the historian can never be sure to what degree intellectuals reflect or affect popular thought. The whole field of popular social thought, even after the refinement of polling techniques, remains a sticky one that requires caution. Nevertheless, observers of different shades of political opinion agreed during the 1930's that some widely held ideas were becoming increasingly doubted.

An old and optimistic assumption, so prevalent and commonplace in America that it went almost unnoticed, was that the world in general and the United States in particular was ever progressing. Only a few die-hard reactionaries such as Federalists like Harrison Gray Otis and out-of-the-way intellectuals such as Brooks Adams had dissented from the almost universally held view that progress was inevitable. There might be a temporary halt in America's forward march, people thought, but only a temporary one, and the direction was certainly forward.

Most people never abandoned their faith in progress despite the mess in which the nation and the world found themselves. President Roosevelt called a volume of his speeches *Looking Forward,* and the official name of the 1933 World Fair at Chicago was The Century of Progress. The Chicago fair well symbolized the confusion many Americans had about progress. Its technological and scientific exhibits indicated a splendid improvement in man's ability to control and employ natural forces. Yet the fair, held on the shorefront of America's second city, only emphasized the slums, the poverty, and the general social sickness of Chicago. At least some visitors to the fair wondered if progress in medical knowledge compensated for widespread hunger and if efficiently harnessed mechanical horsepower offset the gray grimness that permeated the society whose economic inefficiency was so obvious. Certainly, few people rejected hope for progress, although many lost their confidence about it.

Another widespread social assumption that suffered retreat during the depression was what might be called Horatio Algerism. It had long been a fundamental belief of Americans that the degree of "success" that a person enjoyed was a fairly accurate index of his ability and character. Calvinism and Darwinism had left most Americans with the assumption that the most successful people had achieved their status because of superior qualities and determination and that "failures" were the result of personal inadequacy, with the various levels between the extremes being the result of degrees of competence and virtue. In such a view of society, if taken to its logical conclusion, there was no such thing as social injustice; there was only personal strength or weakness. This was the social assumption implicit in the 119 novels written by the immensely popular Horatio Alger (1834–1899), which boys continued to read avidly at least through the 1920's.

But the contracting economy of the 1930's was not conducive to continuation of the belief. Many a highly able person of exemplary character found that the assumptions of Alger no longer rang true. Perhaps you could keep a good man down after all. At least it so appeared to many a good man who saw himself and others like him suffer defeat after defeat in efforts to build themselves a decent life.

Many people—indeed, more than ever before with the possible exception of the late nineteenth century—were ready during the 1930's to adopt new and radical political and economic programs. Socialist and Communist candidates and organizations gained support such as they had never enjoyed before. Despite the huge upsurge in radical thought and action, which no one would deny, still one might argue that the depression set off less of a radical response than might be reasonably expected. When the economic order showed itself to be so utterly inadequate as it was, particularly during the winter of 1932–33, it would appear that only a nation of particularly cautious people would wish to preserve the essence of that economic order, even in modified form.

During the decade itself and during the Cold War following World War II it appeared to most people that the 1930's had been "the red decade." During the late 1960's and thereafter, a period of affluence, the perspective changed. Beginning about 1965 an erosion of social assumptions considerably more significant than that of the 1930's began to become apparent, dwarfing in retrospect the importance of the earlier social disillusionment and discontent. The social or economic drop-out, voluntary drop-out, hardly existed during the 1930's if he existed at all. The kicked-out were plentiful; to drop out on purpose was almost unthinkable. Criticism of the traditional family structure was seldom if ever heard during the depression. Hardly anyone doubted the wisdom of the work ethic. In a day that was so terribly difficult materially, people yearned for more creature comfort rather than rejected it, as some were to do thirty years later. Particularly when one considers such fundamentals, surely more basic than how a person votes or what he thinks of the economic order, and compares the depression decade with the years following 1965, he might justifiably conclude that the earlier era was conservative.

Education

One of the most deplorable aspects of the Great Depression was its effect upon the education of children and young people. During the first two years after the crash schools were not seriously damaged, but by the fall of 1931 the restricted financial situation of local government began to affect education. Even in some of the larger cities, school boards cut teachers' salaries, shortened the school year, and ceased instruction in art, music, and physical education. The 1932–33 school year was the worst. By the end of March, 1933, so many schools had run out of money and closed their doors that about 335,000 children were out of school. The poorer states were the hardest hit. In Alabama four-fifths of all the rural schools for white children were closed, as were 1,318 schools in Georgia. In Arkansas over 300 schools were open for only sixty days or less for the whole academic year. Even in relatively rich Ohio almost every public school system in the state had to shorten its term by a month.

Many municipal governments, in effect, placed the burden on the teachers. Salaries fell to rock bottom. In Iowa the minimum salary, which in many towns actually was the maximum compensation, was $40 a month. Oklahoma established maximum salaries; a school board in that state could not legally pay an experienced elementary teacher with a bachelor's degree more than $85 a month, or $680 a year. Several cities opened the school year in the fall, spent the available funds until they were exhausted, and then told the teachers they could either leave or finish the year without pay. The most widely publicized school disgrace was in Chicago, where in May, 1931, the city began to pay its teachers in "tax-anticipation warrants." When the city had money again, the teachers could redeem the warrants for cash. But meanwhile they and their families had to eat. Banks accepted the warrants at from 12 to 20 per cent discount until the spring of 1932, when the financial plight of Chicago was so desperate that banks would not accept the warrants at all. Teachers, with understandable bitterness, pointed out that the coal dealers who supplied the schools with fuel were paid in cash. It was not until World War II that all the back pay was given the teachers in the nation's second city.

The cutbacks in school programs came in the face of growing enrollments, particularly in the high schools. Young people were aware that if a job should become open it probably would go to a person with a high school diploma, and over the country thousands of boys and girls who in the 1920's would have left school at the earliest permissible age stayed on until graduation. There was little else for them to do. A trend toward universal high school education had been underway for three or four decades; the depression merely accelerated it.

With thousands of young people in high school whose limited intellectual capacities and poor motivation would have excluded them in an earlier day, the schools were forced to operate somewhat differently. At one time the function of the high school was to prepare young people for the college and university. But in the 1930's the high schools were filled with students who had no thought of higher education. The educational needs of these young people were somewhat different from those who would go on to the campus. The high schools had two alternatives: they could keep the old college preparatory curriculum and water it down to a point consistent with the capacities and interests of the students or they could segregate the students who planned to quit after graduation and endeavor to prepare them for their careers and adult life. Actually, most high schools chose combinations of the two alternatives.

The colleges and universities also felt the strains and pressures of the Great Depression. In the depression's early years enrollments declined as students and their families found themselves unable to finance higher education. National enrollments for the 1933–34 year were 8 per cent lower than they had been in 1930–31. But the next year enrollments began to increase, and they climbed steadily for the rest of the decade. In 1940–41 almost one and a half million students were on the nation's campuses, between one-seventh and one-sixth of the college-age population. This, incidentally, was a new record.

Students decided to go to college or stay in college for many of the same reasons that their juniors elected to stay in high school. If one had to be economically idle because of business stagnation, he might as well spend his time in a worthy manner. Students with little money usually chose to go to tax-supported institutions, which supplemented FERA and NYA funds with student loans to the best of their financial ability. College people found new devices for cutting expenses to the minimum. A few farm boys took cows and chickens to college with them, and cooperative eating and housing groups became common.

Because so many students were sacrificing pleasure, comfort, and even health to stay in college, there were larger numbers of serious students on the campuses than there had been in the 1920's. Rah-rah and antics by no means disappeared, but a new mood prevailed in most colleges during the depression decade. Certainly, students of the 1930's had a greater interest in social, economic, and political problems than their older brothers and sisters had displayed. Political clubs and discussion groups, many of them leftist in nature, were more active than they had ever been previously. An increased number of students chose to study history and the social sciences, a reflection of heightened concern for such matters that was stimulated by the depression.

The Press

Newspapers and magazines, one of the most important agencies affecting the education of adults, had their own troubles and developments during the 1930's. Newspaper circulation did not decline significantly during the early depression and by 1937 sales topped the figure for the 1920's. Revenues from advertising fell sharply because advertisers had tighter budgets and because radio commercials took a larger part of the advertiser's dollar. A few newspapers went under altogether, the most famous being Pulitzer's New York *World* which quit in 1931. Mergers with less straitened newspapers became common. About 48 per cent of the independently published newspapers in business in 1930 were gone by 1941. By that time only about 120 American cities had more than one newspaper management, although frequently the merged management continued to publish the former papers, usually one morning and one evening and sometimes even one Republican and the other ostensibly Democratic. By 1940 newspapers owned about one-third of the nation's radio stations. In some communities a single firm had a monopoly on all the local news outlets.

With such consolidation, a tendency toward uniformity of editorial opinion was no surprise. And the opinion was usually conservative. In 1932 60 per cent of the nation's dailies supported Hoover's re-election; in 1936 the number supporting the Republican candidate rose to 63 per cent and in 1940 to 75 per cent. Since Roosevelt won all three of these elections handily, there was considerable talk about the "failing power of the press." Politics is an inexact science and we do not know precisely how much influence a newspaper wields in determining the citizen's vote, but it appears likely that newspapers continued to condition their readers' political positions.

Another development that tended toward uniformity of opinion was the increased syndication of columnists. Walter Lippmann, who joined the New York *Herald-Tribune* after the *World* closed, was syndicated to an estimated ten million readers. Some of the other widely read columnists of public affairs were Dorothy Thompson, Eleanor Roosevelt, who began her "My Day" in 1935, the conservative David Lawrence, and the sensational Drew Pearson and Robert S. Allen. Easily the most violent of the prominent columnists was former sports writer Westbrook Pegler, who was given to apoplectic anger at the mere mention of Roosevelt.

The tabloid newspapers, begun right after World War I, grew tremendously in number and circulation during the 1930's. Although they cleaned themselves up considerably after the collapse of Bernarr Macfadden's New York *Daily Graphic* in 1932—this tabloid was so smutty that it was generally called the Daily Pornographic—most tabloids were sensational in nature and characterized by many photographs, a twelve-year-old vocabulary, and a conservative to reactionary editorial policy. There were a few exceptions. One of them was the relatively dignified Chicago *Times,* an evening paper that supported Roosevelt. Another was the experimental *PM,* founded by Marshall Field III in New York in 1940. *PM* did not accept advertising, was never a financial success, and was consistently left Democratic in its policies. The sensation of the tabloids influenced most regular newspapers which also gave considerable space to stories of superficial importance but of morbid public interest. Two of the biggest such stories of the 1930's were the kidnapping of Charles A. Lindbergh's son and the subsequent apprehension and trial of the kidnapper and the birth in 1934 of quintuplets to a French-Canadian family named Dionne. Newspapers devoted miles of newsprint to the five little Dionnes. The tremendous change in American journalism was to be seen by comparing the treatment of the Dionne sisters to newspaper coverage of the live birth of quintuplets to a Schenectady woman in 1833. The New York press in 1833 had seen fit to devote only ten lines to the multiple birth, despite the juicy fact that the children were born out of wedlock.

The tabloids had a parallel development in magazine publishing when the picture magazines got off to a blazing start with Henry Luce's launching of *Life* in 1936. *Look* and several other imitations soon were on the newsstands, but *Life* continued to lead the field. From the first its formula was to have a scattering of almost everything so as to appeal to as broad a market as possible—a kind of magazine smorgasbord with a little politics, art, science, sex, and sport, all larded with human interest and simplified and accompanied by good photographs. Almost everyone from the highbrow to the illiterate could find in it something of interest. In some ways Luce's older venture, *Time,* was a magazine tabloid. A newsmagazine begun in the 1920's that became a giant in the 1930's, *Time* featured a highly unusual writing style, many photographs with snappy captions, and concise simplifications. It, too, had imitators, notably *Newsweek* begun in 1933.

The pocket-sized monthly *Reader's Digest* was the publishing sensation of the decade. At the start of the depression it had about 250,000 circulation; by the war it approached 7,000,000 copies, counting foreign language and Braille editions, and was the most widely circulated magazine in history. It condensed all kinds of articles from other magazines, but its emphasis was on the folksy and the optimistic. When it undertook a crusade against evil, the object of its concern was always something about which there would be little disagreement such as automobile accidents and microbes. Late in the 1930's it began to affect the content of other periodicals by "planting" articles in them for later condensation in its own pages.

America continued to produce a vast variety of magazines of all levels of quality, most of them with small circulations, despite economic conditions. The specialist, the esthete, and the intellectual could find plenty to whet his interest. Yet the huge commercial success of the tabloids, picture magazines, and digests, all of which appealed to the lowest common intellectual denominator, indicated a development that was to become a cultural crisis after the war.

Leisure in the Depression

By 1929 much of American entertainment had become commercialized. People had learned to prefer the pleasures that cost them money. But in the 1930's most people had less money to spend for their leisure, and some had no money at all for such purposes. Of course, the more expensive ways to pursue pleasure, such as luxury travel, nightclubbing, and some outdoor sports like golf and yachting, did not disappear, for not everyone was broke. As conditions improved, more and more people resumed the costlier pleasures of a happier era. But for most people cost was an important factor throughout the period and seriously limited the possible range of entertainment.

Books

The least expensive way to spend one's leisure time was by reading—if one could get books free. The sale of books dropped precipitously, but library circulation took a sharp turn upward. The American Library Association estimated that the public libraries of the country acquired about four million new borrowers from 1929 to 1933, and the circulation of their books increased by almost 40 per cent. Libraries, however, suffered from the same financial problems as the public schools. Most cities cut their library budgets. Some bought no new books at all; the Chicago public library had no budget for book purchases for three consecutive years. Public libraries were crowded places throughout the depression as many Americans learned what some of the more intellectual bums had long known: the public library was a warm place to idle away many pleasant hours.

Radio

Another almost free leisure activity was radio listening. In 1929 a radio cost about $100; 12,000,000 families owned one. During the 1930's manufacturers put out small wood or plastic table models that sold for about $10, and by 1940, 28,000,000 homes had one or more radios, 86 per cent of the population. One 1937 survey indicated that the nation's radios were turned on an average of four and one-half hours a day.

While radio was quite inexpensive to the consumer, it was by no means uncommercial. In its commercialism lay most of its problems. Radio stations and networks were in the business of selling their services for profit, and advertisers bought their services to increase their own sales. The entertainment and edification of the radio listener were secondary to monetary gain. The listener was important, to be sure, but as a potential customer. These being the ground rules of the business, the widest possible audience for a program was the producer's aim, for that meant the largest possible number of potential purchasers of the advertiser's product. Thus radio programs, like tabloid newspapers, tended to appeal to the lowest common intellectual denominator.

Some of the radio programs, particularly during the daylight hours when "soap operas" dominated the air, were downright bad; the great majority were fairly pleasant (to most people) pieces of fluff, not very memorable one way or another; only a few programs merited critical praise. Music was on the air more than one-half of a station's time. The enormous radio demand for popular music was far more than composers could meet with a consistently creditable product. Although some of the "hit tunes" of the 1930's were of sufficient quality to be deservedly revived time and again since then, most of them lie fortunately forgotten. In the later evening hours when there was little or no commercial demand for radio time, many stations, particularly in the big cities, ran broadcasts from dances, and, through these broadcasts, a new interest in jazz grew. Theretofore, jazz was relatively little known among most white Americans. During the 1930's it increasingly influenced popular music, and by the end years of the decade dance bands found that young people especially preferred jazz to the popular sentimental ballad.

The major networks, Columbia Broadcasting System and the National Broadcasting Company, made one experiment in musical education during the 1930's that indicated something of radio's powers. In 1930 CBS began Sunday afternoon broadcasts of the New York Philharmonic. NBC in 1931 began broadcasts of the Metropolitan Opera Company's Saturday matinées, and in 1937 it organized its own symphony orchestra with Arturo Toscanini as conductor. These ventures were at first financial losses, but the networks persisted and the audiences grew steadily. A poll in 1939 indicated that ten million people listened to serious music broadcasts and that a majority of people, except those on the farm and in the lowest income brackets, enjoyed such broadcasts and were happy that radio music was not exclusively popular. It is impossible to know how many of these people merely thought they should like serious music and how many actually did, but sales of tickets to concerts and of "classical" recordings improved.

Movies

Hollywood enjoyed a boom despite the depression. Movie tickets were not very expensive—usually fifteen cents at the theaters that showed "second runs"—and the theater operators provided a lot of escape for the money, frequently with two feature films, a newsreel, and a short subject. Many theaters attracted customers with such inducements as "bank night," at which the lucky winner of a drawing would receive cash if he were present, bingo, and free cheap dishes. An evening at the movies was by far the most popular away-from-home entertainment.

Movies had a cultural problem similar to radio's. Maximum profits demanded mass audiences, and tailoring a film for a mass audience limited its intellectual and artistic quality. As one prominent Hollywood producer put it, "The picture industry is no different from the underwear business, for example. It is completely governed by the law of supply and demand." Movie-goers who had seen scores of mediocre pictures understood the comment well enough. As in radio, the production volume was too great to be consistent with quality. Each year the major studios turned out hundreds and hundreds of quickly conceived and executed screen plays on a mass production basis, films so full of clichés they were entirely predictable. When a film maker did employ a new artistic device he was usually imitated so widely, if the new idea were commercially successful, that the innovation soon became hackneyed. The volume of films was greater than was warranted. Exhibitors were driven to the double feature by Hollywood's insistence upon block booking. The film companies insisted that exhibitors accept their film rentals in blocks of fifty titles; if they refused they would be denied the titles they wanted. The only way exhibitors could use such a volume was to show double features and change their programs frequently, usually twice a week. In 1940 a group of exhibitors went to the courts to stop block booking, and with the help of the Department of Justice arranged a compromise that cut the block size to five.

The economic pressure for mass audiences seriously hampered the artistic expression of Hollywood. An experiment might be financially disastrous if the public did not like it, and producers were careful to avoid themes and ideas that might alienate any substantial part of the potential audience. For example, the more expensive productions had to have a large foreign sale to make a profit, and criticisms of totalitarianism were few until the late 1930's because such films were not permitted in Germany and Italy. The rulings of the Hays office (an agency instituted by the film makers to police the morality of screen plays, headed by President Harding's postmaster-general, Will Hays) were so mechanical that they ridiculously hampered valid artistic expression while frequently falling short of their original purpose. It is not surprising, given this economic framework, that Hollywood's contributions in the 1930's were for the most part limited to techniques of production.

American movie producers, of course, came forth with some movies of quality despite themselves and their system. Charlie Chaplin's "City Lights" (1931), "Modern Times" (1936), and "The Great Dictator" (1940) were memorable, as were "I Am a Fugitive from a Chain Gang" (1932), "The Informer" (1935), "Dodsworth" (1936), and "Citizen Kane" (1941). These films, however, were not notable commercial successes on their first release. The big money-makers were musical comedies, which were turned out by formula, or Hollywood versions of popular novels, which had a built-in market and which usually disappointed viewers who had read the book.

The Culture of
the Great Depression

It is a primary duty for Americans today to be nationally self-conscious, to seek an answer to the question, What is America? If we cannot answer that, we cannot hope to make the real America come true.

HERBERT AGAR, 1935

Chapter Thirteen

In the 1920's most intellectuals and artists had felt apart from the mainstream of American culture, aliens in their own land. Indeed, hundreds of them found both material and spiritual life more compatible in France. The Great Depression changed this situation quickly. It was not just that the crash dried up the expatriates' flow of checks from home, for those who stayed in America during the Coolidge era found, as much as the expatriates, that after the depression they were no longer alienated from society. It was not that intellectuals, or anyone else, found the United States more attractive during depression than during prosperity; it was only that some of the things to which intellectuals had objected during prosperity, such as Rotarian optimism, blatant materialism, and glorification of dollar success, were now subdued if not gone.

One cannot summarize the cultural developments of a people as diverse and dynamic as Americans in a few words or even a few thousand words. Nevertheless, as one examines literature, the arts, and scholarship during the depression decade, he is struck by two main threads: social protest and a kind of cultural nationalism with a strong element of regionalism. Two songs illustrate well these threads. In the mid-1930's the International Ladies Garment Workers Union sponsored a musical show written and produced by needle trade workers called *Pins and Needles* that did well on Broadway and went on national tour. Its hit song was "Sing Me a Song of Social Significance." Then at the end of the period Hollywood filmed John Steinbeck's *The Grapes of Wrath*. The score relied heavily on "Red River Valley," haunting, sad, and distinctively Great Plains and American folk music.

Fiction, Drama, and Poetry

Most of the big names among the disillusioned authors of the 1920's "Lost Generation" seemed unable to come to terms with depression society. Sinclair Lewis' ridicule of small-town Philistines seemed irrelevant to most readers in the 1930's. Babbitts still existed by the score and Main Street shallowness and pettiness had not disappeared, but somehow Lewis struck readers as old hat. The horses that Lewis had flayed so excellently were not dead, but they were pretty sick. America's most famous author in 1930 when he became the first United States citizen to win a Nobel prize for literature, Lewis was a tragic misfit by the end of the decade when he appeared as an actor in a road company that played an embarrassingly poor farce of his called *Angela Is Twenty-Two*. His anti-fascist novel, *It Can't Happen Here* (1935), which sought to prove that it could happen here, enjoyed a vogue when the WPA Theater Project dramatized it and produced it simultaneously in several cities, but it did not by any means match the impact of his earlier novels. Although Scott Fitzgerald improved as a literary craftsman during the 1930's despite alcoholism and hack work in Hollywood, his *Tender Is the Night* (1934) and *The Last Tycoon* (1941) were not fully appreciated until several years after his death in 1940. Eugene O'Neill, America's most famous dramatist, produced nothing important in the decade after *Mourning Becomes Electra* in 1931, although he too won the Nobel award in 1936.

The most exciting new novelist of the 1920's, Ernest Hemingway, was only a partial exception to the intellectual irrelevance of the lost generation. Of his books during the depression only *For Whom the Bell Tolls* (1940), in which the hero was an American fighting with the Spanish Loyalists, smacked much of the mood of the thirties. *Death in the Afternoon* (1932), a paean to bull fighting, seemed, when it appeared, to be something left over from a long-ago day. Except for the *Bell,* it was Hemingway's literary virtuosity rather than his themes or his thought that kept him in the front ranks of American fiction during the decade.

The Social Critics

John Dos Passos, whose postwar novels had marked him as one to be watched, started the decade's theme of social criticism with a roar with the first volume of his *U.S.A.* trilogy in 1930. The trilogy amounted to an impressionistic, left-wing history of America from the beginning of the century into the early depression. Its mood of anger toward economic privilege and political phoniness well matched the feeling of its readers and was an enormous success. Dos Passos was also a major innovator in technique with his profiles of actual figures inserted into the novel and his placement of characters into historical context with what he called "The Camera Eye."

Perhaps the greatest novelist of the 1930's was California's John Steinbeck whose *The Grapes of Wrath* (1939) was a truly major work. His novels during the depression were full of social criticism, his characters were the dispossessed, and his sympathies were clearly with the down-and-out against their exploiters. Yet compassion rather than anger or rebellion was the dominant emotion that ran through his pages, and he was almost sentimental in *Of Mice and Men* (1937). That he was not a politically naïve primitive, as some people thought until his masterpiece appeared in 1939, was indicated by his novel about a strike of California agricultural workers, *In Dubious Battle* (1936). Most of all, Steinbeck was not doctrinaire. His characters were believably real people, not caricatures and not merely sociological specimens. For this ability to portray human situations in certain segments of American life, he received the Nobel Prize for Literature in 1962.

Social criticism on Broadway became commonplace during the thirties. In the year of the crash, Elmer Rice partly foreshadowed the direction of the theater for the next several years with his *Street Scene,* and he became more frankly political with *Judgment Day* and *Between Two Worlds.* Maxwell Anderson, collaborator on the best antiwar play of the 1920's, was another notable playwright critic of society. His *Both Your Houses* (1933) dealt with the conflict between practical politics and idealism, and *Winterset* (1935), a dramatic comment on the Sacco-Vanzetti case, became probably the best known "depression play" after it was made into a successful motion picture. Robert Sherwood, one of the least critical of the prominent dramatists, wrote an incisive social commentary on war in *Idiot's Delight* (1936). Lillian Hellman's *The Little Foxes* in 1939 was later than most of the bitter dramatic attacks on capitalism. The outstanding theatrical production of the decade that voted the other way was George M. Cohan's 1937 musical satire of the New Deal, *I'd Rather Be Right.*

Poetry, once the special form for sentimentality and later for obscure experiment, expressed much of the 1930's social discontent and criticism of the *status quo.* Archibald MacLeish, then an associate editor of *Fortune* and later Librarian of Congress, in 1937 had an antifascist poem, *The Fall of the City,* dramatized on radio, and the following year he put out a combined picture book and long poem entitled *Land of the Free* in which he made clear his dissatisfaction with much in that land. Edna St. Vincent Millay, once the darling of flaming youth, began to burn her candle at both ends over social questions and in 1937 published *Conversations at Midnight.* In this volume symbols of different economic interests and political points of view argued their cases, and the conservatives lost the argument.

Readers of a later generation who come across this critical literature sometimes make the error of dismissing it as Communist propaganda. It was not. Writers, almost by definition, are sensitive people who articulate more widely-held views, and in the depression dissatisfaction with the *status quo* was a majority sentiment. There were Communist propagandists, of course, and some of the writers mentioned here flirted with Communism as a possible solution for America's problems, usually only to reject it either as no answer at all or as substituting one set of evils for another. The black novelist Richard Wright is a case in point. For a while in the 1930's, before he became a writer of reputation with his *Native Son* in 1940, Wright was an active member of the party. In an autobiographical piece about his Communist experience in a postwar volume edited by R. H. S. Crossman called *The God That Failed,* Wright described why he became a Communist and why he quit. Interestingly, his motives were constant; he joined the party because he thought that by so doing he could advance a little the cause of human freedom, and he left it for the same reason.

With few exceptions, the Communist literature of the 1930's was not great, essentially because it subordinated people to broad abstractions and made propaganda its main purpose rather than artistic validity. Most of the so-called proletarian novels basically were the old Horatio Alger tales stood on their head— stories in which a revolutionary achievement instead of financial success was the climax. In fact, the personalities of the heroes in Alger and the proletarian novels were remarkably similar. Their impact has been much exaggerated; they had little, mostly because of their poor quality as novels. Occasionally, a Communist produced an effective piece. Perhaps the best example was the strike play by Clifford Odets, a party member at the time, entitled *Waiting for Lefty* (1935).

Cultural Nationalism and Regionalism

Another strong current in American letters after the crash was the Whitmanesque "We Sing America" theme. The current ran alongside social protest in that its emphasis was upon democracy and ordinary people—being for "the little people" and against their being "pushed around" were the clichés of the time—and had in it a strong element of regionalism. Frequently this kind of literature, and the school of painting that was its parallel, was exuberant. Sometimes, in its emphasis upon ordinary people and upon what was distinctively American, it had about it a vaguely mystic primitivism.

The sprawling but intense novels by the sprawling but intense Thomas Wolfe, an uprooted North Carolinian, were of the "We Sing America" current. In *Look Homeward, Angel* (1929), *Of Time and the River* (1935), *The Web and the Rock* (1939), *You Can't Go Home Again* (1940), in which the central character was sometimes named Eugene Gant and sometimes George Weber but was always actually Wolfe himself, ran a persistent concern with family and regional roots and a disquieting uncertainty when wrenched from them. Wolfe had a tremendous talent and might have gone on to other themes had he not died in 1938 when still under forty.

Quite different was the short story writer William Saroyan, who was nevertheless an America Singer. A second-generation Armenian from rural and small-town California, Saroyan's passionate exuberance burst upon the scene with his collection, *The Daring Young Man on the Flying Trapeze* (1934). He was prolific, inventive, democratic, and frequently primitive. Robert Sherwood worked in the same current when he went back to the humble youth of Lincoln for his play *Abe Lincoln in Illinois* (1938), and in that state Edgar Lee Masters continued to write his poems about its people.

Other Writers, Serious and Popular

Some major writing of the 1930's does not fit into the classifications of social criticism and a regional kind of cultural nationalism. William Faulkner sometimes seemed to work in either or both categories, but usually he plowed his own furrow. Two of America's celebrated expatriate poets, T. S. Eliot and Ezra Pound, were quite at odds with majority thought during the depression, Eliot removing himself from the present with Anglo-Catholic fascination for the Middle Ages and Pound obscurely translating classical Japanese poetry and praising Italian fascism.

Many, perhaps most, of the novels published even during the depression's tense years were intended as popular entertainment. The trials of the depression may even have heightened popular demand for escape literature. Easily the most successful novel commercially was Margaret Mitchell's *Gone with the Wind*

(1936), which sold millions of copies and, two years after publication, matched the Bible in sales. It was a good yarn, ably told and romantic, nothing more and not intended to be. The adventure books and westerns of Zane Gray and others flowed by floods from the press and found an audience, and there was the usual seriously intentioned but banal and shallow "soap opera" novel from such as Temple Bailey and Lloyd C. Douglas. The "how to" book came into its own as a big seller during the thirties, the most popular being Dale Carnegie's *How To Win Friends and Influence People*. A kind of Horatio Alger handbook for a corporate age, Carnegie's book in effect advised readers to delude themselves into being sincerely interested in other people until they really were interested or until delusion became habit. Of detective stories there was an abundance. James M. Cain's *The Postman Always Rings Twice* (1934) started the hard-boiled, violent school of detective fiction that came to full flower, if that is the term, after World War II. Poetry had its entertainers and homely "philosophers"—Edgar Guest was America's most widely known versifier—and the theater continued to produce some quickly and properly forgotten plays.

New Trends in Publishing

Some changes in the economics of writing and publishing were significant. Because money was tight, most publishers issued fewer titles than they had before and concentrated on those likely to have a wide sale. The book clubs, which became large enough to influence the trade, furthered this trend. The Book-of-the-Month Club mixed a few serious novels into its middlebrow offerings and by membership bonuses and clever advertising became a vast enterprise. In its wake were several book clubs for specialized interests. Book clubs were a natural depression growth. They offered bargain prices and by briefing the membership on its choices narrowed the likelihood of the reader's buying a book that would not interest him. Probably the clubs broadened the base of the book-buying public.

A more important extension of book buying came at the end of the depression years with the paperback. Inexpensive paperbound books had long been prevalent in Europe, and in America, besides the "dime novel," there had been *Blue Ribbon Books* which sold for a dollar. In 1939 Robert F. de Graff began *Pocket Books*, attractively covered paperbacks held together with a new glue instead of stitching or staples. The books sold for twenty-five and thirty-five cents at drug stores and news stands and attracted buyers who seldom bought books in hard covers. Historical romances and mystery stories were the stock in trade of paperback publishers, who soon became numerous, but they also issued reprints of fictional and nonfictional classics. In 1941 Americans bought ten million paperback books, and the paperback boom had only begun.

Art and Architecture

The depression's mood of hard-headed immediacy brought realistic art back to popular favor, and the modernists, who dominated the art scene in the 1920's, faded into the background until happier times when painters and viewers again felt they could forget society. Modernism by no means disappeared, but social painting and "We Sing America," both with a realistic approach, dominated American painting during the Great Depression. Hard and fast distinctions between the social protest painters and those who concentrated on the American scene are difficult, for the angry protest artists usually painted American subjects and there was at least some social criticism implied in many of the works of those who clearly were America Singers.

The America Singers

William Gropper, Joseph Hirsch, Jack Levine, and Adolph Dehn, of whom Gropper was the best known, perhaps boiled over with social rebellion more consistently than other artists. Gropper's painting "Legislative Paunch," with its arm-waving politicos with skull-like heads and obscene bellies, packed a great blow among people who were disgusted with political action. Hirsch and Levine frequently painted lawyers and policemen in the same bitter fashion, and Dehn pictured wealthy matrons as grotesque and cruel. These artists frequently did cartoons for left-wing magazines (Gropper was at his best in black and white) and some of their paintings were exceptionally high-grade cartoons in color.

Ben Shahn and Philip Evergood were perhaps the most artistically gifted of the angry social painters. Shahn first came to major attention in 1932, when he had a show of over twenty paintings on the Sacco-Vanzetti case. His "Miners' Wives," done in the late 1930's, was a masterpiece. Evergood's "My Forebearers were Pioneers," with its bitter, frustrated, and ruined old-fashioned New England lady, was a painting of major importance.

Equally angry but quite different in his style was Peter Blume, who was what might be described as a social protest surrealist. His most famous painting of the period, "The Eternal City," was a dreamlike composite of life under Mussolini so biting that the Corcoran Gallery in Washington refused to hang it in 1939, perhaps fearing a diplomatic incident. That the ugly, livid-green head in the painting was the Italian dictator was unmistakable.

The 14th Street School of painters in New York (Raphael and Moses Soyer, Edward Laning, Isabel Bishop, and Morris Kantor) painted that seamy district and its people in a general mood of protest but usually without bitterness. The Soyer brothers were more in the tradition of the Ash Can School of before the war, and Moses had studied with Henri. Their training was with different teachers, rather catch-as-catch-can in the settlement houses of the Lower East Side where they had grown up, but they were remarkably alike in their mood of sympathy and tolerance. Moses caught fatigue in the faces of the ballet dancers he so frequently painted, and Raphael's "Waiting Room," with its hunched, tired women and men in T-shirts and three-day beards, compassionately caught the depression's mood of despair. Both of them were masters of catching their subjects at unguarded moments, similar to the candid camera's "slice of life." One of the most remarkable pictures of the school was Kantor's "Farewell to Union Square," done just before he left for New England. He gently painted huge roses the size of six buses across the square's traffic lanes.

The America Singers painted the great cities, the small towns, and the country, although frequently they were thought of as only small town and rural. Edward Hopper painted in all three locales, although he was at his best with his big-city canvases. A contemporary of Bellows but slow to hit his stride and find a public, Hopper first came to prominence in the 1930's. He was trained in the humanistic tradition of Henri but worked out his own feeling for cold light that gave his paintings an uncompromising harshness. Hopper's painting of an all-night cheap restaurant in a big city, "Nighthawks," now at the Chicago Art Institute, caught the kind of loneliness that only a walker in a large American city can feel. The canvas was a major American masterpiece. Reginald Marsh was somewhat similar to Hopper in his subject matter but quite different in his style and mood. Marsh was greatly impressed with the vitality of the urban masses, and he squeezed into his paintings crowds of shoppers in Union Square, Bowery bums, and seekers of diversion at Coney Island. Marsh's statement that "well bred people are not fun to paint" was one many America Singers could endorse.

The best known painter of small-town life was Charles Burchfield of Salem, Ohio, and later western New York State. Burchfield's work wavered between the realistic and the romantic, but during the 1930's he usually worked in a realist vein. One of the best known painters of the mid-twentieth century, Burchfield sometimes seemed to revel in small-town life and sometimes to point up its bleak ugliness, yet certainly he was no Sinclair Lewis with a brush.

The Regionalists

The so-called regionalists of the 1930's received tremendous acclaim, perhaps more than they deserved although they were far above the ordinary in quality. The big names among the regionalists were Thomas Hart Benton, grandson of the great pre-Civil War Missouri senator, Grant Wood, and John Steuart Curry. They were all from the western Midwest, and they all glorified that region and regarded the East, particularly the eastern cities, as stifling, degenerate, and effete. Benton was at his best as a muralist, and he invented a technique of ingeniously overlapping his mural panels that was widely imitated. Grant Wood grew up in Cedar Rapids, Iowa, as an indigenous bohemian, and although small-city Iowa did not produce many bohemians, they were proud of Wood. He made several trips to Paris, and on returning from one of them was commissioned by a Cedar Rapids American Legion post to do a stained glass memorial window. With a fine disregard for the amenities, Wood went to Munich to do the work; but with its war memories still fresh, the post refused to accept a work done in Germany. Wood retaliated with his "Daughters of the American Revolution," a biting artistic satire. His best work was "American Gothic," a portrait of his sister and a friend in the yard of an Iowa farm in the style of fifteenth-century German primitives. Curry was born and grew up on a Kansas farm and as a young man studied at the Chicago Art Institute. He worked as an illustrator for pulp magazines before making the usual artist's trek to Paris and New York, but he did not feel at ease with the expatriates and the would-be expatriates of New York and returned to the region he knew and liked best. Curry painted such dramatic midwestern rural events as baptisms, tornadoes, and fighting boars. The violence in his subject matter frequently lent his work a power it would not have merited on strictly artistic values.

Primitivism

Primitivism in painting had a considerable vogue in the 1930's, perhaps because here modernists and America Singers had a common enthusiasm. The early German and French modernists had been interested in primitivism, and the America Singers believed that the work of the untrained painter most truly reflected the thought of the people. Primitivism also received an impetus from the WPA Federal Arts Project's Index of American Design, twenty thousand plates made by hundreds of artists to preserve earlier American designs in all kinds of materials and all subjects, from elaborately carved circus wagons to weather vanes. The search for genuine living primitives turned up a seventy-year-old former Pittsburgh housepainter and coal miner named John Kane, who had amused himself over the years by painting landscapes and pictures of picnics. Now he found himself the rage of the art world. Horace Pippin, a black from Philadelphia who had been wounded in the war and had turned to a crude kind of painting, originally on paper doilies, for something to do in his enforced leisure, became another idol. But Grandma Moses of Eagle Bridge, New York, became the all-time favorite primitive when she was discovered late in the period. She had a store of thousands of rural landscapes and genre scenes which were snapped up by New York City people with the same kind of adoring attitude toward rural primitives that had characterized the eighteenth-century French court when it dressed as peasant milkmaids and plowboys.

Modernists

Many of the modernists of the 1920's continued with their earlier experiments. Stuart Davis tried to make his painting evoke the same sensation as hot jazz. Georgia O'Keeffe did many cold and precise landscapes of the Southwest that prominently featured bleached cattle skulls and horns. Marsden Hartley reached his greatest powers in his Maine landscapes of the 1930's, and Max Weber gained greater intensity with his jewel-like encrusted colors. Several younger artists who became well known in the 1940's were already experimenting in abstraction. Worth special mention are Irene Rice Pereira and Balcom Greene. Mark Tobey, who settled permanently in Seattle, Washington, in the late 1930's and who thereafter had a great influence on the young artists of the Northwest, had traveled in the Orient. The Far East affected his "white line" style, which was a kind of brush calligraphy.

Art Photography

Art photography, which became highly respected and popular in the 1930's, had counterparts of the modernist, social protest, and America Singer schools of painting. Ansel Adams and Edward Weston, who featured the rocks of the California coast and desert sands, turned their cameras upon interesting wind and water erosions that were close to abstractions. Paul Strand, an America Singer with a Leica, set a whole generation to scouring the country for weathered wood after he published his famous picture of a boarded up window in Red River, New Mexico. Dorothea Lange and the Farm Security Administration photographers, with their tragic portraits of sharecroppers, were akin to the social protest painters.

Sculpture

Modernism in sculpture was generally more popular than it was in painting. Indeed, most of the exciting work of the period was modern. David Smith worked in sharp enameled steel. Hugo Robus and Isamu Noguchi created rounded and beautifully contoured abstractions in the Brancusi manner, and Alexander Calder started a craze with his light, free-swinging, metal "mobiles." Carl Milles, who came from Stockholm in 1931 and remained for most of the decade, used conventional materials and was not abstract, but his stylized, elongated figures represented a departure from the idealized realism that dominated monumental sculpture.

Artists during the Great Depression

Artists of all kinds were hard hit economically during the Great Depression, yet during the decade American society felt it had an economic responsibility to support artistic expression. The most vivid manifestation of this sense of responsibility was the WPA's Art Project. But the artists often shocked and outraged the rather conventional people who held the strings to the money bags, and Congress, after a philistine discussion that did its members no credit, all but killed off the WPA cultural activities in June, 1939. Time and again economic and cultural conservatives objected to the work of a WPA muralist in the local post office or high school. Murals, which were popular during the 1930's, perhaps aroused the great reaction since they were painted in places where they attracted the attention of people who would never go to a gallery or a museum. The Mexican muralists, left-wingers politically and innovators artistically, came in for the lion's share of abuse. When José Orozco did a mural in the Dartmouth College library, the alumni protested vigorously, and when Diego Rivera was commissioned to do murals for the Detroit Institute of Arts, local patriots protested that the Institute had "sold out to an outside, half-breed Mexican Bolshevist." Perhaps the most famous incident occurred when Rivera was fired from his commission at Rockefeller Center. When someone discovered that he had put a head of Lenin into his "Man at the Crossroads of Life," the owners of the real estate pulled the artist down from his scaffold, paid him his fee, and covered the offending head with canvas. They later had the mural destroyed.

The audience for art surely became broader because of the muralists and their controversies and because of the many WPA art classes. The audience also was enlarged by two new and important New York museums. The Museum of Modern Art opened in 1929. Perhaps no other institution in the nation has been so influential in shaping American taste in painting as the Modern, both by its exhibitions and its extensive reprint and publication programs. In 1930 the Whitney Museum of American Art became the first major museum to feature art of the United States exclusively.

Architecture

Functionalism and modernism in architecture came strongly to the fore during the 1930's, particularly in large public buildings but to a lesser extent in homes of moderate size and expense. Wright did his magnificent Johnson Wax Company building at Racine, Wisconsin, during the decade. Perhaps no other building ever brought its designer and its owner greater publicity. The Bauhaus gave up on Hitler's Germany in 1934 and closed its doors. Walter Gropius and Marcel Breurer moved to Massachusetts, and Richard J. Neutra settled in California. A few venturesome families built homes in the "international style" for themselves, clean lined and rather austere boxes that had already found favor here and there in Germany and Scandinavia. Scandinavian architects and city planners had quite an influence in the United States. The "Greenbelt" communities of the Farm Security Administration were a modification of the new small Swedish factory towns, and Williamsburg Houses, an island in the Brooklyn slums, were similar to new Scandinavian apartment buildings in their emphasis on light and air.

Music

Perhaps only because music is not a medium which permits precise expression of ideas, musicians in the 1930's did not put into their art the degree of social unrest and criticism that marked literature. But musical theater did sometimes, as in *Pins and Needles* and Marc Blitzstein's 1937 opera *The Cradle Will Rock,* which was about the labor movement. The outstanding current in American music during the depression years, however, was the kind of cultural nationalism that characterized the writers and artists who have in this chapter been called the America Singers. Musical independence from Europe—although not necessarily hostility toward the European tradition—and effort to stimulate a native musical tradition were the keynotes. Emphasis upon things American was by no means entirely new in the 1930's; the emphasis was only greater and broader than it had previously been.

The composer Roy Harris, himself from an Oklahoma farm, summarized well the thinking of many American men of music:

> . . . We have passed through the initial period of musical culture: that of importing our musicians and our music. We have fulfilled the second period: that of developing our own musicians, who are able in interpreting the music of other nations. We have already entered the third period, wherein the quantity and quality of our musicians and our audiences are ready for a new native music, conceived in the mood and tempo of our time.[1]

---

[1] Personal communication from Dr. Roy E. Harris to author, February, 1963.

Harris himself during the thirties wrote four symphonies, and for *Song for Occupations* (1934) he worked the rich mine of folk tunes. Howard Hanson of the Eastman School of Music turned to seventeenth-century New England for his inspiration in *Merry Mount,* produced by the Metropolitan Opera Company in 1934. Another opera drawing on the American past was *The Devil and Daniel Webster,* the result of the collaboration of composer Douglas Moore and poet Stephen Vincent Benét in 1939. Aaron Copland, soon to become the country's best-known composer, came as close to social criticism as is possible with instrumental music when he contributed the score to the documentary film *The City* (1938), a striking plea for city planning and architectural vision written by Lewis Mumford.

Easily the best-known native opera of the thirties was George Gershwin's operatic version of Du Bose Heyward's play about blacks of Charleston's Catfish Row, *Porgy and Bess.* It was an instant hit when it appeared in 1935, two years before the composer's death, and its simple and strong melodies, capable of being hummed, soon were frequently heard on the radio. "Summertime," especially, came to be well known as dance orchestras added it to their books. Some who regarded themselves as serious music listeners were perplexed by *Porgy and Bess* and its reception. An American music, they said, should come from the people and Americans generally should participate in it. Gershwin's opera met those criteria. But Gershwin was a graduate of Tin Pan Alley, although an unusual one, and he wrote in the idiom of American popular music. Was he just a talented but pretentious routine songwriter, or was he an important harbinger of the new American music? Older conceptions of what constituted highbrow, middlebrow, and lowbrow confused matters.

One of the major aspects of the emphasis on musical nationalism was an unusual interest in folk music. Folk music can be divided into two categories: rural folk songs—mountain ballads, cowboy songs, slave work chants, and so forth— and urban folk music, which was primarily jazz until about 1960. The interest paralleled the movement in primitive art, although much jazz was anything but primitive. Alan Lomax published volumes of the rural folk songs he had gathered on expeditions to backwaters of formal culture. Carl Sandburg, newspaperman, poet, and biographer, displayed his versatility by editing *The American Songbag* and singing for audiences some of the folk songs to his own guitar accompaniment. The WPA's Federal Music Project, begun in 1935 to provide help for 15,000 depression-struck musicians, collected and phonographically recorded folk music in all parts of the nation. The more dedicated jazz fans, professional and amateur, scoured through second-hand stores in search of early jazz records, and a few jazz historians took recording equipment into remote places to get facsimiles of the music of old and obscure jazz musicians before they died. The sales statistics of jazz records attested to its growing popularity, and the presence of bands like Benny Goodman's in Carnegie Hall indicated its growing respectability.

The number of people who had an active interest in music, either folk music of some kind or more formal music, apparently grew during the 1930's. Radio audiences for symphonies and opera became steadily larger. The technical quality of phonograph recording improved considerably, and electrically powered players with automatic record changers made listening to records less of an up-

and-down nuisance than it had been. Sales of records grew as the economy slowly climbed. Early in the depression, music education was one of the first "frills" to be cut from the curriculum of many schools, but when it revived it did so with force. High school bands may not have been paragons of musical virtue, but they did teach young people a little about music and widened interest in it. Music teachers in the schools increasingly tried to teach "music appreciation," frequently with the aid of special educational radio programs. How much permanent effect, if any, the Federal Music Project had is difficult to say, but it did make a serious effort to bring live music to the people. More than one hundred million people attended its programs, which featured music by American composers far more than did regular music groups. If millions of Americans still lived in a musical void except for the simplest rhythms and melodies from their radios, the 1930's laid the foundation for the great upsurge of interest in music that came after the war.

Depression
Diplomacy,
1929–1938

*Most of you know what it means when 100 corpses lie
there, or when 500 corpses lie there, or when 1,000
corpses lie there. To have gone through this and—apart
from a few exceptions caused by human weakness—to
have remained decent, that has made us great. That is a
page of glory in our history. . . .*

GESTAPO CHIEF HEINRICH HIMMLER,
from a speech to his top commanders, 1943

Chapter Fourteen

The Great Depression ultimately had to affect America's relations with other countries. The central fact of economic distress was in either the foreground or the background of developments in American foreign policy from 1930 until Pearl Harbor.

Economic conditions forced both Hoover and Roosevelt to make modifications in the nation's foreign economic policies, although neither departed seriously from traditional objectives. Hoover faced a direct effect of the depression in the crisis over European reparations and war-debt payments. The depression indirectly was a factor in the Japanese Manchurian crisis confronting Hoover since Japan had decided to take a militarist course partly because of economic disruption. Roosevelt faced the problem during his first months in office of whether to combat the depression through international cooperation or through national policies at odds with the desires of other nations. His reciprocal trade program was a frontal attack upon the depression, his recognition of the Soviet Union had economic motives, and his headaches over German and Italian militarism and expansion were due, ultimately, to the depression's effects in Europe.

America's Foreign Economic Policies

During the 1920's there had evolved an irrational but, in the short run, workable scheme of loans, reparations, and war debts. American investors, through Wall Street bankers, lent money to Germany which enabled that country to pay its reparations to the Allies and which in turn enabled the Allies to keep up payments on their war debts to the United States Treasury. The Wall Street crash brought the circular financial complex to an abrupt halt. As the flow of American loans to Germany dried up, the stoppage of reparations and war debt payments was only a matter of time. If the American tariff wall had been lowered, thereby stimulating European imports and building up dollar exchange funds in Europe, payment of war debts might have continued. However, Congress raised the tariff with the Hawley-Smoot Act in June, 1930.

The Moratorium

The international financial crisis came to a head in the spring of 1931 when Austria's largest bank was in danger of imminent failure and an important German bank collapsed. If further banking difficulty developed, foreign holders of assets in the banks would have to call back other loans and thereby jeopardize the whole economic and political stability of Central Europe.

President Hoover then made a startling proposal. Congress was not in session, but after consulting with congressional leaders from both parties, Hoover proposed a one-year moratorium, or postponement, in the payment of international obligations. Subject to the approval of Congress, Hoover announced that the United States would not demand payments on war debts for a year beginning July 1, 1931, if other governments would do the same. Hoover's hope was that in a year free of reparations commitments Germany and Austria could overcome the financial crisis. The European nations agreed, although France resisted for three weeks and thereby worsened the German situation.

When Congress convened late in 1931, Hoover submitted the moratorium for approval and urged the re-establishment of the World War Foreign Debt Commission with authority to negotiate further on foreign debts. Congress approved the moratorium but balked at any step that might further reduce the war debts. So far as Congress was concerned, the United States would expect to receive full payment on the next due date after the end of the moratorium, December, 1932.

Hoping for a long-term settlement, Germany and her creditors met at Lausanne, Switzerland, in June and July, 1932, and reached an agreement by which about 90 per cent of the remaining German reparations bill would be cancelled if the former Allies could get corresponding relief from their creditors. In other words, since the United States was the creditor at the ultimate end of the line, ratification of the Lausanne agreement was contingent upon American cooperation. But Congress was in no mood to change its position. After the 1932 election Hoover vainly pleaded with Roosevelt to use his influence with Congress. When he got no results, Hoover sent the debtor nations notices of payments due December 15, 1932. Most of the debtors met this payment, but except for some subsequent token payments these were the last payments on the war debt. (Finland was a special exception. She had an export surplus to the United States and was able to continue paying her small obligation.) In April, 1934, Congress passed a law sponsored by Senator Hiram Johnson of California designed to punish debtor governments in default. The Johnson Act made it illegal to sell within the United States the bonds or other securities of foreign governments, or their subdivisions, which were in default on debts owed to the American federal government. The measure did not stimulate any further payments from depressed Europe. The Attorney General later ruled that token payments did not prevent a country's being considered in default under the terms of the Johnson Act; thereafter, even token payments stopped.

Recognition of the Soviet Union

Despite Roosevelt's failure to act on Hoover's urging to persuade Congress to accept war debt reductions—motivated probably by political considerations—

and despite his "bombshell message" to the World Economic Conference at London in June, 1933, Roosevelt clearly, at least from late 1933, considered the revival of foreign trade as a direct assault on the depression. In seeking to stimulate American exports and to find foreign markets for American goods as a means of getting the domestic economy on its feet again, Roosevelt was operating within a tradition at least as old as the depression of the 1890's. In 1895 a group of industrialists had organized the National Association of Manufacturers, and the original purpose of the NAM had been to stimulate exports and thereby ease the economic difficulties within the nation that came from the panic of 1893. The search for foreign markets and investments had played a major role in the American decision to embark upon a colonial imperialist role later in the decade. Exports of munitions to the Allies after the outbreak of war in Europe had lifted another depression, and the Webb-Pomerene Act had been designed to give American industrialists a competitive position in foreign markets by exempting their overseas operations from the antitrust laws. One of the Roosevelt administration's first efforts to stimulate exports involved recognition of the Union of Soviet Socialist Republics.

It was a painful fact in the early depression that the Soviet economy continued to grow while the western economies sagged. In the fall of 1932 about one hundred thousand Americans applied for jobs in Russia through Amtorg, the Russian foreign trading organization. Hoover was fully committed to continue the nonrecognition policy toward Russia, but he did yield a little when the Reconstruction Finance Corporation underwrote some cotton exports to the USSR. Roosevelt had not committed himself to nonrecognition, and businessmen from both parties put considerable pressure on the State Department to recognize the Soviet Union so that exports to that country would be facilitated. There were other considerations in Roosevelt's mind besides a foreign market (the logic of recognizing a government of sixteen years' standing, for example, and a hope that recognition might hamper Japan in Manchuria), and he began a correspondence with Soviet leaders looking toward formal recognition. The Soviet government agreed to refrain from spreading propaganda designed to overthrow the United States government, to grant religious freedom and protection in its courts to American nationals living in Russia, and to negotiate the question of unpaid prerevolutionary debts and claims. The United States recognized Russia on November 16, 1933; the Soviet Union's first ambassador to Washington was Maxim Litvinov, hardly a typical Russian leader of the 1930's in that he was Jewish and well acquainted with the western world. The negotiations on debts and claims came to nothing, and Russian-inspired Communist propaganda did not cease. But the hopes of American businessmen to send large orders to the Soviet Union failed to materialize in any significant way.

The Role of the Export-Import Bank

The Export-Import Bank, a government agency that later played an important role in American foreign economic policy, developed directly from the hope to sell to the newly recognized Soviet government. American business firms hoping to export or make investments abroad sometimes found that private bankers considered the risks too great to undertake the financing. Such was the case with many proposed deals with the Russians. Roosevelt established the first

Export-Import Bank under National Industrial Recovery Act authority early in 1934 to finance exports to the USSR. Its original funds came from the Reconstruction Finance Corporation. When the negotiations with the Russians over the debt fell through, the first Export-Import Bank became inactive. Early in 1935 Congress set up "Ex-Im" on a two-year basis, renewing its life each biennium until it made the Bank a permanent independent agency in 1945. By 1938 the Bank began to make development loans to underdeveloped nations. A $5 million loan to Haiti in that year went for improved roads, agricultural experiment stations, and drainage facilities. A $25 million loan to China for the Burma Road, from Chungking to Burma, strategically important in World War II, strengthened China's position against the Japanese. Besides the obvious benefits to the countries involved—helping them to create the capital prerequisite for a more advanced economy—these loans helped to create new foreign markets for American products. Thus "Ex-Im" gradually changed from underwriting of exports to already existing markets to active creation of foreign markets in economically backward areas.

Reciprocity

Secretary of State Cordell Hull's reciprocal trade agreement program was another facet of the New Deal's assault on the depression by stimulating foreign trade. Indeed, the purpose of the June, 1934, law as stated in its preamble was "expanding foreign markets for the products of the United States (as a means of assisting in the present emergency...)." The idea of reciprocity was an old one, and Hull, a traditional low-tariff southerner, pushed the idea vigorously when he took the State Department's direction. He had hoped that reciprocal trade agreements would come from the fruitless London Economic Conference in 1933. Hull saw reciprocity as a precondition to world peace. Commercial rivalry, as he viewed it, jeopardized peaceful international relations, and reciprocity would reduce commercial rivalry.

The Reciprocal Trade Agreements Act of 1934 empowered the executive branch for a period of three years to negotiate agreements with other countries to change by as much as one-half the existing American duties on imports in exchange for reciprocal concessions by the other nation on its duties on American products. Such agreements did not need Senate ratification to become effective. The law further directed that such agreements contain a "most favored nation" clause. That is to say, if an agreement with Venezuela reduced United States duties on certain imports, the United States would be obligated to reduce its duties on those same commodities imported from any other country that did not discriminate against American trade. Venezuela would have the same obligation. Thus, for the commodities included in reciprocal trade agreements, there developed a wide tendency toward lower tariffs.

By the spring of 1939 the State Department had negotiated twenty-one reciprocal trade agreements, not only with Latin American nations and Canada, but with the more important non-Fascist West European nations as well. The precise effect of these agreements on trade and the business cycle was impossible to determine since there were several other variables affecting international trade, but until the recession of late 1937 and 1938 American exports increased more rapidly than the total exports of all nations. The United States increased its relative share in world markets. This was because every trade agreement concluded affected America's important exports while few agreements affected the important exports of other countries. The share of American imports from agreement countries increased more rapidly than those from nonagreement countries, and the Latin American economies became more closely tied with the United States.

"Yanquis" as "Good Neighbors"

Roosevelt in his first inaugural address said, "In the field of world policy I would dedicate this Nation to the policy of the good neighbor—the neighbor who resolutely respects himself and, because he does so, respects the rights of others." From this vague, even meaningless, statement about foreign relations in general came the label used to describe the New Deal's extension of the better manners in Latin American matters instituted during the 1920's.

The Seventh International Conference of American States was to meet at Montevideo, Uruguay, in December, 1933. Latin American nations were eager to get through the conference a resolution condemning intervention by one country into the affairs of another, a proposal aimed particularly against the United States. In 1930 the State Department had published the Clark memorandum which denied that the Monroe Doctrine could be used as justification for American intervention, but at the last conference, in 1928, Charles Evans Hughes as head of the United States delegation had refused to allow a nonintervention resolution even to be discussed. The United States had by no means renounced intervention as a Latin American policy.

Nonintervention and a Multilateral Monroe Doctrine

Secretary Hull, head of the American delegation to the Montevideo conference, surprised the Latin American delegations and fully accepted the nonintervention position. The conference went on to write a Convention on the Rights and Duties of States that included the statement, "No state has the right to intervene in the internal or external affairs of another." The United States signed the convention. Two days later, the President in a speech at home said, ". . . the definite policy of the United States from now on is one opposed to armed intervention." In December, 1936, at a special Latin American conference at Buenos Aires, Argentina (a meeting initiated in Washington which the President himself attended), Hull signed a protocol which forbade intervention "directly or indirectly, and for whatever reason." The Senate approved the protocol without reservation. Nonintervention was the essence of the Good Neighbor policy, but another aspect of it was increased trade between the northern Colossus and the Latin nations.

Simultaneously with its renunciations of intervention, the administration moved to make the Monroe Doctrine multilateral. Enunciated by President James Monroe in 1823, the Doctrine had declared the United States opposed further European colonization in the New World and further European "interposition" into the affairs of American nations. The United States had invoked the Monroe Doctrine upon several occasions. But it had been a unilateral policy of Washington alone. Now, after 1935, when Mussolini's Italy and Hitler's Germany threatened the peace of the world, the United States sought to commit all of Latin America to the Monroe Doctrine's principles.

It was in pursuit of this intention that the administration initiated in 1935 the calling of the Buenos Aires conference. No conference was scheduled until 1938. At the conference the delegates signed documents that called upon Latin American nations to consult one another in situations that formerly would have brought the United States to invoke the Monroe Doctrine unilaterally. Consultation in the face of any threat from outside America to the peace and independence of an American state did not necessarily mean that action would follow, but the step was clearly in the direction of "continentalizing" the old Doctrine.

The Buenos Aires documents did not stipulate just how consultation should be done. At the next regularly scheduled international Conference of American States at Lima, Peru, in December, 1938, the delegates agreed that the foreign ministers of any of the twenty-one American states could call a meeting to consider methods of meeting any outside threat. The American states did in fact meet under this plan: at Panama just after the oubreak of war in Europe in the fall of 1939; at Havana, Cuba, in the summer of 1940 after the fall of France; and at Rio de Janeiro, Brazil, in January, 1942, after Pearl Harbor. All the Latin American powers followed the United States into World War II, although some followed late and reluctantly. The Good Neighbor policy, in effect, paid off in a time of crisis.

Cuba and Haiti

The United States, with but one partial exception in the case of Cuba, observed well the nonintervention policy it had adopted. Most of the Cuban partial exception occurred before the Montevideo conference. Cuba's president, Gerardo Machado, led a tyrannical government over that politically unhappy island when Roosevelt took office. Machado had suppressed a rebellion in 1931 and was still using dictatorial powers in a futile effort to stamp out his opposition. Roosevelt's intervention was diplomatic rather than military, although parts of the fleet did go to Cuba for the announced purpose of being ready to evacuate United States citizens if necessary. The proximity of naval power unquestionably lent weight to the statements of Sumner Welles, the Foreign Service officer who had recently been appointed ambassador to Cuba and whose ostensible mission was to mediate between Machado and his opponents. Welles's real mission was to get Machado to resign. This Welles accomplished in the summer of 1933 with the support of some Cuban army officers. For the rest of the year, the United States helped select the next Cuban president by withholding recognition from those of whom it did not approve. In January, 1934, Carlos Mendieta became president of Cuba with the blessing of the United States, and thereafter intervention ceased. Four months later the United States and Cuba negotiated a new treaty which abrogated the Platt Amendment of 1903. In other words, the United States renounced its treaty right to intervene in Cuban affairs and to supervise Cuban finances. The

Senate ratified the treaty without a dissenting vote only two days after it was signed. The American naval base at Guantanamo Bay was to remain until the right to maintain it was withdrawn by mutual action.

The United States pulled back elsewhere in the Caribbean during the Roosevelt years. FDR inherited a problem in Haiti. Hoover had sent an investigating commission to Haiti in 1930 when internal difficulties flared up there. The commission recommended new elections, and Haiti held its first elections since World War I. Americans relinquished control of Haitian public works to the islanders. A treaty in the fall of 1932 provided for withdrawing American marines and relinquishing control of the Haitian constabulary but for continuation of United States control of Haiti's finances until its American-held bonds were paid off. The Haitian legislature rejected the treaty, objecting to United States financial control. Roosevelt in the summer of 1933 reached an executive agreement with Haiti. The constabulary was to be controlled entirely by Haitians after October 1, 1934, and the marines were to be withdrawn within a month thereafter. Through an American-appointed "fiscal representative," United States control over the customs was to remain, although less obviously, until the bonds were satisfied. Roosevelt in fact withdrew the marines in the summer of 1934, the first time in decades that American marines were not stationed somewhere within the boundaries of a nominally sovereign Caribbean state. In 1941 the United States government withdrew the "fiscal representative." In 1940 a treaty with the Dominican Republic, at the other end of Santo Domingo, relinquished American control of Dominican customs but imposed a lien on the little state's general revenues until its bonds were discharged. An American remained as collector of the customs in Nicaragua until its American loans were repaid in 1944.

The Mexican Crisis

It was Mexico far more than any other Latin American nation that put the Good Neighbor policy to the test. More dollars were involved in the Mexican crisis than elsewhere in the Caribbean. The Mexican revolution progressed in a series of waves, each of them demanding foreign withdrawal from Mexican oil fields and other resources and then subsiding. A wave had subsided in 1927 and 1928 when the clever Dwight Morrow had been the American ambassador. Another wave began to build in 1934 with the election of Lázaro Cárdenas to the Mexican presidency. It came to a crest in early 1938.

Cárdenas accelerated the expropriation (taking national possession with compensation) of foreign-owned agricultural lands and led in the organization of a single large union of Mexican oil company employees. The oil workers' union presented the companies, both American and British, with extensive demands that infringed conventional management prerogatives. The oil companies rejected them. A Mexican arbitration board found the demands just and ordered the oil companies to accept them. Again the companies refused. On March 18, 1938, Cárdenas expropriated the property of foreign oil companies within Mexico. Simultaneously, the anticlericalism of the Mexican revolution aroused intense opposition to the Cárdenas government among Roman Catholics north of the border.

The British broke diplomatic relations with Mexico and did not reach a settlement on compensation of their oil companies' claims until after World War

261

II. The United States, despite the touchy political situation created by American Catholic opposition, lived up to its good-neighbor declarations. Roosevelt's smooth politicking (he even arranged to have his letters in reply to outraged Catholic leaders written for him by a priest); the folksy shrewdness of the American ambassador in Mexico City, Roosevelt's old boss in the Navy Department, Josephus Daniels; and the administration's firmness with the American oil companies saved the Good Neighbor policy.

The American oil companies conducted their own negotiations with the Mexican government. They claimed $260 million in compensation. This the Mexican government rejected, although it did come to terms with the Sinclair Oil Company. The oil companies hoped that the next Mexican president, to be elected in 1940, would be less demanding and were disappointed with the election of Manuel Avila Camacho. Both Cárdenas and Camacho were vigorously anti-Nazi and eager to make some arrangement with the United States before the Western Hemisphere might become embroiled in war with Hitler, but neither would back down on expropriation.

Mexico and the United States signed an agreement on November 19, 1941. The United States agreed to continue purchasing Mexican silver at the world price, to extend Mexico credits through the Export-Import Bank, and to negotiate a reciprocal trade agreement. Mexico agreed to pay $40 million for all American claims exclusive of oil claims. The oil claims were referred to two commissioners, one from each country. The commissioners set the total of the claims at $24 million, payable over several years. Mexico completed the payments in 1949. The United States oil companies protested that they should receive more, but the administration refused to support them further.

Puerto Rico and the Philippines

Latin Americans had a special interest in United States treatment of its Spanish populations in its colonial empire, Puerto Rico and the Philippines. Under the New Deal, the Washington-appointed governors of Puerto Rico made an effort to diversify the economy, to make it less dependent upon sugar. Public works with Washington's financial support both relieved hardship on the island and provided some of the prerequisites for the development of industry. Illiteracy (over 77 per cent in 1898) also handicapped economic growth, and Puerto Ricans put a special emphasis upon elementary education. Their results were gratifying but less than fully satisfactory: illiteracy in 1940 was still 31.5 per cent. The governorship of Rexford Tugwell from 1941 to 1946 brought the island's difficulties to the attention of citizens of the mainland even more. In 1948, Puerto Rico for the first time was permitted to elect its own governor.

The progress of the Philippine Islands toward independence was a confusing one, complicated by Filipino hesitation to be outside American tariff barriers and by United States naval strategic considerations in the western Pacific. In 1932 Congress passed the Hawes-Cutting Act granting the Philippines independence in 1945 with a transitional period until then. Hoover vetoed the measure, and Congress overrode the veto. Manuel Quezon, leader of the Filipino Nationalists, opposed the law because it left American naval bases in the islands and put Filipino products outside the American tariff system. The Philippine legislature rejected the law. There matters stood when FDR became president. In 1934 Congress passed and Roosevelt signed the Tydings-McDuffie Independence Act, which provided for independence on July 4, 1946, and commonwealth status meanwhile. The Filipinos accepted the arrangement in a plebiscite and installed Quezon as their president.

Difficulties with Japan, 1931–1938

In 1931 Japanese militarists embarked upon an expansionist policy on the Asian mainland that eventually led to war with the United States and defeat in 1945. The late 1920's saw shifts in the relative strength of Asian national power and an increase in international tension. In 1924 Dr. Sun Yat-sen, leader of the Chinese revolutionary nationalists, accepted aid from the Russian Communist government and strengthened the Chinese nationalist movement. Upon his death in 1925 his successor as head of the Kuomintang party, Chiang Kai-shek, continued collaboration with the Russians. The central Chinese government extended its authority in the north and hoped to bring reunification with Manchuria. Two years after assuming leadership, Chiang broke with the Russians, and in 1929 and 1930 Sino-Russian relations were severely strained; there was even undeclared warfare before China backed down in the face of superior Soviet strength. But Chinese power in North China was growing. In the winter of 1929–30, the warlord of Manchuria acknowledged Chinese suzerainty. Simultaneously, the Chinese organized a boycott of Japanese goods and began to skirt treaty obligations they had been forced to yield to the Japanese under duress. Japanese militarists, fearful of growing Chinese strength, were eager for action before China became too strong for them to handle.

The Japanese Take Manchuria

Without the consent of the Premier or the Foreign Office, Japanese troops on the night of September 18–19, 1931, seized the Chinese garrison at Mukden, Manchuria, and several key points along the South Manchurian Railway. Their pretext was an explosion on the railroad, which was minor in any case and may have been altogether fictitious. The Kuomintang government of China protested Japan's action to the United States and to the League of Nations. Japan's action was inconsistent with her membership in the League, with the Kellogg-Briand Pact, and the Nine-Power Treaty of 1922, but the League's first action, after the Japanese government promised to withdraw as soon as practicable, was only to request China and Japan to do nothing to irritate the situation. Secretary of State Henry L. Stimson at first was cautious in the hope that American forbearance would strengthen the moderates in the Japanese civil government against the militarists and the army.

When the Japanese army continued its aggressions in Manchuria, President Hoover instructed Prentiss Gilbert, an official in the American consulate at Geneva, to sit with the League Council in discussions of Manchurian matters. Although the decision to cooperate this closely with the League raised eyebrows in the United States, the cooperation had little practical effect. The Japanese ignored the

League's resolution calling for withdrawal of all Japanese troops to the area that they had occupied before the Mukden incident.

Stimson and Hoover did not see eye-to-eye on the proper course to be followed. After he recognized that moderation was having no effect, Stimson was for a policy of nonrecognition of Japanese conquests and was prepared to impose economic sanctions against Japan. Secretary of War Patrick Hurley wanted even to threaten military force, but Hoover was unwilling to go beyond nonrecognition and moral sanctions. Events moved swiftly at the turn of the year. On December 11, 1931, the Japanese cabinet resigned; the new one was more militaristic. On the following January 3 Japanese forces practically completed their conquest of Manchuria. On January 7 Stimson addressed identical notes to Japan and China setting forth what at the time was known as the Stimson Doctrine, since then more generally called the Hoover-Stimson Doctrine because it went no further than the nonrecognition policy upon which the two men agreed and did not threaten economic sanctions such as Stimson favored. The notes declared that the United States would not "admit the legality of any situation de facto nor ... recognize any treaty or agreement ... which may impair the treaty rights of the United States or its citizens in China ... or the international policy relative to China, commonly known as the open-door policy...." The Hoover-Stimson Doctrine was unilateral; Stimson had asked Britain and France to join in his declaration, but each declined.

Then the Japanese attacked the Shanghai area in an attempt to get the Chinese to repeal their boycott, and the British were moved to action for the first time. British naval units joined American ships in going to Shanghai to protect each nation's citizens. Both the United States and Britain stimulated negotiations between China and Japan which in time led to the end of hostilities in the Shanghai area. By the end of May, 1932, Japanese troops in the international city had been reduced to their normal number. But the Japanese did not retreat in Manchuria. Their method of fastening control over the area was to create a puppet state, called Manchukuo, which declared its independence from China on February 18, 1932.

The creation of Manchukuo was a direct challenge to the Hoover-Stimson Doctrine. Five days later Stimson released a public letter to William Borah, chairman of the Senate Foreign Relations Committee, that was intended for the eyes of the Japanese, the Chinese, the League, the British, and the American public more than it was for Senator Borah. Stimson had based his previous condemnations of Japanese aggression upon the Kellogg-Briand Pact. In the letter to Borah he urged that other nations join the United States in nonrecognition and shifted his basis for judging the Japanese to the Washington naval treaties of 1922. The Nine-Power and the Five-Power treaties, Stimson pointed out, released all signatory nations from the treaty provisions if any one of the signatories violated the pacts. In other words, if Japan violated the integrity of China (one of the provisions of the Nine-Power Treaty) America would no longer be obligated to limit the size of her navy. The United States moved its fleet to the Pacific in 1932, but it did not build its navy beyond treaty strength limitations. In fact, until Roosevelt became president there was no effort to keep the navy up to the strength authorized by the Washington treaties.

If the Borah letter had no visible effect upon Japanese policy, it did bring the League around to nonrecognition. In March, 1932, the League Assembly declared League members should not recognize any situation achieved by means contrary to the League Covenant or to the Kellogg-Briand Pact. The League later received the report of its special commission to investigate the Manchurian problem headed by a British subject, the Earl of Lytton. The Lytton report was moderate, urging Chinese sovereignty in Manchuria but protection of Japanese economic interests. The Japanese were not content with its recommendations and on September 15, 1932, recognized Manchukuo as an independent power. When the League advised its members against recognition of Manchukuo, Japan served the necessary two-year notice of its withdrawal from the League.

Roosevelt assured Stimson between the election of 1932 and the inauguration that his administration would continue the Hoover-Stimson policies in East Asia. Roosevelt kept the fleet in the Pacific and announced that it would be built up to treaty strength, but during his first years in office tensions with Japan became less serious. When the Japanese began expanding from Manchuria they encountered stiffer Chinese military resistance, and in late May, 1933, the Chinese and Japanese signed a truce. The truce was not altogether effective, but until 1937 there was no more large-scale military action in East Asia.

The Years Between 1933 and 1937

During these years, however, there were other matters of Japanese-American relations that form part of the background to war in 1941. The two main issues were Japanese efforts to close the open door in China and naval armaments. Over intermittent protests from the State Department, Japan used her control of the Manchukuo puppet government to slam the open door in that part of the Chinese mainland. Manchuria became a private preserve for Japanese trade and capital, and Japan consistently denied she had anything to do with Manchukuo policies that kept trade from other nations out of the area. Japan even proposed to Secretary Hull in 1934 that the United States, in effect, withdraw from the Far East, a "Japanese Monroe Doctrine" for Asia. Although America was at the time making preparations for ultimate withdrawal from territorial control of the Philippines, there was no intention of withdrawing from open-door imperialist policies in East Asia. Hull rejected the Japanese proposal. Continued American determination to retain the East Asian status quo and Japanese determination to make the area a special reservation for her commercial and military interests made an increase in international conflict inevitable. East Asia was an arena of conflict between empires: between American and British, on the one hand, primarily economic or informal in nature rather than colonial, and the Japanese, on the other hand, militaristic and colonial as well as economic.

The Japanese announcement in December, 1934, that they would not renew the naval limitations agreed upon at Washington and London when those agreements expired at the end of 1936 indicated they meant business. Japan did send delegates to a naval conference at London in 1935–36, but the delegates withdrew when the American and British delegations would admit no change in the traditional ratios. The American, British, and French delegations reached an agreement on the size of vessels but not on their number, and early in 1938 these three nations abandoned limitation of any kind by mutual consent. The naval race had begun. In January, 1938, while the economy was suffering from a serious recession, Roosevelt in a special message to Congress asked for the largest naval authorization in the nation's history. The measure passed a few months later.

Japan Resumes War on China

The 1933 truce between China and Japan ended dramatically in a skirmish at the Marco Polo bridge near Peiping on July 7, 1937. (This city was known as Peking until 1928 when the Kuomintang moved the capital from there and re-named the city Peiping. The Japanese called the city by its old name, as have the Chinese Communists since 1949.) The incident at the bridge seems not to have been staged like the one at Mukden in 1931, but the Japanese army used it as an excuse to launch a full-scale offensive in the northern China provinces. The Kuomintang and the Chinese Communists under Mao Tse-tung had recently concluded a truce in their civil war and made a common front against Japan. Japan decided to move before China could become stronger.

Japan enjoyed quick military success. Her method was to bomb major cities and follow the raids with land expeditions. Japan had bombed civilians at Chin-chow, Manchuria, in 1931, Italy had bombed defenseless Ethiopians in 1935, and Germany and Italy had used airplane bombardment against civilians in Spain in their aid to Franco, but most of the world was still repelled by the airplane's bringing war to noncombatants. A photograph widely published in America showed a terrorized Chinese infant crying amidst bomb rubble. Japanese troops took Nanking in December, 1937, and the Chinese moved their capital to Han-kow, which fell in October, 1938, along with Canton. The Chinese retreated to the interior and set up their capital at Chungking. Japan controlled the coastal cities and the principal railroad lines by the end of 1938. But the Chinese armies had not been destroyed and they would not quit. As the Japanese learned, to defeat China in battle to gain control of the strategic positions was one thing; to win a war with all China and to control the whole country, with its vast distances and its enormous population accustomed to a low living standard, were something else.

Though disgusted by Japanese bombing of civilians, the American public was not ready to pursue policies that might lead to war. At an international conference at Brussels in November, 1937, convened to consider what Japan called the Chinese incident or the Chinese affair but never the Chinese war, the American delegation was instructed not to press for economic sanctions because the administration knew the position was more advanced than public opinion would support. On December 12, 1937, Japanese aircraft bombed and sank a United States navy gunboat, the *Panay*, in the Yangtze River although the American flag was painted on its decks and it was obviously an American ship. Japan apologized profusely and quickly made financial restitution for the loss of property and the lives of two crewmen. In 1898, the sinking of the *Maine* had brought a sharp demand for war with Spain. The *Panay* sinking provoked only fear of war. What business, many people asked, did a naval vessel have in convoying Standard Oil Company tankers in the Yangtze? The memory of the horrors of 1917–18 were too strong for most Americans to consider risking war on the other side of the world. Within two weeks after the *Panay* sinking, the whole affair was a closed matter. The most that was done against the Japanese until the outbreak of war in Europe was to aid China (for example, the Export-Import Bank's credit to China for the Burma Road) and to request American airplane manufacturers in July, 1938, not to supply planes to Japan.

Yet the United States government did not retreat from its historic Far Eastern policies. Japan in November, 1938, announced a "new order" in East Asia based on "a tripartite relationship of mutual aid and coordination between Japan, Manchukuo and [Japanese-controlled] China." The State Department protested that such a "new order" could not legitimately annul previous treaty rights, meaning mostly the open-door safeguards in the 1922 Nine-Power Treaty. The United States never abandoned its open-door policy in East Asia; Japan would not abandon its position as the paramount power in the "new order." By the winter of 1938–39, Japan and the United States were completely at loggerheads, but American public opinion was far more concerned with the situation in Europe than it was with Asian tensions.

Fascism in Europe: Hitler and Mussolini

When Benito Mussolini came to power in Italy in late 1922 and instituted his fascist order, majority opinion about him in the United States was not adverse. Many Americans commended Mussolini for driving beggars from the streets and praised him for "making the trains run on time."

Majority public opinion, however, was opposed to Adolf Hitler's National Socialist or Nazi rule in Germany almost from the time the Nazis came to power early in 1933, although Italian Fascism and German Nazism were only national variations of the same totalitarian idea. Hitler's blatant anti-Semitism alarmed many Americans, and millions, remembering the war, feared the resurgence of German militarism. When both Italy and Germany endangered the peace of the world with their expansionist policies, only a small proportion of the American population favored the two nations.

To summarize fascism (both Italian Fascism and German Nazism were generally known as fascism) in a few sentences is not simple. Fascist nations were vigorously anti-Communist. Both Hitler and Mussolini rode to power on middle-class fear of communism, and both their regimes essentially maintained the class systems that had existed earlier. To a degree, then, fascism was "capitalism by violence." But it was not conventional capitalism. The corporate state intervened extensively in the nation's economic life and regulated it. Industrial and landed capitalists accepted fascist regulation in preference to some form of Marxist control. Ironically, fascism had one major similarity to Stalinism: totalitarianism, or the subordination of the individual and all social institutions to the needs of the national state. Hitler's Nazis, for example, urged children to inform on their parents to the authorities. Fascist nations were also extremely militaristic. They glorified the military life and praised war as a means of bringing out the best in a people. Fascists had nothing but contempt for democracy, either in the sense of shared decisions by a wide electorate or in the Bill of Rights' sense of protection of the individual from the state. In sum, fascism was antidemocratic nationalism run riot.

Fascism in Germany was extremely racist, although it was less so in Italy. The Nazis exploited the latent anti-Semitism of the German people in their rise to power and used the Jews as a scapegoat to explain away all of the country's difficulties. At the same time, Nazis exalted the mythical racial purity, "Aryanism," of non-Jewish Germans. Beginning with mob action against Jews, the requirement that they wear identifying clothes, and boycotts of their businesses, German anti-Semitism ended with what the Nazis euphemistically called "the final solution of the Jewish question": killing all Jews and eradicating Jewish culture in all areas under German control. By the time Nazi Germany collapsed in 1945, the Nazis had killed six million Jews, most of them in efficient slaughterhouses, where their corpses were rendered into fat for soap manufacture.

For the first few months after Hitler came to power in Germany (January 30, 1933), he displayed an attitude toward other nations which, while not cooperative, would seem remarkably moderate in retrospect. Perhaps he was only waiting for consolidation of his power within Germany. In March, 1933, he was voted dictatorial powers for four years, and after Paul von Hindenburg's death in 1934 he combined the offices of the German presidency and chancellorship. Hitler at first was even willing to talk about disarmament. A General Disarmament Conference had met first at Geneva in February, 1932. It met again in the spring of 1933. Hitler announced that he was willing to go along with disarmament and to postpone for five years his insistent demands for German arms equality, but he refused to sign any agreements or to consent to abide by majority votes of the Conference members. In October, 1933, Germany withdrew from both the Conference and the League of Nations. A few months later the Conference broke up altogether.

In March, 1935, Hitler declared the Treaty of Versailles limitations upon German armed strength no longer valid, instituted compulsory military service, and began to build the German army toward an announced five hundred thousand men. At the same time he said Germany would continue to respect the rest of the treaty, including keeping the Rhineland as a demilitarized zone. With such promises he managed to prevent France and Britain from presenting a solid front of opposition. Britain three months later even signed a treaty with Germany which allowed the Reich a navy 35 per cent as large as Britain's. In March, 1936, Hitler again took advantage of French-British discord, this time over what to do about Italy's undeclared war against Ethiopia, and he denounced the whole of the Treaty of Versailles, as well as the Locarno Treaty of 1925, and marched two hundred thousand soldiers into the Rhineland. The League of Nations failed to take any action.

Germany's and Italy's increased belligerence and disregard of international agreements caused grave concern in the United States, but the reaction was not so great as it would have been if the citizenry could have known what the end of German-Italian policies would be. In the mid-1930's the American population was far more concerned with domestic problems than with foreign affairs in either Europe or Asia and was undergoing a deep reaction against its involvement in the war of two decades earlier.

Neutrality and Anxiety, 1933–1938

In discussions of foreign policy with respect to expansionist Germany, Italy, and Japan in the 1930's, politicians and publicists used terms of opprobrium for their opponents that did little to clarify the actual situation. All too often, historians since have trapped themselves by accepting these political catchwords without efforts to use them with precision. The most common loosely used term in the lexicon of commentators about foreign policy is *isolationist*, which has described those who opposed colonial imperialism in 1898 and after, who opposed American participation in World War I, who fought ratification of the Treaty of Versailles, who resisted entrance into World War II, and, in recent years, who criticized the United Nations and foreign aid programs. Actually, the term means one who advocates a policy of nonparticipation in international affairs, and very few Americans indeed have advocated such a position. In the context of the 1930's, "isolationism" embraced a wide range of positions. All they had in common was a fear of engagement in another world war. An insignificant number were partisans of fascism (for example, members of the German-American Bund) who, seeing that the United States would not become an ally of Germany or Italy, wanted the nation to stay clear of associations with antifascist governments. Another small group was composed of pacifists, many of them religiously motivated, who believed that violence and war were un-Christian and subversive of all decent values. Most "isolationists" were antifascist but fearful that vigorous opposition to expansionist foreign nations would involve the United States in an unwanted war. Some would have taken a few risks of war to hamper fascism; some would not. Some were for a strong military defense; some were not. To lump all of these positions into any single term is not precise, but some kind of general term is valid on occasion if one remembers that it is loose and general. The term *isolationist* will not be used here because it has become emotionally loaded. *Noninterventionist* is no more precise, but it avoids political passion.

Interventionist also is a loose term, but it is one that has somehow not acquired strong emotional overtones. Almost no one was an open, outright interventionist demanding a quick declaration of war against fascist nations until war began in Europe in September, 1939, and they were few even then. However, especially after the beginning of the European war, an increasing number of people advocated strong aid to the antifascist European nations and actions "short of war" that might result in armed conflict. As with the noninterventionists, the interventionists represented a considerable range of positions, from the quite bellicose to those who genuinely believed that only through cooperation with the western democracies could American belligerency be prevented.

Foreign policy cut across conventional political lines, whether party, regional, ethnic, or ideological. Both major parties, all regions of the nation, and all major nationality and racial groups divided on foreign policy issues. Frequently, debates between interventionists and noninterventionists made bedfellows of political leaders who vigorously opposed one another on domestic matters. Thus, on the interventionist side, the Roosevelt administration worked in harness with conservative eastern and southern congressional leaders of both parties, and the other side displayed the unusual spectacle of Colonel Robert R. McCormick, publisher of the extremely conservative *Chicago Daily Tribune*, agreeing with the leader of the Socialist party, Norman Thomas.

Clearly, in the early and middle 1930's American public opinion was overwhelmingly and vigorously antiwar. Given the depression-induced popular hostility to bankers and manufacturers and what was known about loans to the Allies from 1914 to 1917 and of profits in munitions, it was perhaps inevitable that antiwar sentiment would focus upon the role of business in American entrance into the war in 1917, widely felt to have been a disastrous mistake. In the spring of 1934, the Senate created a special committee, headed by Senator Gerald P. Nye, Republican of North Dakota, to conduct an inquiry into the adequacy of legislation on government control of munitions. For nearly three years the Nye Committee provided headlines and newspaper stories full of sordid details of greed and chicanery in the American munitions business during the war. It was easy for people to conclude that "merchants of death," a favorite phrase of the time, had been solely responsible for America's going to the aid of the Allies. Operating upon the assumption that legislation that presumably would have prevented participation in the war of 1914–18 would prevent entrance into a future war, Congress moved to write a series of neutrality measures into the statutes.

The Three Neutrality Acts

In the summer of 1935 it seemed likely that Mussolini would soon begin a war to expand his colonial empire in North Africa. Roosevelt and Hull had a bill introduced to authorize the president to impose an arms embargo upon the nation he considered the aggressor. Instead, Congress passed the First Neutrality Act, which Roosevelt signed with misgivings on August 31, 1935. This law required the president to impose an embargo on arms to both nations engaged in conflict, created a government board whose special permission was necessary before munitions could be exported to any country, whether at war or not, and prohibited American ships from carrying munitions to or for a belligerent. The president's only discretionary power under the Act was whether or not to warn citizens that they traveled on ships of belligerent nations at their own risk.

Then, on October 3, 1935, well-equipped Italian troops invaded Ethiopia, whose soldiers were armed with the most primitive of weapons. Two days later FDR declared that a state of war existed and thereby invoked the Neutrality Act of 1935. Italy at no time made an official war declaration. In this case the prohibition of arms shipment to both sides probably did not harm Ethiopia, which had no seaport and probably would not have been able to get American arms anyway, although many people at the time thought it did. But, on the other hand, the arms embargo did not hurt Italy to any appreciable extent, particularly in a war against a foe as defenseless as Ethiopia. The Neutrality Act made no provision for an embargo on oil, and it was petroleum products that Italy needed most desperately for her motorized legions and air force. Hull applied a "moral embargo" on oil to Italy, requesting American oil companies to keep their shipments to Italy at normal levels. Hull thought the "moral embargo" was "reasonably successful," but how much American gasoline the Italians diverted from peaceful uses to tanks and army trucks is not known. Mussolini completed his conquest of Ethiopia in May, 1936.

Most of the provisions of the First Neutrality Act were due to expire at the end of February, 1936. Congress passed the Second Neutrality Act on the last day of February. The new measure extended the previous legislation until May 1, 1937, and added some new features. Under the old legislation, the president had been authorized but not directed to impose an arms embargo against any third power that might become involved in war with a nation already embargoed. The new legislation made such an embargo of a third nation mandatory. The new law also exempted from embargo any American nation that became a belligerent against any non-American nation and forbade loans by any person living in the United States to belligerent governments. This last provision was designed to prevent the repetition of such loans as the House of Morgan began to handle for the Allies in 1915.

None of this neutrality legislation mentioned civil wars and thus did not apply when the Spanish Civil War began in July, 1936. In 1931 the Spanish had overthrown their monarchy and established a republic; five years later General Francisco Franco led a revolt against the republican government. Franco and his followers were unmistakably Fascist, although not cut precisely from the German pattern. Franco's revolt was ostensibly directed against communists in the Spanish government, who at the beginning of the Civil War did not control the Spanish state. Fearful that the Spanish war would lead to a general European war, France persuaded other European governments to agree to a nonintervention policy. However, Germany and Italy soon violated the agreement, sent military units to aid Franco, and made Spain a testing ground for their new military techniques. Russia also violated the nonintervention agreement with direct aid to the Spanish government, or Loyalist cause, although her intervention was less extensive than was that of the Fascist powers.

When the European nations decided upon nonintervention, Roosevelt and Hull complied and declared another "moral embargo" upon shipments to either side of the Spanish conflict. No further action was possible under existing law. When Congress convened in January, 1937, Roosevelt asked Congress to extend the neutrality laws to civil as well as international wars. Congress complied hastily. The decision to take a hands-off policy toward the Spanish war—in effect, to aid Franco because denying the Spanish government help made German and Italian intervention decisive—sharply divided the American population. The American Catholic hierarchy approved of the arms embargo to Spain because of the Spanish government's anticlericalism and the support the Spanish hierarchy gave Franco. The American political left, both Communist and non-Communist, vigorously condemned the embargo. The Communists organized the Abraham Lincoln Brigade, and almost three thousand young Americans, all of them anti-Fascist but not all of them Communist, enlisted in this military organization to fight Spanish fascism. Hundreds of thousands of others donated funds to Spanish war relief organizations.

The Third Neutrality Act (May, 1937) extended the main provisions of earlier neutrality laws without a definite time limit. It also gave the president discretionary power in invoking an embargo in the case of a foreign civil war.

Roosevelt never invoked an embargo against Spain, although the administration was close to a decision to do so in the spring of 1938. Interestingly, Roosevelt did not invoke the Third Neutrality Act until war broke out in Europe. He declined to take official recognition that a state of war existed between Japan and China after July, 1937. Apparently, Roosevelt concluded that to "find" the Asian war and thereby make neutrality legislation applicable would have the practical effect of strengthening Japan's hand. Instead, he relied upon appeals to other nations to reaffirm their treaty obligations and to pleas for international morality. Since American public opinion would not support strong measures, the American delegation to the Brussels Conference on the Asian situation was powerless to provide strong leadership.

The "Quarantine" Speech

Indeed, it became increasingly apparent in 1937 and 1938 that noninterventionist public opinion was a thorn in the President's side and that non-interventionists meant to keep the thorn sharp. This antagonism between the public and the President over foreign policy was illustrated by the reaction to Roosevelt's speech at Chicago in October, 1937. In this address, commonly called the "Quarantine the Aggressors Speech," Roosevelt said, "It seems to be unfortunately true that the epidemic of world lawlessness is spreading. And mark this well! When an epidemic of physical disease starts to spread, the community approves and joins in a quarantine of the patients in order to protect the health of the community against the spread of the disease." Such a medical metaphor was not precise language, and no one could say just what Roosevelt had in mind. But whatever he had in mind, the public did not like it. Press reaction to the speech was unfavorable. Later in the month a public opinion poll asked this question: "Which plan for keeping out of war do you have more faith in—having Congress pass stricter neutrality laws, or leaving the job up to the President?" Only 31 per cent preferred the President. The strength behind the Ludlow amendment to the Constitution was another indication of noninterventionist power and distrust of the President's foreign policies. An idea that went back at least as far as the period of American neutrality during World War I, the Ludlow amendment, named for Representative Louis Ludlow, Democrat of Indiana, proposed that a national referendum would be necessary to declare war except in the case of armed invasion of the United States or its territories. Roosevelt had to use great pressure to defeat the proposed constitutional amendment in the House where it failed by only twenty-one votes in January, 1938.

The Munich Pact

Also in January, 1938, the State Department perceived that Hitler's next move would be to absorb Austria under German rule. With public opinion being what it was, Hull only impressed upon the German ambassador in Washington that the United States would not look favorably upon any such aggression. This did not deter Germany whose troops marched into Austria with the aid of Austrian Nazis in March.

In the summer of 1938 Hitler began a war of nerves over the question of the Sudetenland of Czechoslovakia, an area populated largely by German-speaking people. Hitler demanded the area, and the Czechs were willing to fight to keep it since it was vital to the defense of the rest of the country. But Britain, France, and the United States were by no means prepared to go to war to defend Czechoslovakia. Indeed, many British and French leaders regarded Hitler as less of a menace than the Russians. Prime Minister Neville Chamberlain and Premier Édouard Daladier were prepared to go to great lengths at Czechoslovakia's expense to prevent the outbreak of war. Matters came to a crisis in late September. Millions of Americans kept close to their radios to hear the frequent news bulletins. After European heads of state and foreign ministers had conferred both personally and by cable for days without a final settlement, Roosevelt, on September 26, sent messages to Hitler, Chamberlain, Daladier, and President Eduard Beneš of Czechoslovakia in which he asserted that war would only wreck every country involved and urged continued negotiations. Hitler's reply only repeated his previous demands for the Sudetenland. Three days later the State Department urged all other countries to support the American appeal for further negotiations, and Roosevelt personally appealed to Mussolini to use his influence with Hitler. At the last minute, Hitler issued invitations to Mussolini, Chamberlain, and Daladier for a conference at Munich. When Roosevelt heard that Chamberlain had accepted the invitation, he dispatched a cabled instruction to his ambassador at London, Joseph P. Kennedy, to give Chamberlain this oral message: "Good man." On September 30, Chamberlain and Daladier signed a Four-Power Pact at Munich which gave the Sudetenland to Germany in exchange for only a promise from Hitler, who had already broken several promises, to refrain from further demands for European territory. When the gray Chamberlain returned to London, carrying the umbrella which came to be considered a symbol of appeasement, he announced, "I believe it is peace for our time." The same day the State Department in a press release announced that the Munich agreement had brought "a universal sense of relief," but it declared that the United States would not "pass upon the merits of the differences to which the Four-Power Pact . . . related."

War in Europe had been averted—for about eleven months.

Suggestions for Additional Reading

This list of titles is not comprehensive. It is designed for the student and teacher in planning a program of "outside reading." For the historical researcher it is no more than a place to begin. I have tried to include titles my students have found useful over the years and upon which I relied in the preparation of this volume. For more extensive bibliographies the student should consult the *Harvard Guide to American History*, a new edition of which is to appear by 1974, and bibliographies and footnotes in the books cited here.

CHAPTER 1. THE WAR COMES— AND THE YANKS WHO WENT

On the road to war, two works by Charles Seymour, *American Diplomacy During the World War* (1934) and *American Neutrality, 1914–1917* (1935), are the standard works that in general defend the Wilson administration. See, also, Ernest R. May, *The World War and American Isolation* (1959) and Daniel M. Smith, *The Great Departure: The United States and World War I, 1914–1920* (1965). C. Hartley Grattan, *Why We Fought* (1929) is one of the early revisionist works; Walter Millis, *Road to War: America, 1914–1917* (1935) is the most popularly written revisionist book; and Charles C. Tansill, *America Goes to War* (1938) is the most comprehensive. See, also, E. M. Borchard and W. P. Lage, *Neutrality for the United States* (1937); Alice M. Morrissey, *The American Defense of Neutral Rights, 1914–1917* (1939); Harley Notter, *The Origins of the Foreign Policy of Woodrow Wilson* (1937); Arthur S. Link, *Wilson the Diplomatist* (1957); Edward Buehrig, *Woodrow Wilson and the Balance of Power* (1955); and Edward Buehrig, ed., *Wilson's Foreign Policy in Perspective* (1957).

Among the special studies are: On propaganda, Horace C. Peterson, *Propaganda for War* (1939), George Sylvester Viereck, *Spreading Germs of Hate* (1930), and Armin Rappaport, *The British Press and Wilsonian Neutrality* (1950). Two studies of a vital ethnic group are Clifton J. Child, *The German-Americans in Politics, 1914–1917* (1939) and Carl Wittke, *German-Americans and the World War* (1936). Hermann Hagedorn, *The Bugle that Woke America* (1940) is an account of TR and preparedness by his most prolific and ardent admirer. On the peace movement, see Merle Curti, *The American Peace Crusade* (1929), *Peace or War: The American Struggle* (1936), and *Bryan and World Peace* (1931). On the aspects of the decision for war that were popular in the 1930's, see Paul Birdsall, "Neutrality and Economic Pressures, 1914–1917," *Science and Society* (Vol. III, 1939).

Many of the participants wrote memoirs. See Robert Lansing, *War Memoirs of Robert Lansing* (1935); Josephus Daniels, *The Wilson Era—Years of War and After, 1917–1923* (1946); Burton J. Hendrick, *The Life and Letters of Walter Hines Page* (3 vols., 1924–1926); Stephen Gwynn, ed., *Letters and Friendships of Sir Cecil Spring Rice* (2 vols., 1929); James Gerard, *My Four Years in Germany* (1917); Johann H. von Bernstorff, *My Three Years in America* (1920) and *Memoirs* (1936); and Newton D. Baker, *Why We Went to War* (1936).

On the war itself, the best general account is Vol. II of Frederick Logan Paxson, *American Democracy and the World War* (3 vols., 1936–1948). See, also, John S. Bassett, *Our War with Germany: A History* (1919); Elting Morison, *Admiral Sims and the Modern American Navy* (1942); Thomas G. Frothingham, *The Naval History of the World War* (3 vols., 1925–1926); James G. Harbord, *The American Army in France, 1917–1919* (1936); David F. Trask, *The United States in the Supreme War Council: American War Aims and Inter-Allied Strategy, 1917–1918* (1961); and John F. Pershing, *My Experiences in the World War* (2 vols., 1931). Russell F. Weigley, *History of the United States Army* (1967) is important, treats the army throughout its history, and focuses on army organization.

CHAPTER 2. THE HOME FRONT AND THE PEACE

For a general background, Preston Slosson, *The Great Crusade and After, 1914 1928* (1930) and William E. Leuchtenburg, *The Perils of Prosperity, 1914–1932* (1958) give a broad overview. See John Bach McMaster, *The United States in the World War* (2 vols., 1918–1920); Frederick Palmer, *Newton D. Baker: America at War* (2 vols., 1931); and Benedict Crowell and R. F. Wilson, eds., *How America Went to War* (6 vols., 1921).

On industry during the war, see Grosvenor B. Clarkson, *Industrial America in the World War* (1923), a rich store of information; Bernard M. Baruch, *American Industry in the War* (1941); Margaret Coit, *Mr. Baruch* (1957), a readable account with some chapters on the war, and Walker D. Hines, *War History of the American Railroads* (1928). For other aspects of war mobilization, see John M. Clark, *The Costs of the World War to the American People* (1931); Herbert Hoover, *The Ordeal of Woodrow Wilson* (1958), revealing about Hoover also; W. C. Mullendore, *History of the United States Food Administration* (1941); and Herbert Stein, *Government Price Policy During the World War* (1941). For wartime propaganda see James R. Mock and Cedric Larson, *Words That Won the War: The Story of the Committee on Public Information* (1940); George Creel, *How We Advertised America* (1920); Harold D. Lasswell, *Propaganda Technique in the World War* (1927); and James R. Mock, *Censorship, 1917* (1941). On the opponents of war and their difficulties, see Horace C. Peterson and Gilbert Fite, *Opponents of War, 1917–1918* (1957) and Zechariah Chaffee, Jr., *Free Speech in the United States* (1941), both accounts of appalling disregard for civil liberty; David A. Shannon,

The Socialist Party of America: A History (1955); and Ray Ginger, *The Bending Cross: A Biography of Eugene Victor Debs* (1949). For the postwar hysteria, see Robert K. Murray, *Red Scare* (1955) and Richard Drinnon, *Rebel in Paradise: A Biography of Emma Goldman* (1961).

On the Versailles treaty, see N. Gordon Levin, *Woodrow Wilson and World Politics* (1968); Thomas Bailey, *Woodrow Wilson and the Lost Peace* (1944); Ray Stannard Baker, *Woodrow Wilson and World Settlement* (3 vols., 1922); H. W. V. Temperley et al., *A History of the Peace Conference of Paris* (6 vols., 1920–1924); Ruhl J. Bartlett, *The League to Enforce Peace* (1944) on the American background to the League; John Maynard Keynes, *The Economic Consequences of the Peace* (1920), a widely read criticism of the treaty, and a critique of Keynes, Etienne Mantoux, *The Carthaginian Peace, Or the Economic Consequences of Mr. Keynes* (1946); David H. Miller, *The Drafting of the Covenant* (2 vols., 1938); Bernard M. Baruch, *The Making of the Reparations and Economic Sections of the Treaty* (1920); James T. Shotwell, *At the Paris Peace Conference* (1937); Harold Nicolson, *Peacemaking, 1919* (1939); and Paul Birdsall, *Versailles Twenty Years After* (1941). For what historians have written about the conference, see R. C. Binkley, "Ten Years of Peace Conference History," *Journal of Modern History,* I (1929) and Paul Birdsall, "The Second Decade of Peace Conference History," *Journal of Modern History,* XI (1939).

On the Senate's rejection of the treaty, see Thomas Bailey, *Woodrow Wilson and the Great Betrayal* (1945); Denna F. Fleming, *The United States and the League of Nations, 1918–1920* (1932); W. Stull Holt, *Treaties Defeated by the Senate* (1933); Selig Adler, "The Congressional Election of 1918," *South Atlantic Quarterly,* XXXVI (1937); Seward Livermore, "The Sectional Issue in the 1918 Congressional Election," *Mississippi Valley Historical Review,* XXXV (1948); Dexter Perkins, "Woodrow Wilson's Tour," in Daniel Aaron, ed., *America in Crisis* (1952); Kenneth Colegrove, *The American Senate and World Peace* (1943); Henry Cabot Lodge, *The Senate and the League of Nations* (1925); Karl Schriftgiesser, *The Gentleman from Massachusetts* (1944); and John A. Garraty, *Henry Cabot Lodge* (1953). On other aspects of foreign policy at the time, see L. A. R. Yates, *United States and French Security, 1917–1921* (1957); William S. Graves, *America's Siberian Adventure, 1918–1920* (1941); William Appleman Williams, *American-Russian Relations, 1781–1947* (1952); Robert P. Browder, *Origins of Soviet-American Diplomacy* (1953); and the multivolume study by George F. Kennan, *Soviet-American Relations, 1917–1920.*

CHAPTER 3. THE POLITICS OF BUSINESS, 1919–1929

There are several general histories of the United States in the 1920's. The most comprehensive and reliable general work is John D. Hicks, *Republican Ascendancy, 1921–1933* (1960), which has an excellent bibliography. One of the most popular is Frederick Lewis Allen, *Only Yesterday: An Informal History of the Nineteen Twenties* (1931). More perceptive but brightly written is William E. Leuchtenburg, *The Perils of Prosperity, 1914–1932* (1958). Other general histories are Harold U. Faulkner, *From Versailles to the New Deal* (1950); Karl Schriftgiesser, *This Was Normalcy: An Account of Party Politics during Twelve Republican Years* (1948), which votes vigorously Democratic; and Louis M. Hacker, *American Problems of Today: A History of the United States Since the World War* (1938). For conversion to a peacetime order, see James R. Mock and Evangeline Thurber, *Report on Demobilization* (1944).

For Harding, see Andrew Sinclair, *The Available Man* (1965); Francis Russell, *The Shadow of Blooming Grove* (1968); Randolph Downes, *The Rise of Warren G. Harding* (1970); and Robert K. Murray, *The Harding Era* (1969). For the oil scandals, see J. Leonard Bates, *The Origins of Teapot Dome* (1963) and Burl Noggle, *Teapot Dome* (1962).

On Coolidge, see William Allen White, *A Puritan in Babylon* (1938), a masterpiece of popular biography; Claude Fuess, *Calvin Coolidge* (1940), generally sympathetic; Donald McCoy, *Calvin Coolidge* (1967), the best life; Francis Russell, "Coolidge and the Boston Police Strike," *Antioch Review*, XVI (1956); and Gamaliel Bradford, "The Genius of the Average: Calvin Coolidge," *Atlantic Monthly*, CXLV (1930).

On Republicans of various hues during the period, see Malcolm Moos, *The Republicans* (1956); Henry Pringle, *William Howard Taft* (2 vols., 1939); William T. Hutchinson, *Lowden of Illinois* (2 vols., 1957), thorough and scholarly; George W. Norris, *Fighting Liberal* (1945); Claudius O. Johnson, *Borah of Idaho* (1936); Marian C. McKenna, *Borah* (1961); and William Allen White, *Autobiography* (1946). On the Democrats, see Arthur M. Schlesinger, Jr., *The Crisis of the Old Order, 1919–1933* (1957); Frank Freidel, *Franklin D. Roosevelt: The Ordeal* (1954), the second volume of this multivolume life of Roosevelt; James M. Cox, *Journey through My Years* (1946); and David Burner, *The Politics of Provincialism* (1968).

On the La Follette movement of 1924, see Kenneth McKay, *The Progressive Movement of 1924* (1947), the standard work; David A. Shannon, *The Socialist Party of America: A History* (1955); Russel B. Nye, *Midwestern Progressive Politics* (1951); Belle and Fola La Follette, *Robert M. La Follette* (2 vols., 1953); and James Shideler, "The Disintegration of the Progressive Party Movement of 1924," *The Historian* (1951).

On various aspects of agricultural politics, see Robert Morlan, *Political Prairie Fire: The Nonpartisan League, 1915–1922* (1955), a valuable study; Gilbert Fite, *George Peek and the Fight for Farm Parity* (1954), thorough and scholarly; Theodore Saloutos and John D. Hicks, *Agricultural Discontent in the Middle West, 1900–1939* (1951); Harold Barger and H. H. Landsberg, *American Agriculture, 1899–1939* (1951); Grant McConnell, *Decline of Agrarian Democracy* (1953); Arthur Capper, *The Agricultural Bloc* (1922); and Alice Christensen, "Agricultural Pressure and Government Response, 1919–1929," *Agricultural History*, XI (1937).

On electric power struggles, see Ernest H. Gruening, *The Public Pays* (1931); Stephen Rauschenbush, *The Power Fight* (1932); Carl D. Thompson, *Confessions of the Power Trust* (1932); and Preston J. Hubbard, *Origins of the TVA: The Muscle Shoals Controversy, 1920–1932* (1961), definitive on the subject.

CHAPTER 4. THE ECONOMICS OF BUSINESS, 1917–1929

The best general economic history of the 1920's is George Soule, *Prosperity Decade* (1947). Other useful general studies are Frederick Mills, *Economic Tend-*

encies in the United States (1932); Joseph Schumpeter, "The American Economy in the Interwar Period: The Decade of the Twenties," American Economic Review, XXXVI (1946); President's Conference on Unemployment, Recent Economic Changes in the United States (2 vols., 1929); Eli Ginzburg, The Illusion of Stability (1939); and Thomas Nixon Carver, The Present Economic Revolution in the United States (1925), an optimistic view.

Among the special studies, many of which require some understanding of economic theory, are Harold Barger, Outlay and Income in the United States, 1921–1938 (1942); United States National Resources Committee, Technological Trends and National Policy (1937); Simon Kuznets, National Income and Its Composition, 1919–1938 (1941); Edwin Nourse et al., America's Capacity to Produce (1934); Maurice Leven et al., America's Capacity to Consume (1934); and Ralph Epstein, Industrial Profits in the United States (1934). On economic concentration, there is Arthur R. Burns, The Decline of Competition (1936); Adolph Berle and Gardiner Means, The Modern Corporation and Private Property (1932); Harry Wellington Laidler, Concentration of Control in American Industry (1931); George W. Edwards, The Evolution of Finance Capitalism (1938); Charles Chapman, The Development of American Business and Banking Thought, 1913–1936 (1936); William Z. Ripley, Main Street and Wall Street (1927); James C. Bonbright and Gardiner C. Means, The Holding Company (1932); and Norman Buchanan, "The Origin and Development of the Public Utility Holding Company," Journal of Political Economy, XLIV (1936). On specific large corporations during the decade, see Sumner Slichter, "Woolworth," Fortune, VIII (1933), and "A & P and the Hartfords," Fortune, VII (1933); Allan Nevins and Frank Ernest Hill, Ford (Vol. II, 1957); and Keith Sward, The Legend of Henry Ford (1948).

On business thought and advertising, see James Prothro, The Dollar Decade (1954); Morrell Heald, "Business Thought in the Twenties: Social Responsibility," American Quarterly, XIII (1961); and Otis Pease, The Responsibilities of American Advertising: Private Control and Public Influence, 1920–1940 (1958), a pioneering work.

For labor in the 1920's, see Irving L. Bernstein, The Lean Years: A History of the American Worker, 1920–1933 (1960); Philip Taft, The A.F. of L. in the Time of Gompers (1957), and The A.F. of L. from the Death of Gompers to the Merger (1959); Robert Ziegar, Republicans and Labor, 1919–1929 (1969); James O. Morris, Conflict within the A.F. of L. (1959); John S. Gambs, The Decline of the I.W.W. (1932); Felix Frankfurter and Nathan Greene, The Labor Injunction (1930); Edward Berman, Labor and the Sherman Act (1930); David Brodie, Steelworkers in America: The Nonunion Era (1960); William Z. Foster, The Great Steel Strike and Its Lessons (1920); Commission of Inquiry, The Interchurch World Movement, Report on the Steel Strike of 1919 (1920); Matthew Josephson, Sidney Hillman (1952), a poor biography but the best existing one; Samuel Yellen, American Labor Struggles (1936), a useful account of several strikes, some of which were in the 1920's; J. B. S. Hardman, ed., American Labor Dynamics (1928); Sumner Slichter, "The Current Labor Policies of American Industries," Quarterly Journal of Economics, XLIII (1929); David Saposs, "The American Labor Movement since the War." Quarterly Journal of Economics, XLIX (1935); and Lyle Cooper, "The American Labor Movement in Prosperity and Depression," American Economic Review, XXII (1932).

CHAPTER 5. THE FOREIGN POLICY
OF A BUSINESS GOVERNMENT

Work of a general nature are L. Ethan Ellis, *Republican Foreign Policy, 1921–1933* (1968); Frank H. Simonds, *American Foreign Policy in the Post-War Years* (1935); William Appleman Williams, "The Legend of Isolationism in the 1920's," *Science and Society*, XVIII (1954) and *The Tragedy of American Diplomacy* (1959), Selig Adler, *The Isolationist Impulse* (1957); Denna F. Fleming, *The United States and World Organization, 1920–1933* (1938) and *The United States and the World Court* (1945).

For foreign economic policies, see James Angell, *Financial Foreign Policy of the United States* (1933); Herbert Feis, *The Diplomacy of the Dollar: First Era, 1919–1932* (1950); Harold G. Moulton and L. Pasvolsky, *World War Debt Settlements* (1926) and *War Debts and World Prosperity* (1932); the chapter on foreign affairs in Simon Kuznets, *Economic Change* (1953); M. F. Jolliffe, *The United States as a Financial Centre, 1919–1933* (1935); John Madden, et al., *America's Experience as a Creditor Nation* (1957); Benjamin H. Williams, *Economic Foreign Policy of the United States* (1929); and Joseph Brandes, *Herbert Hoover and Economic Diplomacy: Department of Commerce Policy, 1921–1928* (1962).

Merlo J. Pusey, *Charles Evans Hughes* (2 vols., 1951) and Dexter Perkins, *Charles Evans Hughes and American Democratic Statesmanship* (1959) provide a good survey of foreign affairs for the first part of the 1920's. See, also, Thomas H. Buckley, *The United States and the Washington Conference* (1970); Benjamin H. Williams, *The United States and Disarmament* (1931); Merze Tate, *The United States and Armaments* (1948); Robert H. Ferrell, *Peace in Their Time* (1952), on the Kellogg-Briand Pact; James T. Shotwell, *War as an Instrument of National Policy and Its Renunciation in the Pact of Paris* (1929); L. Ethan Ellis, *Frank B. Kellogg and American Foreign Relations, 1925–1929* (1961); David Bryn-Jones, *Frank B. Kellogg, A Biography* (1937); Rodman W. Paul, *Abrogation of the Gentlemen's Agreement* (1936); Russell M. Cooper, *American Consultation in World Affairs* (1934); and Robert H. Ferrell, *Frank B. Kellogg—Henry L. Stimson* (1963).

On relations with specific nations, see Graham H. Stuart, *Latin America and the United States* (1938); Isaac J. Cox, *Nicaragua and the United States* (1927); Harold Nicholson, *Dwight Morrow* (1935); Howard F. Cline, *The United States and Mexico* (1953); Robert P. Browder, *Origins of Soviet-American Diplomacy* (1953); William Appleman Williams, *American-Russian Relations, 1781–1947* (1952); and Frederick L. Schuman, *American Policy toward Russia since 1917* (1928).

CHAPTER 6. THE BUSINESS CIVILIZATION
AND ITS CRITICS

See also the titles cited under Chapter Six in Volume 1.

General works are Harold Stearns, ed., *Civilization in the United States* (1922), an historically important landmark, and *America and the Young Intellectual* (1921). Robert and Helen Lynd, *Middletown* (1929) is a classic analysis of a small midwestern city; see, also, Lewis Atherton, *Main Street on the Middle Border* (1954). Many English and European travelers offered their observations; George

Knoles, ed., *The Jazz Age Revisited* (1955); Andre Siegfried, *America Comes of Age* (1927); J. A. Spender, *Through English Eyes* (1928).

American literature during the decade has attracted much attention. See Frederick Hoffman, *The Twenties* (1955); John Hutchens, *The American Twenties* (1952); Arthur Mizener, "The Novel in America: 1920–1940," *Perspectives USA,* XV (1956); Joseph Wood Krutch, *The Modern Temper* (1929); Frederick John Hoffman, *The Modern Novel in America, 1900–1951* (1951); Maxwell Geismar, *Last of the Provincials* (1947); J. W. Beach, *American Fiction, 1920–1940* (1941); Alfred Kazin, *On Native Grounds* (1942); Malcolm Cowley, *Exile's Return* (1934); and Oscar Cargill, *Intellectual America: Ideas on the March* (1941). The exuberant Mr. Mencken is the subject of Edgar Kemler, *The Irreverent Mr. Mencken* (1950); William Manchester, *Disturber of the Peace* (1951); and Carl Bode, *Mencken* (1969). For other aspects of literature, see William Vann O'Connor, *An Age of Criticism, 1900–1950* (1952); Alan S. Downer, *Fifty Years of American Drama, 1900–1950* (1951); and Louise Bogan, *Achievement in American Poetry, 1900–1950* (1951). For two great literary biographies, see Arthur Mizener, *The Far Side of Paradise* (1959), on F. Scott Fitzgerald, and Mark Schorer, *Sinclair Lewis* (1961).

The "new psychology" that swept America is considered in Frederick Hoffman, *Freudianism and the Literary Mind* (1954); A. A. Brill, "The Introduction and Development of Freud's Work in the United States," *American Journal of Sociology,* XLV (1939); and Lucille Birnbaum, "Behaviourism in the 1920's," *American Quarterly,* VII (1955).

On art and architecture, see Milton W. Brown, *American Painting from the Armory Show to the Depression* (1955), and other titles listed under Chapter Six, Volume 1. See, also, Thomas Hart Benton, *An Artist in America* (1937); Lewis Mumford, ed., *Roots of Contemporary American Architecture* (1952); Carl W. Condit, *The Rise of the Skyscraper* (1952); and Frank Lloyd Wright, *Modern Architecture* (1932), an opinionated personal document.

For music, see titles under Chapter Six, Volume 1, plus Sigmund Spaeth, *A History of Popular Music in America* (1948); Rudi Blesh, *Shining Trumpets* (1946); William C. Handy, *Father of the Blues* (1941); and Winthrop Sargeant, *Jazz* (1946).

CHAPTER 7. THE PEOPLE AND THEIR TENSIONS

For general social history of the 1920's, see Frederick Lewis Allen, *Only Yesterday: An Informal History of the Nineteen Twenties* (1931); Lloyd Morris, *Postscript to Yesterday* (1947) and *Not So Long Ago* (1947); Henry M. Robinson, *Fantastic Interim* (1943); Paul Sann, *The Lawless Decade* (1937); Isabel Leighton, ed., *The Aspirin Age* (1949); and James Truslow Adams, *Our Business Civilization* (1929).

On immigration, see Carl Wittke, *We Who Built America* (1939); John Higham, *Strangers in the Land* (1955); William S. Bernard, *American Immigration Policy* (1950); Kate Holladay Claghorn, *The Immigrant's Day in Court* (1932); and Joseph J. Huthmacher, *Massachusetts People and Politics, 1919–1933* (1959), which puts its emphasis on the political maturation of ethnic groups.

For Negro history, see John Hope Franklin, *From Slavery to Freedom* (1947); E. Franklin Frazier, *The Negro in the United States* (1949); Gunnar Myrdal, *An American Dilemma* (2 vols., 1944); E. David Cronon, *Black Moses: The Story of Marcus Garvey and the Universal Negro Improvement Association* (1955).

For prohibition, see Charles Merz, *The Dry Decade* (1931) and Herbert Asbury, *The Great Illusion, An Informal History of Prohibition* (1950), which is about as informal as a history can be; and Andrew Sinclair, *Prohibition* (1962).

On the family and women, see John Sirjamaki, *The American Family in the Twentieth Century* (1953); Oliver Jensen, *The Revolt of American Women* (1952) and William H. Chafe, *The American Woman: Her Changing Social, Economic, and Political Roles, 1920–1970* (1972). The following sample of contemporary titles will attest to the concern in the 1920's about changing ways: Freda Kirchwey, ed., *Our Changing Morality: A Symposium* (1924); the December, 1926, and May, 1929, issues of *The Annals of the American Academy of Political and Social Science*; John Carter, Jr., " 'These Wild Young People': By One of Them," *Atlantic Monthly*, CXXVI (1920); Viola Paradise, "Sex Simplex," *Forum*, LXXIV (1925); Mary Agnes Hamilton, "Nothing Shocks Me," *Harper's*, CLV (1927); Dorothy Dunbar Bromley, "Feminist, New Style," *Harper's*, CLV (1927); Eleanor Rowland Wembridge, "Petting and the Campus," *Survey*, LIV (1925); William Bolitho, "The New Skirt Length," *Harper's*, CLX (1930); and G. Stanley Hall, "Flapper Americana Novissima," *Atlantic Monthly*, CXXIX (1922).

For "One Hundred Percentism," see David Chalmers, *The Ku Klux Klan* (1966); Emerson Loucks, *The Ku Klux Klan in Pennsylvania* (1936); and Robert Moats Miller, "A Note on the Relationship between the Protestant Churches and the Revived Ku Klux Klan," *Journal of Social History*, XXII (1956). Calvin Coolidge, "Enemies of the Republic: Are the Reds Stalking Our College Women?" *The Delineator*, XCVII (1921) is an example of one hundred percentism by the Vice-President. Bessie L. Pierce, *Public Opinion and the Teaching of History in the United States* (1926) and Howard K. Beale, *Are American Teachers Free?* (1936) discuss pressures on the schools. Ray Ginger, *Six Days or Forever?* (1958) on the Scopes trial. See, also, Walter Lippmann, *American Inquisitors* (1928). For religion's role in the period's tensions, see Norman F. Furniss, *The Fundamentalist Controversy, 1918–1931* (1954); Paul Carter, *The Decline and Revival of the Social Gospel* (1956); and Robert Moats Miller, *American Protestantism and Social Issues, 1919–1939* (1958).

For some of the victims of intolerance, see Felix Frankfurter, *The Case of Sacco and Vanzetti* (1927); G. L. Joughin and E. M. Morgan, *The Legacy of Sacco and Vanzetti* (1948); and James Grossman, "The Sacco-Vanzetti Case Reconsidered," *Commentary*, XXXIII (1962). For Communism during the decade, see Theodore Draper, *The Roots of American Communism* (1957) and *American Communism and Soviet Russia* (1960); and Granville Hicks, *John Reed* (1936).

On the election of 1928, see Oscar Handlin, *Al Smith and His America* (1958); Henry F. Pringle, *Alfred E. Smith* (1927); Edmund Moore, *A Catholic Runs for President* (1956), a work of careful scholarship; Roy Peel and Thomas Donnelly, *The 1928 Campaign: An Analysis* (1931).

CHAPTER 8. THE GREAT CRASH AND
THE HOOVER ADMINISTRATION

For the crash and the early depression, see John Kenneth Galbraith, *The Great Crash* (1955), by an economist who does not write like one when he does not want to; Broadus Mitchell, *Depression Decade: From New Era through New Deal, 1929–1941* (1947), a book basic to this chapter and subsequent ones; Murray N. Rothbard, *America's Great Depression* (1963), a conservative economic analysis; Lionel Robbins, *The Great Depression* (1934); Francis Hirst, *Wall Street and Lombard Street* (1931). For the impact of the depression on human lives, see David A. Shannon, ed., *The Great Depression* (1959); Gilbert Seldes, *Years of the Locust: America, 1929–1932* (1933). For the Hoover administration, see Harris G. Warren, *Herbert Hoover and the Great Depression* (1959); Arthur M. Schlesinger, Jr., *The Crisis of the Old Order, 1919–1933* (1957); Jordan A. Schwarz, *The Interregnum of Despair* (1970); Gene Smith, *The Shattered Dream: Hoover and the Great Depression* (1970); John D. Hicks, *Republican Ascendancy, 1921–1933* (1960); and Albert U. Romasco, *The Poverty of Abundance* (1965). Charles A. and Mary R. Beard, *America in Midpassage* (1939), invaluable for the decade following 1928; Herbert Hoover, *Memoirs* (3 vols., 1951–1952); W. S. Myers and W. H. Newton, *The Hoover Administration* (1936), a defense; Ray Lyman Wilbur and Arthur Hyde, *The Hoover Policies* (1937), another defense by administration officials; the relevant parts of William Appleman Williams, *The Contours of American History* (1961), an exciting and provocative interpretation; the chapter on Hoover in Richard Hofstadter, *The American Political Tradition and the Men Who Made It* (1948); and Irving L. Bernstein, *Lean Years: A History of the American Worker, 1920–1933* (1960).

CHAPTER 9. THE EARLY DEAL

There is a mountain of material on FDR and the New Deal. For FDR in the years immediately preceding the presidency, see Frank Friedel, *Franklin D. Roosevelt: The Triumph* (1956); Bernard Bellush, *Apprenticeship for the Presidency: Franklin D. Roosevelt as Governor of New York* (1951), a definitive work; Arthur M. Schlesinger, Jr., *The Crisis of the Old Order, 1919–1933* (1957); Roy V. Peel and T. C. Donnelly, *The 1932 Campaign* (1935); and James M. Burns, *Roosevelt: The Lion and the Fox* (1956), the best one-volume study of FDR, a political biography.

FDR's published papers include: Samuel I. Rosenman, ed., *The Public Papers and Addresses of Franklin D. Roosevelt* (13 vols., 1933–1950); Elliott Roosevelt, ed., *F.D.R.: His Personal Letters* (4 vols., 1947–1950). Arthur M. Schlesinger, Jr., *The Coming of the New Deal* (1958), Volume II of *The Age of Roosevelt*, treats the material covered in this chapter. See, also, Ernest K. Lindley, *The Roosevelt Revolution: First Phase* (1933); Charles A. Beard and George H. E. Smith, *The Future Comes: A Study of the New Deal* (1933). Among the special studies relevant to this chapter are Leverett S. Lyon et al., *The National Recovery Administration* (1935); E. G. Nourse et al., *Three Years of the Agricultural Adjustment Administration* (1937); Gilbert C. Fite, "Farmer Opinion and the Agricultural Adjustment Act," *Mississippi Valley Historical Review*, XLVIII (1962); G. Griffith Johnson, Jr., *Treasury and Monetary Policy, 1933–1938* (1939); Ferdinand Pecora, *Wall Street under Oath* (1939); and Leo Wolman, Rexford G. Tugwell et al., *America's Recovery Program* (1934).

The best overview of the New Deal is William E. Leuchtenburg, *Franklin D. Roosevelt and the New Deal, 1932–1940* (1963). James M. Burns, *Roosevelt: The*

Lion and the Fox (1956) is excellent to about 1938; Basil Rauch, *The History of the New Deal, 1933–1938* (1944) was one of the first efforts at New Deal history and is still useful; Denis W. Brogan, *The Era of Franklin D. Roosevelt* (1950) is a clever Englishman's view, valuable mainly for an outsider's opinion, as is Mario Enaudi, *The Roosevelt Revolution* (1959); Arthur Ekirch, *Ideologies and Utopias: The Impact of the New Deal on American Thought* (1969); Otis Graham, *An Encore for Reform* (1967); V. O. Key, Jr., *Southern Politics in State and Nation* (1949) is an important study of a relevant subject; Raymond D. Moley, *Twenty-Seven Masters of Politics* (1949) has some interesting insights.

Among the books about FDR are Harold F. Gosnell, *Champion Campaigner, Franklin D. Roosevelt* (1952); Edgar Eugene Robinson, *The Roosevelt Leadership, 1933–1945* (1955), sharply critical and containing an excellent bibliography; Rexford G. Tugwell, *The Democratic Roosevelt* (1957); John T. Flynn, *The Roosevelt Myth* (1948), a right-wing swipe; John Gunther, *Roosevelt in Retrospect* (1950); Robert E. Sherwood, *Roosevelt and Hopkins* (1948), contains many letters and is especially good for the partnership of these two men during the war; Paul K. Conkin, *F.D.R. and the Origins of the Welfare State* (1967); Mauritz A. Hallgren, *The Gay Reformer: Profits before Plenty under Franklin D. Roosevelt* (1935), a criticism from the left; Elliott Roosevelt, *As He Saw It* (1946); Frances Perkins, *The Roosevelt I Knew* (1946); Carroll Kilpatrick, ed., *Roosevelt and Daniels, A Friendship in Politics* (1952).

Among the memoirs and biographical studies of the FDR circle are Hugh S. Johnson, *The Blue Eagle from Egg to Earth* (1935); Marriner S. Eccles, *Beckoning Frontiers* (1951), a useful document; Grace G. Tully, *F.D.R., My Boss* (1949); Raymond Moley, *After Seven Years* (1939); Alfred B. Rollins, Jr., *Roosevelt and Howe* (1962); Harold L. Ickes, *Autobiography of a Curmudgeon* (1943) and *Secret Diary* (3 vols., 1953–1954); Edward J. Flynn, *You're the Boss* (1947); Eleanor Roosevelt, *This Is My Story* (1937) and *This I Remember* (1949); Charles Michelson, *The Ghost Talks* (1944); Samuel I. Rosenman, *Working with Roosevelt* (1952); Vice Admiral Ross T. McIntire and George Creel, *White House Physician* (1946); Daniel C. Roper, *Fifty Years of Public Life* (1941); Lela Stiles, *The Man behind Roosevelt: The Story of Louis McHenry Howe* (1954); Nicholas Roosevelt, *A Front Row Seat* (1953). Donald R. Richberg, *My Hero* (1954) and *The Rainbow* (1936); James A. Farley, *Behind the Ballots* (1938) and *Jim Farley's Story* (1948); Bernard Sternsher, *Rexford Tugwell and the New Deal* (1964).

CHAPTER 10. THE LATER NEW DEAL

Many of the titles listed for the previous chapter are useful for this one as well. Arthur M. Schlesinger, Jr., *The Politics of Upheaval* (1960), Vol. III of *The Age of Roosevelt*, treats in admirable detail the material of the greater part of this chapter.

On the revolt of the right, see Herbert Hoover, *The Challenge to Liberty* (1934) and *Addresses upon the American Road* (1938), as well as his *Memoirs* (3 vols., 1951–1952); Alf M. Landon, *America at the Crossroads* (1936); and George Wolfskill, *The Revolt of the Conservatives: A History of the American Liberty League, 1934–1940* (1962). For the pressure from the left and quasi-left, see Donald R. McCoy, *Angry Voices: Left-of-Center Politics in the New Deal Era* (1958);

Alfred M. Bingham, *Challenge to the New Deal* (1934); Harnett T. Kane, *Louisiana Hayride* (1941), on Huey Long; and T. Harry Williams, *Huey Long* (1970). See, also, Donald McCoy's life of Alfred M. Landon. See, also, two strong books by James T. Patterson, *Congressional Conservatism and the New Deal* (1967) and *The New Deal and the States* (1969).

On various aspects of later New Deal reforms, see Paul H. Douglas, *Social Security in the United States* (1939); Seymour Harris, *The Economics of Social Security* (1941); Grace Abbott, *From Relief to Social Security* (1941); Donald S. Howard, *The WPA and Federal Relief Policy* (1943); James C. Bonbright, *Public Utilities and National Power Policies* (1940); Marion L. Ramsay, *Pyramids of Power: The Story of Roosevelt, Insull and the Utility Wars* (1937); Ellis W. Hawley, *The New Deal and the Problem of Monopoly* (1966); William O. Douglas, *Democracy and Finance* (1940); and Paul K. Conkin, *Tomorrow a New World: The New Deal Community Program* (1959).

On the Supreme Court crisis and the Roosevelt court, see Merlo J. Pusey, *The Supreme Court Crisis* (1937); Joseph Alsop and Turner Catledge, *The 168 Days* (1938); Samuel Hendel, *Charles Evans Hughes and the Supreme Court* (1951); Merlo J. Pusey, *Charles Evans Hughes* (2 vols., 1951); Robert H. Jackson, *The Struggle for Judicial Supremacy* (1941); Edward S. Corwin, *Court over Constitution* (1938); Joel Paschal, *Mr. Justice Sutherland* (1951); Alpheus T. Mason, *Harland Fiske Stone: Pillar of the Law* (1956); Samuel J. Konefsky, *Chief Justice Stone and the Supreme Court* (1945); and C. Herman Pritchett, *The Roosevelt Court: A Study in Judicial Politics and Values, 1937–1947* (1948). Leonard Baker, *Back to Back: The Duel Between FDR and the Supreme Court* (1967) is useful, but William E. Leuchtenburg's forthcoming book on the subject promises to be definitive. See Leuchtenburg's "The Origins of Franklin D. Roosevelt's 'Court-Packing' Plan" in Philip B. Kurland, Ed., *The Supreme Court Review* (1966).

CHAPTER 11. ECONOMIC CHANGE
IN A TIME OF TROUBLE

General works on economic history and special studies on aspects of federal economic policies are Broadus Mitchell, *Depression Decade: From New Era through New Deal, 1929–1941* (1947); Merle Fainsod and L. Gordon, *Government and the American Economy* (1941); Clair Wilcox, *Competition and Monopoly in American Industry* (1940); David Lynch, *Concentration of Economic Power* (1946), a very useful summary of the TNEC reports and hearings; Henry H. Villard, *Deficit Spending and the National Income* (1941); John Kenneth Galbraith and G. G. Johnson, Jr., *The Economic Effects of the Federal Public Works Expenditures, 1933–1938* (1940); Arthur E. Burns and D. S. Watson, *Government Spending and Economic Expansion* (1940); Jesse Jones, *Fifty Billion Dollars: My Thirteen Years with the RFC, 1932–1945* (1951); Harry L. Hopkins, *Spending to Save* (1936); John A. Brennan, *Silver and the First New Deal* (1969), and Kenneth D. Roose, *The Economics of Recession and Revival: An Interpretation of 1937–38* (1954).

On labor, see Selig Perlman, *Labor in the New Deal Decade* (1945); Edwin Young and Milton Derber, eds., *Labor and the New Deal* (1957); Irving Bernstein, *The New Deal Collective Bargaining Policy* (1950) and *The Turbulent Years: A*

History of the American Worker, 1933–1941 (1970); Jerold S. Auerbach, *Labor and Liberty: The La Follette Committee and the New Deal* (1966); Sidney Fine, *The Automobile under the Blue Eagle* (1963); Walter Galenson, *The CIO Challenge to the A.F. of L.* (1960); James O. Morris, *Conflict within the A.F. of L.* (1959); John B. Andrews, *Labor Laws in Action* (1938); Joseph Rosenfarb, *The National Labor Policy and How It Works* (1940); Robert R. R. Brooks, *When Labor Organizes* (1936), *Unions of their Own Choosing* (1939), and *As Steel Goes* (1940); Harold Seidman, *Labor Czars: A History of Labor Racketeering* (1938); J. Raymond Walsh, *CIO, Industrial Unionism in Action* (1937); Edward Levinson, *Labor on the March* (1938); Herbert Harris, *American Labor* (1939) and *Labor's Civil War* (1940); Carroll R. Daugherty, *Labor under the NRA* (1934); and Harry A. Millis and Emily C. Brown, *From the Wagner Act to Taft-Hartley* (1950).

For the TVA and southern problems, see C. Herman Pritchett, *The Tennessee Valley Authority: A Study in Public Administration* (1943); David E. Lilienthal, *TVA: Democracy on the March* (1953 ed.); Howard W. Odum, *Southern Regions of the United States* (1936); Rupert B. Vance, *Human Geography of the South* (1935 ed.); and National Emergency Council, *Report on Economic Conditions of the South* (1938).

Besides the works on agricultural history cited earlier, see John D. Black, *Parity, Parity, Parity* (1942); Henry Wallace, *New Frontiers* (1934); Russell Lord, *The Wallaces of Iowa* (1947); Richard Kirkendall, *Social Scientists and Farm Politics in the Age of Roosevelt* (1966); Arthur F. Raper and Ira DeA. Reid, *Sharecroppers All* (1941); Thomas J. Woofter, Jr., and E. Winston, *Seven Lean Years* (1939); M. S. Venkataramani, "Norman Thomas, Arkansas Sharecroppers, and the Roosevelt Agricultural Policies, 1933–1937," *Mississippi Valley Historical Review*, XLVII (1960); and Howard Kester, *Revolt among the Sharecroppers* (1936).

CHAPTER 12. SOCIETY AND THE GREAT DEPRESSION

General works with a great deal of social history of the 1930's are Dixon Wecter, *The Age of the Great Depression, 1929–1941* (1948) and Edward R. Ellis, *A Nation in Torment: The Great American Depression, 1929–1939* (1970). Robert and Helen Lynd, *Middletown in Transition* (1937) and August B. Hollingshead, *Elmtown's Youth* (1949) are valuable dissections of midwestern communities during the decade. Revealing the assumptions of a stagnant population are such demographic studies as National Resources Committee, *Problems of a Changing Population* (1939) and Walter F. Wilcox, *Studies in American Demography* (1940). For the erosion of social assumptions, see many of the titles cited in Chapter 13 and the novels of the period, particularly those of John Dos Passos, Sinclair Lewis, Thomas Wolfe, John Steinbeck, and James T. Farrell.

On the Negro during the Great Depression, see John Hope Franklin, *From Slavery to Freedom* (1947); Franklin Frazier, *The Negro Family* and his *Black Bourgeoisie* (1957); Walter White, *A Man Called White* (1948), the memoirs of the leader of the NAACP; Elbert L. Tatum, *The Changed Political Thought of the Negro, 1915–1940* (1951); Ira DeA. Reid, *The Negro Immigrant* (1939); Arthur F. Raper, *The Tragedy of Lynching* (1933); Horace R. Cayton and G. S. Mitchell,

Black Workers and the New Unions (1939); Herbert S. Northrup, Organized Labor and the Negro (1944); Bernard H. Nelson, The Fourteenth Amendment and the Negro Since 1920 (1946); Donald Holly, "The Negro in the New Deal Resettlement Program," Agricultural History (July, 1971); and Christopher Wye, "The New Deal and the Negro Community: Toward a Broader Conceptualization," Journal of American History (December, 1972).

On education, besides previously cited titles, see Malcolm W. Willey, ed., Depression, Recovery, and Higher Education (1937); Davis S. Hill and F. J. Kelly, Economy in Higher Education (1933); and Isaac L. Kandel, The End of an Era (1941).

CHAPTER 13. THE CULTURE OF
THE GREAT DEPRESSION

General works of value are Dixon Wecter, The Age of the Great Depression, 1929–1941 (1948); Charles A. and Mary R. Beard, America in Midpassage (1938), the last half of the book; Alfred Kazin, On Native Grounds (1942); Oscar Cargill, Intellectual America: Ideas on the March (1941); Merle Curti, The Growth of American Thought (1943); and Harold E. Stearns, ed., America Now (1938), a quite different assessment from his 1922 venture.

On literature, see the novels and other works of the writers themselves plus Granville Hicks, The Great Tradition (1935); John W. Aldridge, After the Lost Generation (1951); Maxwell Geismar, Writers in Crisis: The American Novel, 1925–1940 (1961); Leo Gurko, The Angry Decade (1947); Milton Crane, ed., The Roosevelt Era (1947); and Joseph Blotner, The American Political Novel (1966).

On the arts and music, see previously listed titles, especially Milton W. Brown, American Painting from the Armory Show to the Depression (1955); and Homer Saint-Gaudens, The American Artist and His Times (1941); Henry Geldzahler, American Painting in the Twentieth Century (1965). John T. Howard, Our Contemporary Composers: American Music in the Twentieth Century (1941); and David Ewen, Music Comes to America (1942).

CHAPTER 14. DEPRESSION DIPLOMACY, 1929–1938

For foreign affairs in the Hoover administration, particularly the Manchurian affair, see Sara Smith, The Manchurian Crisis, 1931–1932 (1948); Reginald Bassett, Democracy and Foreign Policy: The Sino-Japanese Dispute, 1931–1933 (1952); Robert Langer, Seizure of Territory: The Stimson Doctrine (1947); Henry Stimson and McGeorge Bundy, On Active Service in Peace and War (1948); Richard N. Current, Secretary Stimson (1954), critical of Stimson; Elting E. Morison, Turmoil and Tradition: A Study of the Life and Times of Henry L. Stimson (1960), a defense of Stimson; Armin Rappaport, Henry L. Stimson and Japan, 1931–1933 (1963); Robert Ferrell, American Diplomacy in the Great Depression (1957); Alexander De Conde, Herbert Hoover's Latin American Policy (1951); and W. S. Myers, The Foreign Policies of Herbert Hoover (1940).

On foreign economic policy under FDR, see loyd C. Gardner, Economic

Aspects of New Deal Diplomacy (1964); Seymour Harris, *The Economics of Social Security* (1941); Herbert Feis, *The Changing Pattern of International Economic Affairs* (1940); Raymond L. Buell, *The Hull Trade Program* (1938); and Jeannette P. Nichols, "Roosevelt's Monetary Diplomacy in 1933," *American Historical Review,* LVI (1951).

Allan Nevins, *The New Deal and World Affairs* (1950) provides a quick survey. Herbert Feis, *The Spanish Story: Franco and the Nations at War* (1948) and F. Jay Taylor, *The United States and the Spanish Civil War, 1936–1939* (1956); Grayson L. Kirk, *Philippine Independence* (1936) for that subject and Edward O. Guerrant, *Roosevelt's Good Neighbor Policy* (1950); Bryce Wood, *The Making of the Good Neighbor Policy* (1961); Howard F. Cline, *United States and Mexico* (1953); and E. David Cronon, *Josephus Daniels in Mexico* (1960) for New Deal Latin American policy. For the recognition of Russia, see William Appleman Williams, *American-Russian Relations, 1781–1947* (1952) and Robert P. Browder, *Origins of Soviet-American Diplomacy* (1953). See also Manny T. Koginos, *The Panay Incident* (1967).

For neutrality legislation, see Edwin Borchard and William P. Lage, *Neutrality for the United States* (1937) and James M. Seavy, *Neutrality Legislation* (1939). Thomas A. Bailey, *The Man in the Street* (1948), a study of public opinion and foreign policy, treats the neutrality sentiment. See, also, Elton Atwater, *American Regulation of Arms Exports* (1941). William E. Dodd, Jr. and Martha Dodd, eds., *Ambassador Dodd's Diary, 1933–1938* (1941) is the document of the American ambassador to Berlin in the early Hitler days.

Index to Volume 2

Printed in U.S.A.